Against All England

ReFormations

MEDIEVAL AND EARLY MODERN

Series Editors: David Aers, Sarah Beckwith, and James Simpson

AGAINST ALL
England

Regional Identity and Cheshire Writing,
1195–1656

ROBERT W. BARRETT, JR.

University of Notre Dame Press
Notre Dame, Indiana

Manufactured in the United States of America

Library of Congress Cataloging-in-Publication Data

Barrett, Robert W., 1969–
Against all England : regional identity and Cheshire
writing, 1195–1656 / Robert W. Barrett, Jr.
p. cm. — (ReFormations: medieval and early modern)
Includes bibliographical references and index.
ISBN-13: 978-0-268-02209-9 (pbk. : alk. paper)
ISBN-10: 0-268-02209-7 (pbk. : alk. paper)
1. English literature—England—Cheshire—History and criticism.
2. Literature and society—England—Cheshire.
3. Cheshire (England)—In literature.
4. Cheshire (England)—Intellectual life. I. Title.
PR8309.C47B37 2009
820.9'94271—dc22
2008035611

For Anna and Frances with love

CONTENTS

FIGURES

ACKNOWLEDGMENTS

I would first like to thank the many librarians and archivists who assisted me with the completion of this book. I have spent many pleasant hours in the reading rooms of the Bodleian Library, the British Library, the Cheshire and Chester Archives and Local Studies, and the Rare Book and Manuscript Library of the University of Illinois at Urbana-Champaign. Special thanks go to Sally-Beth MacLean and Arleane Ralph at Victoria University's Centre for Research in Early English Drama: by graciously allowing me to consult the proofs of REED's *Cheshire including Chester* volume in summer 2006, they saved me from a number of errors in chapters 2 and 3.

I also want to thank the institutions who funded much of my research. The support of the National Endowment for the Humanities (in the form of a 2004 summer stipend) got me to England at a crucial point in my writing process. In addition, I have benefited from the generosity of the University of Illinois's Campus Research Board on two separate occasions: a Humanities Released Time grant in spring 2004 allowed me to research and write chapter 5, while a spring 2007 Campus Research Board Award covered the costs of the maps and illustrations used in this book.

Credit also goes to the providers of those images. It was a pleasure to work with the permissions staffs of the British Library, the Bodleian Library, Christie's Images, the Hereford Cathedral Library, the Huntington Library, and Marketing Projects. My friend Chris Carter used his expertise in heraldry to produce the wonderful Scrope and Grosvenor arms displayed in chapter 4, and I thank him for his assistance. I especially want to acknowledge the labors of my cartographer, Andy Lawrence of Keele University Digital Imaging and Illustrations Service (KUDIS). His maps of Cheshire and Chester are outstanding.

The core argument of chapter 3 first appeared in "The Absent *Triumphator* in the 1610 *Chester's Triumph in Honor of Her Prince*," *Spectacle and Public Performance in the Late Middle Ages and the Renaissance*, edited by Robert E. Stillman (Leiden: Brill, 2006), 183–210. I am grateful to Rob Stillman for inviting me to contribute my first publication to his collection, and I thank Gaby van Rietschoten of Brill for her permission to reprint a revised version of that material here.

I owe numerous debts to colleagues throughout the academic world, having received valuable feedback from audiences at meetings of the Delaware Valley Medieval Association, the Midwest Modern Language Association, the Modern Language Association, and the New Chaucer Society. The annual International Congress on Medieval Studies at Western Michigan provided me with a regular venue for my work, and chapter 5 greatly benefited from a spring 2004 address to the Fourth Fifteenth-Century Conference here at Illinois.

Less formal, but equally vital, is the advice that I have received on an individual basis from colleagues at other institutions. I therefore want to thank Mary Carruthers, Theresa Coletti, Matthew Fisher, Christina Fitzgerald, Richard Emmerson, Bruce Holsinger, Gordon Kipling, Zachary Lesser, Philip Morgan, and Richard Newhauser for their suggestions and support over the years. David Wallace was the director of the Ph.D. dissertation on which this book is based, and he has continued to be an important influence upon my thinking. Finally, Jennifer Summit merits special attention here, not only for commenting on my work, but also for making me aware that the University of Notre Dame Press was looking for manuscripts that crossed the period boundary between the Middle Ages and the Renaissance.

Indeed, it has been a distinct pleasure to work with Barbara Hanrahan, Rebecca DeBoer, Margaret Gloster, and the rest of the University of Notre Dame Press staff. I particularly want to thank copy editor Matthew Dowd for his careful attention to my manuscript. Kudos are also due to Lynn Staley, my outside reader, and to David Aers, Sarah Beckwith, and James Simpson, my series editors. Their suggestions have made for a better book.

Since this book is an analysis of a regional culture, it seems appropriate to end these acknowledgments with recognition of the local communities that have sustained the project since its inception. Two of these communities—the Department of English and the Program in Medieval Studies at the University of Illinois at Urbana-Champaign—are my professional home. I could not ask for a better set of colleagues and therefore offer thanks to Nancy Castro, Eleanor Courtemanche, Jed Esty, Catharine Gray, Jim Hansen, Cathy Prendergast, Curtis Perry, Tony Pollock, Carol Symes, Renée Trilling, Gillen Wood, and Ted Underwood for their friendship and encouragement. Scott Garner and Danuta Shanzer double-checked my Latin translations—any remaining errors are my own, not theirs. Martin Camargo, Carol Neely, and Lori Newcomb each read my complete manuscript more than once. Their suggestions for revision have been greatly appreciated.

My greatest professional debt, though, is to my senior colleague Charlie Wright. I have been blessed with many excellent mentors over the years, but Charlie is the best of them all. He has been a tireless reader and insightful editor of my prose, shaping the book at every stage of its development. I lack the words to express the full extent of my gratitude for his guidance.

The third and final local community I want to thank is my family. My in-laws, Randolph and Judy Ivy, generously allowed me to use their home in Reading as a base camp for my English travels. My maternal grandfather, Walter Liskow, passed away in 2004, several years after I commenced work on the book. He didn't understand what I was writing about, but was nonetheless proud that his grandson was writing a book. My younger brother, Andrew Barrett, did his time as an assistant professor of political science before jumping ship to pursue a career in government, so he knows only too well the burdens of academic publishing. He and I have commiserated on many occasions. My parents, Bob and Melody Barrett, have never failed me, cheering me on over the years in person and over the phone. (Yes, Dad, the book is done—now you can ask about something else!) Their good wishes merited the dedication of the dissertation version of this project, and I want to reiterate the affectionate sentiments I expressed then.

But I have reserved the dedication of this book version for my two best friends: Anna Ivy, my wife, and Frances Kay Ivy-Barrett, my daughter. Anna arrived at the University of Pennsylvania (and in my life) in fall 1996, just as David Wallace was suggesting that I might consider focusing a medieval English drama dissertation on the Chester plays. She has been with me for the duration of the project, serving as a careful proofreader and, more importantly, as my most valued sounding board. I would not have been able to finish this book without her. Frances showed up in winter 2004, just in time for the final phases of the project. Like her great-grandfather, she is not entirely sure what Cheshire is or means, but she assures me that she is duly impressed to know that Daddy is writing a book. I therefore present this volume to them as a token of my love—a wholly inadequate return for what they have given me.

ABBREVIATIONS

CCALS	Cheshire and Chester Archives and Local Studies
CPTR	*Chester in the Plantagenet and Tudor Reigns*, Rupert H. Morris
E&D	*The Chester Mystery Cycle: Essays and Documents*, R. M. Lumiansky and David Mills
ECCO	Eighteenth-Century Collections Online
EEBO	Early English Books Online
EETS	The Early English Text Society
MED	*The Middle English Dictionary*
OED	*The Oxford English Dictionary*
REED: Cheshire	Records of Early English Drama, *Cheshire including Chester*, eds. Elizabeth Baldwin, Lawrence M. Clopper, and David Mills
REED: Chester	Records of Early English Drama, *Chester*, ed. Lawrence M. Clopper
RSLC	The Record Society of Cheshire and Lancashire
SD	Stage direction
SGGK	*Sir Gawain and the Green Knight*
VCH: Ches.	*The Victoria History of the County of Chester*, eds. B. E. Harris, C. P. Lewis, and A. T. Thacker
VCH: Lancs.	*The Victoria History of the County of Lancashire*, eds. William Farrer and J. Brownbill

Above:
Medieval and early modern Cheshire.
Based on the parish maps in *A New Historical Atlas of Cheshire.*

Right:
The city of Cheshire, ca. 1500.
Based on a map in *A History of the County of Cheshire*, 5:36.

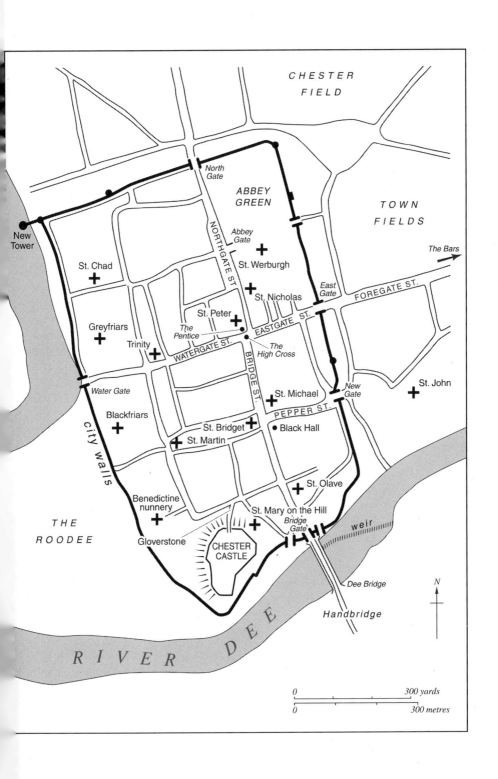

CHESTER
FIELD

North
Gate

ABBEY
GREEN

New
Tower

Abbey
Gate

TOWN
FIELDS

St. Chad

St. Werburgh

The Bars

East
Gate

FOREGATE ST.

NORTHGATE ST.

St. Nicholas

Greyfriars

St. Peter

The
Pentice

EASTGATE ST.

Trinity

WATERGATE ST.

The
High Cross

Water Gate

BRIDGE ST.

St. Michael

New
Gate

St. John

Blackfriars

PEPPER ST.

St. Bridget

St. Martin

Black Hall

city walls

St. Olave

Benedictine
nunnery

St. Mary on the Hill

THE
ROODEE

Gloverstone

Bridge
Gate

weir

CHESTER
CASTLE

Dee Bridge

N

Handbridge

RIVER DEE

0		300 yards
0		300 metres

INTRODUCTION

For centuries, the county of Cheshire was the northern bulwark of the Welsh Marches, one of England's key border zones. As such, it offers an ideal opportunity for a revisionary critique of pre- and early modern English national identity from the vantage point of an explicitly regional literature. The provincial texts under review in this book— pageants, poems, and prose works created in Cheshire and its vicinity from the 1190s to the 1650s—work together to complicate persistent academic binaries of metropole and margin, center and periphery, and nation and region. In addition to the blurring of established spatial categories, the close study of early Cheshire writing and performance also serves to reconfigure England's literary and social histories as processes of temporally uneven accretion. The vantage point of Cheshire demonstrates that the regions of the nation do not move in lockstep from one historical period to the next. Indeed, by covering nearly five centuries of literary production within a single geographical location, I challenge still dominant chronologies of literary history that emphasize cultural rupture and view the Renaissance as a sharp break from England's medieval past. My *longue durée* historicist account of Cheshire writing reveals instead the strategies whereby local writers, texts, and performances maintain regional continuity in response to the administrative pressures of academic and political centers.[1] In the following chapters, regional space/time emerges as a viable alternative to the national space/time that still defines both countries and canons.

Premodern Cheshire's suitability for my project derives from the county's awareness of itself as a community separate from its English and Welsh neighbors. This sense of regional distinction is already fully developed in the oldest extant piece of Cheshire writing, the ca. 1195 *Liber de Luciani laude Cestrie* ("The Book of Lucian in Praise of Chester").[2] Lucian's book is a description of the county town of Chester produced

by one of the monks resident in the city's Benedictine Abbey of St. Werburgh's. In a section of the text glossed *De moribus provincialium* ("On
the character of the provincials," p. 65), Lucian launches into a glowing
account of his fellow Cestrians. Most of the regional virtues he lists are
nondescript ones, common in any encomiastic discourse. But a few qualities stand out as specifically Cestrian:

> Si quis autem petit, vel in pleno, vel in proximo, secundum
> habitationem morum provinciales tangere, instar reliquorum
> viventium pro locis terrarum, ceteris Anglis in parte dissimiles,
> in parte meliores, in parte inveniuntur equales . . . Britonibus
> ex uno latere confines, et per longam transfusionem morum,
> maxima parte consimiles. (p. 65)

> (If anyone wants to compare, either fully or as closely as possible,
> the character of the provincials in relation to that of those liv-
> ing elsewhere, he will find them partly different from the other
> English, partly better, and partly equal . . . confined on one side
> by the Britons and, through a long transfusion of morals, mostly
> similar to them.)

The Cestrians are a hybrid population, neither truly English nor truly
Welsh.[3] Their preconquest Mercian origins connect them with their eastern neighbors, but their daily traffic (marital, mercantile, and military)
with their western neighbors pulls them in the opposite direction.

   According to Lucian, the regional landscape bears primary respon-
sibility for the Cestrians' status as heterogeneous *dissimiles*. Their Anglo-
Welsh *tranfusio morum* is possible due to the liquid nature of the River
Dee, the county's western boundary. The connection between ripar-
ian topography and ethnic instability is not made explicit in *De laude
Cestrie*: the section of the text devoted to the Dee (*De amne diva*, p. 46)
concentrates on the river as a nexus of international trade between
Chester, Aquitaine, Spain, Ireland, and Germany. But we do find a contemporary version of it in Gerald of Wales' *Itinerarium Kambriae*, the
first version of which was completed ca. 1191. In book 2, chapter 11,
Gerald reports that "Item, ut asserunt accolae, aqua ista singulis men-
sibus vada permutat; et utri finium, Angliae scilicet an Kambriae,

alveo relicto magis incuberit, gentem illam eo in anno succumbere, et alteram praevalere, certissimum prognosticum habent" ("The local inhabitants maintain that the Dee moves its fords every month and that, as it inclines more towards England or Wales in this change of channel, so they can prognosticate which nation will beat the other or be unsuccessful in war in any particular year").[4] The territory through which Gerald travels with Archbishop of Canterbury Baldwin in 1188 is a space marked by conflicting allegiances, generally secure within the English *imperium* but always open to Welsh incursions. It is also the zone in which Lucian's hybrid Cestrians dwell: although *De laude Cestrie* is not indebted to the *Itinerarium*, Lucian's *transfusio* does contain a hint of fluidity in its derivation from the Latin infinitive *transfundere*, "to pour out from one vessel into another." Gerald's Dee flows from one channel into another as time passes, marking the historically contingent boundaries of national identities. Lucian and his neighbors exist in a similar state of flux, acquiring Welshness at the expense of their Englishness.

Topography is not the only engine powering Cestrian exceptionalism: the county culture also derives its patriotism from Cheshire's unusual position within the premodern English polity. Post-Conquest Cheshire was a county palatine, an administrative region holding rights and privileges equivalent to those possessed elsewhere by the sovereign (in this case, the English Crown). This palatine designation is technically a back-formation: the first surviving reference to the earl of Chester as a *comes palatinus* comes in 1293, fifty-six years after the 1237 death of John the Scot, the last Anglo-Norman earl.[5] However, while the Cheshire governed by the Anglo-Norman earls from 1070–1237 may not have been a palatinate in name, it effectively was one in practice:

> [T]here appears to be abundant evidence that Cheshire stood apart, in the minds of contemporaries, from England. Although the importance of the county's absence from the Pipe Rolls has been minimized, that absence reflects a considerable degree of independence. Thus there was no royal demesne in Cheshire. The chief administrative official, the justice of Chester, was neither appointed by the king nor responsible to him. The king derived no benefit from scutages or tallages levied in the county. Royal

justices did not visit it; fines and amercements levied there did not reach the king.[6]

Stemming from the Anglo-Norman need for military flexibility in the Welsh Marches, these (and other) administrative distinctions did not immediately vanish with the earldom's annexation by the Crown in 1237, nor did they disappear upon the 1301 creation of Edward, son and heir of Edward I, as the first in a line of royal earls of Chester.[7] Many of them even survived the Henrician political reforms of the 1530s and 1540s, decades that otherwise saw Cheshire subjected to English justices of the peace (1536), national taxation (1540), and Parliamentary representation (1543).[8] These palatine practices remained vital in large part because they were grounded in a pair of county-specific institutions: the county court (presided over by the justice) and the county exchequer (supervised by the chamberlain), both of which continued in one form or another until 1830—and thus into modernity.[9] These two bodies had powers similar to those of their national parallels. For example, "Within the palatinate, the chamberlain occupied a position akin to that of the chancellor in the kingdom: he had custody of the Chester seal and was responsible for making out and sealing writs and charters."[10]

Cheshire's bureaucratic instantiations of autonomy were accompanied by the emergence of an ideology of regional independence, an explicitly palatine discourse. As Geoffrey Barraclough has noted, "perhaps not the least important" outcome of the county's 1237 royal annexation "was to stimulate in Cheshire both a sense of community and a sense of differentiation from the rest of England."[11] The sociopolitical dynamic Barraclough identifies here is crucial to my argument: Cheshire becomes increasingly Cestrian even as centrally located English governments appropriate (or eliminate) its unique institutions. To a large degree, regional identity depends on the loss of regional power, growing in strength as administrative autonomy diminishes. However, as Lucian's comments on Cheshire's problematic Englishness demonstrate above, Cestrian awareness of the county's "sense of differentiation" also predates the earldom's 1237 reversion. This is another key point in my thesis: local identity is always more than an epiphenomenon of cultural nostalgia. It has a material basis in distinct institutions and practices.

Lucian provides us with our first extended (or, rather, nondocumentary) example of palatine discourse in a passage of *De laude Cestrie* glossed *De Lima nemore*, "On the Forest of Lyme." There he writes:

Illud eciam intuendum, qualiter Cestrie provincia, Lime nemoris limite lateraliter clausa, quadam a ceteris Anglis privilegii distinctione sit libera, et per indulgentias regum atque excellentias comitum magis in cetu populi gladium principis quam coronam regni consuevit attendere, et in suis finibus etiam maximas negociorum discussiones licenter ac liberius explicare. (p. 65)

(This also should be considered: enclosed on the other side by the borders of the Forest of Lyme, the province of Chester is, by a certain distinction of privilege, free from all other Englishmen. By the indulgence of kings and the eminence of earls, it gives heed in the assemblies of its provincials more to the sword of its prince than to the crown of the king. Within their jurisdiction, they treat matters of great importance with the utmost freedom.)

If the naturally mercurial River Dee generates a disturbing identity with the Welsh, the legally fixed Forest of Lyme generates a pleasing difference from the English.[12] The cultural distinction produced by the Forest is not entirely innate, relying to a substantial degree on the *indulgentiae regum*. But Lucian's syntax first equates the kings' *indulgentiae* with the earls' *excellentiae* and then subordinates the *corona regni* to the *gladius principis*.[13] Within the *fines* of Cheshire, the latter is attended to *magis . . . quam*, "more than," the former. As a marginal gloss to the passage puts it, "Comiti paret regem non pavet" ("The earl is obeyed, the king is not feared," p. 65).

When the words of the gloss were written (by either Lucian or one of his monastic brethren), Cheshire's *princeps* was Ranulf III (1170–1232), the sixth and greatest of the county's seven Anglo-Norman earls.[14] Many of the quasi-royal offices that come to define the palatinate are first recorded during the forty-odd years of Ranulf's rule. For example, in either 1202 or 1203, Philip of Orby replaced Ranulf de Mainwaring as justice of Chester, the first in "a continuous succession of known justices."[15] Late twelfth- and early thirteenth-century records refer to Earl Ranulf's *camera*, the chamberlain-supervised financial office that came to be known as the Cheshire exchequer by the time of the royal annexation in 1237, five years after Ranulf's death.[16] In developing these institutions, the earl modeled his administration along royal lines. His efforts to establish Cheshire as an extra-English jurisdiction—a space parallel to, but not coterminous with, England—even extended into architecture. The entry for 1225 in the *Annales Cestrienses*, the chronicle of St. Werburgh's Abbey, states that "Item Rannulphus comes Cestrie cepit edificare castrum de Bestan" ("Also Ranulf, earl of Chester, began to build Beeston Castle," p. 54).[17] Dominating the Cheshire plain from its perch atop a steep bluff, Beeston Castle guards the southern and eastern approaches to Chester, "all too obviously defending the county from England rather than Wales."[18]

The local boosterism of *De laude Cestrie* functions as a textual analog to Earl Ranulf's contemporary political activities on behalf of the county and its administration. With the extinction of the earls' line and the county's reversion to the Crown in 1237, palatine discourse necessarily shifts generic contexts, abandoning reportage for what historian Tim Thornton calls Cheshire's "creation myth."[19] At the core of the myth is the ca. 1070 creation ceremony that transforms the Norman viscount Hugh d'Avranches into Hugh I of Chester. Henry Bradshaw's 1521 *Life of Saint Werburge* describes the ceremony as follows:

> With Wylliam conquerour came to this region
> A noble worthy prynce nominate Hug. Lupus,
> The dukes son of Britayne / and his syster son;
> Flourynge in chiualry, bolde and victorious,
> Manfull in batell / liberall and vertuous:
> To whom the kyng gaue for his enheritaunce
> The counte of Chesshire, with the appurtinaunce,
>
> By victorie to wynne the forsayd Erledom,
> Frely to gouerne it as by conquest right;
> Made a sure chartre to hym and his succession,
> By the swerde of dignite to holde it with myght,
> And to call a parlement to his wyll and syght,

To ordre his subiectes after true iustice
As a prepotent prince / and statutes to deuise.
$$(2.1262-75)^{20}$$

Bradshaw, like Lucian a monk of St. Werburgh's in Chester, wrote
some three centuries after his predecessor. But all of the elements of
palatine discourse are present in his narrative: Lucian's *gladium principis* becomes Bradshaw's "swerd of dignite," while the twelfth-century
monk's *coetus populi* turns into his successor's "parlement." According to Thornton, the Cheshire myth "was backed by a concrete symbol, a sword preserved in Chester Castle" and identified as "the very
weapon with which Hugh was created earl."[21] This supposed "swerd
of dignite" had sufficient ideological potency to ensure that it was
"removed to London as a trophy" after Royalist Chester fell to the Parliamentarians in 1646.[22] The removal had a clear spatial symbolism:
in taking the sword, the Parliament of the national center transferred
what Michelle R. Warren calls "a vital artifact of the medieval border
imaginary" to demonstrate its authority over the "parlement" of the
regional periphery.[23] But there were limits to such demonstrations,
signs that the metropole acknowledged the jurisdiction of the margin. Thornton notes that the sword "was soon returned . . . Ashmole
saw it in Chester in 1663."[24] The sword's return redefined its original
plunder, turning the 1646 appropriation of palatine authority into a
momentary rebuke instead of a permanent transformation in political
relations.

　　The legend of the sword also appears in *The Vale-Royall of England,
or, The County Palatine of Chester Illustrated*, a 1656 collection of four six-
teenth- and seventeenth-century Cheshire chorographies published in
London by the Chester-born engraver Daniel King. The Tudor herald
William Smith (ca. 1550–1618) notes in his opening portion of the
text that William the Conqueror gave his cousin Hugh d'Avranches
"the *County Palatine of Chester*, to hold as freely by the Sword, as he held
England by the Crown" (p. 49).[25] In the *Description of the City and County
Palatine of Chester* that follows Smith's account, Chester clerk William
Webb (fl. ca. 1580–1620) provides a Latin version of the same turn of
phrase: "Habendum et tenendum praedict. Com. Cestre sibi et heredi-
bus suis, ita Liberè ad gladium, sicut ipse Rex totam tenebat Angliam

P. M.
Prænobilis Richardi HUGH LUPUS EARLE of CHESTER
Grosuenour de Eaton
ju Comit: Cestr: Eq: aur: fitting in his PARLIAMENT with
et Baroneth, ex Stirpe
Dmitum Cestriæ vt abun the Barons and ABBOTS of
de patet in Archiuus A!
s 2 Regis Ric: 2.d that Countie PALATINE .

130

FIGURE 1   Earl Hugh I and the Cheshire parliament in Daniel King's *Vale-Royall of England* (1656). Illustration opposite p. 130. By permission of the Huntington Library, San Marino, California.

ad Coronam" ("to have and to hold the aforesaid county of Chester for himself and his heirs freely by the sword, just as the king himself holds all England by the crown," p. 130). Accompanying Smith's description of Earl Hugh's creation is an engraving depicting "HUGH LUPUS EARLE of CHESTER sitting in his PARLIAMENT with the Barons and ABBOTS of that Countie PALATINE" (figure 1).[26] Replicating on a local scale the medieval and early modern iconography of the English Parliament, the engraving places the sword of state at the right hand of the crowned and enthroned earl. It also shows the Cheshire parliament—clergy on the earl's right, barons on his left—engaged in the legislative business that distinguishes their county from all others in England. Put another way, the engraving evokes Lucian's *gladius principis, coetus populi,* and *maximae negociorum discussiones.* The twelfth-century cenobite and the seventeenth-century chorographer both share a common interest in the cultural potential of Cestrian topography and Cestrian jurisdiction.

Compiler King's paratext steeps Smith's and Webb's accounts of the earl's sword in an atmosphere of palatine perfection. For example, King's choice of title—*The Vale-Royall of England*—deliberately alludes to a well-known Cheshire landmark: the Cistercian abbey of Vale Royal, founded by Edward I in the centrally located parish of Over on 13 August 1277 and surrendered by Abbot John Hareware to Henry VIII's royal commissioners on 7 September 1538.[27] In a replay of the Dissolution, King appropriates the medieval monastic name and turns it to nationalizing ends, transforming what was once the heart of a county (Cheshire's Vale Royal) into the heart of the country (England's Vale Royal). One of King's commendatory writers, his "Worthy Cozen" John King, makes the national connection explicit: "Your Love unto our Nation is fully evidenced in your graphicall Description of *Cheshire*" (A2r). Yet the work is simultaneously an example of local patriotism: as the Chester-born King insists in his dedicatory letter to Sir Orlando Bridgeman, a former vice-chamberlain of Cheshire, "no *County* in this Nation doth exceed it [Cheshire] for a Succession of *Ancient Gentry*" (A1v). *The Vale-Royall of England* looks to the medieval past for its modern-day justification, arguing that regional culture can come to exemplify the nation. An anonymous dedicatory poem addressed to King emphasizes this point via rhyme: "CHESHIRE, *Palatinates* most Noble Pile, / CHESHIRE, the Glory of the *British* Isle!" (A2v).[28]

The palatine discourse promulgated by Lucian, Bradshaw, Smith, Webb, and King continues to play a role in modern-day Cheshire. Here is the current online description of the Cheshire County Council's coat of arms:

> The Shield displays the trio of golden wheatsheaves on blue which have been associated with the Earldom of Chester since the late 12th century. The Shield is the same as that known to have been used as the City arms of Chester in 1560 and which can be seen on the bridge at Eastgate, Chester. From 1779 this shield was occasionally used as the Chester Assay Office hallmark.
>
> Above the Shield is the closed helm, proper to civic arms, with decorative mantling in the livery colours of blue and gold. The Crest is a royal lion between two ostrich feathers, referring to the Principality and Palatinate, upon a red mural crown alluding to Chester's sandstone walls. The feathers franking the Shield are supported by gold lions derived from the arms of the third and fourth Earls of Chester.[29]

Created in 1938, this device is a deliberate hodge-podge, an assemblage of disparate historical signs into a single genealogical image.[30] The device combines the jurisdictions of Anglo-Norman earldom, royal palatinate, and civic corporation: comital lions share the same space with princely feathers and municipal defenses. Tying everything together (and lying directly in the center of the arms) is Earl Hugh's sword: the blazon for the shield reads "azure a sword erect between three garbs or." To this we can add the county motto: "Jure et dignitati gladii" or "By the law and dignity of the sword."

What the palatine myth promises Cheshire is a regional identity with an unbroken lineage, one in which Earl Hugh's sword continues to guard Cheshire over the course of centuries. But the bricolage of the county arms demonstrates in actuality that juxtaposition and amalgamation—not unity and purity—are the logics at work in Cheshire writing. The cultural continuities examined in this book are products, not essences. They rely on material processes of accretion and adaptation, reclaiming the cultural materials of an earlier generation for use in new historical contexts. The *gladium principis* is one example of this dynamic: Lucian points to the sword as an indicator of local strength, while the Parliamentarians remove it from the county as a means of stressing local subordination. Another instance is the fourteenth-century stone structure of St. Nicholas's Chapel, located at 32–34 Northgate Street in Chester. Built by the Benedictine monks of St. Werburgh's no later than 1348, the Chapel was originally home to both the Guild of St. Nicholas and the parishioners of St. Oswald's (who had formerly met in the nave of St. Werburgh's).[31] After the Dissolution, the building was turned over to the city: it served for many years as the civic Assembly's Common Hall, the mayor and sheriff's Pentice and portmote courts, and the local corn market's spare warehouse.[32] In more recent times, St. Nicholas's took a theatrical turn, serving as a theater, a music hall, and a cinema during the eighteenth, nineteenth, and twentieth centuries.[33] At the time of the writing of this book, the chapel has added yet another identity to its already impressive roster: zoned for retail, it bears the corporate name "Superdrug" above its eastern entrance in large, bold, green letters (figure 2). From the cure of souls to the cure of colds—St. Nicholas's continues to take part in a cultural, topographical, and architectural tradition of modification and accumulation.

The specifically Cestrian nature of my *longue durée* approach differentiates it from the new literary history exemplified by scholars like David Wallace and James Simpson. Wallace locates the end of the Middle Ages in Henry VIII's assault on the monasteries, "the single most important institutional framing for the collection, copying and preservation of medieval texts."[34] Simpson's reversal of Whig periodization concentrates instead on Henry's reorganization of the English polity, arguing "that the institutional simplifications and centralizations of the sixteenth century provoked correlative simplifications and narrowings in literature."[35] Both agree, though, that the 1530s and 1540s are the decades that see out the English Middle Ages. Much of my analysis agrees with theirs: for example, the transition between chapters 1 and 2 relies on Henrician reformations of Cestrian space (the 1506 transformation of the city into a county in its own right) and spirituality (the 1539/40 dissolution of St. Werburgh's).

Wallace's and Simpson's critiques of traditional periodization nonetheless rely more on concepts of nation than on those of region. They

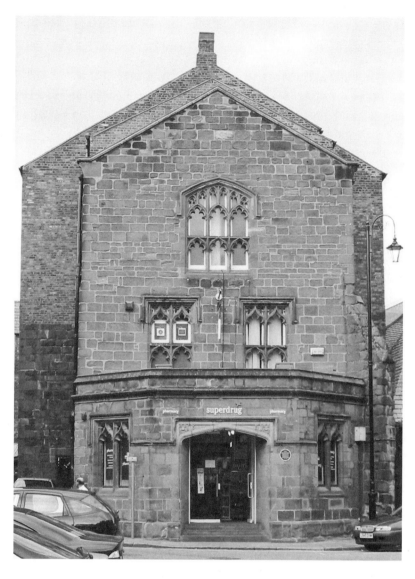

FIGURE 2   St. Nicholas's Chapel (2002). Photograph by Robert W.
Barrett, Jr.

focus on the ways in which powerful centers force subjection upon unwilling peripheries. My regional focus concentrates instead on the irregular distribution of periodization across English space: the historical changes we identify as period markers do not take place inside a single homogenous space, but within a heterogeneous England divided into an assemblage of "parcellized sovereignties."[36] Ralph Hanna's recent argument for a new attention to "the polyvocal and individuated voices of discrete local/regional literary cultures" relies on a consciously ironic dislocation of London, transforming the metropole into another of fourteenth-century England's "vernacular backwaters."[37] In spatial terms, Hanna turns England inside out, exposing its center as one periphery among many. I take an opposite tack, demonstrating peripheral Cheshire's claims to central status.[38] As Thornton points out, Cheshire's marginal position "just beyond the core territory of England" is simultaneously "at the interface—in many ways the centre—of the influence of the various core territories which made up the British Isles in the late medieval and early modern period."[39] Lucian describes three of the "core territories" meeting at this "interface" in *De laude Cestrie*: "Hec igitur Hibernis receptoria, Britannis vicina, Anglorum sumministratur annona[m]" ("This place is therefore a port of receipt for the Irish, a neighbor to the Welsh, and is served grain by the English," p. 65). William Smith adds Scotland to this list when he asserts in his portion of *Vale-Royall* that centuries of military recruiting have made "The name of a *Scot*, odious in Cheshire" (p. 19).

Put another way, Cheshire is a crucial test case for the study not only of medieval and early modern Englishness but of the early modern Atlantic Archipelago as well. Originating in J. G. A. Pocock's call for a "new British history," this emergent field locates what Philip Schwyzer calls its "essence" in its "willingness to challenge traditional boundaries—boundaries, that is, between the histories of different nation-states, and also between academic disciplines."[40] David Baker is more specific: "What drives the British history, I would say, is the demand that apparently distinct entities—call them 'nations'—be considered in their constitutive inter-relatedness."[41] Schwyzer's and Baker's references to "nation-states" and "nations" testify to the implicitly (and traditionally) national focus of archipelagic studies. The field is not intrinsically hostile to regional analysis: three of the essays included in Schwyzer and co-editor Simon Mealor's *Archipelagic Identities* concentrate on specifically regional communities.[42] However, its programmatic assertions reflexively treat the nation as the default unit of analysis. The "hitherto neglected peripheries" that archipelagic specialists like Baker and Willy Maley restore to academic attention turn out to be Wales, Ireland, and Scotland.[43] As for Englishness, it is first (and promisingly) identified as "not a self-generated but rather a relational identity"—but is then immediately redefined as "a matter of complex and often bitter negotiation among the nations of the Atlantic archipelago (England, Ireland, Scotland, and Wales)."[44]

Similar elisions of the regional are present in medieval postcolonial studies. When Geraldine Heng investigates England's "consolidating itself as a nation," she contrasts "national rivals across the sea or ethnic antagonists sharing a border with the English polity—the French, Irish, Welsh, Scots" with English Jewry, "a resident alien community *within* England."[45] The point is well taken, but an opportunity is missed: Heng's concept of "internal others" could just as easily apply to Cestrians and other regional communities subject to "English manipulation."[46] Patricia Clare Ingham makes precisely this point in a discussion of fifteenth-century North-South conflict within England, insisting that "a policy of 'internal colonialism' has consequences for intra-English relations as well as for Anglo-Scots, or English-Welsh, ones."[47] But even Ingham conflates region and nation. At different moments in her work, she refers to "relations between medieval England and the regions of its insular neighbors" and "Regions of the so-called 'Celtic fringe.'"[48] As I show in chapter 4, these are not mere slips of the pen: Ingham's reading of *SGGK*, one that explicitly acknowledges the role of regional Cheshire identity within the text, nonetheless identifies Sir Gawain's passage through the county's hundred of the Wirral as an encounter with colonized "Welsh wildness" and treats it accordingly.[49]

Each of these examples demonstrates the intellectual attraction of what Jeffrey Jerome Cohen calls "big designators like the nation."[50] Region either goes unnoticed as a category of analysis or finds itself transformed into one of many available "big designators" (a group that includes class, ethnicity, race, religion, and sex/gender in addition to nation). The multiregional character of these otherwise crucial categories eclipses the equally necessary concept of the local. England maintains its national coherence because its intranational spaces escape sustained analysis. According to Thornton, the "new British history" ironically "tends . . . to display the same certainties of unity within each of the three kingdoms of England, Scotland, and Ireland which it criticised in the old historiographical elision of England with Great Britain or the British Isles."[51] The same is frequently true of medieval postcolonial studies: Englishness may be put under analytical pressure, placed into dialogue with hitherto neglected identities, but English space emerges largely intact.

Concerns like these explain why I only occasionally cross England's international borders in the chapters that follow. At the moment, Cheshire's position on the Anglo-Welsh interface is in less need of critical attention than its position within the English state. The same can be said of the county's traditional function as a staging ground for invasions of Ireland and Scotland. Cestrians certainly took part in the ethnically targeted "violences and internal colonizations upon which Englishness was founded."[52] But they themselves were often targets of the same process of sociopolitical homogenization, one that sought to minimize regional as well as racial distinctions. This book therefore attends to the intranational tensions between Cheshire and the larger English community.

Over the *longue durée*, we might see that conflict as a net loss for Cheshire, one that ends in 1830 with the fulfillment of Westminster's centuries-long assimilation of local prerogative. This is certainly the position of Michael Bennett and John M. Bowers, the two most vocal advocates for the academic study of medieval Cestrian identity.[53] For these scholars, Cheshire's brief tenure (1397–99) as a principality under Richard II represents the county's heyday, a cultural apex swiftly reduced to mere provinciality at the hands of the Lancastrian usurpers.[54] A sense of catastrophe therefore informs Bennett's description of Cheshire's fifteenth-century "expatriate careerists" as men who "lost their regional identity" to a London-centered cosmopolitanism: "While John Stanley of Battersea . . . commissioned a handsome manuscript full of the latest Chaucerian verse, and while the gifted sons of Hugh Bostock and Hugh Holes indulged themselves in Petrarchan elegancies, their country cousins reverted to the crude, regional chauvinism typical of the later works of the alliterative revival."[55] It also appears in

Bowers's comments on British Library MS Cotton Nero A.x, the unique copy of the *Gawain*-poet's works: "the Cotton Nero collection reflects an aftermath of provincial retreat and reduced means . . . the manuscript was produced for a backwoods manorial culture of the sort created by Cheshire's knightly families such as the Masseys at Tatton, the Grosvenors at Hulme, and the Stanleys at Storeton."[56] Faced with the "utterly provincial" embarrassment that is Cotton Nero A.x, Bowers consoles himself by imagining the book's "jewel-like" and "sumptuous" exemplar, "a deluxe manuscript produced during the period of Cheshire privilege at court, also now long lost."[57] His flight of fancy replays the plot of *Pearl*: Bowers and the poem's narrator are both in mourning for a "long-lost" jewel. For Bennett and Bowers, Cheshire is involuntarily past its prime.

The persistence of the palatine myth suggests otherwise. Each moment of national centralization (such as the case of the 1645 plundering of Chester Castle) triggers local expressions of differentiation (such as King's 1656 publication of *The Vale-Royall*). Administrative assimilation can result in the loss of regional distinction—but it can also stimulate new cultural production. Thornton calls into question the assumption that "strong local identities . . . necessarily mean that localist or even separatist opposition were dominant in politics," reminding us that "Cheshire's origin myth founded the county's position in a monarch's creation, not a separate evolution."[58] His acknowledgment here of Cheshire's peripheral "regard to the authority of the center" bears some resemblance to the work of Thorlac Turville-Petre and Richard Helgerson on the intersection of national and regional identity.[59] In their analyses, regions willingly subordinate themselves to the needs of the nation. Turville-Petre has stated that "local affiliations and interests all have to be interpreted against the image that the nation as a whole has constructed of itself, because the region has a strong urge to identity with the nation that confers on it cultural significance, military and political power, a framework of legal rights, and international prestige."[60] Helgerson concurs, noting that "[t]he particularities, after all, constantly remind us of the whole of which they are part and from which they take meaning, even if only by difference."[61]

I take these cautions into consideration, exploring Cheshire's written and performative traditions for evidence of accord: my exploration in chapter 2 of the Chester Whitsun plays' involvement in the enforcement of Tudor poor law is one example of regional and national cooperation. So is my account in chapter 3 of Cestrian participation in the festivities surrounding Henry Frederick Stuart's creation as Prince of Wales and Earl of Chester. But there will also be moments of contestation, instances in which the interests of region oppose those of nation. The juxtaposition in chapter 5 of *SGGK* with the 1385–91 Scrope-Grosvenor heraldry trial examines regional resistance to centrally coordinated schemes of accommodation. There will even be occasions of intra-Cheshire strife: chapter 1 uses Bradshaw's *Life of St. Werburge* to explore a jurisdictional conflict between the mayor of Chester and the abbot of St. Werburgh's that must finally be resolved by the Crown. In each case, I want to preserve the situation-specific dialectic between these two spatial identities: grounded in the topography of a particular place (even if that site is constantly subject to renegotiation over time), Cestrian identity is nonetheless dialogic. Its inscription in text and performance bears this out, demonstrating the sheer variety of local responses to institutional and cultural initiatives emerging from the center.

My emphasis on the multiform character of regional culture—its simultaneous awareness of local and national contexts—leads me at last to the title of this book. *Against All England* is a phrase taken from the sixteenth-century ballad *Bosworth Field*.[62] In the poem, a tyrannical Richard III spends 112 of the text's 656 lines assembling a mighty army in defense of his crown against Henry Tudor. These troops are an explicitly national force: Richard's messengers have been recruiting them "throughout England ffar & neere" (line 218). Faced with the unprecedented size of this host, the pro-Tudor poet exclaims:

> had wee not need to Iesu to pray,
>> that made the world, the day & night,
> to keepe vs out of bale and woe?
>> 2 shires against all England to ffight,
>
> & maintaine HENERY that came ffor his right,
>> & in the realme of England was ready bowne!
>> (lines 337–42)

Henry's only allies against Richard are the noble Stanleys and the members of their Cheshire and Lancashire affinities. This passage crystallizes the book's project in two ways. First, it communicates the strong sense of Cestrian exceptionalism that informs the texts I study: "2 shires" have the power to defeat "all England."[63] Second, the poet's remark exemplifies the complex intertwining of regional and national identities discussed in the pages to follow: even as the Tudors strip away many of Cheshire's palatine prerogatives, *Bosworth Field* confidently claims that royal power is wholly dependent on local support. The preposition "against" is key here, conveying both contrast and contiguity. Regional identity is simultaneously oppositional and compliant: protective of the advantages afforded by their marginal position on the Anglo-Welsh border, medieval and early modern Cestrians nonetheless imagine themselves as central to England's construction as a nation.

Against All England's account of the Cestrian imaginary falls into two sections, each organized around a particular regional space and the texts/performances that it produces. Part 1, "Chester the City: Contesting Urban Space in Monastic Writing and Civic Performance," contains three chapters devoted to the articulation of local identity within the walls of Chester. This urban emphasis is compatible with larger, regional concerns: the palatinate institutions of the castle attracted numerous suitors from all over Cheshire, while the city markets served as an entrepôt for the entire county. Moreover, rural gentlemen held civic offices throughout the period under study, and urban merchants and artisans celebrated their economic successes by acquiring land in the countryside.[64] City and county were intimately connected. Part 1 therefore begins in chapter 1 with the medieval "invention" of the city by its Benedictine monks, moves in chapter 2 to the Whitsun plays' sixteenth-century lay appropriation of monastic space, and ends in chapter 3 with a seventeenth-century pageant that honors the city as much as, if not more than, its nominal royal subject. Complementing this focus on local interaction is a careful attention to the interplay of urban and national identities—whether those conjunctions are the result of print publication in the capital (chapters 1 and 3) or legal promulgation in the provinces (chapter 2).

Chapter 1, "From Cloister to Corporation: Imagining Chester in Benedictine Encomium and Saint's Life," concentrates on Lucian's *De laude Cestrie* and Bradshaw's *Life of St. Werburge*. Lucian's Latin *encomium urbis* reads Cestrian topography through biblical exegesis: the city's streets and buildings become scripture made manifest. Bradshaw's vernacular *Life* opts instead for a somatic approach, conflating the body politic with the inviolate body of its patron saint. What unites both authors is their investment in local politics: Lucian confirms St. Werburgh's twelfth-century dominion over Chester by treating the city as though it were a product of the monastery's *scriptorium*, while Bradshaw attempts (and fails) to defend the Abbey's jurisdiction against sixteenth-century civic encroachments by redefining its foes as the latest in a long line of secular threats to the virgin saint's sacred body. The chapter concludes with a consideration of the London publication of the *Life* in 1521: local disaster gives way to national success as the monastic idea of cloistered Chester finds itself deployed by King's Printer Richard Pynson against foreign Lutheranism.

The Dissolution of 1536–40 puts paid to monastic ideas of Chester. The Abbey's transformation into an Anglican cathedral creates an ideological vacuum in the city, one quickly filled by the civic corporation and its Whitsun plays. Lawrence M. Clopper has argued that the Chester plays represent the city's victorious appropriation of the monks' spiritual mission.[65] In chapter 2, "Grounds of Grace: Mobile Meaning and Processional Performance in the Chester Whitsun Plays," I give Clopper's thesis a topographical dimension, following the plays on their processional route around the city—a path that remaps Chester in accordance with civic, not monastic, desires and designs. Each performance station on this route is an urban site with unique cultural resonances and uses, and thus each play takes on different meanings as it moves from station to station. Two plays receive particular attention: the Tanners' *Fall of Lucifer* and the Glovers' *Blind Chelidonian; the Raising of Lazarus*. I read the Tanners' play in relation to perambulatory ritual and systems of oligarchic franchise: expelled from a Heaven which the pageant simultaneously defines as urban space, Lucifer functions as a figure of disenfranchisement, a potential touchstone for the city government's ongoing struggle with the palatinate exchequer over questions of jurisdiction. My analysis of the Glovers' play tracks the blind beggar of John 9:1–38 as he and his pageant wagon move from station to station, literally violating the spatial restrictions on paupers established by the mayors of Chester in conjunction with the Crown's national poor laws.

Chapter 3, "*Chester's Triumph*: Absence and Authority in Seventeenth-Century Civic Ceremonial," concludes the civic section of *Against All England* by focusing on Chester ironmonger Robert Amery's 1610 triumph in honor of Henry Frederick Stuart upon his creation as Prince of Wales and Earl of Chester. Amery's show represents a self-conscious attempt by a regional culture to participate in the national celebration of the prince's creation. It therefore serves as evidence against the claims of scholars like Peter Womack that the emergence of the commercial stage in London means the end of provincial performance in England.[66] London pageantry and Westminster policy certainly challenge Chester's self-celebration, but they do not overwhelm it. At the same time, chapter 3 deals with a disturbing absence at the heart of the 1610 triumph: because Prince Henry was nowhere near Chester on the day of performance, Amery's show becomes a royal entry without a royal presence. As a result, the pageant becomes the site of an internal civic struggle to take the prince's place and appropriate his authority. Amery participates in this conflict, taking advantage of a pun on his surname to insert himself into the performance as Love, victor in a battle against an Envy all too reminiscent of his local rivals. In a sense, the corporation's sixteenth-century success in assuming control over Chester's self-image threatens to undo that image in the early seventeenth century through factional infighting.

In part 2, "Cheshire the County: Destabilizing National Identity in Regional Romance," I leave behind the city of Chester, concentrating instead on the production of regional identity at the county level. The cultural vehicle for this process is the romance, the same genre that Heng links to "the projection of a national community and its future."[67] What I show in this section of the book is that romance can just as easily unsettle ideas of the nation, especially at moments of crisis or reorganization within the English polity (for example, Richard II's baronial troubles, Henry VII's usurpation of the throne, and the Civil Wars of the 1640s)—the very moments that Turville-Petre identifies as essential to the production of "national unity."[68] In Turville-Petre's reading of the thirteenth and early fourteenth centuries, nationalist discourses resist cultural "disintegration" because they effectively transcend many of the alternate identities that generate intranational conflict in the first place.[69] National identity comes to dominate all others because it serves "the interest of all sides, whatever their political agenda."[70] The texts I explore in part 2 complicate Turville-Petre's narrative of progressive domination, either by discounting the possibility of a truly national community (chapter 4) or by insisting on the nation's dependence on the virtues of specific regional communities (chapter 5). Political crises may provide the center with opportunities for the propagation of English identity, but they also give a region like Cheshire a chance to strengthen its own self-image.

The cultural processes at stake in these emergences are fluid and subject to frequent renegotiation—dominance depends on the needs of the historical moment. This is why chapter 4, "Heraldic Devices/Chivalric Divisions: *Sir Gawain and the Green Knight* and the Scrope-Grosvenor Trial," deliberately (and seemingly counterintuitively) sidesteps the attempts of scholars like Bennett and Bowers to provide the *Gawain*-poet with a Cheshire pedigree and thus to read his poems as instances of regional pride and ambition. I opt instead for an exploration of the part that locations like the Wirral play in the poem: region in *SGGK* is less an identity to be celebrated than a problem to be solved. We see this ambivalence in the chapter's opening analysis of the Scrope-Grosvenor controversy, a battle over an inadvertently shared set of arms between the Cheshire knight Sir Robert Grosvenor and the Yorkshire knight Sir Richard Scrope. The evidence given in the Scrope-Grosvenor case suggests that chivalric honor has a topographical basis, that a knight's identity may be more regionally focused than hitherto assumed. These topographies of honor inform *SGGK*: Arthur's champion finds that his pentangle device is not universally comprehensible, that the identities of the center (Camelot) are called into question by those of the margins (the Green Knight's castle of Hautdesert). Indeed, the poem's finale turns inward, establishing intraregional community at the expense of interregional community. National coherence is questioned, but so is regional intelligibility.

The works under discussion in chapter 5, "Two Shires against All England: Celebrating Regional Affinity in the Stanley Family Romances," are more positive about the chances for regional and national rapprochement. These texts—a cluster of fifteenth- and sixteenth-century

romances and ballads devoted to the Stanley family, Cheshire magnates
and Earls of Derby—concentrate on two historical moments: the deposition of Richard at Bosworth Field in 1485 and the bloody English victory
over the Scots at Flodden Field in 1513. Both battles are crucial to the
Tudor dynasty's nationalizing ambitions, yet the Stanley family romances
insist on the part that local affinities play in establishing national hegemony: it is the valor of the Stanleys and of their Cheshire and Lancashire
retainers in each encounter that makes the victory of England possible.
Highly localized and regionally chauvinistic, the romances nonetheless
had a surprising transregional appeal: *The Stanley Poem* appears in one of
London antiquarian John Stow's numerous collections, while a Flodden
poem contained in the 1517–39 commonplace book of London mercer
John Colyns sings the praises not only of Sir Edward Stanley, but "maney
a Royall man of the Weste Contre" as well.[71] The chapter confirms this
complex interplay of national and regional identities by examining a tri-
angulated attempt to produce a new Stanley romance based on the 1644
Parliamentarian siege of Lathom House, the Royalist Stanleys' family
seat. Private journals written by members of the garrison provide a local
take on the command of Countess Charlotte Stanley, wife of James Stanley, seventh Earl of Derby, while public newsbook accounts coming out
of Oxford and London debate the proper generic framework for understanding the Countess's actions. National disaster once again generates
an opportunity for the exercise of regional identity.

The epilogue to *Against All England* returns to St. Werburgh's,
taking up two twenty-first-century cultural productions linked to the
Abbey. The first is 2006 Cheshire Poet Laureate Andrew Rudd's "Chester Cathedral," a sonnet published as part of Rudd's online anthology
of Cheshire verse, *Lines on the Map*. "Chester Cathedral" meditates on
the place of St. Werburgh's in Cestrian history, establishing a transhistorical yet spatially grounded connection between Roman legionaries,
medieval monks, and modern tourists. The second of these modern-
era creations is the 2007 St. Werburgh Festival, a nine-day celebration
of the ca. 907 translation of the saint's relics from Hanbury to Chester. The climax of the festival involved the 21 June entry into Chester
of the saint's "relics," brought to the city from Hanbury by a group of
local dignitaries costumed as monks. What unites Rudd's sonnet and
the St. Werburgh Festival is their enactment of a distinctively regional

tradition grounded in the disparate Cestrian histories discussed in this book: monastic, civic, theatrical, aristocratic, and antiquarian. Separated by nearly two centuries, the poem and the procession nonetheless deploy the same accumulative strategy for the generation of local identity. They blend what were once distinct cultural narratives, turning old stories to new ends. In this, they are the literary and performative analogs of St. Nicholas's Chapel, amalgams that testify to the ongoing vitality of Cestrian culture.

Part 1

Chester the City

*Contesting Urban Space in Monastic Writing
and Civic Performance*

CHAPTER ONE

FROM CLOISTER TO CORPORATION

Imagining Chester in
Benedictine Encomium and Saint's Life

THE HISTORY OF CHESHIRE WRITING BEGINS IN THE PRECINCTS OF
the Benedictine abbey of St. Werburgh in Chester, founded in 1092 by
Hugh Lupus, the first Anglo-Norman Earl of Chester, and St. Anselm
of Bec.[1] The monastic works produced therein are not only among
the oldest extant Cheshire texts (and thus a likely point of departure);
they are also texts about Chester and Cheshire, texts deeply invested
in the creation and transmission of specific localities. Text and context
explicitly fuse in Cheshire's medieval monastic writing: the foundation
of the county's literary tradition is simultaneously the foundation of its
local identity. As my introduction has shown, Lucian's *De laude Cestrie*
acknowledges the cultural distinction generated by Cheshire's position
on the western border of England—a "geographic alterity" that produces "centricity and global supremacy" for the monastery (and the
larger regional community to which it belongs).[2] *De laude Cestrie* is also
the foundational text for a more tightly focused monastic topography

devoted to the city of Chester. Beginning in the 1190s with Lucian, the abbey's conceptualization of civic space is still active in the early 1500s when monk Henry Bradshaw writes his *Life of Saint Werburge*. This chapter concentrates on these two Benedictine authors, whose positions near the opposite ends of the monastery's historical lifetime (1092–1539/40) make them ideal subjects for a *longue durée* study of a monastic genealogy of urban imagining and its construction of space in specific social forms.[3] Lucian's and Bradshaw's texts both construct an ideal Chester in which urban space and sacred space are simultaneous and indistinguishable. In St. Werburgh's Chester, the various social estates live in harmony, united by their veneration of the saint's relics and their respect for the monks' wisdom. The local landscape undergoes exegesis, its physical features translated into spiritual signs and holy objects.

As I shall argue, however, Lucian's and Bradshaw's attempts to depict their frontier city on the River Dee as a type of the New Jerusalem coincide with their efforts to intervene in local political struggle on the monastery's behalf, to shape the conditions of conflict to their own side's advantage. In the last decade of the twelfth century, Lucian's monastic-urban ideal faces little opposition; his abbey shares social dominance and urban power with the earl's palatinate, and no other group within the city has sufficient material and ideological resources to construct a rival arrangement of Cestrian space. Embroiled in legal battles with a civic corporation interested in expanding the scope of its authority, Bradshaw's sixteenth-century abbey has no such luxury—it must aggressively pursue its interests. I will focus on the conflict that most concerns Bradshaw in the *Life*: the 1506–9 controversy over the implications of Henry VII's city charter for the rival jurisdictions of the mayor and the abbot. At the heart of this dispute is a contest between competing images of the city, between Chester as an extension of monastic space and Chester as a site of accumulation and merchant capital. Moreover, this second Chester has become a county in its own right, a newly nationalized space produced as part of the Tudor monarchy's larger project of geopolitical realignment.

The city's revised inclusion in the emergent Tudor state also provides an explanation for the *Life*'s 1521 publication in London by King's Printer Richard Pynson. In the transition from manuscript to print and from regional center to metropolitan capital, monastic Chester finds itself confronted by national spaces and appropriated to national ends—in this case, the English reaction against Martin Luther in the 1520s. With their entry into emergent Reformation discourse, St. Werburgh's relics—focal points for the old idea of the city—receive a new and vulnerable meaning: nineteen years after Pynson deploys Bradshaw's *Life* in defense of catholic orthodoxy, the abbey will be dissolved, its shrine destroyed, and its texts scattered. The 1539/40 dispersal of the abbey's library signals the end of the monks' urban imagination. Monastic Chester surrenders to a civic vision of the city, and the textual tradition inaugurated by Lucian's *De laude Cestrie* gives way to a rival reading of local space, an alternative corpus originating instead in Mayor Henry Gee's Assembly Book.

THE CLOISTERED CITY: ALLEGORICAL TOPOGRAPHIES IN LUCIAN'S *DE LAUDE CESTRIE*

Written ca. 1195 in the cloister of St. Werburgh's (and uniquely preserved in Oxford's Bodleian Library MS Bodley 672), Lucian's *De laude Cestrie* represents one of the earliest English instances of urban *descriptio*.[4] The text celebrates the city and its inhabitants, carefully combining urban observation with learned *encomium urbis*.[5] In the process of lauding Chester, Lucian brings his own locality into being—he creates Chester as a specifically situated, specifically ideological space. As he says, "Michi permittat proxima tangere, vicina cantare" ("I'm privileged to touch upon things close by, to sing of these environs," p. 59).[6] His singing has a distinctly religious cast: Lucian devotes more than half of *De laude Cestrie*'s 195 folios to homilies on the virtues of the clerks, monks, and nuns of Chester. He particularly concentrates on the monastic offices of abbot, prior, and sub-prior, repeatedly enumerating their duties and praising their dedication to Benedictine principles.[7]

This ecclesiastical emphasis signals monastic Chester's conflation of secular and sacred space. Lucian acknowledges a profound spiritual and material continuity between St. Werburgh's and the other urban structures and institutions of Chester. This sense of connection derives in part from the topographical, economic, and legal position of the monastery: by the 1190s (just a century after its foundation), St. Werburgh's properties quite literally enveloped the city, and the abbey complex itself occupied almost the entire northeastern quadrant of Chester.[8] But Lucian also relies on his reading of the Bible (what he calls *scriptura nostra*, p. 49) to define urban space. He asks us to imagine Chester in our mind's eye (*Ecce . . . civitatem nostram* or "Look! . . . our city," p. 49), identifying the city as the material realization of Job 5:6, "nihil in terra sine causa fit" ("nothing upon earth is done without a cause," p. 49).[9] Here divine purpose guides urban history: Chester's buildings exist to remind Cestrians of their cosmic place in God's universe as well as of their Christian duties.

Lucian's audience of would-be urban exegetes are nominally *meos cives* ("my fellow citizens," fol. 15r).[10] Throughout the text, he equates *lectores* ("readers") with *habitatores* ("inhabitants"), asking at one point, "Que percipit lector, nonne perspicit habitator?" ("Doesn't the inhabitant observe what the reader perceives?" p. 59). He thus defines his readership in spatial terms: for example, a reference to the divine establishment of St. Peter's parish church as a *memoriam . . . in centro urbis* ("a memorial . . . in the center of the city," p. 44) is accompanied by the gloss "Probet oculis suis habitator" ("the inhabitant may verify this with his own eyes," fol. 11v). But we should be careful about identifying Lucian's primary audience with the laity who make up the bulk of medieval Chester's population. His ideal reader is more than a mere *habitator*: Lucian writes instead for the *clericus inhabitator* ("clerical inhabitant," p. 67) and the *literatus Cestrie habitator* ("literate inhabitant of Chester," p. 56).[11] The Latinity of *literatus* suggests the practical limits to Lucian's audience: in spite of his gestures toward a more inclusive audience, the Cestrians he addresses are effectively the local clergy.

By recognizing that Lucian's intended readers are actually a minority within the larger community he claims to address, we gain a better understanding of the deliberate deformations his spatial hermeneutic works on the cityscape of Chester. Consider the following description of a spectator standing in the marketplace at the city center:

Nam siquis stans in fori medio, vultum vertat ad ortum solis,
secundum ecclesiarum positiones, inveniet Iohannem Domini
precursorem ab oriente, Petrum apostolum ab occidente,

Werburgam virginem ab aquilone, Archangelum Michaelem a
meridie. Nichil illa scriptura verius, "super muros tuos Ierusalem
constitui custodes." Nichil hac evidentia dulcius, cui tales Deus
contulit servatores. Sollempne munus: suave misterium. Confortat
animos et pascit intuitum. (p. 47)

(Now, if someone is standing in the middle of the marketplace,
let him turn his face toward the rising of the sun: according to
the positions of the churches, he will find John the precursor
of the Lord in the east, Peter the apostle in the west, the virgin
Werburgh in the north, and the Archangel Michael in the
south. Never was there a scripture truer than "upon thy walls, O
Jerusalem, I have appointed watchmen." Never was there a sweeter
testimony to those whom God gave such servants. Solemn gift,
sweet mystery! It comforts souls and feeds the mind.)

As the passage reveals, Lucian has reconfigured the act of reading as
motion and gesture—the physical structures of Chester are a *misterium* in need of explication. Turning in space, this spectator carries out
that process of exegesis, bearing witness to the literalization of Isaiah
62:6 ("super muros tuos Ierusalem, constitui custodes") and to the
city's material confirmation of divinely inspired prophecy. Lucian uses
Isaiah's *Ierusalem* to remind his readers of Chester's place within typological history, its double identity as successor to the prophet's Old Jerusalem and as type of the New.[12] The spectator's movements replicate
Christian chronology: his panorama begins in the east with St. John
the Baptist, then turns west to the apostolic age of St. Peter, north to
the missionary era of St. Werburgh and the Anglo-Saxon saints, and
finally south to St. Michael's apocalyptic battle against the Devil.

However, those motions and sights are only possible in the allegorical Chester of Lucian's text. In the material Chester of the 1190s,
no such vantage point exists. There was indeed a medieval market at
the intersection of the city's primary streets, but standing in that space
would put St. Peter's directly to the north of the spectator, not to the
west.[13] Another candidate for Lucian's *forum* is the marketplace outside
the Abbey Gate, the site of the monks' summer fair.[14] As the symbol
of the abbey's economic dominance over the citizens of Chester, this

location has the advantage of playing to Lucian's sense of monastic superiority. Nevertheless, it too is disoriented in relation to the text: St. Werburgh's lies to the east of this *forum*, not to the north, and St. Peter's is now directly south of the spectator, the same direction as St. Michael's. Lucian's *forum* is thus best seen as an imaginary space, an ideological amalgam of Chester's physical center and its political center (identified by Lucian as St. Werburgh's). *De laude Cestrie* functions as textual "urban renewal," shifting portions of the city's topography around in an attempt to consolidate the abbey's influence.

This spiritualization of the urban is central to Lucian's aims in *De laude Cestrie*. The work opens with what initially appears to be a clear separation of institutional space and power. Lucian has stopped to rest in the porch of St. John's after a hard morning's work in Chester Castle and the *curia comitis* ("earl's court," p. 38).[15] Tired out by his efforts *pro causis et utilitatibus monasterii* ("on behalf of the abbey's business and profit," p. 67), he meets with his clerical patron and reflects on the day's experience in overtly spatial language: "castellum tedio set ecclesia solatio fuit; in definicione negocii distulit me turgiditas et superbia secularium, set refovit honestas et amor domesticorum, et quicquid lesit aula principis, lenivit uberius atrium Precursoris" ("the castle was tedium, but the church was solace. While handling my business, the pride and pomp of secular things overwhelmed me, but the decency and love of homely things restored me. Whatever the hall of the prince injured, the porch of the Precursor healed more fully," p. 38). *Castellum* and *ecclesia*, *aula* and *atrium*—topography and architecture govern Lucian's spatial imagination here, causing him to conclude that "in uno turbamur, in altero consolamur" ("in the one, we are confused; in the other, consoled," p. 39). At this point in the text, the division of space is also a totalizing division of labor: exhausting yet necessary struggle in the earl's political sphere, refreshing and voluntary peace in the precincts of the church.

Yet these carefully delineated boundaries quickly break down as Lucian reorganizes Cestrian space along monastic lines. He tells his readers that the Benedictines have been placed in Chester (*in urbe placuit*) by the saint herself so that they might tend to *suorum civium curam*, "the care of her citizens" (p. 57). The hospitality of the abbey's table addresses the community's bodily hunger and need for human fellowship: "Ideo miramur Cestrenses monacos, quia iugi iocunditatis sue opere non lassantur. Provincialibus hilares, procul venientibus alacres, prompti visceribus et patentes" ("Therefore we Cestrians admire the monks because they are never exhausted by the labor of the yoke of their hospitality. They are pleasant to their fellow Cheshiremen, cheerful to those coming from afar, accessible and at the disposal of their dearest friends," p. 57).[16] At the same time, Chester's spiritual necessities find their way into the monks' liturgical practice: "Quorum cordibus atque vocibus assidue Deus laudatur, virgo memoratur, civitas roboratur" ("Their hearts and voices continually praise God, venerate the saint, and strengthen the city," p. 57). In passages such as these, Lucian suggestively links a project of urban maintenance to the obligations and duties of the Benedictine rule. Monastic largesse (generated, we should remember, by the abbey's numerous tenants in and outside of Chester) and monastic prayer join together to provide the city's inhabitants with temporal sustenance and spiritual guidance. *De laude Cestrie* conceives of Chester as a fantasy space in which citizen and monk live alongside one another in amity and unity. In such a context, action against the interests of St. Werburgh's becomes inconceivable in any terms other than those of ingratitude and sin. Indeed, Lucian finishes his book on a note as aggressive as it is apocalyptic, mentioning on folio 196v the fallen cities of Babylon, Sodom, and Gomorrah to remind Cestrians of what happens to a community that transgresses against the will of God (or that of his servants). Stopping in the midst of a quotation from Job 18:17–18, the manuscript of *De laude Cestrie* ends ominously: "Memoria illius pereat de terra et non celebretur nomen eius in plateis. Expellent eum de" ("Let the memory of him perish from the earth and let not his name be celebrated in the streets. They shall drive him from . . . ").[17]

   Lucian's integration of city and cloister is at its strongest in a section of the text labeled *de Roma et Cestria collatio* ("a comparison of Rome and Chester," fol. 28). This *collatio* belongs to a much longer meditation (some 31 folios) on St. Peter and appears to stem from Lucian's interest in the saint's Roman connections. Here Lucian translates his earlier distinction between castle and church—busy tedium versus restful solace—into purely ecclesiastical terms. He replaces imperial Rome (he has already told his audience of Chester's position *Romani servans limitem imperii* or "guarding the boundaries of Roman power," p. 45) with papal Rome. Yet the Vatican he describes proves identical in character and function to Earl Ranulf III's *curia*:

> Qui sibi romam elegit ut dictaret; cestriam ut defenderet. Ibi statuens generalem tronum; hic constituens speciale templum. Inde scribens iura legum; hinc nobis subueniens a gemitu laborum. Ibi causidicus litibus altercantium; hic carissimus laudibus amantium. Coruscabitur obtutibus romanorum; sed complectibitur affectibus anglorum. Expetitus de omnj orbe ad negocia populorum; exoratus de omni corde precibus humilium et piorum. Rome rutilat in cathedra potestatis; apud nos redolet ex gratia pietatis. (fol. 28r)

> (He [Peter] chose Rome for himself so that he might dictate laws; he chose Chester so that he might protect it. There he establishes his universal throne; here he builds his local temple. There he writes the statutes of the law; here he comes to release us from the groans of labor. There as a partisan he engages in the struggles of adversaries; here as the favorite he takes part in the praising of lovers. He will gleam in the eyes of the Romans, but he will be embraced by the affections of the English. [There] he is required to attend to the business of all the peoples of the world; [here] he is beseeched by the prayers of every humble and dutiful heart. In Rome, he shines in the seat of power; here with us, he exudes the grace of piety.)

The juxtaposition of Roman law and Cestrian peace in this passage maintains the content of Lucian's earlier binary opposition even as it alters the referents. In Rome, Peter is *doctor atque dissertor* ("teacher and disputant," fol. 28v); in Chester, he is *nobis patronus atque protector*, ("our patron and protector," fol. 28v). To some extent, Lucian merely widens the scope of his initial observation—the earl's juridical power lies along the same continuum as the pope's, but the latter manages the affairs of all Christendom, a jurisdiction greater than that of a single city and county in the Welsh Marches.

Nevertheless, the shift to a larger geographical context has the effect of collapsing local difference and thereby unifying urban Chester as a thoroughly monastic space. Lucian concludes the *collatio* thus: "Ibi denique tumultus et negotia; hic tranquilitas per ocia. Roma igitur in robore; Cestria in requie" ("Finally, there one finds tumult and toil; here, tranquility through retirement. Therefore in power in Rome, while at rest in Chester," fol. 28v). Or, as the gloss to this passage puts it, *in Roma auctoritas in Cestria affectus* ("authority in Rome, affection in Chester," fol. 28v). Rome and its pomp represent the world from which Chester retires, a move that parallels a given individual's withdrawal into monastic space and regular life. For the moment, the cloister is no longer separate from a city which stands off against it and inadvertently oppresses it through bureaucratic tedium—let alone an urban space economically oppressed by the privileges granted to the monks by the earl, their supposed opposite. Lucian instead uses the vocabulary of monastic discourse to shift the abbey's legal and political boundaries, to make them coterminous with those of Chester itself. His idea of Chester as a holistic site of worship subsumes prior divisions of social space, reconfiguring the city as monastery.

Lucian supports this revision of Cestrian locality through a carefully deployed series of formal and linguistic operations. For example, he fills *De laude Cestrie* with rhetorical triads, groups of threes designed to convey the image of triple identities subsumed within a greater unity. M. V. Taylor suggests in her introduction to the text that these triads may derive from the verse forms of Chester's Welsh neighbors (p. 13). However, Lucian's spiritualization of space suggests a more likely origin: the heavenly Trinity. Indeed, the idea for *De laude Cestrie* comes from the anonymous patron's suggestion that Lucian meditate on the *tercia consonancia* of Chester's Latin name, *Cestria* (p. 44). The text stresses this point: Lucian notes that "tripliciter in civitate trisilliba contulisti" ("in three ways you suggested the three syllables of the city," p. 38), and a marginal gloss agrees that *Cestria trisilliba est*. He goes on to tell us that Chester *in tribus videatur esse constructa* ("seems to have been built in three parts," p. 41)—a turn of phrase that links the physical action of building (*constructa*) to the implicitly spiritual division of space. The multiplication of triads here at the start of *De laude Cestrie* directs our attention to those which follow. Lucian gives us (among other triads) the three divisions of St. John's (*literatus episcopus, liberalis archidiaconus, lucidus clerus* or "a learned bishop, an honorable archdeacon, and an enlightened clergy," p. 41); the three estates of the city (*probitas procerum, pietas civium, religio monarchorum* or "the righteousness of its leaders, the piety of its citizens, and the devotion of its monks," p. 41); and the three food sources of Chester (*insula Hibernorum . . . vicinia Britonum . . . provincia Anglorum* or "the island of the Irish, the neighborhood of the Welsh, and the province of the English," p. 44). This proliferating series of threes serves to strengthen Chester's trinitarian associations. The city once again enters typology, its microcosmic triple structures pointing to the threefold divinity which orders the universe and establishes macrocosmic structure.

Lucian also relies on the practice of what Taylor calls "allegorical or symbolic etymology" (p. 15)—that is to say, etymology in the tradition of Isidore of Seville's seventh-century *Etymologiae*.[18] Lucian inquires into the derivation of words and finds that linguistic change corresponds to sacred history. Thus, for example, he argues for the derivation of *Cestria* from the phrase *Dei castra* ("camp of God," p. 51).[19] In this particular etymology, Lucian reveals some awareness of Chester's Roman past (as well as an ability to construct accurate etymologies on occasion—"Chester" really is the Anglicization of Latin *castra*). But he also modifies that Latinate history with *Dei* in order to show how the city's very identity, its historical name, is indebted to divine inspiration. *De laude Cestrie* contains several more such etymologies, the most important of which may be Lucian's explanation of *Wereburga*. Relying on his knowledge of contemporary English (what he calls the *lingua Saxonica* or "Saxon tongue," p. 64), Lucian translates *Wereburga* as *tuens urbem* ("the one defending the city," p. 55).[20] Inscribed within the name of its patron saint (as Old English *burg* or "enclosure, fort, walled town"), the city of Chester enters into a relationship of somatic identity with Werburgh—her saintly body signifies the urban community.[21]

Indeed, through its paradoxical combination of virginity and maternity, its *felix sterilitas et beata fecunditas*, Werburgh's body generates the citizens needed to populate her city: "Nullum peperit filium et numerosum producit populum, quem ampla basilica et aula veneranda vix capiat" ("She gave birth to no son, but brought forth a numerous people which the spacious church and the sacred hall could scarce contain," p. 54).[22] Epitomized by her shrine and relics, Werburgh's spiritually fertile body creates the body politic, albeit one that almost exceeds the urban space available to it.[23] In Lucian's account of a disastrous 1180 fire within the walls of Chester, the citizens are explicitly aware of Werburgh's linguistic and bodily equation with their city, calling on the saint for deliverance because "non est in populo tam simplex necque fatuus, qui tunc nesciat ethimologiam nominis eius" ("no one among the people is such a simple fool that he doesn't know the etymology of her name," p. 55).[24] Their prayers are answered (and their philological skills rewarded) when the monks carry the saint's shrine through the city streets and miraculously extinguish the flames. The relics' processional presence saves not only the bodies of Werburgh's citizen-children, but also the buildings of the urban body materially linked to her holy remains.

The conflation of Cestrian space and incarnate spirit continues in Lucian's use of allegorical topography—that is to say, his reading of the city's physical landscape as the literal level of scripture. For example, Lucian's designation of St. Peter as guardian of the western Watergate receives its authorization from the Gospel narratives of Matthew 4:18–20 (Christ makes Peter a *piscator hominum* or "fisher of men") and Matthew 14:25–33 (Peter attempts to walk on the water alongside Christ). In this passage, the text syntactically links Chester's everyday *captura piscium* ("the catching of fish") with the saint's eternal business of the *conversio populorum* ("conversion of the people," p. 51). Lucian then amplifies this allegorical connection, finding the *salus animarum* ("health of souls") in the *salo aquarum* ("current of the waters," p. 51). Actual topographies shape Lucian's exegesis here: located in the center of Chester, St. Peter's occupies one end of Watergate Street, the main route to the city's medieval quays.[25]

Lucian also amplifies his allegorization of Chester's *forum*, identifying it with both manna from heaven and Christ's own body offered up as the Host:

Hoc simul intuendum quam congrue in medio urbis, parili positione cunctorum, forum voluit esse venalium rerum, ubi, mercium copia complacente precipue victualium, notus veniat

vel ignotus, precium porrigens, referens alimentum. Nimirum ad
exemplum panis eterni de celo venientis, quo natus secundum
prophetas "in medio orbis et umbilico terre," omnibus mundi
nationibus pari propinquitate voluit apparere. (p. 47)

(At the same time it must be admired: how fittingly God willed in
the middle of the city, positioned equidistant to all the rest, that
there be a market of things for sale—where, faced with a pleasing
abundance of goods, and especially of provisions, the local or the
stranger may come, bringing money and taking away nourishment
in return. In other words, a type of that eternal bread sent from
heaven, born—according to the prophets—"in the middle of
the globe and the center of the earth" because he wished to be
equally close to all the nations of the world.)[26]

This passage revisits an earlier discussion of what the manuscript margin designates as *de situ Cestrie*, "the site of Chester" (p. 45). In this
section of *De laude Cestrie*, Lucian notes that Chester's geographical
position permits it to observe the world (*orbem prospicit universum*, p. 45).
From this central vantage point—indeed, from the very same spot in the
marketplace that our aforementioned spectator occupies in his mobile
contemplation of Isaiah's *misterium*—one may survey the entire globe:
"Que a ventis quattuor portas quattuor habens, a oriente prospectat
Indiam, ab occidente Hiberniam, ab aquilone maiorem Normanniam,
a meridie eam, quam divina severitas, ob civiles et naturales discordias,
Britannis reliquit angularem angustiam" ("With four gates for each of
the four winds, Chester looks out at India in the east, Ireland in the
west, Norway in the north, and, in the south, that narrow corner which
divine severity has left to the Welsh on account of their civil wars and
natural discords," p. 45).[27] Lucian's expanding frame of reference calls
to mind the spatial organizations of the medieval *mappae mundi* and
their orientation around the "global centre" of Jerusalem.[28] However,
in *De laude Cestrie*, it is Chester, not Jerusalem, that serves as *omphalos*
to the world.

In a section of the text identified as *de trivio Cestrie*, "on the crossroads of Chester" (p. 63), Lucian follows up on his reading of the city as
omphalos with an exegetical account of its suburbs. The *trivium* in ques-

tion lies outside the city's Eastgate. In yet another instance of a triad, this junction marks the point at which what is now Foregate Street splits up into three roads (*trinus viarum*, p. 64), all leading away from the city in different directions. One road runs due east to the nearby village of Christleton. Lucian quickly capitalizes on this destination's allegorical potential: Christleton becomes the *Villam Christi*, and its eastern location signifies Christ's status as the *verum orientem* or "true east" (p. 64). To journey there is to enter allegorical space: "To conclude, there is nothing more profitable, nothing better, than to walk straight and live straight [*recte incedere ac recte vivere*] on the road from the gates of the city [*porta urbium*]" (p. 64). The road to Christleton is indeed the straight and narrow path of Matthew 7:14.[29]

The village's eponymous affiliation with Christ also suggests that it represents the New Law, a connection confirmed by the description of the second, right-hand (*dexteram*, p. 63) road, the one heading south to Aldford. Lucian picks up on the Old English *eald* in Aldford's name and describes the village as *alter locus quem vocant incole Veterem Vadum*, "another place which the locals call the Old Ford" (p. 64). He states that travelers who choose this path *contra scripturam prohibentem*, "against scriptural prohibition," face the dangers of *superba iusticia*, "the proud justice" (p. 64) of the Old Law (as *Veterem* suggests). Even more dangerous is the third road, the path leading north and left (*a sinistris*, p. 64) to Hoole Heath, one of Cheshire's three avowries, sanctuaries established by the earl for felons from other counties of England.[30] Lucian refers to Hoole Heath as the *Vallem Demonum* or "Valley of Demons" (p. 64). Clearly punning on the English "Hoole" as "hell," he describes the Heath as *locum de latibulis insidiantium*, "the place of those lying in wait" (p. 64). He notes as well that Hoole Heath can only be reached *inter errores*, via spiritually suspect "errors" or deviations from the straight and narrow *regiam viam*, the "royal road" which implicitly serves as the highway of the heavenly King (p. 64).[31]

The most extensive fusion of local landscape and allegorical signification appears in Lucian's exegesis of Chester's ancient Roman street plan. The four major streets of medieval Chester—Northgate, Eastgate, Bridge, and Watergate Streets—come together in the vicinity of St. Peter's. As mentioned above, their intersection is not a perfect one: while Eastgate and Watergate Streets are indeed continuous,

Northgate and Bridge Streets never actually meet. St. Peter's gets in the way: the south end of Northgate Street lies to the east of the north end of Bridge Street. In *De laude Cestrie*, Lucian literally makes ends meet, transforming Chester's streets into yet another *misterium* for his readers to contemplate:

> Habet etiam plateas duas equilineas et excellentes in modum benedicte crucis, per transversum sibi obvias et se transeuntes, qui deinceps fiant quattuor ex duabus, capita sua consummantes in quattuor portis, mistice ostendens atque magnifice, magni Regis inhabitantem graciam se habere, qui legem geminam novi ac veteris testamenti per misterium sancte crucis impletam ostendit, in quattuor evangelistis. (pp. 46–47)

> (Chester has two excellent streets, equal in length and similar to the blessed Cross because they cross over one another. They thus become four streets from two, and they end in four gates, mystically and magnificently revealing the in-dwelling grace of the great King, he who revealed the double law of the New and Old Testaments fulfilled through the mystery of the holy Cross in the four Gospels.)

Here Lucian makes Chester's cruciform streets evoke the Crucifix, a connection he repeats several times throughout the text. For example, we learn that God is a *protector* to the *cives* of Chester because *plateas eorum in modum gloriose crucis aptavit*, "he prepared their streets in the manner of the glorious Cross" (p. 47).

Several pages later Lucian links topography to typology, reminding his readers of Elijah's Old Testament encounter with the widow of Sarephta (3 Kings 17:8–24). In the biblical narrative, the prophet comes upon the widow gathering sticks (*colligens ligna*) for her fire (3 Kings 17:10); a few verses later, she tells Elijah that she has but two sticks (*duo ligna*, 3 Kings 17:12). Lucian relates these *ligna* to the timbers that Pilate's soldiers use to form the *crucis vitale signum et venerandum misterium* or "the life-giving sign of the Cross and a sacred mystery" (p. 53). But the widow's sticks also anticipate the streets of Chester. The first stick, which we metaphorically "hand over to the precursor of the

Lord and his gatekeeper" (*tradamus unum precursori Domini atque ipsius portario*, p. 53), clearly corresponds to Eastgate (St. John's) and Watergate (St. Peter's) Streets, the city's eastern and western thoroughfares. The second stick, which we "commit to the virgin and to the Archangel" (*committamus virgini et Arcangelo*, p. 53), refers to Northgate (St. Werburgh's) and Bridge (St. Michael's) Streets, Chester's north-south axis. Lucian thus locates Chester within typological history: the widow's Old Testament *ligna* prefigure the New Testament *ligna* of the Cross, while Chester's stick-streets point back to the moment of Christ's passion.

However, St. Werburgh's Chester is more than a cruciform city. It also occupies the center of a cruciform region, a cross-shaped territory that spans the Anglo-Welsh border, subordinating national identity to a distinctly monastic Christianity:

> Illud etiam intuendum qualiter ipsum virginis monasterium ambiatur quatuor mansionibus alborum monacorum, qui reginam celi profitentur Dominam, ad consolationem presentis exilii, et requiem futuram. Nam a fronte, et a tergo, et a lateribus ad evidentissimum modum crucis, competenter et pulcre distinctis spaciis, a quatuor monasteriis, velut preconum laudibus comendatur, ut almum et album sit, quicquid medium invenitur. Quippe instar vitalis ligni et dominici patibuli, que ab oriente in occidentem protensa sunt, paululum longiora sunt, et que ab aquilone in austrum, iuxta tranversum crucis lignum, brevia sunt. (pp. 58–59)

> (Consider also how the very monastery of the virgin is surrounded by four houses of white monks, all of whom profess the queen of heaven as their Lady as consolation for their present state of exile and for their future repose. From the front, the back, and the sides, fittingly and with nicely defined spaces, in the clear pattern of a cross, the abbey is extolled by the four monasteries, as if by the praise of heralds, with the result that whatever is found in the middle is kind and white. Of course, like the life-giving wood and Lord's gibbet, those houses that run from east to west are a bit longer, and those that run from north to south, much like the transverse beam of the Cross, are short.)

We know that this grouping of monasteries (Benedictine in the center, Cistercian at the four extremities) crosses the border between England and Wales because Lucian or a commentator has helpfully written *Cumbermare* and *Basinwerc* in the interlinear space above *fronte* and *tergo* respectively. Combermere is a Cistercian house located to the southeast of Chester in English Cheshire; Basingwerk is a house found to the northwest in Welsh Flintshire. By shifting both houses out of position to occupy an east-west axis centered on Chester, Lucian performs a spatial deformation akin to that which he works on the city's streets and churches.[32] He thus trumps regional identity as easily as he does civic selfhood.

In addition, he (or one of his subsequent readers and annotators) provides the text with a visual complement to these ideas of Chester and Cheshire as cruciform spaces. The bottom margin of folio 60v in the Bodley 672 manuscript contains a cross (figure 3). Placed just below the words *uirginis monasterium ambiatur quatuor mansionibus alborum monacorum* ("The monastery of the virgin is surrounded by four houses of white monks"), this cross functions as a map depicting the geographical positions of the four Cistercian monasteries closest to Chester. Here Combermere lies in the east, and Basingwerk in the west—just as the glosses to *fronte* and *tergo* indicate. The map also provides readers with specific identities for the two remaining monasteries from the text. These are Poulton in the south and Stanlaw (or *locus benedictus*) in the north.[33] The cartographer (either Lucian or another monk of the abbey) places St. Werburgh's (*Cestria*) at the center of this cross, in the space occupied on its sacred original by the incarnate body of Christ. Lucian's allegorization of Chester's streets as symbols, signs, Testaments, and Gospels supports such an identification, amplifying the text's sense of the city's topographical link to the Word made Flesh. Somatic systems thus connect seemingly disparate levels of materiality and textuality. In *De laude Cestrie*, Chester the city is simultaneously Chester the book and Chester the body. Moving through the former leads directly to the interpretation and contemplation of the latter two Chesters; the simple act of walking around the city replicates the textual practice of the exegete. As another one of Lucian's glosses puts it, *In Cestria est evidens in plateis*: "In Chester, it is made manifest in the streets" (p. 53).

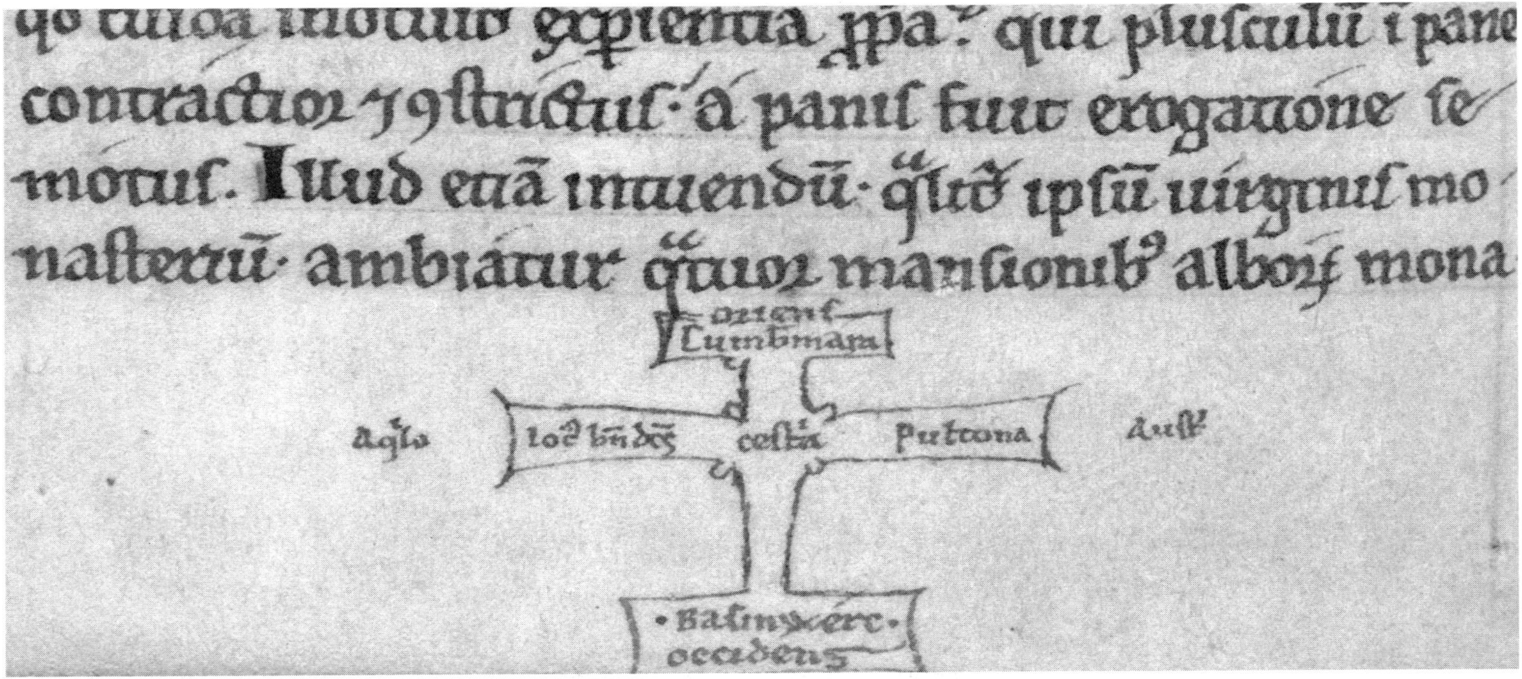

FIGURE 3   The cruciform map in the margin of Lucian's *De laude Cestrie* (ca. 1195). MS Bodley 672, fol. 60v detail. By permission of the Bodleian Library, University of Oxford.

Rechart(er)ing Chester: Bradshaw's *Life of Saint Werburge* and the Politics of Urban Space

Approximately three centuries later in *The Life of Saint Werburge* (written in Chester ca. 1506–13), local monk Henry Bradshaw uses similar strategies of embodiment to convey his sense of Chester as a site of organic and spiritual unity.[34] He claims that St. Werburgh's city is "A place preordinat by our sauiour / Where her body shulde rest and worshipped be, / Magnified with miracles next our ladie" (2.264–66). However, because his text is explicitly hagiographic, Bradshaw concentrates solely on the miraculous and affective potential of Werburgh's enshrined relics. *De laude Cestrie*'s exegetical techniques hold little interest for him. Instead he opens Book 2 of his *Life* with an elaborate account of the saint's translation from her initial burial place in Hanbury, Staffordshire, to Chester.[35] The text tracks Werburgh's shrine through the city streets and describes in detail the procession which accompanies it: "ministres of god" (2.277), "lordes" (2.282), "cite3ens" (2.285), "virgins" (2.288), "widowes and wyues" (2.290), and "all the commonte" (2.292) turn out "in ordre togyther" (2.346) to welcome the saint to Chester. Bradshaw connects this sense of hierarchical social sequence to the display of proper secular respect for ecclesiastical and hagiographic authority: "The lordes the cite3ins and all the commons / Mekely submytted them-selfe to the shryne" (2.302–3). He subsequently reveals the powerful benefits of such obedience when he narrates how, on two separate occasions, the presentation of the shrine at the Northgate put a halt to Welsh and Danish attacks on the city.[36] In addition, Bradshaw's retelling of Lucian's 1180 fire narrative adds a significant detail to the tale's end: "Vnto her shryne the people all went, / The clergie before, in maner of procession . . . Sayeng full sadly 'we shall neuer able be / The place to recompense for this dede of charite'" (2.1675–76, 1680–81). Lucian's emphasis on allegorical etymology disappears here, but the citizens of Chester are still no fools. For Bradshaw's townsfolk, the social power of the holy body remains intact, if not heightened: "For it is well knowen, by olde antiquite / Sith the holy shryne came to their presence, / It hath ben their comfort and gladnes, truly" (2.1710–12).

This new element of the impossible debt, of a charity so great that it can never be matched, sets up the major distinction between Lucian's and Bradshaw's texts. Lucian never acknowledges the possibility of discord between the citizens and the monastery, nor does he need to do so: generously endowed by the Norman earls and secure in its rights, his abbey has the political upper hand. When he writes *De laude Cestrie* ca. 1195, the liberties of Chester's medieval guild merchant have only just been confirmed (ca. 1190–93) by Earl Ranulf III.[37] The clerks of St. John's and the earl's men are the only potential opponents facing St. Werburgh's, and his text takes pains to emphasize their friendly relations with the monks. Bradshaw, on the other hand, includes the idea of impossible recompense as a preemptive strike against a citizenry all too ready to enter into conflict with the abbey—and all too capable of winning that struggle. Increased political strife within fifteenth- and sixteenth-century Chester means that Bradshaw cannot afford to maintain wholly intact his predecessor's assumption of urban accord. This anxiety splits open his text, qualifying his presentation of an idealized Chester united under the spiritual guidance of its monks ("The faith of holy churche dyd euer there endure / Without recidiuacion and infection sure," 2.452–53).

The most explicit moment of rupture in the *Life* occurs in chapter 22 of Book 2, a section of the text entitled "A charitable mocion and a desyre to all the inhabytauntes within the countie palatine of Chestre for the monasterie." This chapter depicts an abbey attacked on all sides by greedy, grasping locals, all of whom seem to have utterly forgotten the litany of the saint's miracles Bradshaw has been rehearsing for dozens of pages prior to this moment:

> Some other haue be, parauenture on late,
> Studious to disquiet the place, the company,
> And diuers libertes haue alienate,
> Also tolled their franchis fraudulently,
> From the sayd place well knowen in memory;
> Suche mysdoers we moue in conscience blynde
> To mende their wronges, lest payne come sodeynly:
> Wherfore to the monasterie be neuer vnkynde.
>
> (2.1874–81)

Terms such as *libertes, alienate, franchis,* and *the sayd place* belong to the discourses of the charter, the law, and the transaction, and Bradshaw takes great care here to remind the ungrateful citizens of their financial and legal obligations to the monastery. As an earlier passage indicates, these obligations are legion:

> Many helde their landes of the sayd monasterie
> By tenure grand-seriante and some by homage,
> By tenure franke-almoigne other by fealtie
> With seruice de chiualere and some by escuage,
> Some by petit-seriant and by tenure burgage,
> As in their euidentes and grauntes they may fynde:
> Tres maners de rentes with tenure villenage:
> Wherfore to the monasterie be neuer vnkynde.
> $(2.1770-77)^{38}$

The chapter's appeal to Cestrians' sense of juridical propriety depends on the citizens' acknowledgment of the historical primacy ("well knowen in memory") of the abbey's rights and claims. Those who would cheat the monks out of their just desserts are informed that "the place had their fraunches and fredom / Afore the sayd cite a hundreth yere and one" $(2.1358-59).^{39}$ Bradshaw thus claims the authority of textual (and thus monastic) tradition: "The erle gaue the place many great fredoms / Within Chestre cite whiche ben known of olde, / With singular priuileges and auncient customs . . . (in writyng as we fynde)" (2.1786–88, 1791).

The stanza's penultimate phrase "lest payne come sodeynly" makes a different sort of appeal, for Bradshaw is not afraid to threaten his audience with divine retribution. In chapter 22, he makes his point in terms both plain and universally applicable:

> There was neuer man of high nor lowe degree,
> Lorde, baron, knyght, marchaunt, and burges,
> Attemptyng to infringe their rightes and liberte,
> Remaynyng in the same malice and wyckednes,
> But if they repent shortly theyr busynes
> Askyng absolucion to theyr conscience blynde,
> Vengeance on them doth lyght, doutles:
> Wherfore to the monastery be neuer vnkynd.
> (2.1842–49)

Book 2 of the *Life* provides its readers with numerous examples of precisely how "Vengeance on them [might] lyght." In chapter 13, barbaric invaders assaulting "the parke of Vpton, / Saynt Werburge landes" are crippled and struck blind on account of "theyr malice and myschief agaynst her possession" (2.999–1000, 1011). Nor are rapacious foreigners the only foes so punished. In chapter 19, Richard, the second Earl of Chester, is "peruerted" by his wicked wife Matilde and plots to steal the abbot's "maner-place of Salton / with the appurtinaunce" (2.1511, 1512–13). Answering the abbot's prayers for assistance, Werburgh apparently brings about the famous sinking of Prince William's White Ship in 1120, drowning Earl Richard, Matilde, and all of its passengers, "cruell ennemyes vnto her place" (2.1583). Chapter 22's "charitable mocion" refers back to this second incident in its final stanza, mentioning "some drowned in water colde" (2.1894) in its list of all the dire fates met by the abbey's enemies.

Bradshaw's *Life* is thus not simply "designed to promote pilgrimage to particular shrines," as Eamon Duffy suggests,[40] so much as it is calibrated to effect change on the level of local politics. It directly intervenes in the long-running struggle between the mayor and the abbot for control of Chester, a struggle that came to a head in the decade preceding Bradshaw's 1513 death (the latest possible date for the composition of the *Life*). Although there were a great many points of contention between the two parties (such as the abbey's control over all trade in the city during St. Werburgh's fair, an issue specifically mentioned by Bradshaw in 2.1786–93), I would like to concentrate on the bitter controversy surrounding the conflicting jurisdictions of Chester's local courts.[41] This dispute directly engages the issues of access, space, and power at work in the *Life*'s defense of monastic privilege.

In 1506, Henry VII granted Chester a new charter.[42] Known as the Great Charter, this document formally restructured the city's civic government, granting control to an assembly led by the mayor. Chester itself was reconfigured and repositioned in the national body politic, "the said city, and the suburbs and hamlets of the same, and all the ground within the precinct and compass of them" becoming a county "distinct and separate from our county of Chester."[43] Only the king's castle (appropriated by the Crown when the earls' male line died out in 1237) and its immediate precinct (an area of Chester known as

Gloverstone) were exempted from inclusion in this new urban county. Among other grants and confirmations, the city corporation received control of all courts within its newly reaffirmed boundaries and thus came into direct conflict with the abbey. Dating back to its foundation, St. Werburgh's charters endowed the monastery with extensive properties in and along Northgate Street. These charters also gave the monks the right to hold a court of their own to which their tenants could be attached for all manner of offenses: as Earl Hugh's 1092 charter asserts, "volumus ut sancta Werburga habeat per omnia curiam suam, sicut comes suam" ("we wish that St. Werburgh have her own court in all things, just as the earl has his own").[44] The monks had a bad habit of deliberately attaching citizens under the mayor's jurisdiction, and abbey tenants frequently relied upon the monastery court (located just outside the city walls at Northgate) to avoid prosecution by the civic authorities.[45] In the early 1480s, Abbot Richard Oldham (1453–85) was actually indicted by the mayor's portmote court "for encroachments and removing the city boundaries about the Northgate"—evidence of a monastery interested in aggressively and even illicitly expanding its own spaces of power.[46] The Great Charter's revision of Cestrian space gave the mayor the legal justification he needed to unify all courts within the city, and a 1507 incident in which officials of St. Werburgh's arrested and fined two men for fighting in Northgate Street provided him with the excuse he needed to shut the abbot's court down.[47]

Two years of legal wrangling ended with the 7 August 1509 decision by Henry VIII's royal arbitrators to give the mayor and the city a complete victory.[48] The abbot's tenants were redefined as citizens under the corporation's control (item 14); city sheriffs, coroners, and even ordinary Cestrians repairing the city walls were given direct access to the monastery precinct whenever necessary (items 8, 9, 12, and 20); and the mayor at last saw the abbot's court removed to the monastery proper and severely reduced in jurisdictional scope (items 5, 15–16, and 18). The penultimate item (item 19) of the arbitrators' award establishes the "limitts of the said monasterie" in exacting detail:

> That the limitts of the said monasterie should begin at the greate
> west gate thereof, within the same gate, and soe followinge
> within the said wall of the monasterie, northward, nigh unto

the towne wall of the said citie, and soe following within the
said towne wall unto the posterne in the same wall goinge into
a place called the caleyard or covent garden, accordinge to the
walls and ditches of the same, and soe to retorne againe to the
said posterne, and from thence followinge within the said towne
wall southward towards the Eastgate street against the end of a
stone wall that abutteth nigh upon St Warburge lane, that lyeth
from the abbay towards the Eastgate streete, so from the stile,
followinge within the ould wall that abutteth nigh upon the said
towne wall, unto the church stile unto the west end of the newe
church stile, at the west ende of the newe church, includinge
the newe houses built at the same because they be inhabited
by citizens haveinge theire entrie and regresse unto and from
the said houses towards the streete of the said citie, and soe
followinge by the said newe houses northward within the wall of
the said monasterie, unto the said great west gate, where the
limmitts began.[49]

Item 19 effectively puts an end to the monastic topography of Chester.
It transforms Bradshaw's description of "the great compas of the sayd
abbay, / Enuired with walles myghty to assay" (2.97–98) into a belated
attempt to counteract the (now) legal penetrations of those "walles
myghty" by the magistrates and citizens of Chester.[50] His exemplary
narratives also prove to be ineffectual fantasies, even those seemingly
targeted at the jurisdiction issue. Chapter 12 of Book 2 describes how an
innocent young Cestrian "was arrest and taken of a lyght suspicion / By
the officers and rulers of the sayd towne" (2.950–51). These wicked
urban "ministres" (2.954) sentence their prisoner to death by hanging,
but relent when Werburgh sends a dove from Heaven to cut the young
man down and return him to life ("The tortuous turmentours cessed
their tyranny," 2.980). The saint's intervention repudiates corrupt
civic justice, and Bradshaw makes sure to give us a concluding image
of a city united in joyous celebration: "The deuout citeȝens approched
them nere, / Went all to the shryne the virgin thankyng; / The belles
were tolled for ioy of this thyng" (2.986–88).

Unfortunately for Bradshaw and his fellow monks, no such happy
ending is in store for the abbey. The early sixteenth century saw the

torturing tormentors continue their tyranny, practicing "subtell policy and wrong-feyned euidens . . . proued periury and fals collusion" (2.1852–53) for the sole purpose of "Defraudyng the right of the holy monastery" (2.1861). Bradshaw implicitly characterizes the 1509 award as a "wronge iugement / Agaynst their [the monks'] libertes, in conscience blynde" (2.1870–71), but, right or *wronge, blynde* or clearsighted, the arbitrators' decision stands. A new, royally authorized topography remaps Chester street by street, confining and constraining the monks in both spatial and political terms. Bradshaw's "charitable mocion and a desyre" in chapter 22 protests the Crown's decision and urges the citizens to recreate the imagined community of the idealized past, but ultimately fails to restore the abbey's flagging fortunes. Another idea of Chester wins out, one increasingly centered neither on Lucian's allegorical crucifix nor on Bradshaw's holy shrine, but on the Pentice building, the site of the mayor's crownmote and portmote courts.[51] This structure, built onto the south wall of St. Peter's ca. 1288, is the material emblem of post-1509 Chester.[52] Its very name inscribes a politics of appropriation: as David Mills points out, *appentis* means "that which appends to a building," that which is added on.[53] In the Pentice, secular, urban government mediates and manages access to spiritual experience—one must pass through the spaces of the mayor, his officers, and his courts in order to worship. In this recharted (and re-chartered) Chester, the marketplace is no longer a stable in Bethlehem, nor are the streets the body of Christ broken for you. After 1509, the *corpus Christi* and the relics of St. Werburgh begin to make room for a Chester embodied anew as the corporation.

That process of displacement culminates in the abbey's surrender to the king's commissioners on 20 January 1539/40.[54] The Dissolution is the end of the monastic imagination of Chester: after 1540, the abbey's urban topographies disappear, their textual bases transferred to the private collections of Tudor antiquarians (Lucian's *De laude Cestrie* enters the Bodleian Library in 1601) and their material, architectural traces appropriated by emergent institutions and administrations. St. Werburgh's becomes Henry VIII's new Cathedral of Christ and the Blessed Virgin Mary on 4 August 1541; its St. Nicholas Chapel, the Chester Assembly's Common Hall in 1545.[55] The civic Assembly offers us the clearest sign of monastic Chester's passing: Mayor Henry Gee has the first of the city's Assembly Books produced during his 1539–40 term of office.[56] This work, a compilation of civic records and orders, signals a new beginning to the city's traditions of oligarchic writing. In it, Mayor Gee commemorates the temporally coterminous occasion of St. Werburgh's surrender with an account of his 1540 perambulation entitled "THE MEYRES AND BOUNDS of the circuite of the liberties of the Citie of Chester newly viewed by Henry Gee, mayre of the same citie, by the advyse and consent of his most auncient and discrete brederne."[57] The *circuite* described therein bears some resemblance to that traced by Lucian's surveying subject as well as to Bradshaw's account of Werburgh's processional translation. But it also recalls the royal arbitrators' 1509 walk around the abbey's diminished *limitts*: from the "newly viewed" perspective of the Reformation, no one will mistake Gee's *brederne* for monks.

A MIGHTY FORTRESS: DRAFTING LOCAL HAGIOGRAPHY INTO NATIONAL SERVICE

Politically ineffective at the regional level, Bradshaw's *Life* was revived for a national audience in 1521, the year when King's Printer Richard Pynson had the text published in London. Pynson's decision to print the locally focused *Life* is not as counterintuitive as it initially seems: Bradshaw's prologues speak of his desire to benefit "euery man and woman" (1.111), "the comyn people symple and neclygent" (2.3), and "marchaunt men hauyng litell lernyng" (2.2016). The readers he anticipates in these phrases are most likely the Cestrians referenced by the address in chapter 22 "to all the inhabytauntes within the countie palatine of Chestre." However, it takes very little effort to reconsider them as members of print culture's developing national audience. After all, Bradshaw himself envisions his work as participating in an emergent English canon of "auncient poetes" (2.2020): his envoi sends his "litell boke" (2.2013) to beg pardon of "maister Chaucer and Ludgate sentencious . . . preignaunt Barkley . . . [and] inuentiue Skelton" (2.2023–25).[58] Pynson is sensitive to such strategies, noting on his title page for the *Life* that "the holy lyfe and history of saynt werburge" is "very frutefull for all christen people to rede." This appeal to "all christen people" follows up on

Bradshaw's nascent ambitions toward a wider audience and reaches out to encompass the entire Christian community.

Moreover, two of the three supplemental poems accompanying Pynson's edition of the *Life* make it clear that these Christians are to be identified as English. These pieces, respectively titled "An other balade" and "An other balade to saynt werburge," combine an interest in vernacular translation with a devotion to the cult of saints' relics.[59] In doing so, the poems pick up on cues in the *Life* proper, a text explicitly concerned with issues of translation, whether that means literary translation from the "close" Latin of the church (2.2019) into the English of "rude people" (2.2017) and "the comyn vulgares" (1.84) or the material, bodily translation of the saint's relics from Hanbury to Chester. The Pynson edition poems respond to these concerns: "An other balade" opens with the apostrophe, "O frutefull historie o digne memoriall, / Enbawmed with doctrine of virtues infinite . . . of englisshe exquisite" (lines 1–2, 5), and notes toward its conclusion that Bradshaw "hath translate this legend profitable / And left it for holsome memoriall / To all his sequaces" (lines 30–32). The poem thus celebrates Bradshaw's contributions to "englisshe exquisite" and "our language publique" (line 20). Through terms such as *memoriall* and *Enbawmed*, it also manages to transform Bradshaw into a saint and his book into a relic.[60] "An other balade to saynt werburge" continues this canonizing impulse: "Leue vnto me for a memoriall," its author prays to St. Werburgh, "Knowlege effectuall of thy lyfe pure" (lines 35–36).

What "An other balade to saynt werburge" also does is to locate the print publication of Bradshaw's *Life* in its historical moment. The poem mentions both "dedes catholique" (line 10) and "the catholique papall" (line 14), phrases which resonate in the context of early 1520s anti-Lutheranism. Jennifer Summit describes the theological and textual response to Luther's 1520 publication of *The Babylonian Captivity*:

> Spurred on by Leo X, Henry VIII and the English Bishops launched a counterattack against Luther: in January 1521 Cardinal Thomas Wolsey banned the sale and possession of Luther's books in England, and in May John Fisher delivered a sermon against Luther at St Paul's Cross that was dramatically

staged against a bonfire of Luther's books—the first major act of censorship against printed books in England. In June of that same year, 1521, Henry himself attacked Luther in a work published under his name, *Assertio Septem Sacramentorum.*[61]

Seen in conjunction with the 1521 assault on Luther's books, Pynson's publication of Bradshaw's *Life* in the same year carries an explicit political meaning. Its use of *catholique* relies heavily on the word's connotations of orthodoxy: compare the use of the term in "An other balade" to Bishop Fisher's mention in his sermon of "the catholike doctryne of our mother holy chirch."[62] Both texts signal their opposition to heretical belief and practice. Conjunctions such as these mobilize Bradshaw's formerly local text in defense of the national religious body against a foreign invader, a deployment which bears some resemblance to the textual strategies of the *Life* proper and to the spatial politics of Chester's 1506–9 charter controversy. The Lutheran threat to English Catholicism is "Wherfore to the monasterie be neuer vnkynde" writ on a national scale, an illicit intrusion into England's religious jurisdiction. Pynson's hagiographic *memorialls*—Bradshaw's book and, as I contend, Bradshaw's *enbawmed* body—occupy key sites in the defense of the English nation and its church.

The *Life*'s utility for a nationally coordinated anti-Lutheran approach is most readily seen in Book 2 with the constant depiction of Chester as a city besieged by a host of external foes: "Danes, Gotes, Norwayes, and scottes also, / Pictes and the wandeles, with mony other mo" (2.174–75). These foreign invaders invariably have the citizens on the ropes until the moment when Werburgh and her monks intervene. For example, chapter 5 focuses on a pre-Conquest assault by the Welsh, twisted Britons whom Bradshaw describes as "Euer to the saxons hauynge inwarde hate" (2.687) and "Ennemies to englisshemen" (2.692). The Welsh army invests the city, and the canons of St. Werburgh (the Benedictine monks' Anglo-Saxon predecessors) respond by assigning the saint's shrine to guard duty on the city walls. Shortly thereafter, a miracle ensues: when an impious Welshman strikes the shrine with a stone from afar, both he and his comrades are struck blind. The Welsh withdraw after first vowing "in euery coost / Saynt Werburge landes to meynteyne alway" (2.725–26).

In other words, divine power protects monastic jurisdiction—at least as far as Bradshaw's immediate political aims are concerned.

Chapter 7 tells a similar story, albeit one that substitutes Danes and Scots for the Welsh as enemies. Here the identification of the shrine with the city is even greater: as the citizens go out of their minds with panic, the canons of St. Werburgh place her shrine "Agaynst theyr enemies at the sayd northgate" (2.773). Now the shrine is no longer on the walls, an appendage to the city's defenses—instead, it effectively replaces them, standing in for the city gate. In a replay of chapter 5, the shrine bears the brunt of the pagan assault, losing "a corner, curiously wrought" (2.784) to an enemy missile. The perpetrator of this blasphemy is immediately torn to shreds by "the deuill" (2.787), a gruesome spectacle that causes the pagan kings to rethink their military strategy. They quickly flee Chester, "Callyng on this virgin fast for grace and mercy, / Promyttynge neuer after to retourne agayne / To disquiete her seruauntes and cite, in certayne" (2.797–99).

This repeated equation of shrine and civic defense is key to Bradshaw's arguments in Book 2 on the abbey's behalf. For example, in chapter 3, he describes the foundation of Chester thus:

> This 'cite of legions,' so called by the Romans,
> Nowe is nominat in latine of his proprete
> Cestria quasi castria / of honour and pleasance:
> Proued by the buyldynge of olde antiquite
> In cellers and lowe voultes / and halls of realte
> Lyke a comly castell / myghty, stronge and sure,
> Eche house like a toure, sometyme of great pleasure.
>   (2.400–406)

Compare this passage to Bradshaw's chapter 16 account of Earl Hugh Lupus's founding of the abbey:

> The founder also buylded within the monasterie
> Many myghty places / conuenient for religion,
> Compased with stronge walles on the west partie
> And on the other syde with Walles of the towne,
> Closed at euery ende with a sure postron,

In south part the cimiterie inuironed rounde about,
For a sure defence ennemies to holde out.

(2.1346–52)

This description of the monastery-as-castle corresponds almost exactly to the spatial parameters of the monastic jurisdiction "invaded" by the civic corporation upon its 1509 legal victory. Given the ca. 1506–13 composition period for the *Life*, Bradshaw's image is a nostalgic one, a fantasy of a time when the monastery's boundaries were inviolate and under the abbot's control.

Nevertheless, it is precisely in this combination of penetration anxiety and holistic fantasy that Bradshaw's *Life* anticipates the emergent anti-Lutheran discourse of the 1520s. At the beginning of Book 2, Bradshaw introduces the "cruell danes" (2.131) as the second of "two plages of pestilence" (2.128). Later on, in an attempt to extend the abbey's claims back into the pre-Saxon era (well before the date of the city's own first charter), he states that "sith baptym came to Chestre cite . . . The faith of holy churche dyd euer there endure / Without recidiuacion and infection sure" (2.449, 452–53). Bradshaw's language of plague and infection anticipates that used by William Warham, Archbishop of Canterbury, in an 8 March 1521 letter to Cardinal Wolsey concerning the discovery of Lutheran heresy at Oxford.[63] Warham begins by reporting to Wolsey that he is "enformyd that diverse of that Universitie be infectyd with the heresyes of Luther and of others of that sorte" (p. 239). These "new doctrynes" are "pestilent" (pp. 239, 240). Worst of all, they threaten to expose Oxford's shame to the world:

> For pytie yt wer that through the lewdnes of on or two cankerd members, which as I understand have enducyd no small nombre of yong and incircumspect foles to geve ere unto thaym, the hole Universitie shuld run in thinfamy of soo haynouse a cryme, the heryng wherof shuld be right delectable and plesant to the open Lutheranes beyond the See, and secrete behyther, wherof they wold take harte and confydence that theyr pestilent doctrynes shuld encrese and multiply, seyng bothe the Universities of Inglande enfectid therewith. (pp. 240–41)

Warham's fears apply the language of infection to a new enemy from "beyond the See": instead of Bradshaw's Danes, we have "open Lutheranes." Instead of threatened Cestrians, we have the endangered and specifically national "Universities of Inglande." The paradigm of external threat that Bradshaw uses against his abbey's civic opponents is the same one that the English government of the 1520s seeks to apply to Lutherans.

Even the discourses of defense are identical. When Anglo-Saxon Edgar becomes king of England in chapter 15, he sets a watch on the North Sea: "Many shyps were made vpon the kynges cost / To serche by the se all his lande about, / That no alian entre in no-maner cost, / By policie and manhod to holde all his ennemies out" (2.1157–60). Cuthbert Tunstall asks for a similar policing of the nation's borders in his 29 January 1521 letter to Wolsey. As the English ambassador to the court of Emperor Charles V, Tunstall was well aware of the controversy surrounding Martin Luther. He therefore sent Wolsey an urgent missive, recommending that "yor grace may cal befor you the printers and bokesellers and gyff them a strayte charge that they bringe noon off his bokes into engelond, nor that they translate noon off them into english, lest therby myght ensue grete troble to the realme and church off england."[64] Tunstall was particularly worried about the heretical power of Luther's 1520 *Babylonian Captivity*: "I pray god kepe that boke out off englond."[65]

Wolsey appears to have listened to these warnings: by April 1521 (three months after Tunstall's letter and a month after Warham's), a ban on the sale and possession of Lutheran books was public knowledge.[66] One month later the authorities called in all copies of Lutheran texts—they were gathering the fuel for the bonfire that would serve to illumine Bishop Fisher's 12 May 1521 sermon against Luther. The sizeable pile of Lutheran books burned at St. Paul's Cross suggests that many English "printers and bokesellers" were insufficient guardians against "alian" encroachment. New defenses were needed, and King Edgar's ships found a contemporary replacement in King Henry's *Assertio septem sacramentorum*.[67] Henry began the *Assertio* in April 1521 (assisted by Thomas More and other English scholars and theologians).[68] Enough of it was finished by 12 May for Fisher to reference the work in his sermon and for Wolsey to wave a copy of it before the gathered crowd's eyes.[69] Henry's royal book was meant to do more than watch the English coast: instead, its mission was to travel "beyond the See" and take the fight directly to the German heretics.

The curious thing about the June 1521 publication of the *Assertio* is that its publisher was Richard Pynson—the same Richard Pynson who published Bradshaw's *Life*.[70] Bradshaw and the anti-Lutheran authorities have more in common than a shared discourse of threat and defense: they share a publisher. As the King's Printer, Pynson was the logical choice to publish a royally authored text like the *Assertio*. But Pynson also had a long-standing interest in hagiographical texts, printing at least seven individual saints' lives (including Werburgh's) during his career.[71] In 1516, he also published the encyclopedic *Kalendre of the New Legende of Englande*, an "overtly nationalist" collection of native saints lives.[72] Jennifer Summit identifies Pynson's hagiographies as evidence for a flourishing Catholic print culture in the years leading up to the 1534 Act of Supremacy.[73] She even goes so far as to read rival publisher Henry Pepwell's November 1521 publication of extracts from *The Book of Margery Kempe* in the context of that year's anti-Lutheran efforts, calling Pepwell's Kempe "an agent of inoculation against Lutheran heresy."[74]

I would like to make a similar claim for Pynson's printing of Bradshaw's *Life of St. Werburge*. The text's specific month of publication remains unclear (and may never be determined), but the letters of Warham and Tunstall suggest that a strong government interest in using the press to combat Luther was developing as early as February 1521. Pynson's official status as King's Printer would have placed him at the forefront of such an effort, lending an anti-Lutheran cast to all of the books he published that year. Bradshaw's *Life* ends with a colophon acknowledging that the book was "Imprinted by Richarde Pynson / printer to the kynges grace / With priuilege to hym graunted by our souerayne lorde the kynge." This royal *imprimatur* suggests that the *Life*—with its fortress mentality and talk of strong defense against foreign foes—would have been understood by its publisher, his royal contacts, and his audience to be an integral part of the anti-Lutheran effort.

Ultimately, intentionality and exact timing matter less than the fact that the *Life*'s 1521 publication took place in a context of heightened awareness of heresy, a horizon of reception that gave new meaning to the text's previously local and regional anxieties over jurisdiction. The defense of the abbey's rights readily transformed itself into a defense of Bishop Fisher's "catholike doctryne." The explicit mention of "dedes catholique" in "An other balade" takes Bradshaw's discourse of spatial inviolability and inflects it in appropriately anti-Lutheran directions— but it must be noted that the *Life* was primed for such appropriations from the moment of its composition. Its local utility was always already national.[75] We could read Pynson's publication of the *Life* with a post-colonial sensitivity to the ways in which the periphery serves up raw materials to the center: the printer of the metropole appropriates the regional saint's life for national ends. Alternately, we could read the London publication of the *Life* with regional historian Tim Thornton as the Chester abbey's attempt to gain a propaganda advantage in a local property dispute between its tenants and Cardinal Wolsey's Cheshire clients.[76] But there is also value in complicating these narratives of open conflict and appropriation: what if we instead read the 1521 publication of the *Life* as a moment of exchange and negotiation between region and nation? If we accept Thornton's argument about Wolsey, we can see how Pynson offers the monks of St. Werburgh's a platform for their protest. But we can also recognize the potential Bradshaw's text holds for the emergent anti-Lutheran effort. Local celebration and regional assertion do not have to come at the expense of national definition, and vice versa. Cheshire texts can speak for England.

CHAPTER TWO

GROUNDS OF GRACE

*Mobile Meaning and Processional Performance
in the Chester Whitsun Plays*

THREE MOMENTS IN TIME AND A SINGLE POINT IN SPACE MARK THE
ideological transformation of urban topography in medieval and early
modern Chester. Each of these moments focuses on Chester's city center, the space formed by the intersection of Chester's ancient Roman
streets. Attempting to appropriate the culturally advantageous centrality of this crossroads, all three moments place a surveying subject
in the site and then task that subject with the imaginative (re)construc-
tion of the city. I have already discussed the first of these moments in
the previous chapter: Lucian's ca. 1195 positioning of his reader *in fori
medio*, "in the middle of the market" (p. 47), with the accompanying
request to read the churches of Chester as the literal sense of Isaiah
62:6, "Upon thy walls, O Jerusalem, I have appointed watchmen." The
third and final moment in the series comes nearly five centuries later in
King's 1656 *Vale-Royall of England.* In a section of the anthology entitled
"Of the Major, Aldermen, Sheriffes, and Officers of the City," William

59

Smith observes that the mayor of Chester "remaineth most part of the day, at a place called, *The Pendice*; which is a brave place builded for the purpose, at the high Crosse, under St. *Peters* Church, and in the middest of the City, in such a sort, that a man may stand therein, and see into the Markets, or Four principal streets of the City" (p. 39).[1] The medieval monk sees Chester's main intersection as an opportunity for exegesis and contemplation, while the early modern antiquarian views the city center as a locus of economic activity and quasi-Foucauldian surveillance. Each writer's vision is nonetheless shaped by a shared awareness of local topography.

Historically situated between these two moments—and linking them together—is a sequence in Play 5 (the Cappers' *Moses and the Law; Balaam and Balaack*) of the Whitsun plays, Chester's sixteenth-century biblical cycle.[2] Here, in a retelling of Numbers 22–24, the pagan king Balaack takes the prophet Balaam to the summit of a mountain in Canaan (no doubt represented by the pageant wagon) and orders him to curse the Israelites encamped below. But the play expands the performance sphere to incorporate its early modern audience, and Balaack's hated Israelite enemies are simultaneously the Christian citizens of Chester: "Lo, Balaham, now thow seest here / Godes people all in feare" (5.272–73).[3] The anachronism of the king's deixis also has an anachoric component: the plains of Moab (Numbers 22:1) are transformed into three distinct locations identified by Balaack as "Cittye, castle, and ryvere" (5.274). Uttered in 1575 from atop a pageant wagon opposite the Pentice (the second station in the cycle plays' traditional route through the city streets and probably the only site of performance in this, the cycle's final year), Balaack's speech describes the three local landmarks potentially visible to the actor who occupies the same central location as Lucian and Smith's hypothetical observers: the southern half of the *cittye* of Chester, the *castle* of the earl, and the channel of the *Ryvere* Dee.[4]

Moreover, in an attempt to compensate for its inability to accurately represent the three mountains of the biblical narrative, the Cappers' play-text instead directs the actors portraying Balaam and Balaack to turn and face three different points of the compass—a curious echo of Lucian's own directive to his readers to spin in place (*vultum vertat*, p. 47).[5] Disgusted by Balaam's initial failure to curse the Israelites, Balaack leads him *ad borialem partem montis*, "to the northern side of the mountain" (SD 5.303+), and orders him to try again. But this second attempt also fails. Balaam has nothing but praise for what he sees: "A, lord, that here is fayre wonninge: / halles, chambers, great likinge, / valles, woodes, grass growinge, / fayre yordes, and eke ryvere" (5.304–7). Once again England is substituted for Canaan. Instead of the desert tent city of Numbers 24:5 (comprised of *tabernacula* and *tentoria*), Balaam's actor gestures toward many of the architectural and topographical features mentioned in his speech: the gardens and *yordes* located within Chester's city walls as well as in its Northgate Street suburbs, the Wirral countryside, and the Dee estuary lying beyond them.[6] His catalog of "fayre wonninge" functions as a succinct urban *encomium*—Lucian's *De laude Cestrie* writ small.

A variant reading in local clerk William Bedford's 1604 manuscript of the plays (Bodleian Library MS Bodley 175) replaces in line 306 *valles* with *walles*, further intensifying the local resonance of Balaam's words with a potential allusion to Chester's famed city walls.[7] The combination of Cestrian topography and biblical prophecy in this sequence suggests that Play 5 has a civic function in addition to its more catechetical concerns. Lawrence M. Clopper has argued that the late medieval English cycle plays can be usefully understood as "signs of corporate identity and supremacy."[8] The careful blocking of Play 5 with regard to its local surroundings supports that assertion, as does Balaam's complaint upon being presented by Balaack with the assembled crowd of Israelite-Cestrians: "How may I curse here in this place / that people that God blessed hasse? / In them is both might and grace, / and that is ever well seene" (5.280–83). *Place* and *grace* combine *here* in celebration of the city and its citizens—whose worth is self-evident, communicated by the spectacle of the plays' performance ("that is ever well seene").

This chapter therefore argues that the Chester mystery cycle and its sixteenth-century performances are mediating elements in the city's long transition from monastic to mercantile regimes of space-time. The Whitsun plays signal a shift from an *urbanitas* defined by immersion in exegetical and hagiographic practices to one in which the rites of *corpus Christi* and Pentecost are infused with, and appropriated by, the oligarchic ideology of the civic corporation. That ideology is itself further modified, not only by the various responses of the performers and spectators toward the pageants' textual matter, but also by the material environment of the procession route and its play sites. Locating the Whitsun plays involves more than placing them within a given moment in Tudor history and culture; it requires their situation within the local spaces of Chester as well as the recognition that these spaces inflect performance even as performance shapes them in turn.[9] The transhistorical prophecies and typologies at work on the audience in Play 5 are deeply implicated in the social and ideological struggles that same audience experiences in its daily life. Tudor Chester is ancient Canaan (or the hills above Bethlehem, or even the New Jerusalem), but the reverse also holds true. As Patricia Badir puts it, "Wherever it is in the city, the stage becomes a socially transformed place in which the quotidian alters representation as it is altered by it."[10]

To demonstrate this point, the chapter opens with a Chester-specific account of what Badir calls urban drama's "unruly plurality," tracing the cycle's route from station to station.[11] I examine each location in turn, giving an account of its history, its topography, and the site-specific practices that inform its complex of meanings.[12] This section of the chapter also considers the procession route as a whole: in its internal survey of Chester's four main streets, the Whitsun play procession negotiates a variety of competing jurisdictions and administrative units (wards, parishes, liberties, etc.). The individual pageants signify differently as they move to new nodes of urban power and privilege, responding to and intervening in what Sarah Beckwith refers to as "the politics of mobility and access."[13]

The remaining two sections of the chapter function as case studies, combining this attention to the intersection of space and performance with carefully delineated accounts of a given pageant's location within time and socio-historical process. The first of these sections considers Play 1, the Tanners' *Fall of Lucifer*, in relation to perambulatory ritual and systems of oligarchic franchise: expelled from a prelapsarian locale which the pageant simultaneously defines as urban space, Lucifer functions as a figure of disenfranchisement, a potential touchstone for the city's ongoing struggle with the palatinate exchequer over matters of jurisdiction. The chapter ends with a consideration of Play 13, the Glovers' *The Blind Chelidonian; the Raising of Lazarus*. Here I track

the blind beggar of John 9:1–38 as he and his pageant move from station to station in violation of the spatial restrictions placed on paupers
by the sixteenth-century mayors of Chester in accordance with Tudor
poor law—a clear instance of national and regional coordination. In a
pageant thematically invested in issues of spatial and legal transgression (Lazarus's resurrection is a boundary crossing in its own right),
both the blind man and Christ challenge oligarchic control of motion.
Play 13 exemplifies the potential for political disruption inherent in
processional drama.

Performing Place: The Whitsun Plays' Route and the Topographical Transformation of Meaning

Processional drama in its fullest sense appears to have emerged in Chester during the years 1521–32, the decade in which the "whitson playe"
mentioned in the 1521 agreement between the Founders-Pewterers and
the Smiths became the "plaiez" announced in William Newhall's 1532
"Proclamacion for the Plaies."[14] It is likely that the pre-1520s "whitson
playe" was a Passion play performed in a single day on the grounds of
St. John's outside the city walls.[15] Moved to Whitsuntide at some point
between the years 1472 and 1521, this play was formerly the climax
to Chester's celebration of the feast of Corpus Christi.[16] As the cycle's
Early or Pre-Reformation Banns indicate, the play—"sett forth by the
clergye / in honor of the fest" (lines 162–63)—followed a "solempne
procession" (line 158) in which "the blessed Sacrament" (line 161) was
carried through the streets of Chester:

> Many torches there may you see,
> marchaunty and craftys of this citie
> by order passing in theire degree—
> a goodly sight that day.
> They come from Saynt Maries-on-the-Hill
> the churche of Saynt Johns untill,
> and there the Sacrament leve they will
> the south as I you say.
>
> (lines 168–71)[17]

The procession route described here is centuries old: Lucian speaks *de processione que sit festis diebus a clericis Cestrie inter duas basilicas* ("of the procession made on feast days by the clerics of Chester between the two churches," p. 63). By retracing the footsteps of their twelfth-century predecessors, Chester's late medieval and early Tudor guildsmen preserved the twin poles of Lucian's monastic topography well into the sixteenth century (the Corpus Christi procession seems to have continued without interruption until its assumed suppression in 1548). The celebrants first descend the hill from St. Mary's, the church traditionally associated with the castle and the Earl of Chester's *aula principis* (Lucian remarks that the *comes caput civium*, "the earl, head of the citizens," attends services there *cum sua cura*, "accompanied by his court," p. 61). Moving north along Bridge Street, turning right at the Pentice, and exiting the city proper at the Eastgate, the procession finally arrives at St. John's, Lucian's *atrium Precursoris*. The path from aristocratic *auctoritas* to ecclesiastical *affectus* therefore turns out to have had quite a long life indeed, even if the earl gives way to the mayor as *caput civium* and the members of the guild merchant replace the palatine *cura*.[18]

When the cycle play does make its 1520s move to a three-day performance beginning on Whitsun Monday, it also shifts to a new route. Local antiquarian David Rogers describes it thus in his 1609 *Brevary or some fewe collections of the cittie of Chester*:

And thei first beganne at the Abbaye gates. And when the firste pagiante was played at the Abbaye gates, then it was wheled from thense to Pentice at the Highe Crosse before the maior. And before that was donne, the second came; and the firste wente into the Watergate streete and from thense unto the Bridge streete. And so one after another, tell all the pagiantes were played appoynted for the firste daye. And so likewise for the seconde and the thirde daye . . . And when the had donne with one cariage in one place, theie wheled the same from one streete to another: firste from the Abbaye gate to the Pentise, then to the Watergate streete, then to the Bridge streete. through the lanes, and so to the Estegate streete.[19]

This itinerary ignores both St. John's and the castle precinct, concentrating instead on St. Werburgh's ("the Abbaye gates") and on the city center ("Pentice at the High Crosse before the maior"). David Mills writes that "The route thus symbolically linked the two new centres of power in the sixteenth century, the expanding abbey, later to become the cathedral, and the recently completed Pentice . . . It signaled a collaboration of church and town, but also of the changing centres of power, as opposed to the older centres emblematized in the Corpus Christi procession."[20] Given the monks' thorough defeat in local politics in 1509, one might quibble with Mills's description of "the expanding abbey," but his general point stands, supporting Clopper's argument about the cycle play's position within an emergent repertoire of assertive civic rituals, "signs of corporate identity and supremacy."[21]

Indeed, the Whitsun plays encode the same oligarchic ideologies at work in the mayor's perambulations (as we saw in the previous chapter). The pageants pass through the main streets of Chester, marking them as the city's own—like perambulation, processional performance extends civic authority to cover the city, symbolically unifying what is in practice an internally divided assemblage of wards, jurisdictions, districts, and liberties.[22] But neither the plays nor, for that matter, their ritual analogs can be seen as purely oligarchic performances. Sarah Beckwith's work on the York cycle addresses topography's resistance to the corporate imagination, the way in which it pushes scholars "to go beyond the notion of an integrated and wholesome body being traced onto the city as if it had no resisting shape, no already delineated contours, no marked and contested spaces."[23]

Put another way, the physical structures of the city are as materially fragmented and divided as the social and religious bodies of its inhabitants—in York or in Chester, each space functions as what Beckwith calls "the literal ground of competing definitions, at once of possession and usage."[24] These "competing definitions" are themselves irregularly distributed among, and subscribed to by, the heterogeneous audiences assembled for a given ritual's performance. Claire Sponsler notes how, "In this setting of mutually powerful cohesion and division, where each individual in all likelihood formed alliances with several different groups simultaneously, performances must have meant different

things to different spectators, and these differences might well have
been irreconcilable."[25] Faced with overlapping allegiances and exclu-
sions, the performance's producers cannot guarantee universal (and
accurate) reception of their intentions: "Onlookers at a medieval performance, who may have had no choice in the matter of what they saw
performed, need not have acquiesced to its view of reality or may only
have recognized its authority, not its desirability."[26]

Topography bears as much responsibility for the "mixed responses"
of the audience as does the crowd's social heterogeneity.[27] As an intersection of what Beckwith calls the city's various "webs of signification,"
each performance site displays a diverse range of meanings (official and
otherwise), "patterns of inclusion and exclusion, of core and periphery" established prior to a given performance and derived from the
activities of those who utilize or even just pass through the location in
question.[28] Processional staging ritually links that site to other stations
along the same route, leading Beckwith to ponder "ways in which the
material space of York must have set up interesting interactions as the
pageants rolled by the different temporary stages of their procession."[29]
For example, the Pavement, York's last station, chief market, and most
public site of judgment, elicits the following response from Beckwith:
"What significance would the Last Judgment have if it were performed
in such a place? Would it be different from the performance, say, of
the Crucifixion or of the various jurisdictions, especially of the secular
ones, that tried Christ in the plays? Would the differing versions of
justice indict or underwrite (more likely both) the mayoral administration?"[30] Her questions here are surely the right ones to ask of performance on the Pavement proper: as each pageant enters the site, it
engages differently with the range of meanings inhabiting that space.

Implicit in Beckwith's mention of the York cycle's "different temporary stages" is the radical potential of processional drama to further
complicate interpellation and reception. Not only does the Last Judgment pageant differ in meaning from the Crucifixion play as enacted
on the Pavement—it differs from the version of the Last Judgment performed at the very first station of the cycle, Holy Trinity Priory, and
from all of the versions carried out at all of the intervening stations. The
pageant wagon moves through the streets of York from station to station, greeting new audiences and new environments along its journey.

At each new stop, it takes on different meanings, both from the other pageants presented at that station and from all of its other incarnations played throughout the city that day. As Beckwith and others (like Marvin Carlson) have argued, plays, pageants, and rituals are always implicated in the socio-semiotic processes and topographical conditions which generate the space of theater.[31] What processional staging as realized in York and Chester does is to multiply that interaction, to coordinate it (effectively or otherwise) across a variety of times and spaces. Meaning is effectively mobile, shifting in response to changes in location.

Once this point is understood, the full magnitude of Beckwith's claim that "it would be hard to think of a theatrical space that is as polysemous as York's" becomes clear.[32] The York cycle registers not only the differences between the various social groups and forces competing throughout the city, but also its own internal, site-specific deviations. The totality of the play experience exceeds the capabilities of any single spectator (or critic, I suspect): try doing the math for up to fifty-one pageants performed at twelve stations over the course of a single day, remembering to factor in those changes that take place over several centuries in both the guilds' individual play-texts and the overall roster of pageants! Chester's situation is somewhat easier to conceptualize, even if the numbers remain daunting ones: twenty-four pageants spread out over three days across five locations generate approximately 120 play situations available for consideration in a given performance year. Polysemy also exists on the banks of the River Dee.

This is particularly apparent at the site of the first station: "the Abaye gates, where the monks and Churche mighte have the firste sight."[33] Discussions of this station typically focus on the local clergy in the audience, usually to establish their continued, post-Reformation support for the Whitsun plays, and not on the site itself.[34] Mills has gone a bit further, reminding his readers that the cycle's first station was also the traditional home of the city's Midsummer fair, run first by the abbot and then, after the Great Charter controversy of 1506–9, by the mayor.[35] However, despite a brief caution that the city's "Midsummer celebrations should therefore be evaluated against this political background," Mills has little else to say about the socioeconomic conflicts that mark the first station's material environment.[36] Clopper's most recent account of the first station is likewise hesitant. Initially describing the corn market (the space outside the Abbey Gate) as "an equivocal space for performance," he then asks a series of intriguing questions: "Is the first performance in the Cornmarket intended to express lay authorization of the plays to the monks within the abbey? Or is a tacit acknowledgment that the laity is ready to be corrected should the abbot find anything objectionable in the performance?"[37] But he never provides any answers to these queries, swiftly finishing up his analysis of Cestrian politics and moving instead to a discussion of biblical drama in Newcastle-upon-Tyne.

Taking some time to fully consider the first station's topographic specificities and political possibilities is thus necessary. In the aftermath of the corporation's 1509 victory over the abbey, the locus of conflict shifts away from the monastery's walls to Northgate Street proper and the corn market.[38] The latter was quite possibly the most visible index of the 1509 civic victory over St. Werburgh's. Chester's city courts had always operated independently of the abbot's court, patiently or petulantly enduring his challenges to their authority, but the town fathers had never before been able to hold the Midsummer fair in the corn market under their own auspices. Audiences viewing the plays at the first station could not fail to notice the corn market's position relative to the pageant wagon, and the sight no doubt served as a bitter reminder of defeat to any monks watching from atop the Abbey Gate throughout the 1520s and 1530s.

As a locus of performance, then, the corn market called spectators' attention to the abbey precinct's history as a site of both jurisdictional debate and economic exchange. It also served as the stage for the much more quotidian performance of the city's internal class divisions, as evidenced in this paraphrase of Mayor Henry Gee's 1533 order concerning the sale of corn within Chester:

Wednesday and Saturday were Chester's market days, when "foreigners" were allowed to trade in the city on payment of toll. Corn was only to be sold in the market after the market bell had been rung. Private citizens had the first choice, then after one o'clock, the bakers could buy and between two and three o'clock, others could purchase corn. No-one was to buy barley to make malt before one o'clock and sellers were not to solicit for custom. Any corn not sold during the market was stored at the Common Hall until the next market day to prevent unlicensed sales.[39]

I will return to Gee and his central role in sixteenth-century Chester's civic self-assertion below, but for the moment I want to emphasize the order's careful coordination of time, space, and socioeconomic status. It draws clear distinctions between what it calls the classes of *citizene* and *comon people*, freeman and foreigner, regulating both groups' access to and behavior within the marketplace. Motion inside the corn market is highly restricted, functioning almost as if it were a variety of theatrical blocking: "mayster mayre stratelye commandyth that no maner of person ne persons coming in to this citie apon the markyt daye to sell corne and all manar of grayne shall not goo abrode in the saide markyt to disturbe nor let the same but shall pacyentlye stand by his or there corne and grayne which they have ther to sell."[40] As the phrase "coming in to this citie" suggests, Gee's regulations are primarily aimed at those individuals—the so-called *comon people*—located outside of Chester's franchise (and thus effectively outside of the city, even though they may live within its walls).[41] Linked to the corn market via spatial proximity and local tradition, performance at the Abbey Gate therefore participates in Beckwith's "politics of mobility and access," potentially excluding some spectators even as it includes others, all in relation to the audience members' respective locations within Chester's social hierarchy.

I should add here that the corn market and the Abbey Gate were themselves subject to material change over time. For example, R. V. H. Burne has raised the intriguing possibility that the completion of the abbey's west front—with its depiction of the Assumption of the Virgin— was timed to coincide with a performance of the Wives' Assumption play at the Abbey Gate in honor of Prince Arthur's visit to Chester in August 1498/99.[42] Other alterations to the material fabric of the first pageant station were far less celebratory. The 1574–75 controversy over the relocation of the corn market house is particularly instructive for my purposes here: on 7 May 1574, the building in question, built in 1556 during the mayoralty of John Webster, was moved by order of Mayor Richard Dutton from its position on the west side of Northgate

Street to a new spot directly "under the bushop's howse."[43] Dean Richard Longworth was not amused: he and the cathedral chapter "served with process the workmen and bound them in bonds not to work it, divers were comitted to the Castell three days."[44] King's *Vale-Royall* reveals that they also initiated a suit against the city in the palatinate's exchequer court, "claiming the ground whereon the house standeth, to be theirs" (p. 87) and bringing yet a third local power base into the dispute. In the end, Chester blinked: faced with what it termed "suites & other inconveniences," the corporation reversed itself on 7 January 1575 and ordered the house returned to its original location "for the avoidinge of the said enconveniences."[45] A deal was subsequently cut on 15 April 1575 in which former Mayor Dutton agreed to build a new corn market house in exchange for the right to transfer the old building to any one of his own properties. The actual removal took place in July 1576, and the original market house spent its twilight years in a quarry just outside Northgate as Chester's first house of correction for paupers.

The corn market dispute did not have an immediate impact upon the production and reception of the Whitsun plays: the 1574 start of the controversy appears to have missed the last performance of the cycle at the Abbey Gate by two years.[46] The incident nevertheless qualifies Mills's sense of the implicitly amiable "collaboration of church and town," revealing that mayor and corporation had interests directly at odds with those of dean and chapter. Cooperation between the two groups was likely and indeed necessary if the plays were to succeed in a given year—but cooperation in one area did not rule out conflict in another, and audiences outside the Abbey Gate would potentially be cognizant of both. Put another way, the space supposedly allotted to St. Werburgh's in the division of the stations was in practice a heterogeneous location, subject to local politics and topographical modification. Performance before the Abbey Gate could speak to a shared sense of civic and Christian ideals, but it could also be understood as a critique aimed at any number of targets.[47]

Play 14, the Shoemakers' *Christ at the House of Simon the Leper; Christ and the Money-lenders; Judas' Plot*, is particularly suggestive in this regard: it contains the Entry into Jerusalem episode which Martin Stevens has identified as essential to English cycle drama's "obsession with civic ceremony and self-celebration."[48] But unlike York this spectacle of urban unity is immediately undercut, first by Christ's prophecy of a sinful Jerusalem's destruction ("Noe stone with other in all this towne / shall stand," 14.218–19, a particularly dire augury for a city as identified with its walls as Chester was) and then by the Cleansing of the Temple episode (which Chester is alone among extant English cycle plays in providing). Play 14 ends not with celebration, but with Christ's attack on the moneylenders ("You make my Fathers wonnynge / a place of marchandize," 14.227–28) and the Pharisees' negotiations with Judas.[49]

The possibilities for audience response multiply swiftly in this more complex narrative structure: if we can assume (for the moment) that the Cleansing of the Temple episode is extant in the 1530s avatar of the Whitsun plays, we can imagine Abbot John Birchenshawe (restored to his position in 1529) being treated by the city council to a biblically authorized warning against any attempts to regain the monks' lost economic privileges. Alternately and simultaneously, ecclesiastical spectators (monastic or otherwise) might understand the episode as a critique of the corn market and the citizens' activities therein (after all, the Shoemakers could save money by dressing the two moneylenders as local merchants, something their designation in the manuscripts as Primus and Secundus Mercator supports). There is also a potentially sectarian element to the play, one expressed in Caiaphas's fears that failure to silence Christ will lead to political disaster ("so shall the Romanes come anon / and pryve us of our place," 14.311–12). In the context of the ongoing Reformation, "Romanes" is hardly an innocent signifier for either the churchmen (abbot, bishop, dean) watching from atop the Gate or the lay Cestrians assembled in the marketplace below.[50]

Finally, we should note the staging possibilities that emerge from the intersection of Play 14 and the Abbey Gate station. The pageant wagon (called the "Jerusalem-carryage" in line 129 of the Late Banns) transforms itself into several separate *loci*: the house of Simon the Leper, the city of Jerusalem proper, the temple, and the *domus* of Caiaphas. With its elaborate steeple, the Shoemakers' carriage alludes to the site of performance: its church-like structure resembles in miniature the more prominent towers of St. Werburgh's.[51] The use of the *platea* in the Cleansing sequence of Play 14 represents an even more intense localization of the cycle drama. The extant stage directions appear to place Christ at street-level at the start of the scene (e.g., *Et cum venerit ad templum, descendens de asina dicat vendentibus, cum flagello,* "and when he will come to the temple, let him say to the merchants as he climbs down from the ass with a whip in hand," SD 14.224+), and the merchants' dialogue suggests that they too may be standing at the foot of the pageant wagon. Complaints such as "What freake is this that makes this fare / and casteth downe all our warre?" (14.229–30), and "My table with my money / is spread abroade" (14.234–35) describe the actor portraying Christ as he overturns the merchants' tables, scattering their goods (props for which the Shoemakers paid "iiij d" in 1550).[52]

While this action could be staged atop the pageant wagon (Christ could first dismount and then climb up onto the wagon), it seems just as feasible to play out the scene on the street, putting the merchants' prop tables in close proximity to the actual spaces in which Cestrians set up their own market tables twice each week.[53] That connection is strengthened by the semantic expansion of the merchants' goods from the explicitly financial *mensas nummulariorum* of Matthew 21:12 (manifest in Play 14 as "my table with my money") to the more generic terms *warre* (14.230, 251) and "chaffere . . . that was so great of price" (14.362, 364). The Shoemakers' 1550 accounts entry supports the text in this regard: the four pence worth of "marchantes ware" mentioned therein probably consists of objects acquired in Chester prior to the performance—items conceivably purchased near or in the area of the corn market itself.

But they might also stand in for the sorts of wares purchased not outside the Abbey Gate but in the Ironmongers' shops underneath the Pentice (the second station) or in any of the businesses lining the main streets of Chester (the third, fourth, and fifth stations—the Shoemakers and Corvisers had their shops in the Northgate Street and Bridge Street Rows respectively). When the Jerusalem carriage moves south down Northgate Street and turns left (west) toward the High Cross to perform before the mayor and the aldermen, it shifts its range of meanings as well, generating different interpretative possibilities at its new performance site. The sense of dramatic synergy between represented and lived space remains intact, but the Abbey Gate and the Cleansing of the Temple give way to a new focus on the Pentice and the Entry into Jerusalem.[54] Staging is again substantially responsible for this change in emphasis: the raised playing surface of the pageant wagon mirrors the elevated position from which the civic dignitaries watch the play. It therefore assists audience members (including said dignitaries) in identifying points of correspondence between on- and off-stage authorities. The six Citizens who welcome Christ to Jerusalem may begin the Entry sequence up on the *locus*, replicating within the play sphere the spatial dynamics of the performance site as a whole. If the Citizens are also dressed in the equivalent of their Sunday best (possibly even in scarlet robes and tippets similar, if not identical, to those worn by the mayor and the alderman in their own ceremonial processions), then Chester's oligarchs are faced with the spectacle of themselves.

When their dramatic doubles step down into the street to spread their garments and palm branches on the ground before Christ, the civic officials find themselves included in a political gesture with local implications. Audience members may read the performers' collective action as a humble assertion of holistic community—or, more cynically, they may understand the actors' evocation of the city's corporate body as nothing more than a temporary gesture of appeasement, reserved for festive occasions and ignored throughout the rest of the civic year. The apocalyptic vocabulary of the Jerusalem prophecy of Luke 19:41–44 certainly establishes a cognitive framework for this latter response: *devotyon* (14.223) will fail, resulting in Jerusalem's being "destroyed, dilfullye dryven downe" (14.217). That dire process is immediately initiated in the Conspiracy sequence that follows the Cleansing episode, and the Jewish authorities (civic and ecclesiastical) who conspire "this ylke shrewe for to assayle" (14.319) occupy the same performance space as the celebratory Citizens.

The performance of Play 14 at the High Cross therefore inserts itself into the repertoire of practices surrounding Chester's administrative and ceremonial center.[55] It intervenes in local politics, offering the citizens (i.e., freemen) in the audience an idealized mirror image even as it dramatizes anxieties about the loss of jurisdiction and the corrosive effect of money upon civic unity. The play also situates itself at the intersection of urban and regional, even national, politics: the Pentice was the locus of official festivity in Chester, a space dedicated to the entertainment of royal and noble visitors from beyond the city walls. Some were local magnates: the Stanley Earls of Derby were routinely feasted in the Pentice throughout the sixteenth century.[56] Others were national figures: in June 1584, Robert Dudley, Earl of Leicester and chamberlain of Chester from 1565–88, was "honorablye received & had a speech at high crosse by master mayor and Cittizins in theire scarlettes & velvett Coates . . . and after banquited in the pentise."[57] Similar entertainments were provided for Robert Devereux, Earl of Essex, in 1599 and James I in 1617.[58]

Performances of the Entry into Jerusalem episode at the cycle's second station therefore take advantage of the site's ceremonial function, inserting themselves into a time-honored series of aristocratic entries. Play 14 relies on the audience's familiarity with these ceremonies, evoking traditional practice in a self-aware and explicit attempt to generate a traditional response. In doing so, the Chester Entry into Jerusalem resembles those staged in York and other cities. However, it also takes advantage of Chester's local history: every chartered borough in England belonged in some sense to the king's honor and could thus potentially imagine itself as the Jerusalem of Palm Sunday. But Chester's long-standing status as chief city of the king's palatinate county of Cheshire (reconfirmed by its 1506 Great Charter elevation to county status in its own right) made this allegorical connection even more meaningful. As a result, Play 14's emphasis on Christ's regality ("Hit seemes well hee would be kinge / that casteth downe thus our thinges," 14.241–42) resonates even more powerfully with Cestrians' deep sense of local prestige.[59] The pageant engages with both past and present, relying on the material structures of the Pentice, St. Peter's, and the High Cross to coordinate its evocation of multiple temporalities.

Our access to the details of that mediatory process relies upon the first and second stations' long history of political and topographical privilege. The abbey and the Pentice are local power centers, equipped with archives dedicated to the recording of their own social importance. Moreover, these archives reinforce one another, preserving the details of their respective institutions' feuds and alliances. The three remaining, nonofficial stations have been less fortunate: aside from Rogers's street designations, there is little evidence of their specific locations. In a sense, once a pageant wagon leaves the High Cross and heads down Watergate Street to the third station, it effectively moves out of historical view. John Marshall offers one possible reason for the latter stations' relative invisibility in Rogers's *Brevary*: "His [Rogers's] apparent vagueness about the other stations may indicate that . . . the venues or stations could alter for each performance."[60]

Although the exact mechanism for choosing Chester's third, fourth, and fifth stations remains unknown, the method used by the York cycle reveals how a contemporary community went about solving the problem of venue. As Meg Twycross has shown, the majority of York's play stations were annually auctioned off, with the highest bidder for each station acquiring the privilege of having the cycle performed at his door—along with the lucrative benefit of selling seats and refreshments to would-be spectators.[61] While there is no clear evidence for this particular practice in Chester, there is also no obvious reason why it could not have been adopted. Late medieval and early modern Chester was as prone to this sort of honor competition as York was, and Mills's optimistic claim that the Chester cycle was "a more communal event than York's" requires qualification.[62] When he states that "Chester's plays belonged to the clergy, to the aldermen, and to all the citizens, not to an elitist group," he downplays the city's less-than-communal aspects: its system of exclusive franchise, its reliance on electoral co-option and oligarchy, and its tendency toward bitter infighting.[63] Politically speaking, the Whitsun plays did belong to an elitist group, even if they gestured toward a more inclusive idea of community. It seems highly plausible, then, that Chester's carefully policed regime of social differentiation would inform the placement of the nonofficial stations. The city producing the plays does not necessarily correspond to the city watching them.

Many of these issues are at stake in the one record we do have for performance at a nonofficial station: the 5 June 1568 memorandum of the *varyaunce* between John Whitmore and Anne Webster "for and concerning the claime, right, and title of a mansion, rowme, or place for the Whydson plaies in the Brudg-gate strete within the Cyty of Chester."[64] According to this document, Webster and "other the tenuntes" had apparently rented a room from a George Ireland in Bridge Street for the purposes of watching the Whitsun plays. Whitmore's argument was that the property in question (Marshall identifies it as the Blackhall, a house standing on the southeast corner of the intersection of Bridge and Pepper Streets) was his to let and that Webster owed rent to him, not to Ireland.[65] Mayor Richard Dutton (then in his first term) and William Gerrard, the city recorder, heard out both parties and ruled that, because Webster and her fellow tenants had previously rented the room on two occasions without incident (most likely the 1561 and 1567 performances of the cycle), she could have access to the space again for the upcoming 1568 production of the plays. After making it clear that her occupancy of the room did not prejudice anyone's long-term claims to the property, Dutton and Gerrard ordered the scheduling of a post-Whitsunday "Indifferent enquest" to determine ownership; if Whitmore's claim was determined to be the better one, then Webster would be required to pay Whitmore rent at the 1568 rate.

As I noted above, the dispute in question is not direct evidence for anything like York's wholesale auction of stations. However, it does suggest that, by the 1560s, viewing the Whitsun plays was effectively integrated with economic exchange, that better seats were available to those willing to pay for the privilege. Moreover, at least two of the three individuals named in the memorandum had personal or historical connections to Chester's civic elite. Marshall's research leads him to identify Anne Webster as the widow of John Webster, the mayor who built the original corn market house in 1556, and Alan Nelson has detailed John Whitmore's gentry status: "By the sixteenth century the Whitmores had moved from Chester to the neighboring Thurstanton [*sic*]: from their burgher status of the fifteenth century, they had become a substantial, landed family."[66] Whitmore's ancestors appear to have included several mayors of Chester: John de Whitmore, senior (three terms, 1370–73); John de Whitmore, junior (five terms, 1373–74, 1399, 1412–15); and William Whitmore (two terms, 1450–51, 1473–74).[67] In addition, the name of Whitmore's uncle (also known as John Whitmore) is linked to a Bridge Street tenement on a 1542 list of Chester's sixteen customary tenants, citizens "who by their tenure were bound to watch the city for three nights in the year, Christmas Eve, Christmas Day, and St. Stephen's Day."[68] Marshall notes that, as some of "the highest ranking and wealthiest citizens" in Chester, the customary tenants were accustomed to working by proxy: they typically arranged for substitutes to take their place as armed watchmen, and they were also quite willing to lease their tenements out to others (such as George Ireland, who was in turn ready to sublet the disputed room to Webster).[69]

Social connections and positions such as these indicate the extent to which Anne Webster's decision to watch the Whitsun plays was caught up in the city's politics of prestige and precedent. Whitmore wanted his rent money, but he also seems to have wanted Webster, Ireland, and the civic authorities to affirm his civic honor by acknowledging his status as customary tenant and landed gentry. He may not have been alone in this regard: observing that the customary tenants' properties were strung out along the Whitsun play procession route (five in Watergate Street, four in Eastgate Street, four in Bridge Street, and three in Northgate Street), Marshall suggests that these properties may have been the sites of the three nonofficial stations. As he puts it, "performance before properties in which the City held an interest seems a strong possibility."[70] If Marshall is correct in his surmise, then the Whitsun plays are implicated in—but not necessarily contained by—oligarchic politics at every stage of their journey. Even if the nonofficial stations are not directly linked to the customary tenants, we are still left with a renewed sense of the extent to which the streets of Chester are marked as political spaces. Reception of the plays outside of the official stops is more than innocent spectatorship: it unfolds within a context of, among other things, furtive ambition (Ireland's desire for the "civic honour and privilege" to be had in the subletting of a customary tenant's property) and affronted dignity (Whitmore).[71]

The plays also operate within gendered space, as Anne Webster's decade-long history of spectatorship indicates.[72] Performances at the Abbey Gate and the High Cross take place in what are largely male-identified sites. Thus Mayor Webster's 1556 reconfirmation of Mayor Gee's 1533 corn market ordinance retroactively genders the earlier order's "every maner of person or persons comynge unto this markyt" as implicitly masculine buyers and sellers: "every person and persons within this Citie which do lacke corne or grayne for ye foryture of his or ther houses and be myndyd to bye the same in the markett shall upon the markett daye eyther himselfe or his wyfe buy such corne and grayne as he doth laycke."[73] The distinction drawn here between *person* as male citizen and *wyfe* as female subordinate establishes the degree to which the corn market was ideologically marked as a male space, even if its gender was mixed in practice.[74] The same can be said for the explicit targeting of first-station performance toward the all-male audience of the clergy, monastic or otherwise, and for the second station's orientation toward the city fathers, the elite among Chester's overwhelmingly male franchise. Mary Wack has been particularly attentive to the ritual marking of the Pentice as masculine space: writing about the shot, the weekly meeting of the city's officeholders for first a drink in the Pentice and then a hierarchical procession to Sunday Mass, Wack juxtaposes the custom's assertion of "a fraternal bond through the drinking" with its ludic inversion in Play 3's depiction of Mrs. Noah and her community of female gossips.[75]

The remaining three stations are more ambiguously gendered, if only because they appear to move from the category of the official to the domestic and the private (Marshall's caveat about customary tenants and a civic investment in the sites notwithstanding).[76] The Blackhall may or may not have been John Whitmore's property on paper, but for the performances of 1561, 1567, and 1568, it was Anne Webster's space in practice. The elevated male dignitaries of the first and second stations give way here to a female spectator, raising the question of how response to the Whitsun plays differed along gender lines. What would Anne Webster think of Eve's involvement in the Fall (Play 2) or Mary Magdalene's washing of Christ's feet (Play 14)? What responses might she have to Play 12, the Butchers' *Temptation; the Woman Taken in Adultery*?

Wack has already offered answers to similar questions concerning the reception of such figures as Mrs. Noah and the Alewife of Play 17, the Cooks' *Harrowing of Hell*.[77] She reads these female characters as thoroughly implicated in "Chester women's sense of lost economic opportunity and lost civic identity resulting from the legislation of the 1530s," legislation that required women to indicate their marital status via their dress, to restrict their attendance at birthing and churching ceremonies, and to forego working as tapsters between the ages of fourteen and forty.[78] Where Anne Webster fits in this history of economic and social loss is unclear: more research needs to be done on her specific identity and history, research that could help us to locate her responses more effectively.[79] But she was potentially affected by all of these laws, and her gendered participation in the cycle complicates the question of the plays' reception even further. Simply by sitting at a window along Bridge Street and watching the performance, Webster reminds us of the presence within the audience of those problematically related to or outright lacking civic franchise—women both single and married, foreigners, apprentices, servants, vagrants, beggars, and so on.

Criticism of the Chester cycle cannot take place in only the space created by scholars' juxtaposition of abbey and Pentice, the official poles of church and state.[80] These sites of urban authority must first be examined for their own internal contradictions, and then read further against the competing cultural authorities and alliances at work in the nonofficial stations. The play Anne Webster saw on Bridge Street during Whitsunweek 1568 was not the same as the play Mayor Dutton saw at the Pentice or Dean John Piers from atop the Abbey Gate, even if the play-text remained the same from site to site. Nor was it the same as the pageant John Whitmore might have seen if he had succeeded in his attempt to evict Webster from the Bridge Street "mansion." The processional performance mode of the Chester cycle demands a localizing, tactical approach, one in which analysis follows the pageant wagons on their path through the city, keeping pace with shifts in topography and in audience. As we shall see in the following short studies of individual pageants, it is this emphasis on processional drama as process that enables a fuller understanding of the Whitsun plays. Locating the cycle in history means little if we fail to pay sufficient attention to the specific details of its multiple cultural and topographical locales.

DISENFRANCHISING THE DEVIL: OLIGARCHIC CONFLICT IN THE TANNERS' *FALL OF LUCIFER*

The critical tradition surrounding Play 1, the Tanners' *Fall of Lucifer*, is one such opportunity for a historicist intervention along newly localized lines. The pageant begins with an oft-cited speech in which God describes his omnipotence and then narrates his creation of heaven (1.1–51). Commentary on this passage emphasizes its sources in late medieval theology and philosophy, particularly its debts to fourteenth- and fifteenth-century nominalism.[81] Furthermore, when scholars do address the speech's sociopolitical implications, they read it as a display of aristocratic power relations. For Jean Q. Seaton, Play 1's "heaven is imagined as God's court, with himself as sovereign lord and Lucifer as his chief courtier."[82] Norma Kroll goes even further, explicitly identifying God and Lucifer "not as absolute sovereigns but as feudal lords who require the personal cooperation and political support of their subordinates in maintaining the integrity of their governments."[83] Finally, while John D. Cox does argue that the devil of the cycle plays "is invariably identified with power and socially privileged individuals: land-owners, courtiers, bishops, lawyers, merchants, wealthy yeomen," he nonetheless characterizes Lucifer's fall in Play 1 as primarily "a palace, not peasant revolt."[84]

Clopper's ca. 1521–32 dating of the play's entry into the cycle undercuts such "feudal" readings.[85] Indeed, Play 1's likely emergence during the decade that Clopper associates with "the civic government's new prominence" suggests that the pageant's politics might be more productively read alongside the oligarchic ideologies and institutions that enable its self-consciously urban performance.[86] Such an approach prompts a reconsideration of the fourth stanza in God's opening speech (1.36–51). Responding to his earlier claim that "all blisse is in my buyldinge" (1.14), God devotes this stanza to the material act of *buyldinge* or construction. He assumes the role of architect, announcing that "a biglie blesse here will I builde, / a heaven without endinge, / and caste a comely compasse / by comely creation" (1.38–41). The key term in this passage is *compasse*, glossed by Lumiansky and Mills as "a bounded area" (in accordance with the *MED*'s sense 3b of *compas*).[87] The "comely compasse" that God casts in Play 1 may therefore allude to the pageant's site of performance: the walled city of Chester, "a bounded area" of great importance to the cycle's local audience.[88] This idea of *compasse* as a discrete space recalls the earlier use of the word in Bradshaw's *Life of Saint Werburge*: "the great compas of the sayd abbay, / Enuired with walles myghty to assay." Bradshaw's reference to "walles myghty" also has a thematic echo in God's Play 1 creation of the angels as sentinels: "Nyne orders of angells, / be ever at onste defendinge" (1.42–43).[89] The pageant imagines limits for "a heaven without endinge" even as it brings that supposedly infinite space into play.[90] The "comely compasse" therefore places spatial limits on the nominally infinite "heaven without endinge." It situates God's "biglie blesse" within Chester's own history of topographical imagination, one that began in the 1190s with Lucian's decision to connect Isaiah 62:6 to the *custodes* and *mures* of his home city.

Some sixty lines later, the pageant activates additional meanings of *compass*—*MED* senses 2a, "A circle, a circular area . . . *wenden in ~*, to

go in a circle," and 3a, "Circumference, perimeter; outline, contour"—
when the actor playing God announces his intention to go forth and
view "his" creation:

> For I will wende and take my trace
> and see this blesse in every tower.
> Iche one of you kepe well his place;
> and, Lucifer, I make thee governour.
> Nowe I charge the grounde of grace
> that yt be set with my order.
>
> (1.110–15)

The mention here of "this blesse in every tower" is an even clearer reference to Chester's urban defenses. But what makes this passage most
representative of Play 1's oligarchic politics is its nod toward the city's
own series of perambulatory rituals. God's *trace* along heaven's ram-
parts (whether it was actually performed or simply left to the audience's
imagination) mimics both Mayor Gee's 1540 tracing of "the circuite of
the liberties of the Citie of Chester" and the ceremony's 29 December
1574 repetition under the direction of Mayor Dutton.[91] Watching from
the vantage point of the Pentice, the mayor, the sheriffs, and the aldermen could not fail to notice the similarities between God's exercise of
spatial authority and their beating of the bounds: at one point, Lucifer
refers to his fellow angels as "sennyors one every side" (1.178), incorporating the *sennyors* watching the performance within the show itself.[92]
By emphasizing God's divine *trace*, the passage transforms heaven into
a chartered borough and works carefully to delineate its socio-spatial
order.[93] It requires that each citizen of heaven "keep well his place," and
it places Lucifer in charge as *governour*, a position comparable to that of
the mayor. God's commands establish jurisdictional authority by defining its present spatial limits ("Touch not my throne by non assente,"
1.91), and they organize topography in accordance with social hierarchy: God's "ground of grace" is a material space infused with divine,
implicitly oligarchic authority—what God calls "set with my order."

In Play 1, Lucifer short-circuits that order, leapfrogging his way up
the heavenly (and, by analogy again, the civic) hierarchy to seize God's
position at the top. His rebellion engages with local anxieties about

political ambition; moreover, it does so in deliberately spatial terms, figuring revolt and presumption as violations of a clearly delineated topography. The performance is organized around God's *cheare* (1.87) or *throne* (1.91), an elaborate piece of stage furniture occupying the central position atop the pageant wagon. Lucifer, his servile doppelganger Lighteborne, and the other angels may also have their own lesser seats, visibly and physically separate from the divine throne. Their presence within God's urbanized heaven and atop the wagon is thus conditional: the Angels ask God to "Graunte us thy grace ever to byde here" (1.81), and the Archangels follow suit with the chiasmatic refrain "Here for to byde God grante us grace" (1.82). Access to the play's city of God ("ever to byde here") is termed *grace* within the play-sphere, and this *grace* is in turn connected to the urban franchise controlling access to Chester's most powerful and exclusive urban community. Put another way, heaven is the "ground of grace," just as Chester is an exclusive *grounde* which limits full citizenship only to those whom it grants *grace*.[94]

To violate the spatial regulations of that *grounde* as Lucifer does is to risk disenfranchisement (i.e., the loss of *grace*). As God says, "I have forbyd that ye neare shoulde; / but keepe you well in that stature. / The same covenante I charge you houlde, / in paine of heaven your forfeyture" (1.106–9).[95] The loyal Cherubim echo this warning in terms whose application to the pageant's spectators is readily apparent: "Our lorde comaunded all that been here / to keepe there seates, bouth more and lesse" (1.138–39). Failure to do so results in an expulsion from the body politic: Lucifer, identified after his fall as Primus Demon, laments that "we have forfayted our grace!" (1.233). This *forfeyture* transfers the offender to the extramural jurisdiction of hell, created by God at the start of the play and designated as "a dongion of darkenes which never shall have endinge" (1.74). Cast out from God's urban "biglie blesse" for their excessively proud attempt to emulate God's authority, the demons become trapped within a series of parodic reenactments of heaven's spatial politics. Before his fall, Lucifer had abandoned his socially defined seat to occupy God's throne; afterwards, in postlapsarian hell, he is ironically a perfect occupant of his proper place: "I ame so fast bounde in this cheare / and never awaye hense shall passe, / but lye in hell allwaye here" (1.271–73). Moreover, as the Secundus Demon (no doubt performed by the actor playing Lighteborne) angrily reports, the devils must continue to beat the bounds and engage in civic perambulations: "And even heither thou hast us broughte / into dungeon to take our trace" (1.234–35). Even a damned jurisdiction is still a jurisdiction.

We see a similar dynamic at work in Chester's sixteenth-century battles over jurisdiction and franchise. As discussed above, the city was internally divided into a number of competing political units, some under the control of the mayor and his Assembly, some under the governance of other bodies, both in and external to Chester.[96] Lucifer's Play 1 fall stems from his violation of heaven's spatial proprieties, and much the same could be said of those Cestrians who crossed jurisdictional boundaries. The fifteenth and sixteenth centuries saw multiple Assembly orders prohibiting citizens from suing one another in "foreign" courts (such as the palatinate exchequer) to the detriment of the city's own portmote and Pentice courts.[97] Cestrians wishing to do so were required to first seek out a license from the mayor; failure to acquire that license could (and often did) result in a penalty of disenfranchisement.[98] This happened to Foulk Aldersey in 1562 when he went to the chamberlain of Chester's exchequer court in order to pursue an action for debt against alderman Thomas Green (Green would become mayor for 1565–66) and found himself first committed to ward and then disenfranchised.[99]

Indeed, the Aldersey family had a history of disenfranchisement: Foulk's brother John was disenfranchised in 1574 for resorting to the exchequer court, and his father William appears to have been at or near the center of Chester's most prominent sixteenth-century jurisdictional controversy, the 1572–74 dispute between the city and the palatinate authorities over the city charter's disposition of the courts.[100] This particular case is relevant here, not only for its revelation of the spatio-political fault lines traversing the city, but for its apparent origin in a 1572 petition asking Leicester, then the chamberlain of Chester, to restore the election process outlined in the Great Charter (and subsequently ignored by Chester's emerging oligarchy).[101] Aldersey's disenfranchisement in 1574 (the year in which, as Smith explains in King's *Vale-Royall*, "the Controversie between the *City* and the *Vice-Chamberlain*, was fully set abroach," p. 86) was primarily due to his inclusion among the plaintiffs seeking action in the exchequer.[102] In a personal petition to Leicester, William described the "hostility mortall and most cruell malice" which accompanied his loss of freeman status:

. . . disenfranchised 28 Jan. at an assembly and deprived of office
of Alderman and Justice of the Peace, upon Saturday last paste
commanded by Thos. Wever, Sergeant of Peax of citie, and Thos.
Bildone, one of serjants of mace, to shutte downe the wyndowes of
his shoppe, not permittinge him to occupie the trade of a citizen,
and on Sunday last of January called him before him [Mayor
Richard Dutton] in the Pentice, utterly forbydedinge him to
resorte to the said pentice or to take the place apperteyninge to
an Alderman and Justice of Peax, or to have any other trade, and
greatly blamed him for repaireing into his presence the same day
at the same tyme and taking the place of an Alderman with his
murrey gowne and velvett tippett and intendeth verie shortly with
force and violence to shutt up the wyndowes of the said shoppe,
and to imprison him to his utter undoing and impoverishment.
Has no remedy by common law in the city, as Mayor is chief
officer.[103]

While Aldersey's complaint is of course calculated to derive maximum
sympathy for his position, it nonetheless stands as a testament to the
spatial practices and divisions at work in Tudor Chester. Disenfranchisement has a topographical dimension: Wever and Bildone order
Aldersey to close up his shop, Mayor Dutton exiles him specifically
from the Pentice and more generally from "the place apperteyninge to
an Alderman and Justice of Peax"—there may be reference in this latter phrase to Aldersey's privileged spatial position in a variety of civic
rituals, including his spot at the Pentice for the performance of the
Whitsun plays.

Indeed, Dutton appears to have been particularly incensed by
Aldersey's insistence on showing up in ceremonial dress at the Pentice
for the city fathers' weekly shot: Aldersey's decision to resist his disenfranchisement by violating both spatial and sumptuary prohibitions
immediately precedes the report of the mayor's threat to imprison him,
most likely in the city's Northgate jail. William's self-designation earlier
in the petition as "Ald., Iremonger and Merchant Venturer" testifies to
a further entanglement of space, commerce, and authority: many of the
Ironmongers' shops were traditionally located underneath the Pentice
itself.[104] It is not clear if Aldersey's own shop was adjacent or in prox-

imity to the Pentice, but the possibility that it was suggests just how total the spatial disruption of disenfranchisement might be.

The controversy ended happily enough (at least where the Alderseys were concerned), for by early 1574 the privy council had decided in favor of the exchequer and ordered William's restoration to the franchise, along with that of his son John.[105] King's *Vale-Royall* states that this took the form of a public—and theatrical—ceremony: "The same day [19 April 1574] Mr. *William* and *John Aldersey* came to the *Common-Hall* before the *Mayor* and all the *Citizens*, and desired to have their former Liberties. Upon whose Request they were Restored; the first, to his Aldermanship, and his son a *Merchant* as he was before" (p. 87). Again, location matters: banished from the economic and ceremonial space of the Pentice several months earlier, the Alderseys regain their franchise before the eyes of their elite peers in the equally official site of the Common Hall. The restoration ceremony operates in a fashion similar to Chester's other civic performances, publicly staging the city's idealized sense of itself as a holistic community.

That ceremony is of course also a record of civic disunity: restoration of franchise necessarily implies a former breach or lapse in the polity. It is likewise possible to imagine the ambivalent responses of the Alderseys (Foulk, John, or William) as they watch a pageant like Play 1 at the second station in the 1560s and 1570s, especially during the cycle's last performance in 1575. As members of Chester's governing elite (William served as mayor in 1560–61, Foulk in 1594–95, and John in 1603–4), they have a stake in what Robert Hanning calls Play 1's "heavy and explicit emphasis on obedience to an established order."[106] They can identify with God's subject position and with the sentiments of the loyal angels, the desire to properly "keepe there seates." But sympathy for the pageant's oligarchic discourse potentially juxtaposes itself with an awareness of their status, however brief, as targets of that discourse. The Alderseys might apply the Principalities' warning to Lucifer ("Yf that ye in thrall you bringe, / then shall you have a wicked fall; / and alsoe your ofspringe, / away with you they shall all," 1.150–53) to themselves, especially with regard to the passage's evocation of sin's consequences for the family—access to the franchise cost the children of freemen nothing, while apprentices and foreigners had to pay. Disenfranchisement risks placing the Aldersey line in the latter category.

According to Hanning, Play 1 suggests "that Lucifer's sin is recreated each time we behave selfishly toward another who deserves better of us."[107] I would like to historically locate that statement, qualifying its assumptions of the generic and the universal. Putting Play 1 in its oligarchic context, watching it from the Pentice station alongside Cestrians previously banned from that very spot—these approaches to the text and its performance allow us to recognize that Play 1 puts the self-centered subject of Hanning's comment at odds with the civic community's obligatory fantasy of unity. It suggests, not only to the Alderseys in the audience, but to all would-be Alderseys, that social transgression is intolerable. In doing so, however, it must also admit that such actions are possible, that civic authority is not complete. The evocation of Cestrian politics in heaven's prelapsarian space may serve the purpose of demonstrating "the reality and finality of heaven's control of non-heavenly space," but the spectators watching at the Abbey Gate or the Pentice (or perhaps even at the other stations) are well aware that such spatial control is itself contestable.[108] The Alderseys may be devils for a time, but in the end, they and their allies successfully fight their way back into heaven.

"Your neighbour borne in this cittie": Breaking Tudor Poor Law in the Glovers' *Blind Chelidonian*

The Tanners' *Fall of Lucifer* concentrates on inter-elite conflict, inaugurating the Whitsun play sequence with a sumptuous, if pointed, drama about the necessities of social hierarchy and political obedience. Tucked away in the middle of the cycle's second day of performance, Play 13, the Glovers' *Blind Chelidonian; the Raising of Lazarus*, takes a different tack: its inclusion of Caecus, the blind beggar of John 9:1–38, reveals a pageant anxious about the presence of the poor within Chester's walls. Previous scholarship on the play minimizes that anxiety, focusing instead on the Glovers' promulgation of a specific theological message. For example, Peter W. Travis sees Play 13 as both a demonstration of God's *potentia absoluta* and a meditation on the contrast between physical and spiritual blindness.[109] More recently, David Mills claims that the play focuses on "the necessity of practical charity."[110] He cites as key evidence the speeches uttered by Caecus and his Boy upon their entry into the playing area:

> [PUER] (ducens Caecum)
> If pittie may move your jentyll harte,
> remember, good people, the poore and the blynd,
> with your charitable almes this poore man to comforte.
> Yt is your owne neighbour and of your owne kynd.
>
> CAECUS
> Your almes, good people, for charitie,
> to me that am blynd and never did see,
> your neighbour borne in this cittie;
> helpe or I goe hence.
>
> (13.36–43)

Here both actors speak directly to the audience, making a didactic appeal whose point can hardly be missed. In particular, the identification of Caecus as the audience's "neighbour borne in this cittie" evokes Matthew 22:39 ("And the second is like to this: Thou shalt love thy neighbor as thyself"), putting the full force of Christ's New Law behind the play's message of charity.

However, as the continuing action of the play makes clear, Christ's commandment is anything but easy to follow. Miraculously healed after his encounter with Jesus, Caecus is immediately accosted by two of his Neighbors and hauled off to the Pharisees' court. There he is accused of being "a knave of kynde / that faynest thyselfe for to be blynde" (13.141–42)—that is, a false beggar and idle vagabond.[111] The Pharisees threaten him with judicial mutilation (in this case, the *contrapasso* punishment of reblinding), and he is saved only by the testimony of his aged parents that he "blynd was borne" and "could never bye nor sell" (13.179, 187).[112] What I want to argue in this closing section of the chapter is that, while Mills is right about Play 13's interest in "practical charity," he nevertheless overlooks the evidence that said charity was the focus of intense political activity in sixteenth-century England.[113] Almsgiving was subject to constant legal classification and reclassification, both in Chester and in the nation as a whole.

To understand the meaning of Play 13, we must therefore examine the shifting status of charity, tracking changes in Tudor poor law and considering how the pageant's horizon of reception alters in response. In other words, we must read the play diachronically and dynamically instead of assuming (as do Mills and Travis) that meaning and interpretation statically resist historical change. Moreover, we must examine the play in its spatial dimension: what are the effects of processional performance on the reception of Play 13? I hope to show that the pageant changes its meaning when it moves from the first station at the Abbey Gate to the second station at the Pentice. As we have seen, each of these sites brings with it a different set of sociocultural associations, associations that stem not only from the site's unique topography but from the different social roles the site plays outside of Whitsunweek.

A brief account of Tudor poor law and its manifestations in Chester (particularly during the years 1530–75, the period corresponding to the performance of the Whitsun plays essentially as we have them today) is necessary at this point.[114] Henry VIII's 1531 Act Concerning the Punishment of Beggars and Vagabonds was the first English poor law to prohibit open begging within local jurisdictions.[115] Earlier laws (going all the way back to the Black Death and the 1351 Statute of Laborers) had been content to control movement between jurisdictions (what Paul Slack has called "the principle of parish settlement").[116] The 1531 Act changed this, transforming begging into a tightly restricted activity reserved for locally licensed paupers only. It also required that surveys of the poor be taken to determine who was eligible for licensing. Paupers and beggars would be divided into categories of the deserving and undeserving poor at the smallest level of jurisdiction: the individual parish or urban ward.[117]

In Chester, the 1531 Act eventually took form as Mayor Gee's 1539 Assembly order concerning the poor (Gee in fact explicitly references "the houlsome statute and lawes of our sovereigne Lorde the Kinge," p. 355).[118] The key provision of the order is a clause announcing the mayor's desire that "the nomber and names of all indigent and nedye mendicant people shalbe serched knowne and wrytten and therupon dyvydit in xv parts and every of them assigned to and what ward they shall resorte and beg within the saide citie and in no other place within the same" (p. 355). Begging out of ward is criminalized: "yf eny of the indigent and pore nedye beggars at any tyme in any other place within this citie out of the warde to them assigned as is aforesaid then the same beger so offendinge to be ponyssed by the mayres discrecyon" (p. 356). We see here how national law becomes local policy: civic officials undertake the surveillance of the poor for the state.[119]

We see something else if we consider the 1539 order's inclusion within Chester's Assembly Book. The order is accompanied therein not only by a "tabull" listing Chester's Tudor wards, "viewed and set out by the Wurshipfull Henry Gee, Mayre of the said Citie," but also by the document (discussed at the end of chapter 1) recording Gee's 1539 perambulation of Chester's "Meyres and Bounds . . . newly viewed by Henry Gee."[120] In other words, the division of Chester's poor is part and parcel of a more general survey of Chester's extra- and intramural jurisdiction. The elite perambulations that delineate the city's corporate body are accompanied by an equally thorough surveillance of its most marginal bodies, those excluded from the franchise.[121]

Gee's 1539 order also co-opts citizens as agents of the state, forcing them to assist civic officials in the management and control of the urban poor. For example, the order mandates that each household maintain a list or *byll* of its ward's licensed beggars: "ther names to be wryttyn in a byll and sett up in every mans house within every warde for knowledge to whome they shall geve ther allmys and to no other" (p. 356). It also states that householders are to apprehend unlicensed beggars and turn them over to ward officials for punishment:

> if anye other person or persons com to anye man or womans
> dore house or person to begge not having his name in the byll
> within that mans or womans houses then the same man or
> woman to geve unto the same begger no manar allmys or relefe
> but rayther to bringe or send him to the stockes within the same
> warde or else to deliver him to the constable of the same warde or
> thaldermanes deputye. (p. 356)

Citizens shirking this duty are subject to fine (twelve pence for "the use of the common box," p. 356) or imprisonment ("for defaut of payment therof the same man or woman so offendinge to be commyttyd to the warde by the mayre tyll it be payde," p. 356). The latter punishment threatens to turn citizens into doubles of their spatially restricted mendicant neighbors.[122] This regulation of individual charity was anticipated in Henry VIII's 1536 Act for the Punishment of Sturdy Vagabonds and Beggars (which required parishes to organize regular collections for the poor) and echoed in subsequent statutes' numerous warnings against casual charity.[123]

When Mayor John Smith reconfirmed Gee's order in 1555, he tightened its spatial restrictions by urging licensed paupers to "remaine and continue in ther houses workinge to the uttermoste of ther power for the sustenation" (p. 357).[124] Instead of going out in the streets to beg, they are to wait at home and "receve such Relief and allmes as shalbe appoynted by the said maire" (p. 357). By modifying Gee's original order in this fashion, Smith made it clear that post-1555 Cestrian charity was the city government's prerogative, not that of individual citizens. Smith was also sure to specify that the city's charity was conditional: otherwise legitimate paupers who persisted "in the going abrode in the begginge as aforesed" were to be stripped of their alms and made subject to whatever additional punishments "as by the sead maire shall be thoughtt convenent" (p. 357).[125]

How do these national statutes and local orders affect our understanding of Play 13's performance and reception? They first of all reveal that Caecus's begging becomes increasingly problematic over time, no matter how justifiable it may seem due to the audience's superior knowledge (superior, that is, to that of the Neighbors and the Pharisees) of Caecus's legitimate infirmity. Performances before the publishing of Gee's 1539 order might be seen by audience members who looked down on open begging and wished for tighter restrictions—but those audiences had no local, legal support for such attitudes. After 1539, Caecus's insistence that he is "your neighbour" resonates with more than the Golden Rule: it alludes as well to the intricacies of ward-specific licensing. Caecus identifies himself as our "neighbour" so that we will not mistake him for an unlicensed, idle vagabond. By 1555, however, that he is out on the street begging at all is a mark against him—at least in Mayor Smith's book. He should instead be at home, doing whatever useful labor he can and expecting civically authorized alms.

The Neighbors' response to Caecus's miraculous healing is equally affected by the changes in charity's legal status. In the 1530s, their exchange about Caecus's identity is not particularly resonant:

PRIMUS VICINUS
Neighbour, if I the trueth should saye,
this is the blynd man which yesterdaye
asked our almes as we came this waye.
Yt is the verey same.

SECUNDUS VICINUS
No, no, neighbour, yt is not hee,
but yt is the likest to him that ever I see.
One man to another like may bee,
and so is hee to him.

(13.81–88)

After 1539, their dialogue with one another (and their subsequent interrogation of Caecus in 13.93–118) becomes part of the mandated process whereby they must ascertain that this beggar is on the *byll* posted in their houses. Spiritually blind to the power of Christ's miracle, they refuse to accept Caecus's account of his healing and hasten to carry out their civic duties. As the Second Neighbor says, "Thou shalt with us come on this waye / and to the Pharasyes these wordes saye. / But yf thou would these thinges denye, / yt shall helpe thee right nought" (13.115–18). Local audiences would well be aware of the penalties awaiting the Neighbors if they failed to act in accordance with Gee and Smith's statutes.

At the same time, we know that many contemporary Englishmen and women disagreed with the restrictions Tudor poor law placed upon charity: audience members sharing such views might see the Neighbors' actions as less-than-principled expediency, especially since they would be implicated in those actions by the Neighbors' self-identification as fellow spectators of Caecus (i.e., "the blynd man which yesterdaye / asked our almes as we came this waye").[126] This latter view resembles the virtuous Christian response that Mills posits, but our survey of Tudor poor law lets us see that even orthodox responses to the Chester plays develop within the paired contexts of national and civic politics. There can be no uniform response to the drama—only a changing continuum of responses corresponding to shifting subject positions within the urban community.

So much for a consideration of how Play 13's meaning alters over time. What about its sensitivity to space? Because the Abbey Gate was also the site of first the abbot and then the dean's courts (and thus served as the city's most visible symbol of ecclesiastical jurisdiction), peformance at that initial station could turn the pageant into a crtique of excessive clerical authority. For example, summoned to appear before the Pharisees (who are probably dressed in spare church vestents), Caecus's mother laments, "Alas, man, what doe we heere? / Must we afore the Pharasyes appeare? / A vengeance on them farre and neare; / they never did poore men good!" (13.161–64). Her husband replies, "Dame, here is no other waye / but there commandment wee must obeye, / or elles they would without delaye / course us and take our good" (13.165–68). We cannot say for certain how the play's clerical spectators would have responded to such speeches, but we can see that the words of Caecus's parents take on extra significance when uttered in a space defined by church architecture and subject to ecclesiastical power.

Once Play 13 moves to the second station, its meaning shifts as well. The Pentice was first of all home to the High Cross. Knocked down by Parliamentarian forces during the Civil War and restored in 1975 to its position in the city center, this market cross was an assembly point for forced labor, as seen in this passage from Gee's 1539 order:

> . . . all manner of idle persons being able to laboure abyding within the saide citie and not admytted to live by allmys within the saide citie shall every workday in the morning in the tyme of wynter at vi of the clock and in tyme of somer at iiii of the clock resorte and com unto the highe cross of the saide citie and there to offer themselves to be hyryd to labour for ther leving accordinge to the kinges lawes and his statutes provided for laborers. (p. 356)[127]

Able paupers refusing to report for work were subject to a penalty similar to that levied against citizens assisting licensed beggars out of ward: "to be commyttyd to warde . . . ther to remayne unto such tyme he or thay so refusing hathe founde suffycent suerties to be bounden by recognisance before the saide mayre in a certene sume" (p. 356).[128] Over time, the punishments meted out to sturdy beggars grew harsher:

Henry VIII's 1531 Act authorized flogging in addition to extant policies placing vagabonds in the stocks; Edward VI's 1547 Act for the Punishment of Vagabonds and for the Relief of the Poor and Impotent Persons legalized the enslavement of the able poor, reserving a "V" brand for the chests of any paupers fleeing such servitude; and Elizabeth I's 1572 Act for the Relief of the Poor and Impotent added such penalties as burning through the ear and hanging.

Throughout the fifteenth and sixteenth centuries, the area outside the Pentice also featured one of Chester's most prominent loci of punishment, the pillory.[129] Hangings took place on the gallows outside the city walls in the suburb of Boughton, but the pillory still provided Cestrians with ample spectacle: the various floggings, humiliations, and mutilations permitted by law would be carried out on its surface or in the street nearby. For instance, it is quite likely that Dorquea Coork's whipping and branding as a vagrant "according to statute" took place here in 1572 (the same year as the Whitsun plays' penultimate performance).[130] In such a setting, the First Pharisee's violent exclamation that "This knave can nought but prate and lye; / I would his eyes were out" (13.151–52) acquires additional, locally inspired—and highly sinister—emphasis.

In conclusion, it is clear that the Chester Whitsun plays do not move through neutral space-time, but though sites marked by lived experience, heteroglossic discourse, and material topography. This is what the study of local and national Tudor poor law brings to the analysis of Play 13: the ability to recognize, however fitfully, some of the circumstances shaping audiences' expectations at any given instance of performance. Thus, to give one last example, in the post-Gee era, the passage of the Glovers' pageant wagon through the city streets from station to station is simultaneously a transition along and across the ward boundaries listed in Gee's 1539 *tabull* (most of which fall to one side or the other of a given street or lane). Caecus first appears before the Abbey Gate, "begging" in what is roughly the intersection of St. Oswald's, Corn Market, and Northgate wards. As he moves to the second station, he passes through St. Oswald's ward and arrives in front of St. Peter's and the Pentice—the point where five wards meet: St. Peter's in the east, St. Bridget's and St. Michael's in the south, and St. Martin's and Trinity in the west. Performance at the neighborhood stations take place along the border between St. Martin's and Trinity (the Watergate Street station); at the intersection of St. Bridget's, St. Michael's, St. Olave's, and Beast Market wards (the Bridge Street station); and finally on the line between St. Peter's and the Eastgate ward (the Eastgate Street station).

Caecus's liminal motion thus runs directly counter to the spirit of Mayor Gee's order and of all the statutes, local and national, that accompany it. Such ordinances seek to control motion, to limit the poor within designated ranges (and ultimately to remove them from both ranging and public view altogether via confinement to hovel or house of correction). But Play 13 forces the issue, not only by moving its beggar from one ward to another, but by neglecting to ever situate performance within a given ward in the first place. Its practical refusal to observe official boundaries in staging its performance of biblical narrative is a telling spatial parallel to the heterogeneous mixing of audiences and structures assembled at each station.

This is especially so in the pageant's depiction of Jesus: Play 13 has the villainous characters speak of Christ and Caecus in identical terms. The blind man is a "sinfull knave" who "faynest . . . to be blynde"; Jesus is denounced as "a sinner and that we knowe, / disceavinge the people to and froe" (13.193–94). Likewise, just as the Neighbors interrogate Caecus's identity, so too does the First Jew (most likely played by one of the actors portraying the Neighbors) demand that Jesus establish his credentials: "Say, man that makest such maistrye, / or thow our sowles doe anoye, / tell us here appertly / Christ yf that thou be" (13.235–38). The first line of this passage implies that Jesus's *maistrye* is a social pre-sumption, a troubling accusation in light of contemporary anxieties over vagabonds' existence outside the labor economy of apprentice and master (not to mention the ideological investment of guilds like the Glovers in such an economy).[131] We might also note that the use of *appertly* in 13.237 belongs to the pageant's thematic schema of light and darkness, blindness and sight.[132] The physically blind Caecus has the faith and spiritual insight required to recognize Christ's divine *maistrye* ("I honour him with hart free, / and ever shall serve him untill I dye," 13.233–34), while the sighted Neighbors, Pharisees, and Jews reveal their spiritual blindness to the truth of his miracles.[133]

But *appertly* also connects Christ in some degree to the questions of identity and verification at the heart of Tudor poor law, questions exemplified by the repeated use of surveys to distinguish the "impotent poor" from the "valient idlle" and in the official insistence on beggars' possession of valid licenses.[134] The assertion of Thomas Wilson, one of the 1572 Act's parliamentary supporters, that "it was not charity to give to such a one as we know not, being a stranger to us" belongs to this cluster of anxieties, as does Play 13's assurance that Caecus is "your neighbour borne in this cittie."[135] The pageant dramatizes the techniques by which local governments carried out such identifications, separating strangers from neighbors and foreigners from freemen. But Jesus's own status in the play as a wandering troublemaker (deceiving the people "to and froe") and low-class criminal (the Second Jew calls Christ *rybauld* in 13.262, and the First Jew threatens to tear his laborer's *tabret* or "tabard" in 13.300) destabilizes the social binary Caecus embodies. By the time Play 13 moves into its second episode, the Raising of Lazarus, it has given its audiences a Christ who functions very much like the vagabond Caecus is accused of being, a Christ who crosses boundaries and moves about of his own accord (his spectacular vanishing from the stage in SD 13.284+ is emblematic of that motive power, related to Caecus's liminality in kind if not in quality). In one sense, this Christ is no problem: as the Son of God and Savior of mankind, Jesus has royal authority and prerogative. He can do as he wills, go wherever he wishes. However, admitting that does not require us to forget the care Play 13 takes in describing him as a vagrant akin to Caecus, lowest of the low.

CHAPTER THREE

CHESTER'S TRIUMPH

Absence and Authority in Seventeenth-Century Civic Ceremonial

---

ON 23 APRIL 1610, ST. GEORGE'S DAY, THE CITY OF CHESTER PUT
on a show (subsequently titled *Chester's Triumph in Honor of Her Prince* for
pamphlet publication).[1] The occasion marked two inaugurations: the
running of the first St. George's Day race in Chester as well as Henry
Frederick Stuart's upcoming creation as Prince of Wales and Earl of
Chester.[2] Produced by local ironmonger and sheriff-peer Robert Amery,
the show was a triumphal procession, complete with death-defying
acrobats, flying gods, and local boys disguised as allegorical personi-
fications. It moved down either Northgate or Eastgate Street, paused
in front of the High Cross and the Pentice to entertain the mayor and

An earlier version of this chapter appeared as "The Absent Triumphator
in the 1610 *Chester's Triumph in Honor of Her Prince*," in *Spectacle and Public Performance in the Late Middle Ages*, ed. Robert H. Stillman, 183–210 (Leiden: Brill,
2006).

the assembled aldermen, and then passed west down Watergate Street with the civic authorities following in its wake.[3] Exiting the city via the Watergate, the procession entered the Roodee, a large tidal meadow used by Cestrians for a variety of ceremonial and recreational purposes. There the show was met with a thunderous cannonade of greeting from a group of ships anchored in the nearby River Dee. Guarded by 240 "brauely furnished" soldiers (A4v), the audience first watched a mock-battle between a pair of ivy-clad savages and a fire-breathing dragon and then cheered on two races and a "running . . . at the Ring" (B1r).[4] Characters from the procession presented the winners with their prizes (two silver bells and a silver cup respectively), and the show ended with a return to the Pentice building for a sumptuous feast in honor of the local gentry.[5]

Amery's show appears to have been a great success. Richard Davies, the local poet who wrote the performers' speeches, called it "a people-pleasing spectacle" (A2v), and antiquarian David Rogers can still recall specific details of "the charge and the solemnitie made the first St Gerges daye" twenty-seven years later in the ca. 1637 redaction of his *Brevary*.[6] But there was something missing from the show, something crucial to its generic self-designation as a "Triumph" (B4r). Simply put, there was no guest of honor. *Chester's Triumph in Honor of Her Prince* is missing its prince: Henry Frederick Stuart was nowhere near Chester on St. George's Day. Instead, he was in the south of England, giving his cousin Prince Frederick of Brunswick a tour of various military sites. John Nichols places the two princes at the Tower of London on 20 April 1610 and at Woolwich Dockyard, visiting the still unfinished *Prince Royal*, on 25 April 1610.[7] A trip to Chester was clearly not on Henry's itinerary that April.

Scholars like David M. Bergeron and David Mills have noted his absence in their accounts of *Chester's Triumph*, but no one has yet gone beyond the mere registration of this fact to discuss its ramifications for the show's sociopolitical goals.[8] In the first part of this chapter, I want to directly address the absence (and absent presence) of Henry Frederick Stuart. As I will show, Amery's pageant assumes that the prince is pres-ent and capable of taking part in the performance, either as spectator or actor (or as both). However, this sort of virtual presence still leaves an actual vacuum at the center of the show, a performative void available for filling by other authority figures and other, more local concerns. Prince Henry's absence destabilizes the generic affiliations of the Chester triumph, transforming a procession that to some extent assumes the form of a royal entry into a primarily Cestrian affair implicitly engaged in an oligarchic conflict contained by the city walls. As Henry recedes from view (or, rather, fails to materialize in the first place), a *psychomachia* conflict between the figures of Love and Envy comes to dominate the dramatic action of the show. What begins as a celebration of a royal heir's creation as Prince of Wales ends up a meditation on local strife, a performative act that raises the possibility of its own negation.

The final speech of *Chester's Triumph* (delivered by the boy playing Chester, the figurehead for civic self-representation) seeks to banish the discord evoked by Envy, promoting instead a sense of social integration and amity. But this same speech also cancels Love's victory over vice, implicitly recognizing ongoing civic conflict as "fact." The second part of the chapter therefore turns to a variety of civic and antiquarian records in order to clarify the role *Chester's Triumph* itself plays in local competitions over honor and finance. A pun is crucial to my analysis here: Amery takes advantage of a variant spelling of his name (Amory) to insert himself into the show as *Amor* or Love. Love's battle against Envy does more than reflect Amery's own struggle against his fellow Cestrians: it is an active part of his efforts to not only solidify but expand his civic status. The text of the show counters Prince Henry's absence by enhancing Amery's presence at others' expense—*Chester's Triumph*, we are told, is "a memorable and worthy project, founded, deuised, and erected *onely* by the most famous, generous, and well deseruing Citizen, Mr. ROBERT AMERIE" (A3r, my emphasis). At the same time, the city records demonstrate opposition to Amery's program of self-augmentation, actions taken to rein him in (if only in favor of promoting someone else). Indeed, the absent *triumphator* is less a rupture in an otherwise steady pattern of authority than an opportunity to recognize "the close-mouth'd rage of emulous strife" already at work in early modern Chester (C2r).

The third and final section of the chapter expands this claim, considering the effects of Envy on a regional scale. Amery's decision to publish *Chester's Triumph* in pamphlet form in June 1610 (two months after the show's initial performance in April) indicates a desire to take part in the national, London-centered celebration of the prince's 4 June creation. Mills has suggested "that Amory [*sic*] expected honours or preferment as a consequence" of pamphlet publication, that the show's entry into print culture is just another instance of "self promotion through display."[9] Given the utility of these arguments for my own in this chapter, I do not wish to downplay their probability. But they do overlook the extent to which Amery's triumph insists on the ability of Cestrians in toto to represent the nation. *Chester's Triumph* is simultaneously England's triumph: Amery's deliberate deployment of nationalizing tropes and figures undercuts modern critical assumptions about the early modern provincialization of urban drama and performance outside of London. Publishing in the capital can signify the subordination of margin to metropole,[10] but it can also assert the periphery's right to speak for, if not as, the center. In a sense, the pamphlet publication of *Chester's Triumph* brings us full circle, back to Lucian's twelfth-century presentation of Chester as global *umbilicum*. Amery's seventeenth-century evocation of centrality will not go unchallenged— but it must be noted.

ABSENCE AND AUTHORITY IN *CHESTER'S TRIUMPH*

Scholars of royal entries and civic triumphs have observed that the presence of the triumphal honoree (or *triumphator*) was an essential element of late medieval and early modern pageant practice. Bergeron and Gordon Kipling both stress the extent to which pageant-masters situate the *triumphator* within the performance space: Bergeron identifies the honoree as an "active participant in the outcome of the dramatic presentation," while Kipling describes him or her as "the protagonist of a drama which takes all London as its stage."[11] As Kipling's use of "protagonist" suggests, the *triumphator* is also the central figure in pageant drama, the performer around whom the entire show revolves. Indeed, without the presence of the *triumphator*, "the meaning of the event would be incomplete."[12] This necessary presence functions on both ideological and performative levels: "Elizabeth, or whoever the honoured person, is not only the thematic centre, but also the dramatic centre of the pageant entertainment."[13] The body of the *triumphator* becomes the organizing and authenticating principle of the overall performance, the material presence that offers spectators "significant compensation" for their otherwise fragmentary experience of ceremonial procession.[14] The honoree unifies the dramatic action, providing a common focal point for the multiple and necessarily limited perspectives of the audience.[15]

Bergeron's reading of the *triumphator*'s relation to the pageant audience resembles Stephen Orgel's description of the spatial dynamics at work in the Stuart masque:

> Jones's stage subtly changed the character of both plays and masques by transforming *audiences* into *spectators*, fixing the viewer, and directing the theatrical experience toward the single point in the hall from which the perspective achieved its fullest effect, the royal throne . . . through the use of perspective the monarch, always the ethical center of court productions, became in a physical and emblematic way the center as well.[16]

City streets are of course organized along different spatial principles than Inigo Jones's masquing stage, but the pageantry described by Bergeron and Kipling remains similarly focused on the figure of authority. Such shows depend on the *triumphator*'s presence for their coherence and, in doing so, organize the dramatic experience along hierarchical lines.[17] Absence therefore generates a crisis within the pageant performance: without a stable, central locus of attention, spectatorship becomes necessarily diffuse and distracted. The triumphal experience is once again a partial one, hardly conducive to the ideal of holistic community such performances are intended to present. The anxiety generated by James I's ongoing reluctance to participate in public rituals (whether civic triumphs or royal entries) is thus understandable: by strategically withholding his presence, James denied civic governments the royal body they needed to authorize their own spectacles of power.[18]

However, not all moments of absence originate in explicit conflicts over access to authoritative presences. The actual, physical body of the monarch (or, in the case of *Chester's Triumph*, the prince) can only occupy one material location at a time—it cannot be present at every ceremony requiring its authorization. Alternative strategies for the ceremonial performance of presence were therefore developed and put into practice. Roy Strong's account of the Order of the Garter's early modern observance of St. George's Day provides us with a particularly relevant instance of these strategies in operation:

> The statutes of the Order of the Garter as revised by Henry VIII made provision for the observance of the annual Feast by Knights absent from court; the Knight was bound to erect the arms of his companions in a nearby chapel or church in the same manner as it was done in the Chapel Royal at court, in imitation of the choir stalls at Windsor. He was further to wear the robes of the Order and to attend services and ceremonies corresponding to those staged at court.[19]

Principles of "imitation" and mimetic correspondence shape this remote Garter ceremony, allowing the Garter knight to achieve a sort of virtual presence through the use of symbolic objects and gestures. The knight uses heraldic arms to transform his local religious space into a type of Elizabeth's Chapel Royal. He takes part in a metonymic ritual, performing as if he were present at court or, to be more accurate, as if the court were present at his location. Strong sees this practice as ·a projection of royal authority on a national scale: "Under Elizabeth these occasions became opportunities for display on a lavish scale, opportunities for a manifestation of the ritual of royalist chivalry in the remoter parts of the realm or even abroad."[20] That is to say, St. George's Day (the date of the Garter ceremonies) serves as the temporal locus of a widespread series of celebratory rituals, stretching from Liverpool to the Netherlands, all focused on the body of the monarch and thus all implicated in a single, royally constructed idea of the nation.[21]

Chester's Triumph relies on similar strategies of virtuality in its celebration, not only of St. George's Day, but also of the prince's creation.[22] The list of performers provided by the pamphlet text describes in some detail the riders bearing the arms of both King James and Prince Henry: these shields, "very richly Haroldized" (A3v), become the functional equivalents of the arms Strong discusses in his account of the Garter observances. Their presence in the procession offers Cestrians the virtual presence of the royal figures their devices represent, a correspondence strengthened by the long-established equation of heraldic imagery with aristocratic identity in the chivalric tradition. Fame's opening address supports this connection, explaining to the audience how "these Worthies (noted by their shields) [James, Henry, and St. George] / Are (by my conduct) thus ariued here" (B2r). Her remarks speak to the difficulty of establishing virtual presence: "I *Fame* . . . Haue brought them thus, as t'were against the hill / Of highest *Lets*, to celebrate this *Day*!" (B2r).

The speech that follows (Mercury's) increases our sense of the royal presence within Chester. In fact, this oration has proven to be so convincing in its evocation of Henry's attendance that at least one modern critic appears to have accepted its claims at face value.[23] At the start of the speech, the messenger of the gods, himself identified in song as a "Prince" (B2v), descends "in a Cloude" (most likely from the top of St. Peter's or one of the buildings adjacent to the High Cross) and reports to the audience that his divine mission is "To visite Him whose rare report hath rung / Within their [the gods'] eares" (B2v–B3r). Mercury continues, identifying this "Him" through gesture and direct address:

> And to this place, directed by their Powres,
> I am ariu'd (in happy time I hope)
> To find this happy God-beloued Man.
> And loe behold on suddaine where I spie
> This Fauorite so fauor'd of the Gods:
> I will salute him with such courtesie
> As best beseemes a wight of such account.
> All haile to thee high Iustice Officer;
> *Mercurie*, Nuntius to the Powres diuine,
> Hath brought thee greetings from their Deities.
>
> (B3r)

Acknowledging his Cestrian surroundings ("this place"), Mercury more specifically locates his objective ("loe behold on suddaine where I spie") and calls out to him ("All haile to thee"). Although the passage lacks an explicit stage direction, the line "I will salute him with such courtesie" suggests the precise nature of the gesture that the boy playing Mercury would then make. It also functions as the first step in its addressee's incorporation within the dramatic field of the triumph: Mercury's salute transforms the "high Iustice Officer" into Kipling's "protagonist." The entire oration prepares the audience for Camber's specific praise of Henry ("God blesse Prince HENRY Prop of Englands ioy," C1r), a laudatory speech that offers spectators an identity to hang upon Mercury's "wight of such account."

But Mercury's performance ultimately fails to fill the real-time performative gap resulting from the prince's absence, the dramatic vacuum immediately confronting the audiences gathered alongside city streets and around the High Cross. The Henry virtually participating in the procession still has to compete for recognition.[24] The material fact of his absence (anticipated in the speech's vague deixis) leaves an opening in the ideological and performative field of the pageant, an empty space available for appropriation by other authorities. The show leaves spectators to their own devices when choosing who will occupy the prince's place. After all, Fame identifies not one but three "Worthies" in her inaugural address. Moreover, when she introduces Mercury, her addressee is equally indeterminate: "Then for th'encrease of this triumphant Mirth, / I'le inuocate the Gods Embassadour, / To be the President of Heau'n to Earth; / And, from the Gods, salute your Gouernour" (B2r). In the local context of Chester, and in the immediate material context of performance, "your Gouernour" proves to be an elusive figure. It certainly could refer to the newly created prince in his capacity as Earl of Chester and thus to his traditional authority over Cestrians. But the phrase could also identify King James, one of Fame's three "Worthies" and the subject of a direct address by Britaine: "Great *Britaines* Greatnesse . . . We doe ascribe vnto thy Match-lesse worth . . . And while me (*Britaine*) *Neptune* shal embrace, / Ile ruine those, that spight thee, or thy Race" (B4v). Britaine precedes Camber in both the procession of riders and the sequence of speeches, carefully preserving James's hierarchical dominance over his popular son.[25] The awarding of prizes after the race and tilt takes place along similar lines, with Britaine (James) handing out "the better Bell" and Camber (Henry) presenting "the second Bell" (D1r). Joy, the final speaker in the pageant procession, ends her oration with an echo of Britaine's: "Wherefore auaunt; that all the I'le may sing, / Now *Enuies* gone, in peace w'enjoy our King" (C4v). In the pre-race portion of *Chester's Triumph*, James, not Henry, literally gets the last word.

Nevertheless, James is also nothing more than a virtual figure, present only via the operations of symbolic object and speech. The phrase "your Gouernour" is therefore most easily appropriated by those authorities in attendance at the show's performance, the mayor of Chester and his magistrates. The figure of Chester begins her speech with a direct address to this elite audience: "Haile sage Spectators, haile yee reu'rend Sires, / Haile yonger Brutes, whose worth self *Worth* admires, / Whose ardent Loues both to the place, and vs, / Constraines our Loues to entertaine yee thus" (B3v). While the gentry assembled for the race and tilt are no doubt included in Chester's address (perhaps as the "yonger Brutes"), the civic authorities watching the performance from the Pentice are the best candidates for the "sage Spectators" and "reu'rend Sires" interpellated by the oration's first line.[26] Immediately following Mercury's recognition of the "high Iustice Officer" whose presence works to ground the dramatic and ideological action of the triumph, Chester's speech proposes additional, local candidates for the ambiguous "Him" pointed out minutes before. If we look back at Mercury's description of the "God-beloued Man," we can see its pliability of reference:

> And know (deere Sir) thy deedes and good deserts,
> Thy well disposed nature, Minde, and thought,
> Thy zealous care to keepe their Lawes diuine,
> Thy great compassion on poore wights distrest,
> Thy prudence, iustice, temp'rance, and thy truth,
> And, to be briefe, thy vertues generall,
> Haue mou'd them all from Heau'n, with one assent,
> To send Me downe, to let thee vnderstand
> That thou art highly in their Fauors plac'd:
>
> (B3r)

The "vertues generall" listed in this speech prove to be precisely that: virtues general enough to apply to both royal figures and civic officials. They could describe Prince Henry, King James, or Mayor William Leicester—each man a "high Iustice Officer" in his own right. But the spatial and mimetic effects of performance, combined with the prince's absence, make it more likely than not that Leicester will be the recipient of Mercury's gesture of acknowledgment.

In addition, the mayor, his officers, and his colleagues in the Chester Assembly are doubly represented in the triumph's dramatic action. First, Chester's speech places them in roles reminiscent of those played by late medieval and early modern *triumphatores*; second, Chester herself embodies the corporate community ruled by these city fathers. The performative doubling of the city's representation suggests that, when Chester speaks in *Chester's Triumph*, she speaks as much to herself as she does to either king or prince. Certainly, this is the effect conveyed in part by "Chesters last speech," the final oration of the entire triumph. Inviting "each noble worthy, and each worthy Knight, / To close their stomåcke with a small repast" (the Pentice feast mentioned above), Chester concludes with a "solemne vow" marked as communal through its use of first person plural pronouns: "whilst *we* breath, *our* hearts shall honour you" (D1v, my emphasis). This corporate city-self dramatically dislocates Joy's earlier celebration of the king, replacing national consciousness with an emphasis on local hospitality and local affairs. The elite spectators on the Roodee end the show by taking part in a feast held within the building representing the institutions of Cestrian authority. Multinational royalty (James as King of England, Scotland, and Ireland; Henry as Prince of Wales) is not forgotten, but the structures of locality effectively contain it and appropriate it to their own ends.

In *Chester's Triumph*, this local appropriation causes a series of identifiable shifts in the show's ideological content and dramatic practice. The first six orations of the triumph (Fame, Mercury, Chester, Britaine, Camber, and Rumor) form a static procession, concentrating on the celebration of St. George's Day in a variety of intersecting geographical and cultural spaces (England, Wales, Chester, Britain, Christendom). However, beginning with Peace's speech and its mention of "ciuill Mutinies" (C2r), the drama of the show increasingly relies on dialogue and interaction between its emblematic figures.[27] The center of this performative activity is the gorgon-like Envy: the second half of *Chester's Triumph* (running from Peace's speech all the way through the race and tilt to Chester's closing remarks) devotes itself in one way or another to Envy's destabilizing presence as well as to the various attempts to dispel that presence, to transform it into absence. A common figure in early modern civic ceremonial, Envy epitomizes the civic pageant's deployment of the English morality play tradition to resolve specifically urban anxieties.[28] Peace's anticipatory condemnation of Envy reveals the social forces, positive and negative, that the vice represents:

> I'll rend the close-mouth'd rage of emulous strife,
> And wound Distraction, with Connexions knife.
> And when damn'd Malice comes but once in sight
> I, with a vengeance, will suppresse her straight.
> I'le send pale Enuie downe to hell with speed,
> Where she vpon her Snakes shall onely feed.
> . . . .
> Which being done I'le send that base infection
> (Whose onely vertue is but base) Detraction
> Her to associate; where they both shall liue
> As long as hell can life with horror giue:
>
> (C2v)

Here Envy embodies social jealousy and political backbiting; she personifies the competitive drives ("emulous strife") that threaten to undermine the continued stability of urban government. In mercantile oligarchies like Chester (or London), the social and generational hierarchy of offices becomes a locus of self-aggrandizement, aggression, and desire. Those individuals located at its bottom seek to rise to the top, displacing others—both predecessors and colleagues—in their acquisition of political power and authority. Conversely, those at the top seek to maintain their control of the system, keeping their junior magistrates in place and insisting upon the measured, regular pace of governmental promotion. Both the vertically oriented language of Peace's speech (*suppresse, downe, base*) and its shift in attention from the national struggle of peoples (the Scots and the English) to the intimacies of "Domestick strife" and the administrative complexities of "this blessed State" (C2v) replicate this political structure. They present Envy as an aggressive, hostile social climber whom Peace, the representative of legitimate civic authority, must "suppresse . . . straight" and send down to her proper place in the triumph's hierarchy of virtues and vices (the dramatic parallel to Chester's own social hierarchy). Envy's lowly origins are confirmed by Peace's insistence upon the "base" status of "associate" Detraction.

Chester's Triumph therefore resembles other contemporary treatments of Envy within civic ceremonial. For example, the procession in Thomas Dekker's 1612 *Troia-Nova Triumphans* takes the new Lord Mayor of London, doubled in the pageant drama by the allegorical figure of Virtue, past the ominous castle of Envy in Cheapside en route from St. Paul's to the Guildhall.[29] When the Lord Mayor returns to Cheapside on his way home, Envy and her minions threaten the mayoral party once again. The forces of Virtue (and civic order) are ready for them this time: twelve gunmen accompanying the Lord Mayor discharge their weapons into the air, defeating Envy. The twelve soldiers are symbolic representatives of London's Twelve Great Companies, and James Knowles has thus read *Troia-Nova Triumphans* as a statement of oligarchic solidarity upon the occasion of the new Lord Mayor's election.[30] The dramatic action of *Chester's Triumph* follows a similar pattern: Love's debate with Envy ends with the vice's banishment to "the depth of deepest Stigian flood" (C4r) at the virtue's command, and Joy's concluding speech widens the scope of Envy's exile, naming all of the other speakers in the show in order to stress their shared role in Love's process of exclusion and condemnation.

It is almost as if Joy strips Envy of her civic franchise: "*Enuie* auaunt, thou art no fit Compeere / T'associate these our sweet Consociats heere" (C4v). Joy's oration makes it clear that "Compeere" and "Consociats" include her fellow personified virtues, but the terms may also be applied to the elite audience watching the show from the Pentice. Presumptuous, slandering Envy is expelled from their company as well. The show finally carries out Peace's promised act of suppression, restoring to the streets of Chester the "mutual concord datelesse" and "peace-procured praise" that come from the alliance of Love and Peace (C2r). The relevance of such an alliance to urban concerns is confirmed early on, when Peace vows that "No forraigne Nation shall affront their force / As long as I direct them in that course. / All rash dissentions and litigious braules, / I shall expell from their vnshaken walls" (C2r).

Even though the first couplet evokes England through the phrase "No forraigne Nation," the second couplet is explicit in its reference to the legal battles and religious struggles which divided the supposedly uniform corporate space of the city, a unity made manifest in the passage's mention of "vnshaken walls," the material marker of late medieval and early modern *urbanitas*.[31] Thus the *psychomachia* of *Chester's Triumph*, like that of *Troia-Nova Triumphans*, resolves civic struggle in favor of a virtue that it defines as oligarchic order. Both shows stage dissension and strife in order to represent vice's active expulsion from the city community, a community whose unanimity is then spectacularly asserted. The triumphs posit that virtue's victory is total.[32]

But Envy's defeat in *Chester's Triumph* ultimately proves to be a limited and contingent one, a dramatic fantasy subsequently undone within the field of performance itself. In retrospect, this outcome seems inevitable: Envy may be a vice, but its character as "emulous strife" reveals its structural necessity to the very institution it threatens. Emulation is an essential element in the repertoire of oligarchic procedures and practices comprising urban government; the political aspirant follows a well-worn and clearly marked path to authority, the *cursus honorum* that ideally culminates in his assumption of the mayoralty.[33] The jealous desires driving Envy are also those assisting his emulative progress up the hierarchical ladder. Anthony Munday's 1604 Lord Mayor's Show, *The Triumphs of Re-United Britannia*, provides us with some London evidence for this alternate understanding of envy as an essential social force. Describing the Britannia's Mount pageant for his readers, Munday offers an "explanation" for its method of propulsion: "Corineus and Goemagot, appearing for the more grace and beauty of the show, we place as guides to Britanniae's Mount, and being fettered unto it in chains of gold, they seem (as it were) to draw the whole frame, showing much envy and contention who shall exceed most in duty and service" (lines 188–94).[34] Here "envy and contention" directly motivate "duty and service"—in Munday's show, "Britanniae's Mount," the figure of the nation, only moves forward due to the efforts of the monstrous figures "fettered unto it." *The Triumphs of Re-United Britannia* reconfigures Corineus and Goemagot's legendary antagonism as socially productive competition.

Evidence for similar connections between envy and social competition can be found throughout *Chester's Triumph*, especially if we
remember the inaugural motives informing the entire show. First of all,
Amery's celebration of Henry's imminent creation ends up undercut by
Envy's mention of her desire "To see a Sonne the Butcher of his Sire . . .
Or else to see a Father sucke the blood / Of his owne Spawne" (C3v).
These grim images should not be read as knowing nods to the tension
between King James and Prince Henry, but their evocation in a triumph
honoring royal father and royal son nonetheless casts a momentary pall
over the show.[35] The second inauguration, Amery's establishment of an
annual race and tilt, swiftly falls under Envy's jealous influence as well.
This slippage first appears in Peace's speech. There she establishes an
analogy between athletic and civic competition, a connection symbol-
ized by the wreath of the champion: "I'le binde their Loues with true
Loues Gordian knot, / That rude *Dissentions* hands vndoe it not: / And
with a Wreath of euer-during Baies, / Crowne all your browes with
peace-procured praise" (C2r). The language of binding and unbind-
ing at work in this passage is immediately echoed in Peace's double-
edged image of "Connexions knife." Technically the personification of
social concord, Peace nonetheless wields a blade that divides in order to
unite: the factionalism signified by "Connexions knife" ties urban elites
together even as it serves to cut out and exclude inferiors (evoked in the
passage by the knife's wounding of the "rude" and thus explicitly lower-
class Dissention).[36] Chester's St. George's Day games are ludic practices
marked by social class—urban and county elites provide the horses for
the race and take part themselves in the tilt. The wreaths awarded to
the winners are symbolically identical to those given to Peace's social
victors, the urban oligarchs who join together to maintain exclusive
rule over the city. In games, just as in civic politics, there are those who
end up with "the better Bell" and those who must be content for now
with "the second Bell."

The show also acknowledges Envy's social necessity (or at least its
social inevitability) when it sends its audience mixed messages about
Fame's ability to transmit honor to posterity. Introducing the presentation of prizes, Fame claims that she will preserve the winners' names
"within her booke . . . till Time stayes his course . . . Maugre Detraction

and fell Enuies spight" (D1r). Here it is Judgment Day, and not "fell Enuies spight," that will ultimately bring a close to the victors' fame—an
end which they as Christians are understood to accept. Envy's conju-
ration by Love appears to be eternal in duration. But four speeches
later, Chester completely overturns Fame's sentence: "No Action,
though admir'd for Excellence, / No Practize, though of high'st pre-
heminence / That can escape the Poliphemian eye / Off Enuie, that
for euer lookes awry" (D1v). Now it is Envy who remains eternally vigi-
lant, and, unlike Fame, she has no limit of Doomsday placed upon her
surveillance (she simply looks on jealously "for euer"). Having restored
Envy to the thematic and social space of the triumph, Chester tries to
once again exclude the vice, telling her elite audience that "Onely your
Loues, which are our fairest markes, / Must muzzle Enuie" (D1v). But
the transfer of responsibility for exclusion onto the spectators remains
a conditional one, dependent on their favor and, no doubt, on their
satisfaction with the show, race, and feast provided them.

Finally, even these elite viewers are susceptible to Envy's appeal,
for Chester acknowledges that "the Fury barkes vnto the best" as well
as the least (D1v). Envy is therefore more than a vertical phenomenon.
It operates horizontally as well, extending laterally within elite levels of
civic government and city culture. The vice's return to *Chester's Triumph*
demonstrates both her ineradicable dramatic presence and her necessary civic function. It reveals the social costs which accompany Prince
Henry's absence in Chester on 23 April 1610: the performative and
political spaces he fails to occupy represent both an opportunity and
an instability. Multiple authorities struggle to appropriate the prince's
presence to their own ends, but the very fact of their conflict delineates
the limits of the *triumphator's* own authority. In *Chester's Triumph*, all
authoritative presence—royal, civic, moral—is rendered contingent.
Someone else is always waiting to take your place.

LOVE AND ENVY IN THE URBAN ARCHIVE

Of course, there is still one candidate for *triumphator* missing from my
analysis of authority's absence in *Chester's Triumph*: Robert Amery, the
show's producer. As I mentioned at the start of the chapter, Amery takes

advantage of a Latinate pun on his surname (Amery = *Amor* = Love) to
cast himself in his own show. The pamphlet version of the triumph
hints at that equation in its closing lines:

> If any Reader shall desire to know
> Who was the Author of this pleasing show:
> Let him receaue aduertizement hereby
> A Sheriffe (late of *Chester*) AMERIE.
> Did thus performe it; who for his reward,
> Desires but Loue, and competent regard.
>   ROBERT AMERIE.
>   (D2r)

We've already seen Mills's hypothesis that the primary audience or
"Reader" for Amery's "self-promotion through display" was Prince
Henry.[37] I think it just as likely that Amery has a specifically local audience in mind here. *Chester's Triumph* did seek out the prince through
print publication in London, but it was performed in Chester first. The
triumph is therefore not only the record of an individual citizen's love
toward Prince Henry, but of the performative processes whereby urban
"Loue," the ideological fantasy of civic unity, is generated—and of that
citizen's claim to individually personify that social force, to locate its
authorizing power within his own act of authorship (Amery makes it
clear that he, not Davies the poet, is "Author of this pleasing show").[38]

Amery's self-authorizing performance has its critics. After all, as I
have argued above, Love's defeat of Envy is only temporary. But there's
a clearer sense of opposition to Love's (and thus to Amery's) schemes at
work in the debate sequence. Asked by Love to define "the solace Enuie
counteth deepe," the vice responds with an extensive wish list of hor-
rific acts (C3v).[39] However, even Envy has her limits:

> But to behold a ranke of rustick Boyes
> Shewing as childish people childish toyes
> To grace a day with; O it grates my gall
> To heare an apish Kitling catterwall.
> Is it not harsh to heare a Marmoset squeake
> Vpon a stage a most vnioynted speake?

And then to heare some ignorant Baboone,
Sweare that this Monky did surmount the Moone.
When as the Infants best is too too bad,
And which to heare would make a wise-man mad.

(C3v–C4r)

This is an amazing speech, one that threatens to undermine the entire show: what Envy denounces here is the very performance her audience is attending.[40] She attacks triumphal discourse, redefining praise of the *triumphator* as nothing more than claims that some monkey "did surmount the Moone," a slander that includes in its scope Prince Henry, King James, Mayor Leicester, and all of the other candidates for the absent *triumphator*'s authority. That said, the passage's primary target appears to be Amery himself (in his capacity as pageant-master). Put another way, Amery uses *Chester's Triumph* to stage an assault on his own authority: as Envy says earlier in the scene, "he that thinks that Loue can e're be wise, / Hath neither iudgement, wisedome, wit, nor eies" (C3r). We might therefore read the debate between Love and Envy as Amery's apotropaic preemption of criticism. Opposition to the show (and to the civic self-promotion that it celebrates) is demonized as the ranting of a foul she-monster, and Love (Amery) emerges victorious.[41]

Chester's reluctant acknowledgment of Envy's inevitability qualifies Amery's achievement—the ironmonger's assumption of Love's identity personalizes the point I made earlier about Envy's civic necessity. The pageant's conclusion suggests Amery's awareness of the limits to his self-authorization, and so (in retrospect) does the debate: you only ward off what you fear and expect to encounter. As Amery's life-records demonstrate, he was no stranger to the social dynamics epitomized by Envy. Admitted to the civic franchise on 16 January 1597/98, Amery was the son and grandson of former sheriffs.[42] He became a common councilman in 1604, and was a leavelooker in 1605–6 and a sheriff in 1608–9.[43] His career in government apparently reached a plateau at this point: from 1609 until his death on 21 September 1613, Amery is listed in the Mayor's Books as a sheriff-peer, an unofficial office between sheriff and alderman.[44]

We know as well that he was caught up in several instances of intrafranchise conflict: for example, on 20 October 1609, a merchant named Charles Leeche accused Amery of diverting dirty water into his courtyard on numerous occasions.[45] More seriously, on 12 April 1605, Amery and two other men were ordered to submit to the Assembly for either pardon or punishment because they had pursued "forraine suites . . . withowte the licence of the Maior" against their fellow free-men in the palatinate's exchequer court—the same crime for which (as we saw in chapter 2) the Alderseys had been disenfranchised in the 1560s and 1570s.[46] Finally, there is the case of the five shillings Amery was fined on 29 November 1611: "And at the same Assemblie Mr Robert Amerie for giuinge diuers vncivill speeches vnto the said Mr Button to the disturbance of this Assembly was fyned in fyve shillinges and ordered to pay the same to the vse of the Maior and Citezens of the said Cittie accordinglie."[47] What Edward Button, a wealthy Chester inn-keeper, did to merit "diuers vncivill speeches" from Amery is unclear, but we do know that he had just been "elected and chosen to be Alder-man in steed and place of William Brocke Esquier learned in the lawes late Alderman deceased."[48] Did Amery feel passed over at Button's elec-tion and lash out?[49] Was he simply launching yet another offensive in an ongoing and otherwise unrecorded feud? Whatever the answer to such questions, Robert Amery's "uncivill speeches" bear a striking resem-blance to the "ciuill Mutinies" evoked by Peace in her St. George's Day speech (C2r). The man who would be Love certainly knew how to play the part of Envy.

To be fair to Amery, his fellow citizens proved equally adept at portraying "Loues Misanthropos" (C4r).[50] We see an inkling of their antagonism in the document identified in British Library MS Har-ley 2150 as "The maner of the showe that is if god spare life & health shalbe seene by all the behoulders vpon St Georges day next being the 23th of Aprill 1610."[51] This text, a single sheet inserted into one of Chester herald-painter Randle Holme II's seventeenth-century anti-quarian collections, is essentially a program for the upcoming event, listing the various participants in their processional order.[52] I cannot identify the precise audience for the document, but I suspect that it may have been presented to the Assembly. My suspicions stem from Amery's signature at the text's end.[53] The list of the show's contents concludes with a direct address inviting commentary on the pageant: "when all is done then Iudge what you haue seene & soe speake on your mynd, as you fynde."[54] The text is then signed by "The Actor for the presente. Robart Amory."[55] Amery's decision to identify himself in his signature as "Actor" is an interesting one: at least three senses of the term (as defined by the *OED*) are potentially active here, and all three are relevant to his involvement in the planning and execution of the 1610 pageant. The first sense of *actor*—"A manager, overseer, agent, or factor"—points to his apparently self-appointed role as pageant-master.[56] This is the Amery at work in "the maner of the showe," laying out his plans for the spectacle. As we've seen above, this is also the Amery who identifies himself in the pamphlet text's signature as "Author of this pleasing show." (There's a third document conveying this sense of *actor*—a 1609–10 petition in which Amery asks the Assembly for money to cover his personal expenses in staging the show—but I want to withhold analysis of that text for the moment.)

The second sense of *actor* evoked by Amery's signature is the one most familiar to us today: "One who personates a character, or acts a part; a stage-player, or dramatic performer."[57] Emerging in the 1580s, this sense was potentially available to Amery. It matters here because of a short poem placed just below Amery's signature (figure 4). The poem reads as follows:

> Amor is loue and Amory is his name
> that did begin this pompe and princlye game
> the Charge is great to him that all begun.
> let him be satisfyed now all is done.[58]

The pun hinted at in the signature of the pamphlet text is made explicit here: "Amor is loue and Amory is his name." Written in the same hand as the rest of the "maner of the showe" (and thus probably of Amery's invention), the quatrain is not an afterthought, but an essential part of the document as a whole. The itemized list of participants is the bill of fare, as it were, and Amery's poem is the bill. Its use of the third person is an attempt to more effectively dun the city fathers: it is a general, unlocalized voice that seeks reimbursement for Amery's expenses, not Amery himself. The voice asserts that Amery's production of the "pompe and princlye game" (the 1610 show) is motivated solely by his

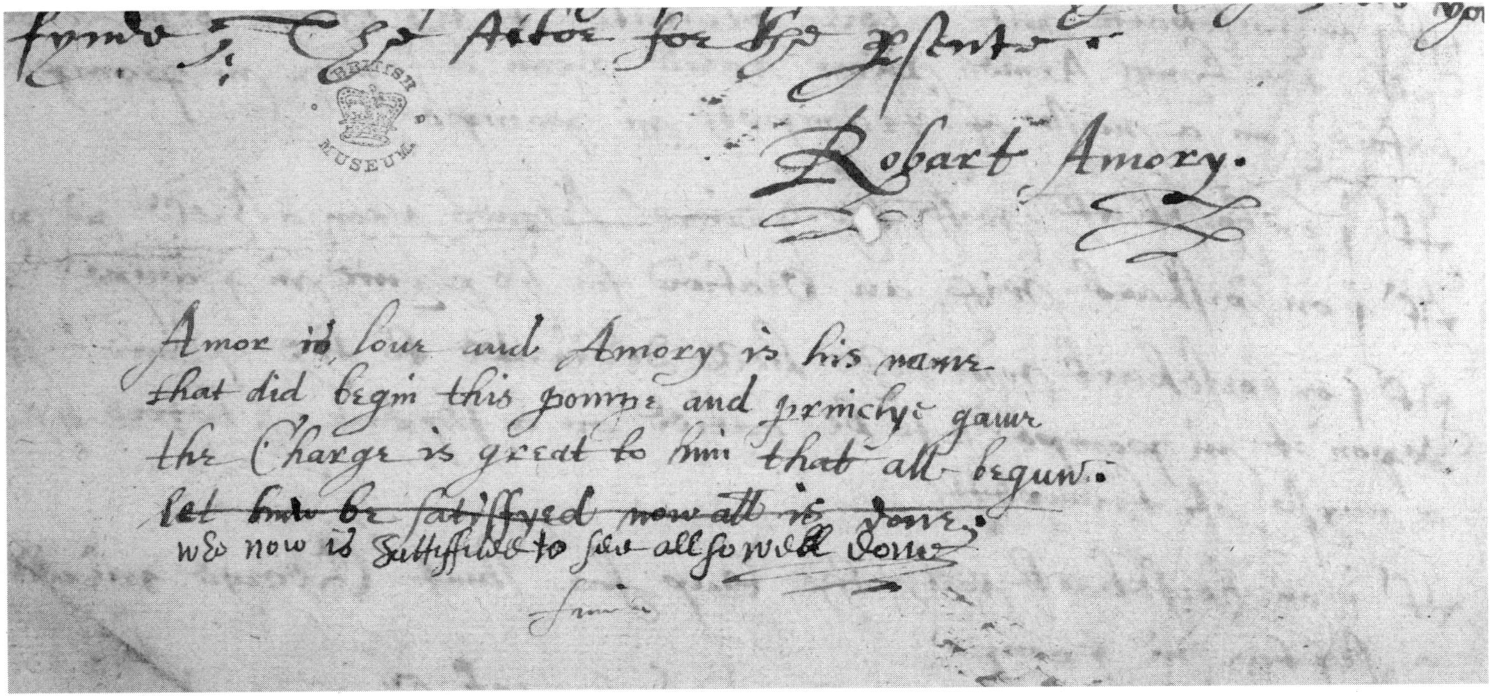

Amor it sour and Amory is his name
that did begin this pompe and ßrinchye gaue
the Charge is great to him that all begunn:
let him be satisfyed nowath ys dou't
wᶜʰ now is Sattisfild to see all so will done

Robart Amory.

FIGURE 4   The signature to Robert Amery's "maner of the showe" (1610). British Library MS Harley 2150, fol. 186v detail. By permission of the British Library.

love for his fellow citizens and for his native city, a love identical to the one acting in the procession proper.

The poem stands out for yet another reason: it subjects the manuscript page to the war between Love and Envy. Civic conflict manifests itself as reinscription, for the last line of the quatrain has been crossed through ("~~let him be satisfyed now all is done~~") and replaced by a new line, "who now is Sattisfited to see all so well done."[59] Attributed to Holme by Clopper,[60] this cancellation transforms the poem's meaning: instead of an imperative request for compensation on Amery's behalf as actor (in both of our first two senses of the term), we now have a subordinate clause recording Amery's aesthetic appreciation ("Sattisfited to see") of a task successfully completed ("so well done"). Holme cancels Amery's line of verse, and, in doing so, symbolically cancels Amery's chances of getting his money back. The emendation underscores the extent to which Amery's aggressive performance of identity backfires, evoking defensive self-assertions from his fellow citizens. What Clopper glosses as a bit of routine antiquarian practice turns out to be fairly antagonistic civic politics.

This sense of conflict brings us to the third and final sense of *actor* at work in Amery's Harley 2150 signature: "A pleader; he who conducts an action at law . . . the plaintiff or complainant."[61] Amery's quatrain belongs to the genre of the poetic petition: "let him be satisfyed" requests payment for services rendered.[62] It also anticipates an actual document, "The humble petition of Robert Amerie."[63] Amery addresses his petition "To the right Worshipfull William Leicester Maior of the Cittie of Chester, the Alderman Sheriffes and comen Councell of the same Cittie"—in other words, to his peers (and fellow honor-competitors) in civic government.[64] In it, he claims total expenses of "the some of C li. at the leaste" and asks to be compensated for bearing this financial burden out of pocket ("to this Peticioners greate trouble & Charges").[65] Amery's assumption of this "humble" stance is ultimately a performance equivalent to those on display in *Chester's Triumph*: the actor/ manager producing the show becomes in turn an actor/pleader before the court of Chester's city government.

However, there is a key difference between Amery's petitionary performance and that of his allegorical double in the show. As I have argued above, Love's function is to augment Amery's civic reputation.

The petitioner takes an opposite tack, downplaying aggressive self-promotion in favor of a self-abnegating dedication to Chester's corporate identity. Amery claims that he proposed and carried out his plans "with the lykeinge and approbation of diuers iudicious persons within this Cittie," that he acted "for the good of the same [Chester], at home."[66] He appeals here to the spirit of communal unity and depicts his actions as directly constitutive of that unity. In doing so, he revises *Chester's Triumph*, presenting race and show as exemplars of urban—not individual—pride and self-celebration. He claims to have only ever had two aims: "the seruice of his Maiestie as occasion shall requyre" and "the present delight & Comforte of his people."[67] Moreover, his petition states that the St. George's Day race is to serve as a perpetual monument to Cestrian community: "the greateste parte of the said Charge is bestowed vpon thinges extant, which are to remayne to future ages for the good of the said Cittie."[68] Amery's emphasis here on permanence and legacy speaks to a fantasy of endlessly unified civic purpose. His hope is that, if the Assembly members share this fantasy, they will give him his £100.

That particular gambit failed: written at the bottom of Amery's petition is the stark comment "this peticion beinge read throughte not fitt to passe to eleccion & voices at an assemblie."[69] Non-individualized bureaucratic procedures (the voice of impersonal, wholly communal civic authority) reject Amery's petition, denying him the chance to re-create the dialogic debate he staged in *Chester's Triumph*.[70] The Assembly's refusal to debate the petition is the civic corporation's refusal to do so: Amery is dismissed by the holistic community he claims to celebrate. Any recompense he receives is therefore private in nature—as is the case in a 20 July 1610 petition sent by Mayor Leicester to the Innholders, Cooks, and Victuallers.[71] Therein Leicester makes a personal appeal ("Wee . . . doe entreat and require you") to the company, seeking the contribution of "some competent somme" toward the cost of the show.[72] The mayor's petition even echoes the terminology Amery uses in his "maner of the showe" signature: noting that *Chester's Triumph* "proceded onlie from the *loue* of the said Mr Amerie to this Cittie," Leicester asks the guild to provide something "towardes the *satisfaccion* of the saide mr Amerie" (my emphasis).[73]

The Innholders' response (if any) to this appeal is not extant, but we do have evidence that other companies received similar petitions and acted accordingly. Over the course of the next year, Amery received fifty shillings from the Beerbrewers;[74] thirty from the Cordwainers and Shoemakers;[75] twenty from the Painters, Glaziers, Embroiderers, and Stationers;[76] and ten from the Drawers of the Dee at "master maiors request."[77] His total take amounted to £5 10s., a nice gesture by his fellow citizens, but a far cry from the £100 of personal money he put up for the show. It's possible that the remaining twenty-three companies made similar contributions—documents and records do go missing over the centuries.[78] But it seems highly unlikely that Amery ever recovered the remaining £94 10s. of his expenses. He did continue to look for ways to conspicuously perform his "Love" for Chester: the Assembly Book entry for 1 October 1613, written down ten days after his 21 September death, notes that Amery's children will be allowed to resubmit his petition requesting compensation for "newe worke in the said Cittie for the strykeinge of the quarters of howers neere the high Crosse."[79] The *Mayors List 13* entry for 1611–12 clarifies the nature of this "newe worke": "Mr Roberte Amerye . . . alsoe vpon his owne Cost and Charges Caused the dyeall: and the two knockers at the south syde of St peters steeple to be made and sett vpp. gyvinge warninge: vpon two litill bells."[80] This sort of privately funded civic improvement—whether it takes the form of a clockworks, a horse race, or a streetside spectacle—exemplifies the Janus-like "Love" Amery celebrates in *Chester's Triumph.* Love of self meets love of city, and the performance of civic virtue generates individual honor (and envy).

Seventeenth-century Cestrians were aware of this conjunction of social forces, and I want to end this section of the chapter with one last document testifying to that fact. It is an Assembly Book entry for 17 April 1612, the year of the third St. George's Day race:

Allso at the same Assemblie it is thought fitt and soe ordered that those sportes and recreacions vsed of late within this Citie vpon Saint George his daie, shalbe from hencefourth vsed and Continued in such decent and Comendable manner as by the Maior for the time beinge and his bretheren shalbe appoincted and allowed of as a pleasure or recreation performed and daie by Direction of the Maior and Citizens, and not by anie priuate or particuler person whatsoever.[81]

There is a hint of puritan opposition to sports and games in this entry (indicated by the phrase "decent and Comendable manner").[82] But a comment in the margin clarifies the Assembly's motives in this matter: "The games and recreations on Stt George his day to haue contynuance by the onelie direction of the maior and cittizens."[83] Amery's aspirations for individually directed celebration are dismissed in favor of community control over all spectacles. "Priuate or particular" persons need not apply: the Assembly's order testifies to an anxious awareness of civic pageantry's ability to serve private purposes even as it ostensibly speaks to the public interest. To minimize the social damage epitomized by Envy, Chester's governors limit Love's purview. Public performance is now the sole business of the corporation (a personified abstraction in its own right). Personal reputation is subordinated to the city's fame, and the ideal of the holistic community is used precisely to deny men like Amery the opportunity to celebrate Chester as anything other than the embodiment of official local power. In 1612, *Chester's Triumph* becomes the triumph of Chester.

St. George Speaks Up

Many of my arguments in this chapter depend on the evidence of the show's speeches—what was said on 23 April 1610 provides a key to what Amery may have been trying to achieve locally. But these speeches survive today only because of Amery's desire to address a national audience: *Chester's Triumph in Honor of Her Prince* was entered at Stationer's Hall in London by the bookseller John Browne on 12 June 1610, a little over a week after Prince Henry's 4 June creation ceremonies.[84] Browne is the "I. B." mentioned on the pamphlet's title page: "Printed for I. B. and are to be Sold in Saint Dunstanes Church-yard in Fleete-streete." Browne's *Chester's Triumph* printer, William Stansby, was in turn responsible for the anonymous *Order and Solemnitie of the Creation of the High and Mightie Prince Henrie,* an account of the prince's Westminster inauguration published alongside *Tethys Festival,* a celebratory masque by Samuel Daniel. Finally, *Chester's Triumph* includes an image of an English warship identical to one depicted in Anthony Munday's *London's Love to the Royal Prince Henry,* a third 1610 publication commemorating the creation.

This is more than coincidence: while both images include the signature mark "A," only the *London's Love* ship appears on signature A1r of its respective pamphlet. In *Chester's Triumph*, the ship appears instead on signature D3r, suggesting that Stansby printed the text of Amery's show on sheets left over from Edward Allde's print run of *London's Love*. The bibliographic data thus positions *Chester's Triumph* as part of a small, London-based publishing flurry surrounding the prince during the weeks following his creation.[85]

David Rogers reflects on the show's London publication in the 1637 redaction of his *Brevary*:

> But heare I muste not omitt, the charge and the solemnitie made the firste St Gerges daye, he [Amery] had apoett one. mr dauies, whoe made speches and poeticall verses. which weare deliuered at the highe crosse before the mayor and aldermen, with shewes of his [Amery's or Davies's?] Inuention, which. booke was Imprinted and presented to that ffamos prince Henry, eldest sonne to. the blessed King Iames of famous memorie[86]

Rogers's account presents us with a scene familiar to readers of medieval manuscripts: the author as supplicant, presenting his text on bended knee to his royal patron. It is not clear why Rogers waits until 1637 to mention the St. George's Day triumph (he discusses the race as early as the ca. 1619 version of the *Brevary*), but the manuscript of his text (Liverpool University Library MS 23.5) does contain an interesting alteration at this point: "presented" is actually an interlinear insertion replacing a cancelled "~~deliuered~~."[87] This change is a subtle redefinition of the pamphlet's ultimate fate. If *Chester's Triumph* was only "deliuered" to Richmond in 1610, it may never have reached Prince Henry himself. The absent *triumphator* would be absent once more. Stating instead that the book was "presented" suggests that it passed directly into the hands of its royal dedicatee, an exchange that finally brings Amery's show before the eyes of the "high Iustice Officer" for whom it was originally intended.[88] The pamphlet publication of *Chester's Triumph* thus serves as the trigger for an (admittedly hypothetical) act of belated spectatorship and participation. In a sense, the pageant ends only with Henry's perusal of the pamphlet and its evidence of Chester's love for its earl.

The idea of the pamphlet as "presentation" also points to those questions of nation and region raised at the beginning of this chapter. At first glance, the entry of *Chester's Triumph* into London's book market resembles nothing more than the arrival in London of yet another immigrant from the outer shires. In this analysis, the aforementioned printing of copies of *Chester's Triumph* on sheets left over from the printing of *London's Love* serves as a synecdoche of the ever-increasing subordination of the provinces to the capital: Chester is literally stuck with London's leftovers. Peter Womack sees this national, centralizing dynamic as intrinsic to print culture: "Instead of the institutionally transmitted manuscripts of the religious drama, with their irregular combinations of inter-urban borrowing and local uniqueness, and their habit of mixing scriptural paraphrase together with traditionary [*sic*] or authorial invention, there was now the single authorised text, emanating from the capital and affording equal access to the truth to anyone who could read."[89] The London publication of *Chester's Triumph* could thus be said to testify to the power of the centralized book trade: in the era of print, regional identity (that of the "poore Palatines" mentioned in Davies's dedicatory poem) can speak itself into existence only by journeying to the capital city.

But Womack's understanding of the English print trade owes more to Reformation debates over the nature of the biblical text than it does to any awareness of the specific details of early modern pageant publication. For example, as both David Bergeron and Paula Johnson have argued, "equal access to the truth to anyone who could read" would have had little to do with the publication of show texts: the impresarios of early modern London most likely published their pageants so that relatively small, elite groups might acquire mementos of the occasion.[90] Thus we have dedications of Munday's *London's Love* "To the right honorable, Sr. Thomas Cambell, Knight, Lord Major of this famous Cittie of London: And to all the Aldermen his worthie Bretheren, &c." (A3r) and of Dekker's *Troia-Nova Triumphans* "To the Deseruer of all those Honors, which the Customary Rites of this Day, And the generall Loue of this City bestow vpon him; Sir Iohn Svvinerton, Knight, Lord Maior of the renowmed City of London" (A3r).[91] In both cases, the primary audience for the print versions of these shows is the mercantile oligarchy governing London and not the buying public; as Johnson says, "we know that in some instances the books were not for public sale, but for

the members of the company to distribute or keep."[92] At the moment
of its publication, then, there was no guarantee that a given show pamphlet might circulate widely even in London, let alone drift out to the
far corners of England.[93] Pageants like Dekker's *Troia-Nova Triumphans*
might lay claim to a national audience:

> For to haue bene leaden-winged now, what infamy could be
> greater? When all the streames of Nobility and Gentry, run with
> the Tide hither. When all the Eares lye listning for no newes but
> of Feasts and Triumphs: All Eyes still open to behold them: And
> all harts and hands to applaud them: When the heape of our
> Soueraignes Kingdomes are drawn in Little: and to be seen within
> the Walles of this City. (A3v)

But the spectators they usually had in mind were members of the court
in Westminster.[94] London shows were as intensely local in focus as anything staged in the provinces.

The appearance of *Chester's Triumph* in London therefore has as
much to do with Cestrians' sense of historical continuity as it does with
the material realities of a publishing industry centered on the institutions of the early modern state. The show's dedication "To the High and
Mightie Prince, Henry Prince of Wales, Duke of Cornwall and Rothsay,
Earle of Chester, Knight of the most noble Order of the Garter, &c."
(A2r) evokes a long-dormant feudal relationship central to the identities of both the city and the county of Cheshire. The last prince created
"Earle of Chester" was the future Henry VIII: he received the title in
1503 and held it until his death in 1547.[95] Prince Henry's inauguration
(the first in over a century) thus gives Cestrians an opportunity to celebrate their region. We see this elevation of the local in "Chester to her
Prince," Richard Davies's dedicatory lyric. Given the prominent role
played by Chester in Amery's show, the verse's title turns out to be both
a speech prefix and a stage direction. Davies's individual voice, that of
an "ill Townesman" (his mysterious signature), merges with the city's
communal voice, openly asserting Cestrian exceptionalism:

> Unto the boundlesse Ocean, most dread Prince,
> Of thy surmounting Great magnificence,

Doe we (poore Palatines) from our best hearts,
(Enlarg'd with Loue of thine admired Parts)
Blushing, obiect to thy deepe Iudgments eye,
The fruit (though poore) of rich Loues industrie.
Not that we are Ambitious, or that wee
Can thinke it worthy; of (most worthy) THEE.
But, with our best integritie, to show
The Awfull Duetie which our Loues doe owe,
To thy great Greatnesse; who (beyond compare)
Doth shine so bright in our Loues Hemisphere
That, in thy right, our Hearts, Liues, Limmes and Swords,
Shall stretch our Actions farre beyond our Words.

(A2r)

Seen from the perspective of the verse dedication, then, Chester's
"poore Palatines" do not arrive in London as part of Dekker's indis-
criminate "heape" of provincial Britons. They instead present themselves as regionally distinct vassals performing homage to their liege
lord ("The Awfull Duetie which our Loues doe owe").

The text's reference to feudal forms of polity is confirmed a few
pages later when the pamphlet states that *Chester's Triumph* was staged
"in liew of the Homage, Fealtie, Alleagance, and Duetie, which wee
doe owe and attribute vnto the Kings most Excellent and magnificent Maiestie, his Crowne and dignitie, and to the most vertuous and
hopefull Heire Apparent, the Prince of Wales, with that Noble victor
Saint George, our aforesaid English Champion" (A3r). Since Davies's
dedicatory poem has already reminded readers of Cheshire's palatine
specificity, the feudal terminology used in this passage—"Homage,
Fealtie, Alleagance, and Duetie"—remains local in orientation even
as it participates in a national chivalric discourse centered on King
James and exemplified by St. George, "our aforesaid English Champion." The pageant proper also relies on feudal vocabulary: Camber
promises the audience that, "to our Prince (Great Britaines matchlesse
Heire) / As humbly low, as is his Greatnesse high, / Our liues wee'le
prostrate with our best Deuoire, / To doe what may vndoe the Enemie"
(C1r). "Deuoire" can mean a generic "duty" or "obligation," but it also
has a more specialized meaning of "feudal service or tax."[96] Camber's

use of the term therefore adds an Anglo-Norman and medieval element to his otherwise nationalizing and modern reference to the new Britain created by James's accession. While the posture in all of these passages is one of humble subservience on the part of Cestrians, such insufficiencies are defined entirely in relation to Henry's "surmounting Great magnificence" and "great Greatnesse" (A2r). The British nation plays a minimal part in Chester's performative admission of its inadequacy, and other English cities are nowhere to be seen. Chester's urban competition consists solely of classical cities like Rome and Troy (see below) and biblical Jerusalem. Indeed, when Peace promises that "No massacre nor bloudy stratageme, / Shall stirre in Peaces new Ierusalem" (C2r), she situates *Chester's Triumph* (and Chester) within the long-standing performance tradition linking the civic triumph to Christ's four Advents.[97] Such authoritative associations undercut Womack's argument that the early modern shift to a national economy centered on London robbed the provincial city of its "capacity to represent itself concretely as a type of *universitas*."[98]

The show's trans-temporal connections to distant past and apocalyptic future are matched by a sense of space as broad in scope as that found in London's civic ceremonies. For example, in Munday's 1605 *Triumphs of Re-United Britannia*, the figure of Brute celebrates King James's 1604 accession in mercantile fashion:

> For this Britannia rides in triumph thus,
> For this these sister-kingdoms now shake hands,
> Brute's Troy (now London) looks most amorous
> And stands on tiptoe, telling foreign lands,
> So long as seas bear ships, or shores have sands,
> > So long shall we in true devotion pray,
> > And praise high heaven for that most happy day.
> > > (lines 348–54)

Chester's Triumph mirrors this emphasis on global trade: Davies's dedicatory poem gives us a Chester who, "enlarg'd" with love of the prince's "admired Parts" (a possible reference to both the royal body and the feudal lands which analogously comprise it), can reach "unto the boundlesse Ocean," encompass "our Loues Hemisphere," and boast that, "in thy [Henry's] right, our Hearts, Liues, Limmes and Swords, / Shall stretch our Actions farre beyond our Words" (A2r). The verses combine feudal obligation and global ambition, linking Chester's mercantile elites to Henry's own interests in maritime exploration and expansion.[99] The city's long history as a port is relevant here: the pamphlet text's summary of the triumph's contents includes a reference to "the Ships, Barques, and Pinises, with other vessels, Harbouring within the Riuer, displaying the Armes of S. George, vpon their maine Toppes" (B1r). Marked with the English flag (and thus representative of the nation), these Cestrian ships resemble those that participate in the water shows accompanying Henry's London inauguration. The text of Munday's *London's Love* reports that, on Wednesday, 6 June 1610, "two Merchants Shippes" (D2v) and "two men of warre" (D3r) took part in a mock battle against "A Turkishe Pirate prowling on the Seas, to maintaine a Turkishe Castle" (D2v).[100] Amery's ships fire their guns in joy, not anger (they "discharged many voleyes of Shotte in Honour of the day," B1r), but their inclusion within the show—reinforced by the insertion of the woodcut ship flying the flag of St. George at the pamphlet's end—offers the pageant's audiences, local and London, material confirmation of Chester's active participation within Britain's imperial project.

Chester's Triumph therefore helps to expand our understanding of the development and practice of urban identity in early modern England. The details of the show also serve as a useful corrective to accounts of early modern pageantry based almost exclusively on the evidence and experience of London. For example, writing on London, Gail Kern Paster has identified a "sharp rise in the seventeenth century of an urban self-consciousness brought about by such factors as London's growth in size and population, the expansion of international trade and finance, the establishment of a London social season, and the success of commercial theater."[101] All well and good—until we notice the extent to which the language of center and periphery informs her analysis: "The population of Stuart London, it may be useful to remember, numbered around a quarter million, while the populations of Norwich and Bristol, contending for second place, were well below fifty thousand."[102] London's immense size may indeed help to underwrite the nationalizing claims made by the city's civic ceremonies, but it does not follow that provincial cities like Norwich and Bristol are unable to mobilize equally assertive civic identities.[103]

The same can be said of even smaller cities like Chester. As *Chester's Triumph* reveals, urban self-consciousness is not necessarily a result of economic and demographic expansion. In fact, urban decline and administrative marginalization can also stimulate the production of civic identities and ideologies. Henry's creation as earl did not lead to a restoration of palatine privilege: "The grant of the earldom to Prince Henry, indeed, was followed by the transfer of responsibility for paying the fees of the justices of Chester from the local receiver to the national Exchequer."[104] But the argument of this book is precisely that reductions in political and economic autonomy contribute to localities' sense of themselves as distinct cultural units.

As mentioned above, residual formations play a powerful role in this process: Davies's "poore Palatines" can proudly stand alongside Londoners, compensating for their relative poverty with both a noble record of service and a long-established sense of regional difference (albeit one increasingly undermined at the level of administrative practice). Literal or imagined continuity with the past enables Chester's ceremonial participation in the present. It provides the St. George's Day race with a classical pedigree capable of supporting the decision to present prizes "after the order of the Olimpian Sportes, whereof these were an imitation" (B1r). These "Olimpian" prizes—wreaths of "greene leau'd branches" and "fragrant" garlands (D1r)—complement the silver bells and cups described in both the archival records and the descriptions of the procession. They also figure prominently in Peace's oration: there "Oliue branches" and "a Wreth of euer-during Baies" anticipate the victory of "mutuall concord datelesse" over Envy's "Domestick strife" (C2r).

Moreover, when the figure of Chester greets the show's spectators, she compares the assembled dignitaries to the heroic Marcus Curtius of Livy: "The Romaine *Curtius* Romes great Fauorite, / (Whose daring Death did her from scathe acquite) / Was ne're more Welcome to the Romanes sights, / Then are your selues, to these our choise delights" (B3v). Chester thus reminds the audience of her former name of Deva and her venerable Roman past, a history equal in antiquity and stature to that of London. In fact, Chester even goes so far as to appropriate the capital's Trojan genealogy for local use by identifying the younger members of the audience as "Brutes" (B3v)—the rhetorical strategy that serves as the bread-and-butter of London civic ceremonial. The Troynovant of Dekker and Munday plays equally well in the provinces.

The pamphlet supplements Chester's classical origins with an explicit reference to another of the city's previous identities: "the most Auncient renowned Citie Caer-leon" (A3r). Historical difference collapses in this designation: English Chester turns out to be nothing more than the latest alias for British Caer-leon. The evocation of the city's supposed Celtic name emphasizes its cultural continuity with the British past, a historical connection brought back to life by King James's restoration of ancient British unity. Chester's British lineage helps to account for the near-absence of the Scots from the pageant: James's countrymen make but one brief appearance in Peace's oration ("while the Scotch the English faire entreate, / And me embrace with-all," C2r). When Munday writes *The Triumphs of Re-United Britannia* for a London audience, he makes sure to include Albania alongside Loegria and Cambria; his recreation of the nation within the bounds of the City requires the representation of all three shattered realms resulting from Brute's legacy.

Chester provides a different vantage point, allowing Amery to locate his show within an alternate configuration of national space: in *Chester's Triumph*, the personification of Britain reunified speaks for the king (whom she calls "Great *Britaines* Greatnesse" and "wonder of the North," B4v), Camber celebrates her newly created prince, and Rumor cries out "Saint *George* for England" (C1r). The British nation presented in the show is effectively a fusion of English and Welsh peoples, a combination owing much to Chester's continued awareness of its position within the border zone of the Welsh Marches. Indeed, Amery's particular deployment of national identity may ultimately derive from the same sense of locality that led Lucian to emphasize Cestrians' English-Welsh hybridity in *De laude Cestrie* (if we think back to the introduction for a moment). It certainly participates within the city's long-established sense of itself as a space poised between nations, a locale no less Welsh than it is English. British identity may even function as an appealing compromise, its own carefully negotiated hybridity proving attractive to a population well aware of its simultaneous ties to multiple nationalities.

Amery's investment in puns contributes to the cultural connections made throughout the show: in a passage describing the extent to which Cestrians will physically modify their local space to better serve the needs of the pageant's audience, Chester ends her initial speech with a reference to "that place, / Assigned this Triumph and triumphant Race" (B4r). Here "that place" is most immediately recognizable as the Roodee, the site "Assigned" to the St. George's Day race, the "triumphant Race" and local custom Amery seeks to inaugurate in perpetuity. But Britaine's and Camber's subsequent references in their own speeches to King James's "Race" (B4v) and "Cambers Race" (C1r) cause us to reevaluate the identity of Chester's "triumphant Race." The racing of horses on the Roodee is also the cultural celebration of the city's local specificity, its belief in its divine assignation as a "triumphant Race" in its own right.

The St. George's Day race and show thus call into question the literary history informing the study of early English drama. For example, Womack pays special attention to the apologetic tone taken by the Late Banns of the Chester cycle:

> Chester in the late sixteenth century retained and even enhanced its medieval prosperity, so the abjectness is not simply a symptom of declining resources; rather, the town has been commercially, politically, linguistically and culturally *provincialised*. That is to say, the gaze under which St George blushes and loses his words is that of the metropolis. The urban drama has been swamped by the idea of a centralised national culture.[105]

He can make this claim in part due to the generic biases informing drama scholarship, which has historically treated the cycle plays of Chester and York as artistic entities wholly separate from (and superior to) civic ceremonies like *Chester's Triumph* and *London's Love*.[106] Defining performance genres in historicist terms (as I have done throughout chapters 2 and 3) generates a different story, one in which the closing-down of certain performance options does not necessitate the cessation of all dramatic activity at the local level. Instead, the celebrations of local and civic identity formerly exemplified by the cycle drama are taken up by other ceremonial forms. When Womack says that "St George blushes and loses his words," he is referring to the Cestrian custom of reading the Banns.

Here is David Rogers's ca. 1619 *Brevary* description of the ceremony:

> Also euery yere that these playes were played, on St. Georges day before, was the banes read, which was a man did ride warlike appareled like st. George throughe euery streete, with drume musicke and trumpetes, And there was published that the playes were played that yeare, And that the breife or banes of the playe was reade what euery Company should playe, which was called the Readinge of the bannes[107]

For Womack, the end of the cycle is the end of St. George in Chester.[108] But the last performance of the Whitsun plays in 1575 (and thus the likely last reading of the Banns) is only 35 years prior to Amery's 1610 triumph. It is thus within the realm of plausibility that a young Robert Amery saw St. George riding through the streets. (Expanding our hypothesis to take in Amery's audience makes the association of the St. George taking part in *Chester's Triumph* with the St. George who read the Banns even more likely.) In addition, the prop dragon defeated by Amery's barbaric "Greene-men" (A3v) may have been the same dragon used in Chester's Midsummer Show, a civic ceremony that bridges the gap between the cessation of the cycle and the inauguration of the St. George's Day race.[109] As Mills notes, Whitsun play characters like the Butchers' Devil, the Cappers' Balaam's Ass, and the Innkeepers' Ale-wife were a regular feature of the Midsummer Show well into the seventeenth century.[110] *Chester's Triumph* thus looks back and sideways to other civic dramas, emphasizing local continuities at the expense of national canons and narratives of literary historical rupture. St. George has no intention of shutting up, and Amery's decision to publish his show in London suggests that his voice is loud enough to reach to the capital.

Part 2

Cheshire the County

*Destabilizing National Identity
in Regional Romance*

CHAPTER FOUR

HERALDIC DEVICES/
CHIVALRIC DIVISIONS

Sir Gawain and the Green Knight
and the Scrope-Grosvenor Trial

OF ALL THE TEXTS ADDRESSED IN THIS BOOK, NONE IS MORE
firmly linked in modern scholarship to Cheshire and to regional identity than the late fourteenth-century romance *Sir Gawain and the Green
Knight* (*SGGK*). Studies of the poem's dialect have traditionally concerned themselves with placing *SGGK* on one side or the other of the
Cheshire-Staffordshire border.[1] The scholarly search for the name of
the poem's anonymous author has regional implications as well: while
the *Gawain*-poet's precise historical identity remains unknown, articles
and essays proposing competing candidates have often had the seren-
dipitous side effect of detailing the sociopolitical activities of Cheshire's
local gentry in the decades surrounding 1400.[2] To their number we
might add Ralph Elliott's analyses of the poem's topographical vocabulary as well as his claim to have solved the "mystery" of the Green

Chapel's location.[3] But the most influential strand of regionally focused interpretation over the last twenty years has been the work of historian Michael Bennett: his research concerning Cheshire and Lancashire participation within Richard II's affinity, especially in the period 1387–99, is now routinely cited in discussions of *SGGK*, albeit often as a brief nod in the direction of local and regional context.[4] Bennett's court-centered approach has found its greatest champion in John Bowers, whose historicist readings of *Pearl* derive much of their force from Bowers' assumption of a cultural collision between the Cheshiremen surrounding the king and a variety of anti-Ricardian forces.[5]

The Bennett-Bowers hypothesis responds to the facts of the poem: at a very basic narrative level, *SGGK* is about the encounter between two different communities, each separated from the other by geography and, more controversially, by culture. Like the local focus described above, the socio-spatial division between Camelot and Hautdesert returns again and again in the scholarship surrounding the poem. To give but a few examples of particular relevance to my own discussion below: J. R. Hulbert argues for a vigorous English north holding the line against a sophisticated Francophile south (the classic statement of defiant regionalism); Thorlac Turville-Petre posits a pair of disparate regions that nevertheless come to acknowledge their national unity; and Patricia Clare Ingham describes an imperial England engaged in cultural contestation with colonial Wales.[6] The Bennett-Bowers approach also fits into this model of socio-spatial interaction. In all four cases, center meets periphery. The precise outcome of the encounter may vary from study to study (Hulbert's static stand-off, Turville-Petre's celebration of class-based identity, Ingham's deflection toward misogyny, and Bennett and Bowers' politico-cultural exile), but the basic assumption of spatial difference remains: whatever else it may be, *SGGK* is a text which foregrounds its provinciality.[7]

Analysis of the poem's assertive localism typically begins with the Fitt 2 description of Gawain's lonely journey in search of the Green Chapel:

> Now ridez þis renk þurȝ þe ryalme of Logres,
> Sir Gauan, on Godez halue, þaȝ hym no gomen þoȝt—
> Oft leudlez alone he lengez on nyȝtez

Þer he fonde noȝt hym byfore þe fare þat he lyked;
Hade he no fere bot his fole bi frythez and dounez,
Ne no gome bot God bi gate wyth to karp—
Til þat he neȝed ful neghe into þe Norþe Walez.
Alle þe iles of Anglesay on lyft half he haldez
And farez ouer þe fordez by þe forlondez;
Ouer at þe Holy Hede, til he hade eft bonk
In þe wyldrenesse of Wyrale. Wonde þer bot lyte
Þat auþer God oþer gome wyth goud hert louied.
And ay he frayned, as he ferde, at frekez þat he met
If þay hade herde any karp of a knyȝt grene,
In any grounde þeraboute, of þe Grene Chapel.
And al nykked hym wyth "Nay!"—þat neuer in her lyue
Þay seȝe neuer no segge þat watz of suche hwez
    Of grene.
  Þe knyȝt tok gates straunge
  In mony a bonk vnbene.
  His cher ful oft con chaunge,
  Þat chapel er he myȝt sene.
                   (lines 691–712)[8]

Unlike the errant wanderings of many romance heroes, Gawain's itinerary is both precise and well-known: Malcolm Andrew and Ronald
Waldron observe that Gawain follows the North Wales road on its journey along the coast of the Irish Sea and through the communities of
Bangor, Conway, Abergele, Rhuddlan, and Flint.[9] The critical commentary on this passage is substantial, ranging from narrowly focused identifications of the topographical features mentioned therein to broader
considerations of the route's cultural and historical significance. Thus
Ralph Elliott's decision to place the Green Chapel in the immediate vicinity of Dieulacres Abbey, Staffordshire, leads him to equate
the knightly journey described in lines 699–701 with the Dieulacres
monks' own travels west to their properties on the Welsh border and
back again.[10] Bennett opts instead for a reading attentive to political
strife, emphasizing the part the itinerary played in Richard II's 1399
deposition: "The route of the king and his companions, and indeed the
rest of the bodyguard as they straggled home, must have been close to

that sketched out for Sir Gawain: through unknown country until Anglesey and the coastline of north Wales came into view."[11] Finally, Ingham concentrates on the connections between Gawain's journey and England's ongoing imperial project in Wales: "His route shares a good deal with Gerald of Wales's description of the usual itinerary through Wales, and with accounts of Henry II's 1135 colonizing invasion."[12] Riding through a landscape that registers the substitution of "historically specific English names for Welsh places," Ingham's Gawain serves as a "colonial emissary" from Arthur's imperial center at Camelot.[13]

What interests me most about all three of these influential readings is their imputation of linearity to Gawain's "anious uyage" (line 535). Elliott's extreme localism focuses his attention on only a short segment of the total itinerary, one that connects the Cistercians at Dieulacres to their estates on the River Dee, while Bennett's mournful analysis moves swiftly (and directly) to Cheshire, treating the Welsh features as little more than clues to the poem's Ricardian affinity. Even Ingham (who goes on to discuss Gawain's return home to Camelot) traces what is effectively a straight line heading north and west. At present, Rhonda Knight and I are the only scholars to make explicit notice of the curvature of Gawain's route at this point in the poem: when the *Gawain*-poet reports that "Alle þe iles of Anglesay on lyft half he [Gawain] haldez," he is describing a sharp right turn on Gawain's part, a shift in an eastern direction.[14] Gawain's eyes may be looking northwest toward Anglesey at this moment, but Gryngolet is carrying him eastward, back toward "þe ryalme of Logres" and England—not further away.

Like *Pearl*, *SGGK* is a poem of circles, spheres, knots, and loops, a series of shapes exemplified in the text proper by the pentangle and the green girdle. And again like *Pearl*, *SGGK* relies upon formal structures to generate an atmosphere of circularity and recursion, one in which *forme* ultimately encounters *fynisment* through the repetition of the phrase "þe sege and þe assaut watz sesed at Troye" (lines 1 and 2525) at both ends of the poem. The same narrative structure that designates Troy as the poem's *termini* would also seem to posit Hautdesert as its poetic center, as the one point in the tale farthest from Camelot.[15] But the *Gawain*-poet's careful inclusion of region-specific topography qualifies that placement, reminding audiences that Hautdesert is actually closer to Camelot than other aspects of the poem might have them believe.[16] Presented in *SGGK* as "þe wyldrenesse of Wyrale," Cheshire is itself as much a part of Logres (England) as it is of "Norþe Walez."[17]

Put another way, any spatially oriented reading of *SGGK* must at least triangulate its analysis: those critics interested in interregional relations between Cheshire and the Southeast need to consider Wales's role in the poem as well, while postcolonial scholars would do well to complicate their arguments with a consideration of imperial England's internal divisions. Ingham offers a substantial gesture in this direction with her discussion of Cheshire's status as a well-trafficked frontier zone in relation to the historical work of both Bennett and R. R. Davies.[18] However, as I noted in the introduction, she nevertheless also conflates colonizing Cheshire and colonized Wales. This tendency is clearest in her discussion of the Cheshire district of Wirral: there she is quick to identify the hostile populace described in lines 701–2 ("Wonde þer bot lyte / Þat auþer God oþer gome wyth goud hert louied") with the beasts Gawain encounters in the very next stanza of the poem:

> Sumwhyle wyth wormez he werrez and with wolues als,
> Sumwhyle wyth wodwos þat woned in þe knarrez,
> Boþe wyth bullez and berez, and borez oþerquyle,
> And etaynez þat hym anelede of þe heȝe felle.
>
> (lines 720–23)

Regional men become monsters, and "the wild Wirral" collapses into "Welsh wildness" in Ingham's analysis of the passage: "Dragons, trolls, and giants walk these woods . . . the scene foregrounds not Gawain's strangeness, but the otherness of Wales to Arthur's knight."[19] But more proximate to the Wirral's mention in line 701 are those "frekez þat he [Gawain] met" in line 703, the individuals whom he asks "If þay hade herde any karp of a knyȝt grene, / In any grounde þeraboute, of þe Grene Chapel" (lines 704–5).[20] The poem's "wyldrenesse of Wyrale" is no uninhabited heath; it contains a number of more-or-less mundane *frekez* willing to *karp* with Gawain, persons who occupy approximately as many lines of verse as do their more monstrous neighbors.[21]

Since its complete history has yet to be written, the historical hundred of Wirral may indeed have been what Andrew and Waldron term a "notorious refuge for outlaws in the 14th c." (a phrase echoed by many, if not most, of the editors of *SGGK* since the publication of Henry L. Savage's 1931 article on lines 700–702).[22] But it was also a jurisdiction containing the estates of wealthy landlords like the Abbot of St. Werburgh's in Chester, who spent the 1390s acquiring "permission to crenellate his manor-houses at Saighton, Sutton and Ince, the latter of which had a new banqueting hall and minstrels' gallery."[23] At its very worst, then, the fourteenth-century Wirral was a space of mixed character, one in which lawlessness coexisted with lordship—a description that could apply to just about any location within Cheshire (or much of England, for that matter). The Wirral was engaged with Wales in the sort of colonial and cultural intimacies that Ingham discusses in *Sovereign Fantasies*, but it was not identical to Wales, wild or otherwise, in any straightforward fashion.

In taking such a distinction seriously, this chapter presents my own local reading of *SGGK*, one that addresses the discourse of provinciality inscribed within the poem by examining chivalric culture's own investment in the idea of region. As I will argue, the eastward bend in Gawain's passage (line 544) through Logres, Wales, and Cheshire ultimately leads to the green girdle, "þe bende of . . . blame" (line 2506) and "þe token of vntrawþe" (line 2509) which Gawain brings back with him upon his return to Camelot. Transformed into the *bauderyk* with "A bende abelef hym aboute, of a bryȝt grene" that every knight of the Round Table agrees to wear "for sake of þat segge [Gawain]" (lines 2516–18), the girdle functions as a floating signifier in the poem's heraldic economy. That economy, represented elsewhere in *SGGK* by the conventionally chivalric exchange of names and places of origin, seems at first to unite disparate corners of the realm, to generate what Turville-Petre has called the "cultural cohesion" of the nation.[24] However, Gawain's negative response to the gift of the girdle and to Bertilak's hospitality results not in an interregional union of chivalric equals, but in the limited, intraregional "cohesion" and self-celebration of Camelot.

A similar dynamic is at work in the roughly contemporary proceedings of the Scrope-Grosvenor controversy of 1385–91, the notorious Court of Chivalry case which saw Sir Robert Grosvenor of Hulme, Cheshire, thrown into a legal battle over an inadvertently shared coat-of-arms with Sir Richard Scrope of Bolton, Yorkshire.[25] I look to the Scrope-Grosvenor case not only on account of its Cheshire connection

(Bennett asserts that Sir Robert and the *Gawain*-poet "were almost certainly contemporaries and compatriots" and that Grosvenor therefore makes "an appropriate reference-point in an investigation" of the poet's context), but also because of its obsessive concern for the same issues of chivalry, identity, and heraldry that inform *SGGK*: Scrope and Grosvenor's arms of *azure a bend or* (figure 5) function in ways similar to those of Gawain's pentangle and Bertilak's green girdle.[26] The deponents on both sides of the case included members of the two litigants' multiregional affinities. These men gave witness to noble pedigrees dating back to the Conquest (Scrope's, Grosvenor's, and, in many cases, their own), routinely recalling local muniments and architectural features inscribed with the device under dispute.[27] These material inscriptions of familial identity transferred chivalric honor into a spatially dispersed cultural field, a point of particular importance to my analysis. For if a knight's honor is determined in part by the geographical scope of its material remains, then intraregional affinity becomes a crucial element in the construction of chivalric identity—and the interregional

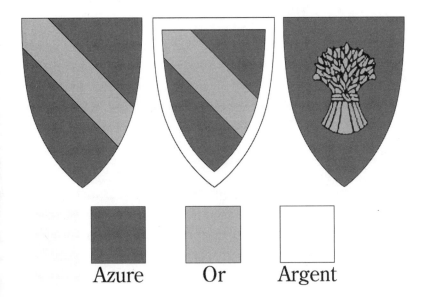

Azure   Or   Argent

FIGURE 5   From left to right: the disputed arms, *azure a bend or*; the Constable's suggested arms for Grosvenor, *azure a bend or, a bordure argent*; Grosvenor's post-trial arms, *azure a garb or*. Illustration by Chris Carter.

intelligibility of the knight's arms serves as a limit to the extent of his power and agency.

Studying Scrope-Grosvenor therefore allows us to recognize how Gawain's identity crisis at Hautdesert—beginning at the precise moment when he relinquishes his arms to Bertilak's servants—resembles in reverse fashion Grosvenor's own struggle in court to establish his name "in straunge contrayez" outside of Cheshire (none of the deponents testifying on his behalf were from locations outside the immediate reach of his home county). As we shall see, the historical case revolves around a knight with no interregional reputation but an unfortunately all-too-familiar set of arms, while the romance's knightly protagonist finds himself in the opposite situation, forced to cope with both an unrecognizable heraldic device and an all-too-notable reputation. Negotiating the hurdles and demands of regional identity will test both knights, fictional and historical.

THE SCROPE-GROSVENOR CONTROVERSY AND CHIVALRY'S TOPOGRAPHIC INSCRIPTION

On 24 November 1385, during one of the preliminary proceedings leading up to the evidence phase of the notorious controversy bearing his name, Sir Robert Grosvenor engaged in a bit of chivalric theater, producing a representation of his coat-of-arms for all in the Court of Chivalry to see:

> Et outre dit qil ne savoit lez queux estoient lez armes du dit monsieur Richard mais mist avaunt en court une escuchon [dazure ove une] bende dor disant et proposant per sa propre bouche que les dites armes sont soens . . . alleggea que monsieur Gilbert Grosvenour venoit ove le Conquerer en Engleterre arme en lez ditz armes et depuis en droit lynee sont descenduz au dit monsieur Robert (p. 37)

> (Moreover, he said that he did not know what the arms of the said Sir Richard were; but produced an escutcheon, *azure a bend or*, before the court, stating and propounding orally that the said

arms were his . . . alleging [as well] that Sir Gilbert Grosvenor had
come with the Conqueror into England, armed in the said arms,
which had since descended in a direct line to the said Sir Robert)

In responding to Sir Richard Scrope's charges that he had earlier "por-
toit ses armes encountre droit" ("borne his arms contrary to right," p. 36),
Grosvenor felt it necessary to supplement both his personal word ("per
sa propre bouche") and the oral history of his family with visual proof
of his heraldic right.[28] The *escuchon* represents in miniature the material
inscription of chivalric identity, the translation of honor into physical
form. What its exhibition before the Court suggests is that the arms *azure
a bend or* must belong to Grosvenor: after all, they are here in his possession, aren't they? Sir Robert's performance has the feeling of an attempt
to short-circuit procedure, to present an example of his proofs before
Scrope has any chance to display his own knightly regalia.

That desire to be the first to produce material witnesses was not
ill-founded: many of the case's approximately four hundred deponents
readily described to the Court the various "sepultures . . . peyntours ve-
rures vestementz et autres evidences" ("tombs . . . paintings, windows,
vestments, and other evidence," p. 40) that they had seen bearing the
arms of either party.[29] The resulting list of armigerous objects and structures is immense. R. Stewart-Brown catalogs some twenty-six different
armorials in his account of the evidence presented on Grosvenor's behalf, while the testimony of the Rector of Medeburn in Lincoln Diocese
alone accounted for sixty-seven depictions of Scrope's arms.[30] Indeed,
the imbalance of evidence between the two sides (one of Scrope's deponents accounts for nearly three times the total number of armorials
attested to by Grosvenor's entire slate of witnesses) offers up a possible
reason for Sir Robert's preemptive strike: if his personal escutcheon was
to have any rhetorical impact on the Constable and the Court, it had to
stand out from the mass of evidence looming on the horizon.

In addition to any tactical role they might play in the proceedings
of the Court, the armorials accounted for in the depositions reveal an
England filled with chivalric signifiers, a national (and, as I shall argue
below, simultaneously regional) topography of honor and franchise.
Familial identity is inscribed upon the land, in manor house and min-
ster, proclaiming itself for all to see.[31] This is the class dynamic to which

Lee Patterson refers in his discussion of the case's 1391 conclusion: "not just the highly public, ceremonial nature of the honor exchanges that constituted chivalric culture but the wholly social, even material sense of selfhood that it presupposes . . . Visibility, even palpability, was required."[32] Patterson is speaking here of the written "schedule" Grosvenor carries during his 16 November 1391 appearance "in full parliament" alongside Scrope. Read out loud by John of Gaunt in Grosvenor's "mother tongue," the document registers Sir Robert's open confession "that he had no knowledge of falsehood, fraud, deceit or reproach of Sir Richard" and that any imputation of such was due to the advice of his counsel and "not out of his own head."[33] To be sure, written records like Grosvenor's "schedule" feature throughout the depositions: Estefan, the Abbot of Vale Royal, mentions "cronicles & anxiens scriptures" in his testimony (p. 253), while Owain Glyndwr answers in the affirmative when asked if he has seen "aucuns charteres ou autres munimentez auncientz ensealez ov sealx eantz les ditz armes engravez" ("any charters or other ancient muniments sealed or having seals inscribed with the said arms," p. 254).[34]

But Patterson's criteria of "visibility" and "palpability" are also easily met by the nonverbal armorials described above. They too serve as sufficient "warrant of its [chivalry's] authenticity."[35] In fact, their very solidity and public presence (multiple witnesses will mention seeing the same armorial) offers them a powerful defense against the charges of forgery to which the written records are all too vulnerable: one of Scrope's exceptions to Grosvenor's evidence involved the accusation that Abbot Estefan's chronicles and ancient writings were deliberate fakes ("Estefan abbe de Valle Real . . . ad forge un discent encountre verite de les auncestres du dit monsieur Robert," "Estefan, Abbot of Vale Royal has forged against truth a pedigree of the ancestors of the said sir Robert," p. 322). Most important for my purposes here, however, is the nonverbal armorial's ability to grant chivalric honor a location all its own. The charter or chronicle speaks to the temporal aspect of a given knight's identity, the antiquity of his family line. The sculpted tomb, painted image, and colored glass of the nonverbal armorials serve to situate that identity in space.[36] Furthermore, they do so in tandem with similar devices, occupying multiple spaces in simultaneous time and thereby extending the aristocrat's honor beyond the immediate purview of its foundation, his person. At its start, the Scrope-Grosvenor controversy threatened to involve the clash of male bodies: Scrope had initially "chalanga [*sic*]" Sir Robert's use of his arms "sur le corps" (p. 38), while Grosvenor's kinsman Sir Ralph de Vernon testified that he would have "chalangee [*sic*]" Scrope himself if the Yorkshire knight had not spoken first (p. 271).[37] But with the Court of Chivalry's decision "deschuer la bataille" ("to forgo battle," p. 39), the honor-struggle resorted to what was effectively a competition of proofs and regalia, one in which the knights' social and translocal bodies stood in for their physical ones. In a sense, Grosvenor lost because he could not muster sufficient spatio-symbolic might to overcome Scrope's own widespread topography of honor.[38]

The mismatch between the two men on these grounds is immediately obvious. Authorized by the Constable and the Court to gather proofs from "diverses paises en Engleterre" ("various counties in England," p. 40), Scrope's commissioners took depositions in localities dispersed across England: Plymouth, Yerdeley, Tiverton, and Abbotsbury in the southwest; York, Aton, Pykering, and Scarborough in the north; Westminster and London in the southeast; Nottingham, Leicester, Lincoln, and Laxton in the north central; even Chester and Lancaster in the northwest.[39] Grosvenor's friends and allies were invariably located in Cheshire: depositions took place in Chester (once at St. John's, once at St. Mary's-on-the-Hill), Stockport, Knutsford, Nantwich, and Sandbach. His commissioners went outside of Cheshire on only three occasions, and two of these—Lancaster Castle and Warrington—were well within the boundaries of the culturally and geographically unified Cheshire/Lancashire region described by Michael Bennett.[40] Coventry was the one location beyond Grosvenor's immediate area of influence to which he sent any commissioners, but the list of deponents examined there reveals a familiar set of Cheshire names (Cotton, Massye, and Bulkeley), suggesting that he was looking to Coventry more for the support of expatriate Cheshiremen than for anything else.[41] Two Welsh voices, those of Owain Glyndwr and his brother Tudor, do speak up for Grosvenor, and the Coventry list of deponents does include the Warwickshire knight Sir William Bagot of "Bagot, Bushy, and Green" fame—but that appears to be the full extent of Grosvenor's multiregional affinity and thus the effective range of his honor as well.[42]

The initial effect of these spatial disparities (Scrope's wide-ranging network of friends, family, and allies; Grosvenor's small-scale regional cluster) is to support what Bennett has recently argued, that "Sir Robert Grosvenor's entanglement with the court of chivalry is symbolic: the local community of honour was being integrated in, and subordinated to, a national one."[43] He sees the 1380s and 1390s, the period in which "the conditions for cultural production in the region became more favorable," as simultaneously and paradoxically the moment "when its regional culture was most under threat."[44] Many of the topographical details of the case do seem to point in this direction: it begins near the Scots border, takes in testimony in an arc ranging from York in the north to Plymouth in the south, and ends in the nation's traditional political center, Whitehall at Westminster.[45] Likewise, Scrope and Grosvenor's ill-fated encounter at Newcastle-on-Tyne takes place in the midst of what is functionally a nation-building moment: Richard's limited invasion of Scotland in the summer of 1385 brought together knights from all over England, creating conditions under which trans-regional bonds might begin to be formed. Many of these men, Grosvenor included, had formerly been on campaign in France; their regular participation in imperial ventures such as the Hundred Years' War and the ongoing exchange of raids with Scotland exposed them to the idea of an England united in conflict against foreign foes.[46] Indeed, the primary reason why Scrope's commissioners were taking depositions in Plymouth in June 1386 was that John of Gaunt was preparing to launch an expedition to Castile, and a good portion of the nation's chivalry was accompanying him thither.

Finally, we might note what seems like a throwaway phrase in Patterson's discussion of Grosvenor's final confession: "Not only Scrope's damaged selfhood but the chivalric community as a whole were thereby declared whole: the ceremony of reparation was performed before *the assembled nobility of England* in Parliament" (my italics).[47] Although Patterson will go on to stress chivalry's localizing resistance to centralization (a point to which I will return below), his statement nonetheless suggests the possibility of reading the controversy's 16 November 1391 denouement in Bennett's terms of national integration and subordination.[48] First, integration: Scrope's repeated insistence that Grosvenor publish his retraction in writing, "making manifest his truth and honour," can be read as an attempt to reestablish a chivalric selfhood understood to be coterminous with the space of the nation—as could Gaunt's decision to stage the two knights' reconciliation during Parliament.[49] As for Grosvenor's subordination (and that of the Cheshire/Lancashire region with which he so closely identified, tied to it as he was by culture and by the trace of his armorial self), it could be located in the public exposure of his mistake in trusting lower-class counsel and defaming Sir Richard. The documentary record notes that Sir Robert answered Gaunt's questions "with a calm countenance," an expressive performance which may be intended to signify the stoic endurance of the chivalric knight.[50] In this understanding of the ceremony's social import, reaffirming community within the parliamentary chamber at Whitehall means rejecting the demands of local honor and acquiescing with the chivalric claims of the nation. One might even read the case's outcome as a historical instance of the "cultural cohesion" Turville-Petre sees at work in *SGGK*: regional knight meets court-identified knight, they battle one another (with words and armorials instead of axes), but in the end they reach reconciliation through their shared acceptance of such hallmark chivalric virtues as "truth and honour"— virtues that transcend the limits of regional affiliation.

But the possibility of reading resentment in Grosvenor's demeanor also suggests the potential for resistance, for a sense of regional identity that resists its mainstreaming. Grosvenor is as alert to the potential of performance as is either Scrope or Gaunt. Faced with the prospect of an impossible fine (originally £466 13s. 4d., it was subsequently reduced by the king to the still unmatchable 500 marks or £333 6s. 8d.), he throws himself upon Scrope's mercy in a move as seemingly calculated as any of his opponent's: he begs for forgiveness of his debt and for Scrope's friendship (in that order). Scrope then takes advantage of this display of weakness to stage his own scene on 11 November 1391:

On which day, before the King in his palace at Westminster,
in the presence of my lord of Guyen [Gaunt], the archbishop
of Dyvelyn, the bishops of London, Cestre and Cicestre, the
earls of Derby, Roteland, Marche, Arundell, Huntyngdoun and
Northumberland, the lords Roos, Neville and Cobham, Sir
Matthew de Gourney and knights and esquires in great number,

Sir Richard and Sir Robert being there in person, Sir Richard, by word of mouth, rehearsed the request of Sir Robert and how he would give his answer in the presence of the King and of my lords of Guyen and Derby, and then told him that the highest and most sovereign things a knight ought to guard in defence of his estate are his troth and his arms, and that in both of them Sir Robert had impeached him.[51]

Grosvenor's subsequent denial of any "knowledge of such defaults to the reproach of Sir Richard" and transfer of blame to his counsel is then swiftly countered by Scrope's recollection of a moment earlier in the case when Grosvenor verbally confirmed the "villanies" at issue.[52] Grosvenor "plainly" states that he knows of no falsehoods to be credited to Scrope, Scrope in turn asks the king if such an admission might be written down, King Richard grants this request, and then, finally, Scrope forgives Grosvenor his fine, embracing him and "promising his friendship"—but all "by command of the king."[53] The embrace's sincerity is further compromised by the final clause in the record: "so that the foregoing words [Grosvenor's confirmation of Scrope's 'truth and honour'] would be entered of record to remain as aforesaid."[54] Whatever "cultural cohesion" is achieved on this occasion is the result of a long, heavily negotiated process.

In the drawn-out, ritualistic series of exchanges between the two men (punctuated by expressions of the king's royal will), no moment seems spontaneous or unscripted. In fact, the record quite effectively blocks the scene. Scrope works his audience of magnates, confirming his own identity in their presence by lecturing Grosvenor on the nature of chivalry (and thus implying the Cheshire knight's lesser command of knighthood's values). Grosvenor is equal to the acting challenge placed before him: Scrope's fine threatens to ruin his estate and patrimony, and he is therefore more than willing to assume the submissive posture required for the penalty's removal. His display of fortitude in the face of Scrope's verbal aggression (his speaking "plainly" responds immediately to Sir Richard's tone of "high reverence") will be matched five days later by his "calm countenance" before Parliament. It is a chivalric performance in time of crisis worthy of Gawain's own at the Green Chapel: "Gawayn grayþely hit bydez and glent with no membre / Bot stode

stylle as þe ston oþer a stubbe auþer / þat raþeled is in roché grounde
with rotez a hundreth" (lines 2292–94).

Grosvenor complemented his passive resistance at Westminster
with his more active decision to choose new arms. In the Constable's
original decision of 12 May 1389 (which found for Scrope), Gloucester had nevertheless partially rewarded Sir Robert by allowing him to
retain (as seen in figure 5) the disputed arms with a heraldic difference: "les armes dazure ove un bende dor ove un playn bordure dar-
gent" (p. 331). By making this concession, the Court of Chivalry was
more or less officially confirming the collective *trawþe* of Grosvenor's
Cheshire and Lancashire affinity. According to the Constable, Scrope's
claim had the greater antiquity, but Grosvenor's was still sufficiently
noble—and so was the regional community that bore witness to Sir
Robert's claim and to its instantiation in armorial form. When Grosvenor went on to reject the Constable's "curtoisie" (as King Richard would
later term it), he was reasserting his right to his original arms and refusing a symbolic modification that would mark his honor (and that of his
family/region) as inferior to Scrope's.[55] Scrope also objected to this
decision (for similar reasons), and the matter was ultimately decided by
the king on 27 May 1390: "que tiel bordere nest difference sufficeant en
armes entre deux estraunges et dun roialme mes taunt soulement entre
cousyn & cousyn privez de sanc" ("such a bordure is not a sufficient
difference in arms between two strangers within one realm but only
between cousins related by blood," p. 351). King Richard's triangulation here of *estraunge, roialme,* and *cousyn* does speak to an emergent
sense of nationhood, but it is a nation caught up in negotiations with
family identity: the distribution of arms owes as much to blood (*sanc*)
as it does to Englishness.

Furthermore, the regional returns to prominence in Grosvenor's
ultimate choice of arms. As Stewart-Brown writes, "It was in consequence
of this decision that Grosvenor, being left without arms, adopted the
single golden sheaf of Cheshire on a blue field, probably allusive to his
supposed relationship to the earls of Chester, one of whom (Ranulf III
de Blundeville) bore three sheaves in his arms."[56] Grosvenor's adaptation
of Earl Ranulf's device (figure 5) seems to me to be an overt assertion
of regional continuity, one that connects him to an even more presti-
gious topography of armorials and links him to traditions of popular

romance and legendry: in *passus* 5 of the B-text of *Piers Plowman*, Sloth's admission that "I kan rymes of Robyn Hood and Randolf Erl of Chestre" (line 396) is quite probably an allusion to the same Earl Ranulf whom Stewart-Brown mentions.[57] Sir Robert's choice may also hint at defiance of King Richard: the Earldom of Chester had reverted to the Crown in 1237 and then been given to Prince Edward (the future Edward I) by his father Henry III in 1254. In 1301 the connection between the monarchy and the earldom grew even tighter with Edward I's decision to create his infant son Edward II Prince of Wales and Earl of Chester, a combination of titles that has remained intact in royal hands to the present day. To assume arms reminiscent of the Earls of Chester (one of whom was the Black Prince, King Richard's father) is to lay a claim to their honor as well as to one's own. In making this decision, Grosvenor was to some degree identifying himself with the king's palatinate of Cheshire and thus appropriating some portion of the king's honor.

Moments of regional and counter-national consciousness like these abound in the Scrope-Grosvenor controversy. For example, let us reconsider the 1386 visit Scrope's commissioners made to Plymouth to take John of Gaunt's deposition: I earlier suggested that a sense of the nation could be detected in Gaunt's status as magnate, particularly in light of his role in orchestrating Scrope and Grosvenor's reconciliation. But Gaunt is in Plymouth assembling his English army for an expedition of extremely personal import: his identity as "le treshaut et puissant prince le Roy de Chastelle et de Lyon" (p. 49) is at stake far off to the south in Castile, and that Iberian title matters to him as much as does any sense of specifically English welfare. Another example: King Richard's 1385 invasion of Scotland is notable to historians in part because it marked the last summons of the feudal levy in late medieval England.[58] Scrope and Grosvenor's fateful meeting thus takes place under the aegis not only of an imperialist expedition, but of a belated appeal to the older, personal loyalties once commanded by the Crown on a regular basis. King Richard's summons operates in the sphere of ancient regional networks of vassalage even as it deploys the idea of an England beleaguered and ready to strike back against its northern foe.

In fact, despite Bennett's tacit assumption that Scrope is a representative of the national "mainstream," Sir Richard's own regional identity is also on display throughout the controversy.[59] While the affinity testifying on his behalf includes witnesses from several counties across the length of England, a substantial number of the deponents are connected to a relatively continuous area between York in the north and Leicester in the Midlands, a political and cultural region that included within its bounds Scrope's seat at Bolton, Yorkshire. Moreover, this region has a name, one which occurs repeatedly in the testimony of Scrope's deponents: "la paiis de North" ("the counties of the North," p. 197). For every witness (like Sir Thomas Walsshe) who comments on how the "publike vois et fame" of the Scropes' arms runs "per tout le roialme Dengliterre" ("through all the realm of England," p. 176), there is another deponent (like Johan Thirlewalle) who reports specifically that the arms are known to any "homme . . . en la paiis de North" ("man . . . in the counties of the North," p. 182). Richard de Beaulieu's testimony raises the possibility that the national "publike vois et fame" mentioned in Walsshe's deposition could be simultaneously understood as regional in nature: Beaulieu refers to the "fame et publike vois . . . per tout la paiis du North" of the Scrope device (p. 187).[60]

With slight modifications reflecting shifts in space and in sentiment, the same phrase routinely appears in the statements of Grosvenor's Cheshire and Lancashire deponents: to give but a single instance of such usage, Owain Glyndwr testified that "en le conte de Cestre et Flynt et autres lieux et contees procheinz publik vois et fame est que les ditz armes ont apperteine et appertient . . . au dit monsieur Robert et a cez auncestres" ("in the county of Chester and Flint and other places and neighboring counties, the public voice and fame is that the said arms have appertained and are appertaining to the said Sir Robert and to his ancestors," p. 255). The formulaic use of these phrases speaks to an awareness of multiple regional communities and a willingness to locate Scrope and Grosvenor at their centers, to link the knights' chivalric honor to local topography. However, these communities of honor are expressly limited in scope: the "publik vois et fame" of Chester is not current in Yorkshire and vice versa. The knight so familiar in his home terrain journeys out in search of *aventure* and finds only ignorance—his identity runs only so far and no further. In a sense, then, the regional "publik vois" is an oral counterpart of the material networks of armorials that register honor's presence in space. They gave chivalry a home base, a site in which its claims were recognized and affirmed, but they also, and by default of their material nature, gave it a set of boundaries as well. If anything, the depositions' discussion of *vois* suggests that speech has similar borders.

None of what I have just argued is meant to imply that the idea of "nation" or "England" is irrelevant to Scrope-Grosvenor and the chivalric crisis it entails: my point is not to simply reverse hierarchies and chauvinistically install the regional over the national. Instead, both here and below in my close reading of *SGGK*, I hope to present the case for a more mixed cultural situation, one in which the regional and the national coexist alongside a great many other categories of identity, all of them jostling for position in a given social context. But if I am aware of the limitations inherent in a regional approach, I am also conscious of the under-examined teleology informing much of the recent discussion of English nationalism in the Middle Ages—of the assumption that the fourteenth century is the essential moment of transition between region and nation, the point at which, say, Cheshire gives way to England in both politics and poetry.[61] As I have claimed above, the Scrope-Grosvenor debate qualifies such a teleology, repeatedly bringing the regional to one's attention even as it attempts to negotiate a national culture of chivalry. Grosvenor's Cheshire identity has been readily recognized by scholars, in part (I suspect) because he was the loser in the case, and the regional is customarily associated with loss, absence, and nostalgia. But Scrope's Northern-ness is also a factor in the controversy: Scrope and Grosvenor's conflict can no longer be written into a familiar narrative of sophisticated Southern encroachment at the expense of a bold, but outnumbered and doomed Northern selfhood. Both men were Northerners, and Northerners in ways that mattered, ways that merited official recognition and registration in the court record. Bennett's understanding of Scrope-Grosvenor as the imposition of a socio-spatial hierarchy with the center at the top is no longer tenable.

We would do better to look at the controversy's spatial politics through an alternate metaphor. Writing about Sir Thomas Berkeley's activities as John Trevisa's patron, Ralph Hanna states the following:

> These [Berkeley's efforts on Trevisa's behalf] suggest that court culture moved *through* London (perhaps with minimal pause), rather than radiating *from* it. Berkeley texts could use the capital

as a way station, one which joined otherwise unrelated courts, and courts which operated at a great distance from one another and from London. London encouraged a disparate national court culture by allowing decentralization, by facilitating a kind of exportable use which joined together quite diverse rural environments. The point seems particularly important for understanding the workings of magnate culture in the period 1370–1425, before London asserted an absolute cultural hegemony.[62]

Although my work on cultural activity in Cheshire during the later fifteenth, sixteenth, and early seventeenth centuries leads me to question Hanna's characterization of post-1425 London's "hegemony" as "absolute," his idea of the capital as a nexus or "way station" has interesting implications for our understanding of Scrope-Grosvenor. It allows us to acknowledge the two knights' local status as Northerners and to see them making use of the Court of Chivalry in a manner similar to Berkeley's utilization of London scribes and booksellers: Westminster mediates the dispute, allowing for the assertion of regional identity on both sides even as it attempts to channel their honor in a direction amenable to its own hegemonic concerns.[63] The latter point cannot be ignored: confronted by a disruptive conflict between a parvenu magnate and a knight whose lower status is nonetheless belied by his leading role in a regional affinity of some importance to the Crown (Cheshiremen will stand for Richard against the Lords Appellant at Radcot Bridge in 1387), the king has a substantial stake in reconciling both men. But if the case's resolution benefits King Richard, it also serves local interests: after all, neither Scrope nor Grosvenor was willing to accept the Constable's ruling on the disposition of the arms, and Grosvenor's modification of the Earl of Chester's is, as we have seen, a multidirectional claim, appropriating a portion of the king's honor for his own.

Turville-Petre builds his case for *SGGK*'s poetics of national cohesion on the foundation of a shared sense of chivalry: "Perhaps we live in the north-west Midlands, or perhaps we live in Logres; the matter is of no consequence because our regionality is subsumed under the international chivalric code to which we all adhere."[64] What Scrope-Grosvenor demonstrates, however, is that regionality will not be subsumed, that adherence to a common code is no panacea for an honor conflict rooted in arms and in the localities whose borders they mark. If anything, the "international chivalric code" only serves to heighten interregional debate through its gathering of what Patterson calls "a dispersed field of autonomous competitors."[65] The instant of horrified recognition which no doubt accompanied Scrope and Grosvenor's first meeting—the detection of your arms on the body of another, of your self invaded, of your identity with a difference—is a direct (and necessary) result of the dispersal Patterson describes. It is also part and parcel of the Trojan diaspora that informs *SGGK* and of the Round Table's self-canceling first encounter with the Green Knight.

"Þou art not Gawayn": The Destabilization of Arms and Identity in *Sir Gawain and the Green Knight*

At first glance, the opening lines of *SGGK* do appear to support Turville-Petre's nationalizing reading of the poem. With the destruction of Troy, "Ennias þe athel and his highe kynde" (line 5) are free to go and build nations of their own:

> Fro riche Romulus to Rome ricchis hym swyþe,
> With gret bobbaunce þat burȝe he biges vpon fyrst
> And neuenes hit his aune nome, as hit now hat;
> Ticius to Tuskan and teldes bigynnes,
> Langaberde in Lumbardie lyftes vp homes,
> And fer ouer þe French flod, Felix Brutus
> On mony bonkkes ful brode Bretayn he settez
>   Wyth wynne
>
>   (lines 8–15)

Turville-Petre sees this sequence of *translationes imperii* as the "foundations for that international court-culture that Arthur most eminently exemplified and Hautdesert strove to imitate."[66] Additional evidence for his claim comes in the form of the poem's statement that the diasporic Trojans have "depreced prouinces and patrounes bicome" (line 6).[67] But our understanding of the Scrope-Grosvenor case allows us to read the first stanza of *SGGK* in a different light, one in which the poem's opening lines represent the ideal (and idealized) deployment of topographical honor. In this chivalric fantasy, each noble *athel* establishes a field of honor identical to his person: there is no difference between Romulus and Rome, Ticius and Tuscany, Langaberd and Lombardy, or (crucially) Brutus and Britain. If you know the region, you know the man—no mistakes or failures of identification here. Moreover, the boundaries of the various *prouinces* are neatly distinct. Marked by material structures (*burȝe, teldes, homes*) similar in function to Scrope and Grosvenor's armorials, these regions are nevertheless free from the far more haphazard distribution of properties that marks the honor of the Cheshire knight or would-be Yorkshire magnate. The Trojan *prouinces* are secure, holistic spaces.[68] Their spatial inviolability anticipates the poem's concern with the invulnerability of male chivalric bodies.[69]

However, as a reading of *SGGK* soon reveals, knightly bodies (and the spatialized arms that represent them) are anything but invulnerable to invasion, division, appropriation, and compromise. The Green Knight is of course the poem's most spectacular instance of male vulnerability, but Gawain will encounter a more serious fate: relinquishing his personal arms at Hautdesert leaves him open to a psychosocial assault upon his *trawþe* and honor, while his subsequent decision to accept the green girdle as his device will result in the direct violation of his physical integrity. Sequence is key here: heraldic vulnerability precedes that of the body. Gawain unknowingly consents to the modification of his arms with the sort of "difference sufficeant" that Grosvenor rejected, and he pays for it with what he perceives to be the loss of his honor. This point is made explicit at the poem's end: "'Lo! lorde,' quoþe þe leude, and þe lace hondeled, / 'Þis is þe bende of þis blame I bere in my nek'" (lines 2505–6). The series of equations in Gawain's statement—green *lace* equals heraldic *bende* equals chivalric *blame* equals the knight's wounded *nek*—represents the sort of outcome that Scrope and Grosvenor were both fighting to avoid. Gawain fails to protect his arms and discovers that to do so is to fail to protect his self. As we shall see, his sense of shame leads him to reject any substantial accommodation with Bertilak and with it any sense of interregional cohesion. According to *SGGK*, accord can only be established within his regional affinity: the Round Table's decision to adopt green baldrics as a sign of their "broþerhede" (line 2516) with Gawain is an attempt at internal, intraregional cohesion, one whose success is questionable. The poem's circular return to Troy in lines 2524–25 recalls its initial evocation of unified chivalric spaces and identities, but formal strategies cannot wholly mask the damage that has been done over the course of the narrative, both to Gawain himself (the figure of the individual honor-man) and to the idea of a unified British nation.[70]

That damage begins to accumulate as soon as the Green Knight bursts through the doors of Arthur's hall at Camelot in response to the king's standing request for, among other things, "sum auenturus þyng, an *vncouþe* tale / Of sum mayn meruayle . . . of *armes*" (lines 93–94, 95, my italics). This movement serves as the poem's first real-time encounter with regional difference, and Arthur's knights are ill-prepared for the interaction forced upon them. Confronted by the Green Knight and his rude demand to speak with "Þe gouernour of þis gyng" (line 225), the Round Table responds with "a swoghe sylence" (line 243). The poet assures us that "fele sellyez had þay sen bot such neuer are" (line 239), that for once they have come face-to-face with a marvel that escapes their collective experience. Certainly their sense of astonishment owes much to the Green Knight's unprecedented green-ness, but we might also locate it in the Knight's deliberate evasion of chivalric intelligibility. His description (along with that of his steed) takes up eighty-five lines, but the only *armes* on display anywhere within that sequence are those covered by his long, green hair: "half his armes þervnder were halched in þe wyse / Of a kyngez capados" (lines 185–86).[71] He does possess "a strayt cote ful streȝt þat stek on his sides" (line 152); surcoats found elsewhere in the poem routinely bear an embroidered version of its wearer's arms (for example, in lines 636–37, we are told that "þe pentangel nwe / He [Gawain] ber in schelde and cote").

However, there is no direct indication that this particular surcoat carries any heraldic information. (Even if we assume that it does, the fact remains that the court does not recognize any such signs.) Several lines later, the text appears to confirm the surcoat's featurelessness: the Green Knight wears "no plate þat pented to armes" (line 204).[72] Literally, this means that he is unarmed, that he wears no armor, but figuratively it also suggests that he fails to signify heraldically. As A. C. Spearing says, "the Green Knight is provided with no equivalent to Gawain's pentangle—no explicit indication of the values to which he is committed."[73] Without that clear indication, his audience can only respond with confusion and silence: on the one hand, the Green Knight displays certain class-specific signs of identity (the aforementioned phrase "kyngez capados" suggests this). On the other hand, he clearly acts in a less-than-courteous fashion throughout the scene, making demands and offering suggestive insults to the assembled Round Table knights.[74] There is no shield to make the court's job easier: while the Green Knight's color scheme fits the rules of heraldry (*vert*, a color, properly goes with *or*, a metal, and vice versa), his garments and accoutrements never put the elements of an armorial device together.

Even after the Green Knight finally does give Gawain and the other knights some information about his identity, that revelation proves maddeningly imprecise. Taking up the axe, Gawain asks the questions all of Camelot has been waiting to pose and have answered: "Where schulde I wale þe . . . Where is þy place? / I wot neuer where þou wonyes, bi Hym þat me wroȝt, / Ne I know not þe, knyȝt, þy cort ne þi name" (lines 398–400). At first, the Knight delays: "quen I þe tape haue," he states, then "smartly I þe teche / Of my hous and my home and myn owen nome" (lines 406, 407–8).[75] In these lines, the poet leaves us in the same position as the Round Table here; like them, we have been waiting on tenterhooks to learn the identity of the Green Knight. His conditional clause teases us with the possibility that we will never know, that the heraldic mystery will remain unsolved—Gawain will decapitate the Knight, and that will be that.

When—courtesy of the power of Morgan le Fay—the Green Knight does survive Gawain's *tape*, resolution is at hand. Always true to its (his?) word, the Knight's severed head provides Gawain, the Round Table, and the poem's audience with the information they have been seeking: "To þe Grene Chapel þou chose, I charge þe, to fotte / Such a dunt as þou hatz dalt—disserued þou habbez— / To be ȝederly ȝolden on Nw ȝeres morn. / Þe Knyȝt of þe Grene Chapel men knowen me mony" (lines 451–54). There is irony in these lines: as I noted earlier, we learn from Gawain's encounters in the Wirral proper that hardly anyone knows of either the Green Knight or his Chapel: "neuer in her lyue / Þay seȝe neuer no segge þat watz of suche hwez / Of grene" (lines 706–8). "Men knowen me mony" is perhaps a subtle dig at the pretensions of Camelot to extraregional knowledge. But there is a stronger irony at work here: like "Romulus," "Ticius," "Langabard," and "Brutus," "Green Knight" is an eponym. The stranger's field of honor, his specific *prouince*, bears his name—a Green Chapel for a Green Knight. The trick is that the Green Knight's topographic identification mocks those of his epic predecessors: if they were paragons of chivalric identity, men whose honor was coterminous with their territory, the Green Knight suggests that such identifications are far more indeterminate than they may at first appear. He gives us a community of honor, but it remains unlocatable. The seemingly intelligible—and identical—signifiers "Green Knight" and "Green Chapel" end up conveying nothing (at least not immediately). If Gawain wants to acquire extraregional knowledge (the basis for any sort of imagined or real cultural cohesion), he will have to quest for it. The Green Knight's subsequent departure from Camelot raises more questions than it answers: "To quat kyth he becom knwe non þere, / Neuer more þen þay wyste from queþen he watz wonnen. / What thenne?" (lines 460–62). The encounter with the other—regional, exotic, foreign—ends in hermeneutic disaster, and Turville-Petre's nationalizing court culture fails its first test in the poem. The possibility of cultural cohesion will now rest on the shoulders (and shield) of the center's representative, Sir Gawain.

The preparations for Gawain's journey are at first glance an indicator of future success. If the Green Knight was an unstable figure of anonymity, Gawain is the essence of intelligibility—a point the arming sequence in Fitt 2 (lines 566–669) works hard to convey. As we watch Gawain slowly (in the poetic sense) don his armor, each line that goes by, each article of clothing that goes on his body, works to establish his holistic selfhood (and, by extension, the holistic integrity of his regionally distinct community). The enclosure of the male body (and the chivalric identities, individual and communal, that this body subtends) is effectively complete by lines 590–91: "When he watz hasped in armes his harnays watz ryche: / Þe lest lachet oþer loupe lemed of golde." The knots are all tied, the buckles all buckled—Gawain is sealed into his armor, ready to face the identity-threatening demands of adventure and the wild.

The presentation of his shield in lines 619–65 is the culmination of this process. This passage situates Gawain firmly within the discursive boundaries of heraldry: "Then þay schewed hym þe schelde, þat was of schyr goulez / Wyth þe pentangel depaynt of pure golde hewez" (lines 619–20).[76] Gawain's arms *goulez* a pentangle *golde* serve to counteract the earlier description of the Green Knight: then, the green and gold amounted to nothing like a coherent heraldic sign; now, the red and gold come together to define the chivalric self.[77] Just as that self is completely encased in armor, so too is the pentangle sealed and seemingly invulnerable: "hit is a figure þat haldez fyue poyntez / And vche lyne vmbelappez and loukez in oþer / And ayquere hit is endelez" (lines 627–29). It therefore "apendez to þat prynce noble" (line 623)—a statement the *Gawain*-poet repeats eight lines later, albeit in what will retroactively be seen as more resonant language: "hit accordez to þis knyȝt and to his cler armez" (line 631).[78] The pentangle passage highlights the effective identification of the knight with his arms; moreover, we are told that it does so with explicit reference to Gawain's reputation, his intercultural field of honor:

> For ay faythful in fyue and sere fyue syþez,
> Gawan watz for gode knawen and, as golde pured,
> Voyded of vche vylany, wyth vertuez ennourned
> > In mote.
> > Forþy þe pentangel nwe
> > He ber in schelde and cote,
> > As tulk of tale most trwe
> > And gentylyst knyȝt of lote.
> > > (lines 632–39)

Gawain's mastery of "þe teccheles termes of talkyng noble" (line 917), so much in demand at Hautdesert, is anticipated here by *lote* or "speech"; his reputation is conveyed via the phrase "tale most trwe." Moreover, the heraldic-somatic link is confirmed in the simile comparing Gawain to "golde pured": the literal gold of the pentangle points to the symbolic gold in Gawain's character. The pentangle device attempts to insure that Gawain "watz for gode knawen," that his noble name is easily recognized throughout the land.[79]

Given the extreme emphasis that *SGGK* places on this description of the shield, it is therefore somewhat surprising to realize that the pentangle utterly fails at its heraldic task.[80] Equally surprising is the location of that failure within the narrative: it lies not with Gawain's acceptance of the lady's gift of the green girdle, nor with his deliberate decision to conceal that gift from Bertilak—both significant lapses in Gawain's chivalric judgment. It takes place instead at the very beginning of Gawain's sojourn in Hautdesert, at the precise moment when he first interacts with any of the regional court's inhabitants. Saved from a case of terminal frostbite by the castle's miraculous appearance, Gawain decides to try his luck: "He calde, and sone þer com / A porter pure plesaunt; / On þe wal his ernd he nome / And haylsed þe knyȝt erraunt" (lines 807–10). Their subsequent exchange reveals the extent to which the pentangle is a failed device:

> "Gode sir," quoþ Gawan, "woldez þou go myn ernde
> To þe heȝ lorde of þis hous, herber to craue?"
> "Ȝe, Peter!" quoþ the porter, "and purely I trowee
> Þat ȝe be, wyȝe, welcum to won quyle yow lykez."
> Þen ȝede þe wyȝe ȝerne and com aȝayn swyþe
> And folke frely hym wyth to fonge þe knyȝt.
>
> (lines 811–16)

Chivalric hospitality functions properly throughout this scene: as Felicity Heal has noted, the porter clearly recognizes Gawain's class position and allows him to dismount inside the gates of Hautdesert, an honor befitting his high status.[81] But the porter's skill at reading the social signifiers of Gawain's armor (and successfully transmitting this information to the court) does not translate into an equal ability to determine the strange knight's individual, heraldic identity. To the porter, Gawain is simply a *wyȝe*—the exact same term Arthur uses in line 252 to first welcome the Green Knight to Camelot ("Wyȝe, welcum iwys to þis place") as well as the word used by the narrator in line 815 to describe the porter. It does not bode well for Gawain to play either the Green Knight or the nameless porter in this reprisal of the entry scene in Fitt 1: from the moment in line 810 when the porter first hails him to the courtiers' discovery in line 906 that "hit watz Wawen hymself þat in þat won syttez," Gawain is as anonymous as his challenger was earlier.[82] The servants confirm this later on when they reenact the Round Table's own questions about the Green Knight's regional origin: "Wheþen in worlde he were, / Hit semed as he moȝt / Be prynce withouten pere / In felde þer felle men foȝt" (lines 871–74).[83] The echo here of "Neuer more þen þay wyste from queþen he watz wonnen" is telling.

As a heraldic device, the pentangle is supposed to prevent such confusion. It is, after all, "a syngne þat Salamon set sumquyle / In bytoknyng of trawþe" (lines 625–26). Moreover, the *Gawain*-poet's insistence on carefully distinguishing between its two names—learned *pentaungel* ("Þat is þe pure 'pentaungel' wyth þe peple called / With lore," lines 664–65) and vernacular "endeles knot" (as the *Englych* people call it)—testifies to the supposed familiarity of the symbol. For all that, it fails to be recognizable at the gates of Hautdesert; only the court's "preué poyntez" (line 902) enables them to ascertain Gawain's identity. The pentangle is a *syngne* or *token* with no practical meaning inside the poem proper. *SGGK*'s extratextual audience can read and comprehend it (the description takes place outside of the text's narrative frame), but the characters overlook it completely.[84] It might be argued that the pentangle is a personal symbol, a private device known only to Gawain and his fellow Round Table knights, taken up for this particular quest.[85] There is indeed a discrepancy between the pentangle and Gawain's other, more traditional (and familial) arms.[86] However, as we have seen, the poem explicitly argues against such a reading, repeatedly linking the pentangle proper to Gawain's public reputation as "tulk of tale most trwe." It is the pentangle's functional role in heraldic exchange that matters to my argument here, not its deviation from romance tradition. And in fulfilling that role, the pentangle fails to signify across regional boundaries—its Camelot meaning does not carry over into the wilds of the Wirral.

The result is a space of uncertainty, a ninety-six line interruption of identity. During that time, Gawain is vulnerable, protected only by the rules of hospitality—and even these work to undermine his chivalric integrity. As Bertilak's servants rush to disarm him, the armorials materially grounding his identity are slowly prised away from him, one by one: "Quen he hef vp his helme þer hiȝed innoghe / For to hent hit at his honde, þe hende to seruen; / His bronde and his blasoun boþe they token" (lines 826–28).[87] This brief detail (the relinquishing of his shield) results in the pentangle's disappearance from the poem for approximately twelve-hundred lines, a second and even more risky gap in Gawain's defenses. A few lines later Gawain loses his surcoat as well: "Þer he watz dispoyled, wyth spechez of myerþe, / Þe burn of his bruny and of his bry3t wedez" (lines 860–61). He is now utterly pentangle-less; none of his arms remain on his person, and he is clad in the clothing of Hautdesert (note *dispoyled* and its echo of the Trojans' ancient conquests in line 6). This change of costume anticipates the Fitt 4 revelation that the green girdle is really the Green Knight's own livery: "For hit is my wede þat þou werez, þat ilke wouen girdel" (line 2358). Indeed, when Gawain does get his surcoat back in the final fitt, he swiftly covers the pentangle with the girdle, incorporating Bertilak's *wede* into his *array*: "Þe gordel of þe grene silke þat gay wel bisemed, / Vpon þat ryol red cloþe, þat ryche watz to schewe" (lines 2035–36). Stripped (however politely) of the signifiers indicating his chivalric identity in this disarming scene, Gawain must fall back on the twin resources of his person and his name. Like the heraldic device which represents its material instantiation, the knight's reputation depends on the deeds of the knight's body for its validity. There should ideally be an exact correspondence between the two: heroic deeds equal heroic fame.

But even as Gawain's identity becomes known throughout Hautdesert, it is already beginning to unravel. The removal of Gawain's armor, his martial self, allows an alternate reputation to come to the fore, one at odds with the self he has so far been careful to uphold. As one courtier excitedly tells another, "In menyng of manerez mere / Þis burne now schal vus bryng. / I hope þat may hym here / Schal lerne of luf-talkyng" (lines 924–27). Hautdesert knows of the great Sir Gawain, but they seem to have mistaken him for his continental namesake. The lady makes this clear to Gawain during her first attempt at seducing him:

> For I wene wel, iwysse, Sir Wowen 3e are,
> Þat alle þe worlde worchipez; quereso 3e ride,
> Your honour, your hendelayk is hendeley praysed
> With lordez, wyth ladyes, with all þat lyf bere.
> And now 3e ar here, iwysse, and we bot oure one;
> My lorde and his ledez ar on lenþe faren,
> Oþer burnez in her bedde, and my burdez als,
> Þe dor drawen and dit with a derf haspe;

And sythen I haue in þis hous hym þat al lykez,
I schal ware my whyle wel, quyl hit lastez,
>   With tale.

(lines 1226–35)

Unlike the pentangle, Gawain's fame precedes him everywhere and is intelligible to all. But what if the *honour* attributed to you is not one you would claim? What if you suddenly find yourself confronted with the presence of a doppelganger? Gawain's dilemma here resembles the one faced by both Scrope and Grosvenor at Newcastle-upon-Tyne in August 1385: secure in the belief that their familial honor (as exemplified in the *azure a bend or* device) was uniquely their own, the two men were suddenly confronted with the fact of duplication, of a second self that mimicked yet was not the original. Likewise, Gawain (who, as we recall, was earlier identified in the pentangle passage "As tulk of tale most trwe") realizes that the lady may have an entirely different sort of *tale* in mind.[88]

Gawain's courteous refusal of her offer takes an unfortunate turn, however. He escapes a potential trap, but only at the cost of personally confirming the split in his selfhood: "I be not now he þat ȝe of speken— / To reche to such reuerence as ȝe reherce here / I am wyȝe vnworþy, I wot wel myselven" (lines 1242–44). The language here is densely packed, but it all amounts to a self-cancellation. By politely rejecting the alternate identity with which the lady presents him and referring to himself only as "wyȝe vnworþy," Gawain actually ends up accepting the porter's earlier designation of him as anonymous *wyȝe*. The intensifying phrase "I wot wel myselven" is rich with irony: Gawain's insistence on self-knowledge here ("I know myself very well, thank you") is in the syntactical service of a self-denial ("I know very well that I'm just an unworthy fellow, and that's all"). After this self-inflicted blow to his identity, it comes as no surprise that the lady is not quite sure with whom she is speaking: "Now He þat spedez vche spech þis disport ȝelde yow, / Bot þat ȝe be Gawan, hit gotz in mynde!" (lines 1292–93).[89]

That denial returns on the second day of the exchange game in a stronger, more explicit form. This time it serves as the lady's opening gambit: "Sir, ȝif ȝe be Wawen, wonder me þynkkez, / Wyȝe þat is so wel wrast alway to god / And connez not of compaynye þe costez vndertake, / And if mon kennes yow hom to knowe, ȝe kest hom of your minde" (lines 1481–84). Her doubt—and her suggestion that Gawain is caught up in forgetfulness and ignorance—comes on a day in which unclothed male bodies are particularly vulnerable (we should always remember that the seduction attempts take place while Gawain is naked in bed, stripped of the social and material defenses clothing brings to bear). Bertilak's boar-hunt has been going on all the while, and the "bor alþer-grattest" (line 1441) that he chases is another double of Gawain's—not so much because the hunted animals are always types of the endangered knight (the critical commonplace), but because the boar is "wearing" the armor Gawain has so carelessly cast off. The huntsmen learn this to their frustration:

> Schalkez to schote at hym schowen to þenne,
> Haled to hym of her arewez, hitten hym oft;
> Bot þe poyntez payred at þe pyth, þat pyȝt in his scheldez,
> And þe barbez of his browe bite non wolde;
> Þaȝ þe schauen schaft schyndered in pecez,
> Þe hede hypped aȝayn weresoeuer hit hitte.

(lines 1454–59)

The overall sense of invulnerability in this passage is heightened by line 1456 and its pun on *scheldez*. According to Andrew and Waldron's glossary, the term is used here to mean "shoulder (of boar)."[90] But the gloss is too quick to ignore the metonymic potential of *scheldez*, to reduce it to anatomy alone. Bertilak's boar is fully armored, completely encased and protected by its shield against attack. In its struggles with the huntsmen, it thus resembles Gawain—he too was caught up in wilderness battles "in his yrnes" (line 729).

But this display of armored integrity is soon followed by the lady's aforementioned questioning of Gawain's identity. She also reiterates the interregional character of Gawain's playboy reputation ("Your worde and your worchip walkez ayquere," line 1521), forcing the modest (and cautious) Gawain to once again deny himself (in both senses of the phrase). The phrases he uses on this occasion make for an even more spectacular act of self-alienation: it would be "a folé felefolde" to sweet-talk the lady, who "weldez more slyȝt / Of þat art, bi þe half, or a hundreth of seche / As I am" (lines 1545, 1542–44). Two conflicting Gawains have become a hundred; the unique, invulnerable self sub-tended by the pentangle has been divided into dozens of generic identi-ties.[91] The text's return to the boar-hunt presents us with a literal (and symbolically parallel) enactment of this splitting of the subject: slain by Bertilak, the boar also ends up cut into pieces. First, his head is hewn off (one in a series of anticipatory decapitations); then, he loses his shield as his *brawen* is sliced off "in bry3t brode cheldez" (line 1611).[92] When Bertilak displays his winnings to Gawain in the hall that night ("He schewez hem þe scheldez," line 1626), we get the message that Gawain fails to receive: shields, even those painted with pentangles, are not impregnable defenses against loss of honor and diminishment of self.[93] Furthermore, when Gawain does finally get his shield back in line 2061, the poet includes an anatomical reference that revisits the knight's perilous similarity to the boar: "His schalk schewed hym his schelde, on schulder he hit la3t." It is a small, realistic detail of a typi-cal knightly posture, but it reveals the extent to which shields blur into shoulders—and thus heraldic arms into men. If the identity-bearing armorial cannot maintain its own integrity, then the chances for the knight whose self it displays (and whose body it guards) are no better.

Gawain's final encounter with the Green Knight activates another shield-centered metonymy, that connecting the knight's shield with the knight's neck.[94] The figure first emerges in the pentangle passage: shown his shield, Gawain "braydez hit by þe bauderyk, aboute þe hals kestes. / Þat bisemed þe segge semlyly fayre" (lines 621–22). When necks finally move to the foreground of the text at the Green Chapel, shields and shoulders are not far behind. We are told explicitly that the Green Knight brings down "þe barbe of þe bitte bi þe bare nek" (line 2310), and Gawain's response to his wounding resembles the violent reaction of the boar's:

> And quen þe burne se3 þe blode blenk on þe snawe,
> He sprit forth spenne-fote more þen a spere lenþe,
> Hent heterly his helme and on his hed cast,
> Schot with his schulderez his fayre schelde vnder,
> Braydez out a bry3t sworde and *bremely* he spekez
>
> (lines 2315–19, my italics)

Compare this passage to the following description of the huntsmen's reluctance to take on the boar and his tusks: "He hade hurt so mony byforne / Þat al þuȝt þen ful loþe / Be more wyth his tusches torne, / Þat *breme* watz and braynwod bothe" (lines 1577–80, my italics). In a sense, Gawain's reaction is a reversal of the boar's: the latter's *breme* attitude precedes his fatal wounding at Bertilak's hands, while the former's *breme* speech responds to the less-than-mortal injury he receives from the very same lord. But the time for armored resistance is past. Gawain brings the pentangle-shield to bear much too late, all on account of the girdle (the garment with which he covered the pentangle in lines 2035–36, as we saw earlier). His less-than-admirable decision to withhold it from Bertilak is a violation of the *trawþe* depicted on his shield; untrue to his host, Gawain is untrue to his arms—and thus to himself as well.

The identity crisis endured in the bedroom returns to haunt him here, in what is structurally, if not materially, a double for Arthur's court at Camelot: the "public" space of the Green Chapel, the heart of the Green Knight's regional territory.[95] Gawain's fear, the motivator for his acceptance of the girdle, causes him to flinch at the Green Knight's first swing of the axe: "Bot Gawayn on þat giserne glyfte hym bysyde, / As hit com glydande adoun on glode hym to schende, / And schranke a lytel with þe schulderes for þe scharp yrne" (lines 2265–67). His earlier failure to live up to the standards advertised in his armorial device is repeated here by the shoulders metonymically identified with that coat-of-arms. Gawain betrays his (heraldic) arms, and his (physical) arms subsequently betray him: "'Þou art not Gawayn,' quoþ þe gome, 'þat is so goud halden, / Þat neuer arȝed for no here by hylle ne be vale, / And now þou fles for ferde er þou fele harmez! / Such cowardise of þat knyȝt cowþe I neuer here'" (lines 2270–73). Cast back into that earlier moment of self-doubt, Gawain does manage to summon his courage and live up to his bargain ("haf here my trawþe," he says to the Knight in line 2287). It is a performance that impresses the Green Knight (he responds to it *muryly*, line 2295) and suggests the possibility of reintegration for Gawain: "So, now þou hatz þi hart holle hitte me bihous" (line 2296).

But Gawain's belated recognition of his divided self (and of his role in its creation) leads to a rejection of such heraldic healing. Even worse, if Gawain risked self-destruction in Hautdesert, he symbolically achieves it here in his rejection of the pentangle and his adoption of the girdle as the new "syngne of my surfet" (line 2433). As he says, "quen pryde schal me pryk for prowes of armes, / Þe loke to þis luf-lace schal leþe my hert" (lines 2437–38).[96] The physical erasure of the pentangle by the girdle (which was a temporary, life-saving strategy in lines 2035–36) is now made permanent and transformed into a *memento mori*: "And þe blykkande belt he bere þeraboute, / Abelef, as a baud-eryk, bounden bi his syde, / Loken vnder his lyfte arme, þe lace, with a knot, / In tokenyng he watz tane in tech of a faute" (lines 2485–88). This passage is full of the lexicon which formerly characterized the pentangle (e.g., *bauderyk* and *tokenyng*); in fact, neither Gawain's shield nor the pentangle is mentioned again in the poem. By changing his arms, Gawain changes himself—if we consider this substitution in chi-valric terms, we will recognize that it is in fact more than a *memento mori*. It is heraldic death.

From one angle, Gawain's decision to alter his device at the poem's end differs substantially from Grosvenor's rejection of the court's *bor-dure* compromise and his subsequent adoption of Earl Ranulf's arms. In appropriating the earl's *garb or*, Grosvenor deliberately (and defi-antly) augments his chivalric identity. Gawain, on the other hand, ini-tially seems to treat the green girdle (the *bend vert*) as an anti-chivalric symbol:

> Bot in syngne of my surfet I schal se hit ofte,
> When I ride in renoun remorde to myseluen
> Þe faut and þe fayntyse of þe flesche crabbed,
> How tender hit is to entyse teches of fylþe.
> And þus, quen pryde schal me pryk for prowes of armes,
> Þe loke to þis luf-lace schal leþe my hert.
>
> (lines 2433–38)

Echoing many *SGGK* scholars, John Burrow has read the girdle as "part of the traditional iconography of penance."[97] In such a view, Gawain's modification of his arms represents a dismissal of aristocratic selfhood and a concomitant move toward a chastened spiritual identity—a dy-namic absent from the conclusion of the Scrope-Grosvenor controversy.

From another angle, however, Gawain's change is entirely intelli-gible in chivalric terms. As David Aers notes of lines 2434 and 2437, "even in his sharpest rhetorical self-flagellation, Gawain sees himself still very much part of the heroic, competitive community . . . The pursuit of prowess and honour, decisive markers of the lay élite, will continue to constitute his life."[98] In both cases, Grosvenor's and Gawain's, a knight rejects a compromise (and compromised) identity offered to him by a higher-ranking aristocrat. The alternate identities the two knights select are not idiosyncratically individual: Grosvenor draws his new device from an established comital tradition, and Gawain makes use of the language of penance to alter his surcoat's signification. But both men opt for difference, for signs that set them apart from their chivalric competitors.[99]

Gawain's choice thus has profound social implications, repercussions that suggest the limits of Turville-Petre's "cultural cohesion" model. Turville-Petre writes that Hautdesert "is provincial only in its geographical location" and "a second Camelot."[100] He sees the *Gawain*-poet's project as one intended "to emphasize the unity of a society in which northerners and southerners are at one in their cultural aspirations, not in order to claim a distinctive place for the region in the nation."[101] Such a reading seems possible to Turville-Petre only because his analysis concentrates on the rituals of hospitality, the "frenkysch fare" that characterizes Gawain's stay at Hautdesert. Seen in such lights, the joy of the provincial court at Gawain's arrival and their pleasant pastimes are indeed highly cohesive elements in a poem obsessed with tying things together.

But knots can be undone, and so can the national unity occasioned by the encounter of two regional cultures. Gawain's less-than-amicable departure from the Green Chapel does not figure into Turville-Petre's argument—an omission that conveniently supports the idea of cohesion. What this leave-taking scene gives us is a national culture that fails to cohere, a hospitality that does not take. Spearing's account of Bertilak's two offers and Gawain's two refusals is my guide here:

> He is absurd too in his petulant rejection of the Green Knight's attempts to comfort him and to achieve a reconciliation. He twice refuses the Green Knight's invitation to return to his castle and be reconciled with the two ladies, and his refusal

may plausibly be seen to stem from his inability to achieve an *internal* reconciliation between his aspirations and his conduct.[102]

Gawain cannot reach an accord with himself, and so Bertilak's promise "With my wyf, I wene, / We schal yow wel *acorde*, / Þat watz your enmy kene" (lines 2404–6, my italics) is met with his notorious misogynist diatribe (lines 2414–28). Gawain attempts to soften his rejection with his usual courtesy ("I haf sojorned sadly—sele yow bytyde, / And He ȝelde hit yow ȝare þat ȝarkkez al menskes!" line 2409), but it is a rejection nonetheless.

Indeed, when Bertilak offers hospitality a second time (as Spearing indicates), Gawain's response is curt rather than courteous:

"Þerfore I eþe þe, haþel, to com to þyn aunt.
Make myry in my hous: my meny þe louies
And I wol þe as wel, wyȝe, bi my faythe,
As any gome vnder God, for þy grete trauþe."
And he nikked hym 'Naye!'—he nolde bi no wayes.
(lines 2467–71)

Here Gawain mimics the close-mouthed answers he got from the men of the Wirral during his search for the Green Chapel ("al nykked hym with 'Nay!'"). It is as if he turns the speech of the region against itself. The two men do embrace and kiss ("acolen and kyssen and kennen ayþer oþer / To þe Prynce of paradise," lines 2472–73) as they take their leave of one another, yet their actions feel perfunctory and in keeping with social form rather than with anything approaching personal warmth. As the poet says, they "parten ryȝt þere / On coolde" (lines 2473–74). Again, Andrew and Waldron are rather literal in their gloss, identifying *coolde* here as "(snowy) ground."[103] The cold surrounding Gawain and Bertilak is not only physical, but personal and emotional as well: earlier in the poem, we have been told that Gawain's departure from Hautdesert is met with "ful colde sykyngez" (line 1982).

Their final encounter is a cancellation of any cohesion they (and their regions) may have managed to achieve. A few stanzas earlier, something like actual regional knowledge had been exchanged. In response to Gawain's request that he reveal his true identity as "lorde of þe ȝonder londe þat I haf lent inne / Wyth yow in worschyp" (lines 2440–41), the Green Knight had complied: "Bertilak de Hautdesert I hat in þis londe" (line 2445). Topography and honor combine here; instead of a parodic riff on Trojan national ambition (the Green Knight and his Green Chapel), Bertilak offers up his locally grounded self (the prepositional phrase "in þis londe" connects name and territory). But the hope of communication and exchange is dashed by the poet's description of their parting: "Gawayn on blonk ful bene / To þe kynges burȝ buskez bolde, / And þe knyȝt in þe enker grene / Whiderwarde-soeuer he wolde" (lines 2475–78). Writing about the essential ambiguity of the Green Knight, Spearing notes of this scene that the poet denies us resolution, that "the mystery remains unsolved."[104] My regional reading of *SGGK* builds upon this observation: we do not end the poem with Bertilak de Hautdesert, the friendly, regional lord, but with the unlocatable Green Knight. The phrase "enker grene" takes us back to the beginning of the poem, back to the mystery knight's alien challenge to the court and to his imputation of a division between the Round Table's reputation and its reality: "He ferde as freke were fade, / And oueral enker grene" (line 150). The possibility of interregional cohesion is gone, lost in the spatial indeterminacies of "Whiderwarde-soeuer he wolde." Once again, Logres is divided into the familiar center of Camelot ("þe kynges burȝ") and the multiple spaces of an unrecognizable, threatening provinciality.[105]

Of course, *SGGK* does continue for two more stanzas. The work accomplished therein is the production (or, to be more precise, the reintegration) of an intraregional affinity. The Round Table's response to Gawain's woeful account of his failure is couched in precisely the language Gawain refuses to extend to his hosts at Hautdesert:

Þe kyng comfortez þe knyȝt, and all þe court als
Laȝen loude þerat and lyflyly *acorden*
Þat lordes and ledis þat longed to þe Table,
Vche burne of þe broþerhede, a bauderyk schulde haue,
A bende abelef hym aboute, of a bryȝt grene,
And þat, for sake of þat segge, in swete to were.
For þat watz *acorded* þe renoun of þe Rounde Table

And he honoured þat hit hade, euermore after,
As hit is breued in þe best boke of romaunce.

(lines 2513–21, my italics)

Acorde with Hautdesert (and with the provinces it represents) is temporary and fleeting in *SGGK*, even if it occupies the bulk of the narrative. Internal, self-confirming *acorde* is the order of the day at Camelot; the provincial sign—the green girdle—is translated into a celebration of the center, a ratification and renewal of their own communal identity.[106] The nation/province split that Turville-Petre considers re-solved is addressed here via the incorporation of the regional into the metropolitan—but unlike Hanna's London, the province gets nothing in return. What *SGGK* reveals in its exploration of regionality is neither cohesion nor full-fledged assimilation (Gawain's insistence on the negative valence of his new arms means that the girdle's meaning remains unsettled), but political struggle, "a kind of authority unknown at Arthur's court: one that is not centered, overarching, and already in place, but multiple, dispersed, and negotiable."[107]

That conflict has its roots in the collision of chivalric selves that is late medieval household culture.[108] Felicity Heal sees the household (represented in the poem by both Camelot and Hautdesert) as a site of competition: "The household provided a theater in which exchanges of power between men of honor could be played out in ritual form . . . the drama of reciprocal relationships between the household and outsiders."[109] Hospitality is thus anything but politically neutral good manners: "Lavish giving between men of honor was thus a powerful form of bonding; it was also a means of competing for status and reputation, a game at which no great lord could afford to lose."[110] This is the *gomen* and the *jest* that Gawain finds himself playing in "þe wyldrenesse of Wyrale," and his shame-filled response to Bertilak's revelations at the Green Chapel are perhaps best understood as his tardy recognition of that political contest, of "the intensifying pressures of gift exchange."[111] Gawain rode forth from Camelot, the representative of his regional culture and the figure of its national ambitions—he expected that his death, however individually unfortunate, would still serve as testimony of his affinity's honor. What he learns instead is that the locals are playing their own games, that accepting gifts involves accepting obligations

he would prefer to avoid—what Christine Chism calls "a mutually implicating transaction with profound stakes for all concerned."[112] Gawain
crosses someone else's heraldic terrain, assuming that he is the invader—
but like Scrope and Grosvenor he comes to understand that the cost of
honor's expansion is the self's own exposure to the invasions of other
honor-seeking selves. In *SGGK*, the national fantasy of "þe endeles knot"
turns out to have been its alienated other, the green girdle, right from
the start. Gawain's entry into regionality is simply the beginning of that
knot's untying and recognition of its own inherent locality.

CHAPTER FIVE

TWO SHIRES AGAINST ALL ENGLAND

Celebrating Regional Affinity in the Stanley Family Romances

THE YEAR 1485 WAS A BANNER ONE FOR HENRY TUDOR, SECOND Earl of Richmond, with his 22 August victory over Richard III at Bosworth Field leading directly to his 30 October coronation as Henry VII. The year was also good to another English aristocrat: Thomas Stanley, the second Lord Stanley. A master of "the tactics of fence-sitting," Stanley earned a share of Henry's triumph without apparently ever striking a blow in anger against Richard.[1] His reward for effectively showing up at the battle's end (or, alternately, for not assisting Richard in any way) was magnate status: Henry created Stanley Earl of Derby on 27 October, three days before the coronation. These two inaugurations fit nicely inside traditional schemes of literary-historical periodization. The Tudors and the Stanleys begin their dynasties even as the English Renaissance begins, new rulers for a new era. Bosworth nominally puts a stop to bastard feudalism and the War of the Roses, while William Caxton's publication of Sir Thomas Malory's *Le Morte Darthur* on

31 July, less than a month before Richard's defeat, signals the rise of print culture, a textual usurpation that matches the political one. The year 1485 is the end of the Middle Ages, the eclipse of the medieval.

Or so the story goes. The new literary histories of David Wallace and James Simpson, discussed in the introduction to this book, argue instead for a rethinking of the transition between the Middle Ages and the Renaissance, a reappraisal in which the Tudor victory at Bosworth is simply an additional (albeit crucial) factor in an ongoing process of cultural transformation. Other scholars demonstrate the post-medieval vitality of supposedly medieval forms: Lawrence M. Clopper's deconstruction of the anomaly of "medieval drama" in the sixteenth century and Jennifer Summit's analysis of gender and Catholic print culture are two examples of this trend.[2] In this chapter, I want to suggest that the family history of the Stanleys counts as yet another complication of traditional periodization—even when that history is encoded in a genre as definitively "medieval" as romance. It makes little sense to say that the Middle Ages came to a close in Cheshire and Lancashire (the heart of the Stanley domain) in 1485 with the emergence of the Tudor dynasty. If anything, the Stanley acquisition of comital rank led to a renewed awareness of regional separation and difference: Thomas's creation as earl gave the two counties their first nonroyal magnate in centuries. The Stanley earls became focal points for regional aspirations (and, to be fair, regional anxieties).

The Stanley challenge to conventional literary history is clearest when seen from the perspective of the *longue durée*. Earl Thomas's great-grandfather, Sir John Stanley of Storeton in Cheshire, first brought prominence to the family as a soldier in the Anglo-French wars of the late 1300s. He established the Stanleys' Lancashire connection in 1385, marrying Isabel of Lathom in spite of opposition from John of Gaunt, fourth son of Edward III and Duke of Lancaster. Sir John possessed "the typically Stanley instinct for choosing the victorious side," receiving the Isle of Man in perpetuity in 1406 for his support of Gaunt's son Henry IV against the Percies.[3] The Isle's "political and legal separation from England" gave the Stanley Lords of Man "all the feudal rights which elsewhere were part of the prerogative of the English crown"— rights similar to those that once gave the Earls of Chester their palatine privilege.[4] Thomas Stanley's 1485 creation as earl, exactly one century after his great-grandfather set the family on the path to preeminence with an aptly chosen marriage, is therefore not an inauguration. It is not even the culmination of one hundred years of "double dealing and unprincipled behavior," the Stanley family trademark.[5] Instead, the earl's creation represents a new stage in an ongoing history, a genealogy that continues well into the eighteenth century and beyond: the last male Stanley in Sir John's direct line, James Stanley, the tenth earl, dies in 1736, and the honor of Derby passes into the hands of a cadet branch of the family—where it remains to the present day. In this timeline, 1485 registers simply as one more confirmation of honor, not as a creation of honor *ex nihilo.*

The Stanley narrative manifests itself in a series of dynastic romances, encomiastic texts that, although they are first written down in the years after Bosworth Field, serve to record long-established family traditions alongside justifications of more recently acquired distinctions. Analyzed in the first two sections of this chapter, these works—the late fifteenth- and early sixteenth-century Bosworth Field poems *Bosworth Field, Lady Bessy,* and *The Rose of England;* the early sixteenth-century Flodden Field poems *Flodden Field* and *Scottish Field;* and a mid-sixteenth-century history of the family entitled *The Stanley Poem*—collectively manage the reputation of the Stanleys and their regional clients, emphasizing triumphs and assuaging disasters. Copied separately at first, and subsequently transmitted throughout the Derby household and the family's regional affinity during the sixteenth and early seventeenth centuries, the Stanley romances are eventually presented *en masse* in the 1640s as a part of the massive Percy Folio (British Library MS Additional 27879).[6] As the third and final section of the chapter shows, the 1640s were also an unsettling decade for the Stanleys, one in which their vaunted instinct for victory appeared to have deserted them. Including the Stanley poems in the Percy Folio becomes one strategy for coping with the contemporary crisis. Another is the attempt, in private journals and public newsbooks, to generate a new Stanley romance out of the raw material of Countess Charlotte Stanley's 1644 defense of Lathom House against the Parliamentarians. Here romance develops in real time, subject to the aesthetic prejudices of the competing sides in the first Civil War.

Writing about the Stanley romances in 1978, David Lawton opined that "the only value of these works is as sociological documents testifying to the Stanley hegemony in the area and the intricate inter-connections of a gentry community around them."[7] To some extent, this chapter is a confirmation of Lawton's point. The Stanley *encomia* do serve as expressions of regional identity, and their primary audience was a local one. The poems put this community on display, equating the grand, multi-regional (and, in some cases, transnational) deeds of the Stanleys with the local achievements of their Cheshire and Lancashire clients. However, as the work of Michael Bennett, John Bowers, Ralph Hanna, and others over the last three decades demonstrates, northwestern texts were not limited to northwestern audiences: Cheshire and Lancashire works went south and east while southern works came north and west. Regional writing becomes national writing insofar as its authors and audiences simultaneously view themselves as members of local and national communities. This sense of multiple, shared identities lets us move beyond an excessively rigid opposition between "nation" and "region." The Stanley family romances testify to more than the mere fact of the Stanley hegemony: they serve as records of individual negotiations between overlapping spatial identities (Cestrian, Lancastrian, northern, western, English, Scottish, etc.). That makes them quite valuable indeed.

FOND FRAY: REGIONAL HONOR AND ROYAL AMBITION IN STANLEYITE ACCOUNTS OF BOSWORTH FIELD

The narrative of Stanley glory begins sometime between 1485 and 1495 with the writing of *The Rose of England*, the shortest of the Stanley poems at 128 lines.[8] Found only in the Percy Folio, the text is a generic mishmash, combining ballad elements (32 *abab* stanzas) with those of allegory (and just a hint of beast fable). The allegory takes its cues from the heraldry of the English aristocracy: in *The Rose of England*, each magnate becomes the animal depicted on his device. The Stanleys are therefore eagles (Thomas Lord Stanley and George Lord Strange) and harts (Sir William Stanley); John de Vere, thirteenth Earl of Oxford, a "blew bore" (line 31); Sir Gilbert Talbot, a hound (the traditional device of the Earls of Shrewsbury); and Sir John Savage of Rock Savage, Cheshire, a "vnicorne" (line 112).[9] King Richard is of course the "bore soe white" (line 32). Henry Tudor is the exception to this practice: the poem presents him not as the Welsh dragon (a connection made in line 25 of *Scottish Field*) but as the Lancastrian "rose so redd" (line 70).[10] All of these plants and animals dwell in an England that is also "a garden greene & gay" (line 1) containing a rosebush "of a mickle price" (line 6), the Yorkist line.[11] Richard's white boar tears up the garden with its tusks, burying the branches of the rose bush "vnder a clodd of clay" (line 19)—possibly a reference to the disappearance of the princes— and seizing the crown for itself. The remainder of the poem focuses on the restoration of the garden (and thus of the nation).

That replanting is made possible by the intervention of the Stanleys, a poetic decision that situates *The Rose of England* well within the bounds of Stanley *encomia*. When the white boar uproots the rose bush, "there came in an Egle gleaming gay, / of all ffaire birds well worth the best; / he took the branche of the rose away, / & bore itt to Latham to his nest" (lines 21–24). That is to say, only the early (and utterly fictional) assistance of Thomas Lord Stanley enables Henry to escape Richard's purge. Moreover, Henry himself plays no part in the action at Bosworth Field. Richard is instead defeated almost exclusively by the Stanleys and their Cheshire and Lancashire retainers:

> then the Egle ffollowed fast vpon his pray;
> with sore dints he did them smyte.
> the Talbott he bitt wonderous sore,
> so well the vnicorne did him quite.
>
> & then came in the harts head;
> a worthy sight itt was to see,
> they Iacketts that were of white & redd,
> how they Laid about them lustilye.
>
> (lines 109–16)

The Earl of Oxford gets a stanza-long nod in the lead-up to the battle (lines 105–8), and Gilbert Talbot gets line 111, but they are the only non-Stanleys to achieve anything of value at Bosworth—another of the poet's pro-Stanley fictions.[12] Indeed, the two lines reporting Richard's death (lines 117–18) and thus the liberation of England from tyranny are balanced by a second pair of lines rejoicing in Lord Strange's escape from almost certain execution at the tyrant's hands: "& the young Egle is preserued, / & come to his nest againe" (lines 119–20). The preservation of Stanley patrimony (George Stanley was father to Thomas, the second Earl of Derby) counts for as much as the preservation of the English polity.

However, the poem more than earns its Tudor stripes, compensating for Henry's absence from the battlefield by stressing his importance elsewhere. We see such pro-Tudor praise in the customary closing prayer on the monarch's behalf: "our King, he is the rose soe redd, / that now does fflourish ffresh and gay. / Confound his ffoes, Lord, wee beseeche, / & loue his grace both night & day" (lines 125–28). We also see it in a nine-stanza episode (lines 57–92) devoted to Henry's encounter with Master Mitton, the defiant "baylye" of Shrewsbury (line 57). Mitton refuses to let Tudor forces into the city until "lettres came from Sir William Stanley of the holt castle" (line 67) authorizing him to do so. The Earl of Oxford wants to behead Mitton for his defiance and loyalty to Richard, but Henry prevents de Vere from doing so: "if wee begin to head so soone, / in England wee shall beare no degree" (lines 75–76). Commending Mitton for his "Loyall service" (line 87), Henry pardons him and moves on to Atherstone and his meeting with the Stanley affinity. Although this nonallegorical episode is stylistically at odds with the rest of the text, it does testify to Henry's worthiness to rule: unlike Richard, whose decision to take Lord Strange hostage reveals his "ffalse craft & trecherye" (line 104), Henry magnanimously spares Mitton.

Of all the Stanley poems, then, *The Rose of England* is the one that most clearly supports the Tudors. Richard is nothing more than a dirty, grubbing "beast" (line 13), and the Stanleys share their spotlight (and line count) with Henry. The poem ends with a vision of the English garden, restored to its former glory: "but now this garden fflourishes ffreshly & gay; / with ffragrant fflowers comely of hew; / & gardners itt doth maintaine; / I hope they will proue Iust & true" (lines 121–24). The Stanleyite narrator's conditional "hope" that the realm's "gardners . . . proue Iust & true" does qualify the Tudor victory, an anxiety that history soon came to justify: Sir William Stanley's 1495 beheading for supposedly and treasonably speaking up in favor of the pretender Perkin Warbeck adds an ironic edge to subsequent readings of Henry's decision to spare Mitton from a similar fate. But such cynicism is still only a possibility at the moment of the text's initial composition in the decade immediately following 1485. *The Rose of England* is an aggressively pro-Tudor poem, one that ultimately subordinates local celebration to national ends.

Bosworth Field tells a different story. Written at the same time as *The Rose of England* and extant in two manuscripts (the Percy Folio and Bodleian Library MS Tanner 306), this 656 line ballad is much more emphatically pro-Stanley than *The Rose of England*.[13] For example, we overhear Henry at Milford Haven telling his followers that stepfather Thomas Stanley's support guarantees victory over Richard: "had I the Loue of that Lord in rich array / that hath proued his manhood soe well att need, / & his brother, Sir William, the good Stanley;— / a better Knight neuer vmstrode steede!" (lines 65–68). Shortly thereafter, the narrator refers to Lord Stanley as "fflower of fflowers" (line 82)— so much for Henry's "rose so redd." Even the ballad's closing prayer reflects the poem's heightened attention to Stanley valor:

> now this doubtfull day is brought to an end,
> Iesu now on their soules haue mercye!
> & he [that] dyed this world to amend,
> saue stanleys blood, where-soeuer they bee,
>
> to remaine as Lords with royaltye
> when truth & conscyence shall spread & spring,
> & that they bee of councell nye
> to Iames of England that is our King!
> (lines 649–56)

We still find a king in this prayer, but he is no longer its subject.[14] Instead, he is an afterthought: pride of position belongs instead to the Stanleys and their kinfolk.

Bosworth Field also increases Stanley honor by adjusting the narrative roles played by Henry and Richard. Although the poem begins like a royal entry (stanzas 2, 4, and 6 each end with the refrain, "& say, 'welcome Henery, right-wise King!'"), it soon shifts much of its focus away from the Tudors. Henry's wish for Stanley assistance leads to a scene in which Sir William Stanley gives Henry a pep talk before the battle: "be Eger to ffight, & lothe to fflee! / let manhood be bredd thy brest within! / & remember another day who doth ffor thee, / of all England when thou art Kinge" (lines 381–84). Like *The Rose of England*, *Bosworth Field* predates Sir William's execution; these lines therefore lack the satirical bite that will eventually come from Henry's failure to remember "who doth ffor thee." But they do undercut Henry's masculinity and hence his authority. Something similar happens during the battle proper. Billed as an encounter "betweene King and King" (line 448), it instead turns out to be a clash between magnate and monarch, one in which Henry must ask his stepfather for the privilege of leading the vanguard against Richard: "King HENERY desired the vaward right / of the Lord stanley that was both wise & wittye; / & hee hath granted him in sight" (lines 449–51).[15] Scenes such as these insist that Henry's victory (and thus his crown) owe more to his allies than to his own efforts. Indeed, at the end of the poem, in a scene central to Stanley family legend, Lord Stanley is the first to get hold of Richard's crown: "the crowne of gold that was bright, / to the Lord stanley deliuered itt bee" (lines 635–36). He then crowns Henry, stating "methinke ye are best worthye / to weare the crowne and be our King" (lines 639–40). Stanley's *methinke* undercuts Henry's triumph: the Tudors sit on the throne of England because a Stanley deems them worthy of occupying it.

The poem subverts Tudor power in yet another way: it augments and complicates Richard's portrayal. As Helen Cooper notes, the Percy Folio Stanley poems demonstrate a "marked resistance to the Tudor demonization of Richard III."[16] *Bosworth Field* in particular is "remarkably even-handed."[17] King Richard is certainly not all sweetness and light in the poem: we still get a scene in which he responds to Stanley defiance by vowing that, "ffrom the towne of Lancaster to Shrewsburye, / Knyght nor squier Ile leaue none aliue" (lines 203–4). But Richard's seemingly genocidal hostility to the Stanleys is less an innate tyranny than it is the result of evil counsel: "wicked councell drew Richard neere, / of them that had the prince in their guiding; / ffor wicked councell doth mickle deere, / that bringeth downe both Emperour & King" (lines 77–80). Jealous of the Stanleys' power ("they may show vpon a day a band / such as may noe Lorde in Christentye," lines 99–100), Richard's counselors work upon the king until he agrees to their plan to hobble Stanley's might by holding Lords Stanley and Strange hostage. Thomas Stanley escapes this fate by falling sick at Manchester en route to Richard's court ("as the will of god is," line 116), but George Stanley finds himself "to ward comanded" (line 138). The text makes it clear that this act of "trecherye" (line 156) is solely responsible for turning Lord Thomas ("hee wold mee & mine into bondage bringe; / therefore cleane against him will I bee," lines 158–59) and his brother Sir William ("he keepeth there my nephew, my brothers heyre . . . that, Richard shall repent full sore," lines 169, 171) against their liege. Henry's personal qualities therefore have nothing to do with the Stanleys' shift in allegiance: in *Bosworth Field*, he is more or less a convenient means to the end of Stanley vengeance upon Richard.

The now (post-Shakespeare) notorious horse scene operates in accordance with a similar dynamic. Frightened by the onslaught of Sir William's forces ("against them no man may dree," line 588), one of Richard's knights presents the king with a horse and urges him to ride away and return "another day" (line 590). But *Bosworth Field*'s Richard is no coward:

> he said, "giue me my battell axe in my hand,
> sett the crowne of England on my head soe hye!
> ffor by him that shope both sea and Land,
> King of England this day I will dye!

> "one ffoote will I neuer fflee
> whilest the breath is my brest within!"
> as he said, so did it bee
>
> (lines 593–99)

His defiant last stand outdoes Henry's performance in battle, contained in its entirety in the statement that "King Henry ffought soe mannfullye" (line 547). The forces of the two men are more evenly matched: the poet's eulogy (lines 625–30) for Richard's standard bearer, Sir Percival Thirwall, is the same length as that (lines 619–24) provided for Henry's standard bearer, Sir William Brandon. In a sense, then, *Bosworth Field* depicts both armies—and thus both men leading them—as effectively identical. If anything does serve to distinguish the two claimants to the throne, it is Richard's ill-advised (in every sense of the term) decision to forego the Stanley assistance that Henry so eagerly accepts. Stanley "councell" (line 655) is the deciding factor in England's destiny.

Bosworth Field reduces Henry's role, equating him with Richard. The early sixteenth-century ballad *Lady Bessy* goes one step further, almost completely eliding Henry from the Bosworth story.[18] In the Percy Folio version of the poem (a second, earlier copy, dated ca. 1600, is extant as British Library MS Harley 367), the Earl of Richmond's first appearance comes in line 701, approximately two-thirds of the way through the poem. Moreover, his visage at that moment is anything but heroic: the porter who admits messenger Humphrey Brereton to Henry's presence points out the earl's "priuye wart, withouten lett, / a litle aboue the chin; / his face is white, the wart is red, / thereby you may him ken" (lines 693–96). There may even be a mischievous allusion to the Tudor rose in the porter's observation that Henry's "face is white, the wart is red." A wholly unprepossessing man, Henry remains a marginal figure for the rest of the poem. After line 788 (the end of his second speech), he speaks only three more times: once to greet Sir William Stanley (lines 901–2), once to bid him farewell (line 914), and once to ask Thomas Stanley for the privilege of leading the vanguard (lines 943–46).

The true catalyst for the action of *Lady Bessy* is its eponymous heroine, Elizabeth of York. The poet spends more time in her "Bower" (line 139) than he does on the battlefield—the actual fighting occupies only 43 lines (four percent of the entire poem).[19] Elizabeth, not Henry, is the mastermind who defeats the tyrannical Richard. When we first see Henry in the poem, "he shooteth at the butts, / & with him are Lords three" (lines 687–88). This sort of shiftless leisure is not for Elizabeth: her opening speech to Thomas Stanley contains a detailed accounting (lines 65–88) of the men and money that the Stanley affinity can muster in support of Richmond. Commenting on the poem's change of emphasis, Helen Cooper notes that the ballad is "very much a fanciful, romance version of history . . . in which Elizabeth herself is cast as the dispossessed heiress, Henry Tudor merely as her knight in shining armour"—exactly the opposite of other Tudor *encomia* that present Henry as the exiled hero of romance come to regain his birthright.[20] Henry will make such a claim in *Lady Bessy*: when he asks to lead the vanguard, he states that "I come for my right" (line 945). But his decla-

ration has already been preempted, first by Elizabeth's masculine desire to be "wroken" (line 26) on Richard for the murder of her brothers
the princes and then by her "prophesye" (line 18) that the Stanleys
"might make me a Queene . . . for Richard is no righteous Kinge, / nor
vpon no woman borne was hee" (lines 54, 56–57). According to Cooper,
such inversions of romance's usual narrative (and gender) patterns provide more evidence for Yorkist bias in the Stanley *encomia*: focusing on
Elizabeth of York demonstrates "that the Tudor claim to the throne
resided principally in Henry's marriage to the dispossessed heiress."[21]
Whatever its source, the poem's focus on Elizabeth marginalizes Henry
at the moment of his triumph.

Sharing pride of place with Elizabeth are the Stanleys. At the start
of the ballad, the poet reveals that "the Stanleys without doubt / were
dread ouer England ffarr & neere" (lines 9–10), second in authority
only to King Richard. *Lady Bessy*'s Stanleyite bias subsequently leads it
to commit anachronism: Thomas Stanley is introduced as "Erle of Darbye" (line 20) before he takes any of the actions that earn him the title
upon Henry's victory.[22] Henry himself acknowledges Stanley power,
telling the King of France that "the Stanleys stout ffor me haue sent,
King of England ffor to make mee" (lines 753–54). The Stanley role in
making Henry king is confirmed at the end of the poem when Elizabeth and Henry are crowned in Leicester: "the Erle of Darbye he was
there, / & Sir william Stanley a man of might; / vpon their heads they
sett the crowne / in presence of many a worthy wight" (lines 1071–74).
Elizabeth's narrative agency occasionally overwhelms the otherwise
"stout" Stanleys, leading the earl's nephew (and Cheshire client) Sir
John Savage to exclaim that "womens witt is wonder to heare! / my
vnckle is turned by your Bessye!" (lines 413–14). But the poem makes
it equally clear that Elizabeth relies on the patriarchal authority of
"ffather stanley" (line 25) to achieve her political goals.

Lady Bessy's generous praise of the Stanleys is accompanied by an
equal investment in the members of their regional affinity. Here the
focus of attention is Elizabeth's trusted messenger, the Cheshire squire
Humphrey Brereton. A member of the Brereton family of Malpas (a
cadet branch of the baronial Brereton family), Humphrey carries the
Earl's messages first to his allies in the regionally marked "north cuntrye"
(line 234) and "west Cuntrye" (line 508) and then to the exiled Henry

across the Channel. Humphrey is thus the character responsible for most of the poem's narrative motion (his journeys back and forth occupy lines 249–798, half of the ballad's length). Although John W. Hales and Frederick J. Furnivall, the nineteenth-century editors of the Percy Folio, confidently state that *Lady Bessy*'s "writer was Humphrey Brereton," modern critics opt instead for "some member of the family or, perhaps more likely, the household of the Breretons."[23] Brereton's costarring role transforms *Lady Bessy*, turning the dynastic romance of the Stanleys into a text with greater social scope: in this poem, Brereton *encomium* piggybacks on Stanley *encomium*. A tearful Derby confirms Brereton's importance, insisting that "my loue, my trust, my liffe, my Land, / all this, Humphrey, doth Lye in thee! / thou may make, & thou may marr, / thou may vndoe BESSYE & me!" (lines 281–84). More subtle (but equally effective) are Humphrey's words to Henry upon his arrival at Bigeram Abbey: "I am come ffrom the stanleys bold, / King of England to make thee" (lines 717–18). His boast is not empty: the fate of England lies in the hands of a humble Cheshire squire, to "make" or "marr" as he sees fit.

Brereton's importance has been noted by critics like Cooper and Lawton. However, the poem's social register extends even further, reaching down into the ranks of the commons. *Lady Bessy* establishes a complicated network of social allegiances and obligations, one in which royal Elizabeth depends on magnate Stanley—who in turn depends on gentleman Brereton. But there is a fourth participant in this chain: the anonymous porter who lets Humphrey Brereton into Bigeram Abbey to speak with Henry. Unlike Brereton, who routinely accepts cash rewards for his messenger services, the porter generously turns down Brereton's offer of "ready gold to thy meede" (line 670), insisting that "I will none of thy gold . . . nor yett . . . none of thy ffee" (lines 671–72).[24] His altruism derives from his own position within the ballad's system of concentric affinities: he is not only "an Englishman" (line 662), but also "a Cheshire man borne . . . ffrom the Malpas but miles three" (lines 675–76). Sent to the "strange countrye" (line 682) of faraway France, Humphrey Brereton suddenly finds himself back home in rural Malpas, welcomed by one of his tenants (as line 672 reveals, the porter knows Brereton by his Christian name). A local connection (the porter's acquaintance with Humphrey) makes a national polity (Tudor England) possible. Henry's victory at Bosworth hinges on the compassion of an unknown and ignoble "Cheshire man." *Lady Bessy* therefore provides a picture of a nation integrated at all levels, from the "comelye Kinge" (line 3) at the top to the "pore cominaltye" (line 4) at the bottom.[25]

That national community is nonetheless regionally inflected, something that becomes clear in *The Stanley Poem*.[26] Also known as *A Historical Poem Touching the Family of Stanley*, this ca. 1560–72 text appears in three manuscripts—Bodleian Library MS Rawlinson Poet.143.II, British Library MS Harley 541, and British Library MS Additional 5830—and one print witness: the 1741 *Memoirs* of John Seacome, a Stanley household retainer.[27] The first two fitts of the poem (nearly 300 lines, or one quarter of the total text) are devoted to the extraordinary exploits of Sir John Stanley, the second son of the Cheshire Stanleys who married his way into the Lathom inheritance in Lancashire. Sir John's adventures are just that, instances of romance *aventure* that have him impregnating "the Turkes daughter" (p. 212) and humiliating "the chiefest of all Fraunce" (p. 210) in the lists. These fantastic deeds are then repeated by his descendants in the third fitt. For example, like his great-grandfather, Thomas Stanley also defeats a foe from "over sea" in chivalric combat, "a man of arms called most dangerous" (p. 229). This mercenary comes to England at the bidding of the Duke of Somerset, Thomas's "mischeevous" father-in-law (p. 228)—paternal opposition similar to that posed earlier in the text by Oskell of Lathom, Sir John's mythical father-in-law.[28] Completing the sequence of foreign challenges is the victory of Sir Edward Stanley, first Lord Monteagle and second son of Earl Thomas, over the "fine musitions" of the "king of Castyle" (p. 252). In a performance rivaling that of "Tristram" (p. 253), Edward reveals that "He had more quallities like a gentleman / Then in all his time had any other mann" (p. 254). Stressing courtesy over chivalry, this incident nonetheless places Edward firmly within the heroic genealogy established by his great-great-grandfather.

But cross-Channel antics like these are outnumbered in *The Stanley Poem* by locally focused incidents. Lancashire sites feature prominently in the poem, particularly in the last hundred or so lines of the text. There the poet gives us an account of all the "edyfices" (p. 265) Thomas Stanley had built in his years as earl, going so far as to provide us with the name of "on Robert Rochdale," the earl's "free-mason" (p. 267). Pride of place is reserved for "fayre Lathum," the Stanley seat:

Such a howse of that age cannot be fownde,
I meane not for the beauty therofe only,
But each office sitte so necessary,
Both fayre and large, and in place so apte and meete,
With each on a fayre well with water full sweete,
Save only the pantry, which therof had no neade,
Butler, seller, kitchin be noble in deade.
King Henry the Seaventh, who did lye their eight dayes,
And of all houses he gave it the most praise,
And his haule at Richmond he pulld downe all,
To make it up againe after Latham hall

(p. 266)

As Henry's presence at Lathom demonstrates, the Tudor story is indeed present in *The Stanley Poem*—but it is no longer the poem's point. *The Rose of England, Bosworth Field,* and *Lady Bessy* all end with Richard's defeat at Bosworth and Henry's coronation. The Stanleys are instrumental in bringing about both of these outcomes, but the Percy Folio poems still ultimately subordinate local stories to national ones, even if that subordination almost resembles conflation at times. In *The Stanley Poem*, the local dominates: the King of England demolishes his palace for the sole purpose of rebuilding it in accordance with the hall of a provincial magnate.

The overall structure of the poem mirrors this regional orientation, beginning with the prosaic matter of how the Stanleys took their name from the Staffordshire manor held by their Audley ancestors and ending with a series of micronarratives about the Earl of Derby's regional stewardship. One of these short sequences deals with the time "when Henry the Seavanth first exaccion did move / Lancashire and Chessyre first fifteene to pay" (p. 269).[29] The locals refuse to pay, and only the intervention of the earl can save them from "the kinges greevaunce" and "some fond commotion" (p. 270). In an action described as "the chiefest thing that gate the people's love," Derby "went to the exchecker and laide down the mony" himself (p. 269). A second micronarrative points out that "For all controversies he found provision" (p. 270). As a result, "fewe for suytes travayled to London," saving "the countrey travayle and much money" (p. 270). Here the region maintains its autonomy, taking care of its own business without any need for arbitration from the center. The poem's most powerful testimony to the strength of the Stanleys' Lancashire and Cheshire affinity (what Andrew Taylor calls "the continued union of neighbourly love and Stanley property") comes in an anecdote dated to "When Lathum manor was made not after longe." (p. 269).[30] In this story, a local gentleman compliments the earl on the hall's imposing fortifications: "My lord, this howse is stronge, / And enemies came neare, they would fall on quaking" (p. 269). The earl gently corrects the gentleman, insisting "I have a stronger wall a making, / that is my neighbours to get theyre god willes all, / To love me truelly, that is a stronger wall!"

Although the poet is willing to admit that some of the earl's neighbors opt out of this "human shield," he nonetheless stresses the price they pay for doing so: "who loved him not gate but losse or shame" (p. 269). This context of regional honor competition has national implications, transforming Bosworth Field, birthplace of the Tudor dynasty, into nothing more than a local dispute writ large. The poet tells us that the Earl of Derby (once again, anachronistically created as such prior to Bosworth) would have led a "quiet life" but for one thing:

> . . . King Edward had a busy brother,
> That was called Richard Duke of Glocester,
> For a fond fray had benne amongeste their tenantes,
> The melancholicke duke tooke to much grievaunce,
> And sware by cockes bludd, quod he, shortly I shall
> Kill the Earle of Darby and burne Lathum Hall.
>
> (p. 233)

The earl responds to Richard's threat, first with a jest ("I will rather meete him in field face to face; / I payed workmen much money for heyre, / I wold be sory to see my house on fyre," pp. 233–34) and then with a show of strength, riding forth to meet Richard's army at Ribble Bridge. No battle takes place, however, because Richard and his men run away "dickduckfarte for feare" (p. 234). The "frindly neighbour warre" (p. 236) between the two magnates continues when Richard recruits Derby and his retainers for an assault on the Scottish city of Berwick. Once again, Richard's "pupose peevishe" (p. 237) makes itself known: as soon as the earl is in position outside the city walls, Richard and his forces decamp, either out of "feare" or "sum mischievous intent" (p. 239), leaving the men of Lancashire and Cheshire alone and outnumbered. But the Earl of Derby turns seeming disaster into glorious success, capturing Berwick and claiming it for England. All Richard gains from the incident is "shame" (p. 239).

The Berwick episode leads directly to an account of Richard's usurpation of his nephew's throne and his oppression of the Stanleys, using proximity to suggest that the events of 1483–1485 are simply the latest stages in Richard's ongoing feud with the earl, a vendetta that Thomas Stanley never actively pursues but always manages to win: "that which he [Richard] wrought to be his confusion / Redounded to the earles honor in conclusion" (p. 247). In *The Stanley Poem*, English history becomes little more than an unintentional side effect of Stanley history, a "fond fray" gone wrong. The fighting at Bosworth Field never even appears in the text: alive and threatening to execute Lord Strange at one moment, Richard is suddenly dead and "naked brought to Leicester" in the next (p. 250). Richmond's triumph is contained within the space of a single line ("At Bosworth did Harry Richards life deprive")—and even then its primary purpose is to save George Stanley: "And lefte the Lord Straunge, thankes be to God, on live" (p. 250). In a sense, *The Stanley Poem* represents the logical conclusion of Stanley *encomium*'s localizing trend, reducing the Tudor myth to a passing afterthought. Bosworth Field is redundant, an origin easily dismissed as nothing more than just another incident in the ongoing narrative of Stanley power.

FLED AND GONE: FLODDEN FIELD AND REGIONAL ANXIETY IN ANGLO-SCOTTISH CONFLICT

There is one battle that the Stanley propagandists cannot ignore: the struggle between the English and the Scots at Flodden Field on 9 September 1513. Celebrated in contemporary chronicles and verse, Flodden Field saw an English army under the command of Thomas Howard, Earl of Surrey, defeat an invading Scots army under the command of King James IV.[31] Since the battle took place near the Northumberland village of Branxton, it was originally referred to as the Battle of Branxton. But King James and his army had left their camp on nearby Flodden Edge to fight the English, and this tactical decision led to the battle's alternate name, the one by which it is known today. Flodden Field was a disaster for the Scots: hoping to wreak havoc in England while Henry VIII was off fighting in France, they ended up losing thousands of men. Among the slain was King James himself.

Far more relevant to Stanley concerns than the Scottish defeat is an incident that took place relatively early in the battle: led by Alexander Hume, third Lord Hume, the Scots left wing charged the English right wing, a force under the command of Edmund Howard, the Earl of Surrey's second son. The English right wing panicked and fled, leaving Howard and his commanders behind to hold off the advancing Scots. Only the sudden appearance of English reserves under the command of Thomas Dacre, second Lord Dacre, kept the Scots from flanking the English center. This near catastrophe looms large in Stanley tradition because the soldiers who ran away were mostly men from Cheshire and Lancashire, the core Stanley territories. The seeming cowardice of the Stanley retainers in the English right wing threatened to undermine the laurels earned by the family and its affinity elsewhere on the field of battle. For the Stanley encomiasts concerned with Flodden (the authors of *Scottish Field* and *Flodden Field*), this situation was untenable. The behavior of the right wing required an explanation: Stanley honor was at risk.

As a result of the poets' attempts at spin control, texts which ostensibly concentrate on international conflict turn out to be records of intranational conflict and its negotiation. The Stanley poems look to participate in the larger Tudor imperial project (one buoyed by the Scots defeat at Flodden and manifest in Henry's own invasion of France). Their participation takes the form of a cultural script: put simply, imperial glory depends on the support of regional affinities. This script is a variation of the national one at work in the Bosworth Field poems.[32] Just as the Tudor dynasty comes to power on the backs of the Stanleys, their cadet branches, and their client families, so too does the expanding English empire. But the right wing's flight at Flodden destabilizes the imperial script, forcing the Stanley encomiasts to generate an acceptable rationalization (what David Lawton terms "an oblique encomium") for what is otherwise regional cowardice.[33] National celebration and regional chauvinism must wait until the internal honor crisis is resolved.

Written no later than 1515 and extant in three manuscripts (the incomplete Lyme MS in the John Rylands Library; the facsimile of the Lyme MS in Bodleian Library MS Dep. c. 130; and the Percy Folio), *Scottish Field* has a particular interest in explaining away the right wing's behavior, for its author was a Cheshireman and thus a party to the dishonor incurred at Flodden.[34] He reveals his identity at the poem's end:

> he was a gentleman by Iesu that this iest made
> which say but as he sayd forsooth, & noe other.
> att Bagily that bearne his bidding place had,
> & his Ancestors of old time haue yearded their longe
> Before william Conquerour this cuntry did inhabitt.
>
> (lines 416–20)

Baguley Hall lies in northeast Cheshire, just across the Lancashire border from Manchester. In the early sixteenth century, its owners were the Leghs—although their occupancy only dated back to 1353, the year that Sir William Legh took position of the estate from his uncle John Baggiley, not to a time "longe / Before william Conquerour this cuntry did inhabitt."[35] Seeing "little reason to suppose that one of these Leghs was not the author," Ian Baird assigns composition of *Scottish Field* to the family.[36] Baird also notes that the Leghs were connected to the Stanleys by marriage.[37] Cheshire's shame at Flodden thus imperils a multitude of dynastic identities: if the Stanleys fall from honor, so too do the Leghs, taking their pre-Conquest "history" with them.

The *Scottish Field* poet therefore deploys a variety of recuperatory schemes in his text. For example, he begins his account of the events of 1513 with a forty-six-line flashback to Bosworth Field and the advent of the Tudors. In this prelude, the Stanleys and their clients are Richmond's lone supporters:

> there were lite Lords in this land that to that Lord longed,
> but of derby that deare Earle that doughty hath beene euer,
> & the Lord chamberlaine that was his chief brother,

Sauage, his sisters sonne a Sege that was able,
& Gylbert the gentle with a Iollye meanye,
all Lancashire, these ladds the ledden att their will,
& Cheshyre hath them chosen for their cheefe Captain

(lines 9–15)

Like its counterparts in the Bosworth poems, this "royall retinewe" (line 23) enables Richard's defeat. Returning to the thrilling days of yesteryear, the opening of *Scottish Field* functions as ideological inoculation: the poet reminds us of Cheshire's most famous victory in order to establish a narrative counterweight to his upcoming account of Cheshire cowardice. Knowing what Cheshire has done in the past ostensibly minimizes the impact of what it has failed to do in the present. The Bosworth prelude thus serves to preempt criticism.

A similar strategy of anticipation resurfaces in the poet's pre-battle description of the English formations. As the Cheshiremen move into position on the right side of the line (the poet mistakenly places them on Surrey's left), they receive a ready-made excuse for their imminent failure:

the left winge to that ward was Sir Eward Howarde,
he chose to him Cheshire theire chance was the worse;
because they knew not theire Captaine theire care was the more,
for they were wont att all warr to wayte vppon the stanleys;
much worshipp they woone when they that way serued,
but now lanke is their losse our lord itt amend!

(lines 264–69)

The blame for failure does not belong to the Cheshire contingent—if they had been able to pick their commander, a Stanley would have led them into battle. As we saw above, this was precisely the case in 1485: "Cheshyre hath them chosen for their cheefe Captain." But they don't have that choice in 1513: as the syntax of the second *a*-verse reminds us, "he chose to him Cheshire." Edmund Howard is the one who makes the fatal (and foolish) decision to deny the Cheshiremen their traditional leader. In grammatical terms, the Cheshire troops are the obedient objects of an incompetent subject.

A similar elision of agency (and thus of responsibility) takes place when the poem's narrative finally reaches the moment of crisis. Burdened with one unfamiliar superior already, the Cheshiremen suffer a second lapse in command:

> then betid a checke that the shire men fledden;
> in wing with those wayes was with my Lord Dacres,
> he ffledd att the first bredd & they followed after;
> when theire Captain was keered away there comfort was gone,
> they were wont in all warrs to wayt on the Stanlyes,
> they neuer fayled at noe forward that time that they were;
> now lost in their loofe our lord it amende!

> (lines 330–36)

Dacre, the historical savior of the right wing, becomes the scapegoat in *Scottish Field*'s account of the battle. This revisionist moment raises an interesting question: if the poet can rewrite history to make Dacre a coward, if he can go on to state against all other evidence that King James "was downe knocked : & killed in there sight / vnder a banner of a Bishoppe : that was the bold standlye" (lines 386–87), why can't he simply overlook the right wing's flight and concentrate instead on the heroism of Sir Edward Stanley's left wing, "a manfull meany" that "will neuer flee for feare that might happen" (lines 361–62)? It may be the case that the Cheshire collapse is already too well known to be denied or covered up. But a more likely answer to this question lies in the need of this local Cheshire poet to shore up his own sense of lost honor. Outsiders are not the poet's primary audience—he is speaking instead to his fellow Stanley clients. His slippage into first-person plural pronouns in lines 314–16 ("then full boldlye on the broad hills we busked our standards, / & on a faugh vs be-side there we seene our enemyes / were mouing over the mountaines to macth vs they thoughten"), line 325 ("they proched vs with speres"), line 328 ("we blanked them will bills"), and line 377 ("wee mett him [King James] in the Midway & mached him full euen") suggests as much. Self-celebration becomes self-recrimination and self-explanation.

The implicit internality of *Scottish Field* gives way in the ballad *Flodden Field* (produced no later than 1521 and extant in the Percy Folio, British Library MS Harley 293, and British Library MS Harley 367) to

an explicit confrontation with extraregional opprobrium—a spatial orientation confirmed by the anonymous author's decision to set his poem
in the midst of the English camp outside Tournai, France.[38] This foreign
location, far from the battlefield at Branxton, means that reactions—
those of the Stanleys, their allies, and their enemies—count for more
than actions in the poem. The initial honor crisis comes when the
Earl of Surrey's messenger arrives in France and tells Henry VIII that
"Lancashire & Cheshire . . . cleane they be fled and gone; / there was
nere a man that Longd to the Erle of darby / that durst looke his enemyes vpon" (lines 37–40). Henry confirms this report with a perusal of
Surrey's written account of the battle (a letter that is eventually exposed
in line 399 as a "wronge wryting") and then impulsively dismisses Lancashire and Cheshire as false recreants: "neuer a one of them is true
to mee!" (line 52). In responding to the king's outburst, the Cheshire
knights Sir Ralph Egerton and Sir William Brereton both attempt to
use *Scottish Field*'s "wrong commander" defense. According to a dubious
Egerton, "if Lancashire and Cheshire be fled & gone . . . it was for want
of their Captaine" (lines 57, 60). Brereton offers Henry an experiment:
"where-soeuer you come in any feild to fight, / set the Earle of Darby &
vs before, / then shall you see wether wee fight or flee, / trew or false
whether we be borne" (lines 73–76). Neither man gets anywhere with
the king. In fact, when the Warwickshire knight Sir William Compton
stage-whispers in Henry's ear that the two Cheshiremen are "cowards"
(line 78), Egerton throws his glove to the ground and angrily challenges
Compton to a duel "Man to Man" (line 82). Only the Earl of Derby's
timely arrival keeps internecine violence from breaking out.

But the plot doesn't move forward—the narrative opts instead to
compulsively replay the scene. Standing in for Egerton and Brereton,
Derby repeats the "wrong commander" defense ("I was not there to be
there Captaine," line 104) and offers to conquer Scotland and France
with "noe more helpe" (line 112) than that of his own regional affinity.
Even as the situation reiterates, it escalates in intensity: this time it is
not Compton but Henry himself who rejects Lancashire and Cheshire
as "cowards" (line 123). Luckily, the earl's next move breaks the pattern: in his defense of regional honor, he eschews the dangerously
intelligible gesture of the *desfiance*. He instead resorts to implication,
deploying a variant of the Bosworth strategy:

who brought in your father att Milford Hauen?
King Henery the 7th forsooth was hee;

thorow the towne of fortune wee did him bring,
& soe convayd him to Shrewburye,
& soe crowned him a Noble King;
& Richard that day wee deemed to dye.

(lines 127–32)

Derby's use of the first person plural pronoun in this passage is a telling detail: "wee" Stanleys did the deeming at Bosworth, killing Richard and transforming Henry Tudor into Henry VII. The speech is a careful but pointed reminder of the dynastic debt that the Tudors owe the earl and his affinity—and for the moment it works. The king regains his equilibrium: "our prince was greatlye moued at that worde, / & returned him hastily againe" (lines 133–34). In *Scottish Field*, the battle at Bosworth has an apotropaic function, anticipating and warding off the shame of Cheshire flight. The *Flodden Field* poet makes more aggressive use of Bosworth: in his text, the memory of 1485 becomes a weapon to be used against an unruly Tudor monarch. The earl fights shame with shame, exposing Henry's lack of gratitude for Stanley deeds done on his behalf.

Because *Scottish Field* focuses on the battle itself, it can downplay the possibility of intranational strife. The Surreys and Dacre are incompetent, but the presence of the Scots foe preserves the sense of something akin to a unified national community:

this layke lasted on the land the length of 4 houres.
yorkshire like yearne men eagerlye they foughten;
so did darbyshire that day deered many Scotts;
Lancashire like Lyons Laid them about;
All had beene lost, by our Lord had not those leeds beene;
but the race of the Scotts increased full sore

(lines 380–85)

Flodden Field opts instead for a model of internal conflict, one in which king struggles with magnate and affinity with affinity. The Howards are

no longer the wrong men for the job. Now they are actively malevo-
lent: as the kindly Duke of Buckingham reminds Derby, "sith King Richard feele, he [Surrey] neuer loued thee, / for thy vnckle slue his father
deere, / & deerlye deemed him to dye" (lines 141–43).[39] In *Flodden Field*,
international conflict is merely a backdrop for intranational strife. The
text immediately confirms this point, pausing the narrative action so
that the earl can indulge in 23 stanzas of topographically oriented *planc-
tus* (lines 145–238). This lament bids "ffarwell" (line 151) to the Stanley
estates in Lancashire and Cheshire, properties ranging from the "bright
bower" of Lathom (line 209) to the "watter gate" of Chester (line 226).
The loss of Derby honor at Flodden threatens to bring about the literal
loss of the honor of Derby, the spatial heart of the poem.

When the plot resumes in line 239, it continues this subordination of the imperial to the regional. Jamie Garsed, one of Henry's yeomen of the guard, has "sticked 2, & wounded 3" of "his fellowes" (lines
243–44).[40] Jamie's crimes are nominally domestic ones, taking place well
within the boundaries of the king's household. But Jamie is more than
a royal guard: he is also a Stanley ward, "brought vp with the Erle of
Derbye" (line 242). Accused of treason by Henry and threatened with
hanging, he confesses that the motivation for his violence is regional in
nature:

> When I was to my supper sett,
> they called me coward to my face,
> and of their talking they wold not lett,
> & thus with them I vpbrayded was.
>
> thé bade me flee from them apace
> to that coward the Erle of Derbye.
> when I was litle & had small grace,
> he was my helpe & succour trulye.
> (lines 305–12)

The insult Jamie personally receives is less offensive to him than the
one offered to the earl—and thus to all of Lancashire and Cheshire.
This general, regionally directed slander is what provokes his murder-
ous outburst: "'to haue the Erle rebuked thus, / that my bringer-vp

forsooth was hee, / I had rather suffer death,' he said, / 'then be false
to the Erle that was true to me'" (lines 331–34). Here Jamie's allegiance
to the earl—his membership in the Derby affinity—trumps his oath of
allegiance to the king. The current, royal relationship gives way to a
prior, regional connection. The shame generated by Cheshire and Lancashire failure at Flodden extends all the way down the social ladder,
tainting commoners like Jamie with the same dishonor that mars their
aristocratic coregionalists.

Jamie's trial is the third of three confrontations in *Flodden Field*,
revisiting the earl's encounter with Henry just as that meeting replayed
the even earlier altercation between the king and the Cheshire knights.
Like his earl, Jamie also has a story that mollifies Henry—the account
of how he came to join the royal guard:

> then after, vnder Grenwich, vpon a day
> a Scottish Minstrell came to thee,
> & brought a bow of yew to drawe,
> & all the guard might not stirr that tree.
>
> then the bow was giuen to the Erle of Derbye,
> & the Earle deliuered it to mee;
> 7 shoots before your face I shott,
> & att the 8th in sunder it did be;
>
> Then I bad the Scott bow downe his face
> & gather vp the bow, & bring it to his King;
> then it liked your noble grace
> into your guard for me to bring
>
> (lines 317–28)

Jamie's little story lacks the epic importance of the master narrative
of Milford Haven, the Tudor myth that Henry must acknowledge if he
wishes to preserve his authority. But both tales share the same plotline:
the Tudors owe their position of power to a member of the Stanley
affinity. The Scottish minstrel threatens English (and thus royal) manhood with his unbendable bow: for Englishmen ("all the guard") in
particular to admit defeat in anything involving archery is to provoke

a national crisis of honor. Jamie's ability to not only bend the bow but shoot and break it averts a Scottish victory.

In fact, Jamie's inset narrative might be see as a micro-Flodden: another English near-disaster at the hands of a Scots interloper, but this time the Cheshire and Lancashire provincials are the ones doing the rescuing. Henry reads the story this way, granting Jamie clemency and announcing that "he that rebuket Lancashire or Cheshire / shall haue his judgment on the next tree" (lines 349–50). *Flodden Field*'s audience is more than capable of connecting the dots here: the "gallow-tree" (line 292) once reserved for regional Jamie Garsed now stands ready to receive the Stanleys' extraregional critics. It therefore comes as no surprise that this small victory for Derby and his affinity is immediately followed by the delivery of a letter from Katherine of Aragon, a missive proclaiming that "Lancashire & Cheshire . . . they haue done the deed with their hand! / had not the Erle of derbye beene to thee true, / in great aduenture had beene all England" (lines 369–72). Katherine's letter restores regional honor. Henry makes Sir Ralph Egerton, the knight insulted by Compton, his "marshall" (line 374) and reconfirms the earl's right to his once-threatened possessions ("the thing that I haue taken from thee, / I geeve it to thee againe whollye," lines 389–90).[41] Stanley pride is also increased by the earl's "verry patient" (line 415) resolution of his intranational feud with the Howards: given the power to judge Surrey, Derby opts for mercy instead ("then is his liffe saued," line 411). This magnanimous gesture leads directly to imperial victory in France, as a rejuvenated Derby (assisted by the Earl of Shrewsbury) takes the city of Tournay "in dayes 3" (line 422). Stanley *encomium* and English destiny are both back on track.

Playing the Man: Reality and Romance in the Civil War Siege of Lathom House

The concentration of the Stanley family romances in the decades surrounding Bosworth and Flodden (the 1480s–1520s) makes the creation of the Stanley family legend roughly coterminous with the tenure of the first few Stanley Earls of Derby: the family's assumption of magnate status necessitates the creation of a myth to naturalize that status, to protect it from contemporary attack. The Bosworth poems rewrite Stanley opportunism as forthright action, while the Flodden texts carry out damage control, responding to a threat that undermines the consolidation of Stanley power. A similar form of crisis management appears to be at work in the decision of the Percy Folio scribe to include the bulk of the romances in his anthology (*The Stanley Poem* is the exception here, appearing nowhere in the Folio). Watermark evidence places the production of the Percy Folio manuscript during the 1640s, sometime after 1642 (the year of the Royalist occupation of Banbury, an event referenced on folios 98r–v).[42] While the precise identity of its compiler is uncertain, his politics have proven easier to grasp: Joseph Donatelli speaks of "a case to be made for the compiler of the manuscript being a Catholic with Royalist leanings, as he copies the manuscript during the Civil War."[43] Donatelli bases this characterization on the Folio's inclusion of "Marian devotions," "Cavalier lyrics from manuscripts which circulated privately," "Martin Parker's enormously popular Royalist song *The Kinge enioyes his rights again*," and "two acerbic satires on Puritans."[44] Collectively comprising what Gillian Rogers calls a "little pocket of contemporaneity," these items are outnumbered in the Folio by late medieval and early Tudor romances and ballads, texts that initially seem ideologically inert and antiquated in comparison.[45] The possibility of a direct connection between the medieval works and the compiler's contemporary interests briefly captures Donatelli's attention ("we may wonder to what extent his copying of medieval romances may be viewed as a political act"), but nothing further is said or done in this direction.[46]

In this final section of the chapter, I would like to follow up on Donatelli's suggestion. The genre of chivalric romance does play a part in Civil War politics, functioning as "a common currency within the political élite," one that "could be adapted, by both sides, to serve diametrically opposed ends."[47] Romance could be consolatory: the 1646 funeral for the Parliamentarian Robert Devereux, third Earl of Essex, deliberately evoked the 1612 funeral of Henry Frederick Stuart, using "archaic chivalric ritual . . . to order and rationalise the traumatic and dislocated politics of 1646 by an act of relocation in the past."[48] Writing about Katherine Philips, Alex Davis observes that "the patterns of exile or obscurity and vindication . . . that structure these works, in which nobility is laid low and enjoys restoration, must have had a certain appeal to the royalist community—dispossessed, anxiously awaiting the moment of its reversion of fortune and the 'discovery' of the true king, Charles II."[49] As we saw in the introduction, the paratext of Daniel King's *Vale-Royall* contains similar expressions of Royalist nostalgia. The Stanley romances in the Percy Folio certainly serve such purposes: disappointed by the less-than-inspiring military performance of James Stanley, the seventh Earl of Derby, the compiler and any other Stanley-ite readers could find solace in the heroic deeds of the earl's ancestors.[50] Such readings might downplay the antagonism, explicit or otherwise, between the Stanleys and the Tudor kings, choosing to concentrate instead on the Flodden texts' imperialist themes (the traditional Stanley opposition to the Scots would be particularly useful in this regard) or on the Bosworth poems' vision of an end to civil war.

However, in the 1640s, romance provided its readers with something more than passive reassurance. The genre also offered scripts for action: J. S. A. Adamson points to "[c]hallenges to personal combat or trial by battle issued by such principal commanders on both sides as the parliamentarians Lord Brooke and the Earl of Essex, or by the royalist Earls of Lindsey and Newcastle."[51] Romance also gave contemporary propagandists a lens through which to view the war. As Lois Potter notes, "The habit of seeing events in literary terms was common to both sides in the civil war, as was the attempt to 'place' those events by assigning them to the correct genre."[52] One such event was the 1644 siege of Lathom House by Parliamentarian forces. Commanded by Charlotte Stanley née de La Trémoille, Countess of Derby, the Royalist garrison inside Lathom held out from 27 February to 27 May (when it was relieved by Prince Rupert and his forces).[53] The various newsbook reports of the siege are augmented by two "eyewitness" accounts: *A Briefe Journall of the Siege against Lathom* (British Library MS Harley 2054) and *A True and Genuine Account, of the Famous and over Memorable Siege of Latham-House* (first printed in Seacome's 1741 *Memoirs*).[54]

Common to all of these texts is an investment in establishing the proper interpretative framework for the siege. Royalist accounts (those found in *A Brief Journall, A True and Genuine Account,* and the newsbook *Mercurius Aulicus*) depict the garrison's resistance as an episode right out of romance. Indeed, the Royalist portrayal of the countess and her commanders resembles that provided of Elizabeth of York and her Stanley advisors by the *Lady Bessy* poet. In each case, an aristocratic woman with unusual military savvy resists tyranny long enough for her lord (Elizabeth's Henry, Charlotte's James Stanley) to return home and restore proper authority. My point here is not to establish a direct link between the Stanley family romances and Charlotte Stanley's actions at Lathom, but to suggest that the countess, her local chroniclers, and Aulicus (a.k.a. Sir John Birkenhead) all made regular use of romance conventions and tropes in their attempts to comprehend the conflict. The siege of Lathom House represents a prime opportunity for the creation of a new chapter in the Stanley legend.

For example, the opening negotiations between Charlotte and Parliamentarian commander Sir Thomas Fairfax on 28 February are depicted in *A Brief Journall* as a particularly fraught instance of *fin'amor*. Identifying himself as a "faithfull instrument," Fairfax attempts to get the countess to "yield" (p. 163). She resists, "indeavouring to gayne tyme by demurhes and protracc'ons of the busines," a strategy "the good Knight" counters by inviting her to a conference at New Park, a Stanley residence a quarter mile away from Lathom (p. 164). Charlotte sees through the trap inherent in this proposal and assumes the role of the cruel fair:

> This her Ladyship flatly refused, with scorne and anger, as an ignoble and uncivill moc'on, returneing only this answer, "That, notwithstanding her present condic'on, she remembred both her Lord's honour and her owne birth, conceaving it more knightly that Sir *Thomas Fairfax* shold waite upon her, than shee upon him." (p. 164)

This interaction, mediated by a series of Pandar-like go-betweens, exposes Fairfax's pretense of gentility, his improper performance of chivalric selfhood. Royalist Prince Rupert provides a far better example of *Frauendienst* at the siege's end:

> The Prince that day not only releev'd but reveng'd the most noble Lady his cosen, leaveing 1600 of her besiegers dead upon the place, and carrying away 700 prisoners. For a perpetuall memoriall of his victory, in a brave expression of his owne

noblenesse, and a gracious respect to her Ladiships sufferings, the
next day hee presented her Ladyshipp with 22 of those collours,
which a dayes before were proudly flourisht before her house, by
the hands of the vallient and truely noble Sir *Richard Crane*, which
will give honour to his Highnes and glory to the acc'on, soe long
as there is one branch of that auncyent and princelye familye
which his Highnes that day preserved. (pp. 183–84)

Like Fairfax, Rupert makes use of a go-between. However, unlike his
Parliamentarian rival, the prince directs his chivalric force against his
lady's oppressors and not his lady. Rupert becomes Charlotte's champion, and his attack on Bolton, a bloodbath for which the Earl of Derby
will ultimately be blamed and executed in 1651, is recast as trial by
combat, complete with heraldic trophies.

In the romance narrative developed by the Royalists, Countess
Charlotte is only partially the *domna* of courtly love. She is also an
Amazon, a *femme forte* capable of undertaking chivalric action in her
own behalf.[55] This identity had long been available to the countess: in
1632, Charlotte posed as the goddess Minerva, complete with spear
and breastplate, for the painter Gerrit van Honthorst (figure 6). In
1644, her chroniclers were quick to pick up on this association. In the
Mercurius Aulicus entry for 17 April, Birkenhead gives a stirring depiction of Charlotte's "matchlesse courage":

and this day sevenight (*April* 10.) this most noble *Countesse* made a
sally out upon the Rebels which was performed so gallantly; that
she killed 45, wounded above 60 more, and tooke two Peeces of
Ordnance, with Colonell *Moores* Colours and Drummes, one who
heretofore hath eaten much bread in *Lathom House*, and therefore
this brave *Lady* caused his Colours to be nayled on the top of
the highest Tower of the house, that all the world may see the
ingratitude of a Rebell.[56]

The syntax here deliberately conflates the actions of the countess with
those of her men (a point the Parliamentarian commentators were quick
to note as we will see below). She is the one striking blows in this sally, killing, wounding, and looting with impunity. Colonel Moore, identified as

FIGURE 6   Gerrit van Honthorst's portrait of Charlotte Stanley, Countess of Derby, as Minerva (1632). © Christie's Images Ltd., 2009.

a treacherous member of the Stanley affinity ("one who heretofore hath eaten much bread in *Lathom House*") is her particular target: she engages in successful honor competition against him, stealing "his Colours" (just as a knight takes the arms of his defeated foe) and displaying them for all to see—a public declaration of her honor and his shame.

The author of *A True and Genuine Account* opts for a more straight-forward account of the countess's Amazonian nature. Charlotte is the one directing the defenses of Lathom: "She therefore caused her Men to be listed under six Captains, whom for their Courage and Integrity, she chose out of the Gentlemen that were in the House to her Assistance" (p. 101). We learn as well that Captain Farmer, made "*Major* of the House" by "her Ladyship," also "received his Orders from her Ladyship" (p. 101). In sum, "This Martial and Heroic Lady Commanded all the Affairs of the House" (p. 102). She knows the tropes of chivalry, issuing a "Defiance" or *desfiance* to the Parliamentarian besiegers: "That as she had not lost her Regard for the Church of *England,* nor her Allegiance to her *Prince,* nor her Faith to her *Lord,* She cou'd not therefore as yet give up that *House*; that they must never Hope to gain it, 'till she had either lost all these, or her Life in Defence of them" (p. 104). Unlike Birkenhead, the author of *A True and Genuine Account* does not depict the countess as directly engaged in combat. But he does show her actively taking part in the defense: "During all this Sharp and Bloody Fight, the Heroic and most Undaunted Lady *Governess,* was without the Gates and sometimes near the Trenches, Encouraging her Brave *Soldiers* with her Presence" (p. 106).

Charlotte is needed on the field of battle, for the foe her men face is also a figure out of romance. The text presents Colonel Rigby, the man to whom Fairfax delegates command when he is called away to Yorkshire, as a pagan Saracen, a creature akin to the Turk of the Percy Folio *Turke and Sir Gawain*: "He denied a Pass to three sick Gentlemen to go out of the *House,* and wou'd not suffer a Midwife to go into the *House* to a Gentlewoman in Travel; nor a little Milk for the support of young Infants, but every way Severe and Rude, beyond the Barbarity of a *Turkish* General" (p. 107). The "beyond" in this statement is crucial. Sir Gawain's Turk can be restored to his original Christian identity as Sir Gromer, "a stalworht Knight" (line 290) who sings "Te Deum Laudamus" (line 292).[57] He can become a member of Arthur's Round Table (a typical romance ending). He can even be installed as "King of Man" (line 322), a title that makes him the Stanleys' mythical predecessor. But such redemptions are denied Colonel Rigby, a villain far worse than any "*Turkish* General." Upon Prince Rupert's arrival in the neighborhood of Lathom House, Rigby can only slink ignominiously away.

Of course, the Parliamentarian accounts of the siege demonize Countess Charlotte in similar ways. One of these is reported second-hand by the author of *A Brief Journall*:

> But their fractious ministers, very dutyfull sonnes of the Church of England, made the pulpitt speake theire designe aloud, one whereof, *Bradshaw*, to the dishonour of that house (*Brazennose*) which had given him more sober and pious foundations, tooke occasion, before his patrons at *Wigan*, to prophane the fourteenth verse of the fiftieth chapter of Jeremy, from thence by as many markes and signes as ever hee had given of Antichrist, proving the Lady *Derby* to bee the scarlett whore and the whore of *Babylon*, whose walls he made as flatt and as thin as his discourse. Indeed, before he dispatch'd his prophecy hee thump't em downe, reserveing the next verse to be a triumph for the victor. (p. 163)

As the chronicler states, Bradshaw's texts here are Jeremiah 50:14 ("Put yourselves in array against Babylon round about: all ye that bend the bow, shoot at her, spare no arrows: for she hath sinned against the Lord") and 50:15 ("Shout against her round about: she hath given her hand: her foundations are fallen, her walls are thrown down: for it is the vengeance of the Lord: take vengeance upon her: as she hath done, do unto her"). His sermon thus treats the siege of Lathom as a Protestant allegory in the making, one that equates the countess (historically a devout Protestant of Hugenot descent) with the Papist "whore" of Revelation 17:3–4.[58] The *Brief Journall* author returns to Bradshaw's allegory in his entry for 23 April, turning the preacher's discourse against him and his Parliamentarian allies. When the besiegers aim their cannons at the Eagle Tower, Lathom's innermost defense and home to the countess's chambers, the Stanleyite chronicler snidely comments that "sure it was theire plot eyther to strike off one of the hornes of the Whore of Babylon, or els to levell one of her hills, the 7 *towres* in the devines sermon being easily found to bee the 7 *hills of Rome*" (p. 176).

The Parliamentarian journalists treating the siege in 1644 are equally capable of appropriating the opposition's language, and nowhere is this clearer than in their response to the Royalists' deployment of romance. John Hall is the leader here; his newsbook *Mercurius*

Britannicus "constantly uses the language of romance to support his contention that his opponents are the victims of a dangerous delusion."[59] Hall particularly stresses the *fin'amor* aspects of romance in his commentary on the siege, misogynistically exaggerating them until courtly love becomes nothing more than the emasculation of men at the hands of licentious females: "what adoe this *Aulicus* keepes with this *Countesse*, to the perpetuall shame and dishonour (as he implies) of the Earle of *Derby* himself, whom they report as I heare from *Oxford*, that had he been Commander in chiefe in the *Countesses* roome, he had delivered up the Garrison long since, as he did the field."[60] Elsewhere he implies "that the Countesse had rather endure extreamity at home, with a few lusty Commanders and Groomes, then live chastly abroad with the Earle himself; well, I am loath to speake what iniquity hath beene committed under the colour of a siege."[61] Chivalric *Frauendienst* becomes foul adultery: "*The Earle of* Derby *returned to* Latham *again, his own house, to the great comfort of his Lady*; hold, you know not that, it may be his Lady had rather have his house then his company, she has Commanders enough with her."[62] As *The Spie*, another Parliamentarian newsbook, wittily notes to its readers, "But you see they are resolute in Sallying as well as the Countesse of *Derby*: She is somewhat like the *Oxford-Countesses*, admirable expert in Sallying against men, as well as dallying."[63]

    Charlotte's martial exploits also come in for censure from the Parliamentarians. What strikes the Royalists as noteworthy bravery registers in the anti-Royalist accounts as an illicit emulation of male identity. For Hall, the countess is an "*Amazonian Dame*" whose "*Masculine Prodigies*" are "more than ever the *Female Lord* himselfe could do with all his *Regiments*."[64] Hall mocks Birkenhead's hyperbolic *Mercurius Aulicus* account of Charlotte's 10 April sally ("is this not very much for a *single Countesse* to do?"); several weeks later (27 May–3 June) he jokes that "there is a little rumour wandring about, that the *Countesse* is not all of one *Sex*, but like the Earles *Principality*, she is suspected to be part of the *Ile of man*, plainly, some think her an *Hermophrodite*, a Lady betwixt two genders."[65] For Parlimentarians like Hall, Royalist romance destabilizes gender hierarchy, elevating women at the expense of men (and thus confirming opposition to Charles I and his uxorious, feminized court). Resistance to royal tyranny becomes a stand for clarity in gender relations, one that pits the "brave *feminine spirits*" of such

Parliamentarian women as "the Lady *Manchester*, the Lady *Waller*, the Lady *Fairfax*" against Countess Charlotte, Queen Henrietta Maria, and the rest of the viraginous "*Generalissimaes* of all the *forces* for Popery."[66] Misogyny is the antidote to romance, "the language of romance being turned on the romantic hero."[67]

At the same time, in a striking confirmation of Adamson's thesis that "chivalric iconography could serve, with equal elasticity, to glamorise Garter Knights and regicides alike," Parliamentarian misogyny has its Royalist counterpart.[68] As Katherine A. Walker says, "it would be more insulting for the opposition to be shown to be defeated at the hands of a woman."[69] *A Briefe Journall* is particularly invested in this Royalist brand of misogyny. For example, when the garrison learns from prisoners captured on a sally that "the purpose of the enemy was to starve the house," the chronicler cannot resist taking a cheap shot at his foes' masculinity: "the com'anders having courage to pyne a lady, not to fight with her" (p. 169). The rebel cannonade is likened to a *Frauendienst* as emasculating as that presented in the Parliamentarian newsbooks: "They first tryed the wall, which being found proof, without much yeildance or the least impression, they afterwards shott higher to beate downe pinacles and turretts, or else to *please the women that came to see the spectacle*" (p. 170). Colonel Rigby is singled out as especially vulnerable to this effeminate desire to display:

> One thing may not heere bee omitted: that day that our men
> gave *Rigby* that shamefull defeate, had hee destined for the
> p'secuteing of his utmost cruelty. Hee had invited, as it is now
> gen'ally confest, all his friends, the holy abettors of this mischiefe,
> to see the house yeelded or burnt, he haveing purposed to use
> his morter gunne with fireballs or granadoes all afternoone; but
> her Ladyshipp before 2 o'clocke (his owne tyme) gave him a very
> skurvy satisfying answer, soe that his friends came opportunely to
> comfort him, who was sicke of shame and dishonour, to be routed
> by a lady and a handfull of men. (p. 180)

Not only is Rigby a man defeated topsy-turvy style by a woman, but—as the echoes here of Charlotte's initial exchange with Fairfax indicate—

he is also a failed lover, incapable of penetrating his lady's resistance and easily dismissed with a "skurvy satisfying answer."

In the short run, the battle to control interpretation of the siege of Lathom House is won by the Parliamentarians. A second siege (ending in December 1645) results in the capture and destruction of the Stanleys' ancient stronghold (neither the earl nor the countess is in residence during this siege). The Parliamentarian newsbook *The Scotish Dove* offers what it thinks is the last word on the subject:

> On Saturday by Letters to the House was certified, that *Latham-house* (that strong Garrison in *Lancashire*) was surrendered: It hath cost much blood at severall times, and it was a place that the *Oxford* Serpent *Aulicus* hath much gloried in, and highly magnified the valour of the Countesse of *Derby* (whose House it was) who it seemes stole the Earles breeches when he fled long since into the Isle of *Man*; and hath in his absence playd the man at *Latham*: but the best man may be conquered, and so is the Lady *Derby*.[70]

The Stanley family legend reaches its nadir here, seemingly ushered into oblivion at the hands of a misogynist pun. With the demolition of Lathom House and the sale of the earl's commandeered properties, the Parliamentarians finally achieve in reality what was always the goal of romance villains like *The Stanley Poem*'s Duke of Gloucester and *Flodden Field*'s Earl of Surrey. Even James Stanley's 15 October 1651 execution for treason resonates with romance: one of the earl's final companions (and possibly one of his last chroniclers) is a Humphrey Baggerley.[71] Baggerley's identity is uncertain, but his name suggests a possible connection to Baguley Hall, home to the "gentleman" who made the "iest" of *Scottish Field*. This earlier "Bagiley" helped save Stanley honor in the aftermath of Flodden. But in the aftermath of the third Civil War, the second Baggerley can do nothing as James Stanley is hung on a gallows built from what an anti-Stanley account of the execution identifies as "the timber of his own House of Latham."[72] The Lathom timbers appear to put an end to romance: the seat of Stanley power becomes the instrument of Stanley shame, and the once noble Earl of Derby dies like a common criminal.

From the perspective of the *longue durée*, though, it is the Stanleys who have the last laugh. James's son Charles, eighth Earl of Derby, is able to recover much of his father's lost territory in the Restoration, and the family relocates to Knowsley Hall, the seat occupied today by Edward Richard William Stanley, the nineteenth earl.[73] The four eighteenth-century editions of Seacome's *Memoirs* bring the Stanley legend to the turn of the nineteenth century—when the emergent form of the novel, itself descended from romance, picks up the story. Bosworth and Flodden are no longer the bywords of Stanley fame; Countess Charlotte's valiant defense of Lathom House becomes the core of the tradition, reaching new audiences through the novels of Sir Walter Scott (*Peveril of the Peak*, 1822) and William Harrison Ainworth (*The Leaguer of Lathom*, 1876). The latest incarnation of the Stanley family legend is the title track on Steeleye Span's 2004 folk-rock album *They Called Her Babylon*. As the song's final verse indicates, the discursive strategies of the Stanleys' seventeenth-century defenders are still operative at the beginning of the third millennium:

> 'Twas in two good months when those rebels did retreat
> They were cast out from the earthworks and driven to defeat.
> With dishonor and in shame, their siege came to an end.
> They were routed by a lady and two hundred loyal men.

This song (and the Stanley tradition it represents) bears witness to several of the arguments of this book: continuity matters, local stories successfully compete with national narratives, regional identities confound traditional periodization. Change is of course possible, something we see in the feminist sentiments of the song's second verse ("The Countess was of noble blood, though not of royalty, / Yet brave and as intrepid as any man was she"), a clear counter to the seventeenth-century misogyny transmitted by the final verse (continuities are not automatically positive in nature). But a careful attention to the voices of the English margins (and Marches) reveals a past more complicated than the established master narratives allow.

EPILOGUE

THE STANLEY TEXTS ARE NOT THE ONLY CHESHIRE-AREA WORKS with a popular presence in the twenty-first century. Moreover, many of these modern versions maintain a distinctly regional identity, even when presented to national and international audiences. Writing in the *Times*, self-described "native of Cheshire" Alan Garner rejects W. S. Merwin's 2002 translation of *Sir Gawain and the Green Knight* as "a limp *Gawain* that portrays a suburban America rather than a Pennine English North."[1] Garner prefers a translator with personal knowledge of the poem's local landscape: "whoever takes on that job should know the feel of the light of those hills and have the speech of millstone grit on the tongue."[2] The dust jacket for the British edition of West Yorkshire poet Simon Armitage's 2007 version follows Garner's lead, describing Armitage's work in overtly regional terms: "It is as if, six hundred years apart, two northern poets set out on a journey through the same mesmeric landscapes—acoustic, physical and metaphorical—in the course of which the Gawain poet has finally found his true and long-awaited translator." In his introduction, Armitage characterizes his work as the deliberate reclamation of a regional text from extraregional appropriation: "although my own part of northern England is separated from Lud's Church by the swollen uplands of the Peak District, coaxing Gawain and his poem back into the Pennines was always part of the plan."[3]

The Cestrian performances discussed in this book are also culturally active. While Robert Amery's 1610 triumph remains defunct, the St. George's Day race he helped to inaugurate is still run on the Roodee today, albeit in May due to the calendar reform of 1752.[4] The Whitsun plays were revived in Chester in 1951 as part of the Festival of Britain and have been produced every five years since then.[5] I saw them performed in a moving two-part musical version by director Robin Goddard at Cathedral Green in 2003. The official website for the modern cycle promises that Goddard's upcoming 2008 performance "celebrates once again Chester's unique cultural heritage and demonstrates its special place on the world stage."[6] The plays literally went global in 2001 with the stunning Wilton's Music Hall production of *Yiimimangaliso: The Mysteries* in London. Making use of an abridged text of the Chester cycle, *Yiimimangaliso* stages the plays not only in Modern English, but also in Afrikaans, Xhosa, and Zulu—the four major languages of South Africa, home to the performers. The production's multilingual script acknowledges South Africa's regional divisions, preserving the cycle's Cestrian localism in spirit if not in letter.

All of the above are instances of the survival and continued cultural relevance of individual Cheshire texts. For the Cheshire myth, the county's sense of itself as a separate and distinct community, we need to look elsewhere. The Cheshire County Council coat of arms (discussed in the introduction) is one piece of evidence for the persistence of some form of palatine culture. We might also consider fiction and poetry. For example, the stories and novels of Merwin reviewer Alan Garner—from his 1960 children's fantasy *The Weirdstone of Brisingamen* to his 2003 mystery *Thursbitch*—frequently take a trans-temporal Cheshire as their setting, shifting from past to present and back again as a means of emphasizing the power of place and landscape to connect otherwise distinct epochs.[7] More recently, Andrew Rudd of Frodsham made the community-wide composition of specifically Cestrian topographical poetry the keystone of his tenure as 2006 Cheshire Poet Laureate.[8] He outlined his plans for a virtual anthology entitled *Lines on the Map* in a 6 March 2006 entry on his blog:

> The idea of this project is a simple map of Cheshire, with dots to represent places. As the mouse moves over these dots, the place name appears. When clicked, the name brings up a poem—normally with some kind of introduction. I would like to see this build up into a comprehensive "poetry map" of the County. I can imagine all kinds of conversations when a resident of Twemlow Green, for example, has a look at the poem connected with their place. It may give unique insights into the way people perceive places, and encourage local poetry.[9]

The 101 poems Rudd collected are now available online as part of the Cheshire County Council's website.[10] Although the texts range in quality from prosaic to profound, they nonetheless collectively represent a coherent articulation of regional identity, Cestrians representing themselves to the global readership of the Internet. In addition, as Rudd's map demonstrates, the Cheshire these local poets evoke is the pre-1972 county: the anthology includes poems on Wirral and Wallasey (currently part of Merseyside) as well as Stockport and Cheadle (now communities in Greater Manchester). Here the lived experience of locality revises the administrative initiatives of the center.

One of Rudd's own contributions to *Lines on the Map* is a poem entitled "Chester Cathedral." Like Lucian and Bradshaw, Rudd conflates the histories of cathedral and city:

> The Romans came and dealt a single card
> beside the river, drilling into line
> a grid of narrow streets. Later, a shrine:
> the city spread out wider, dropped its guard,
>
> soared upwards. In a crowded bay of lights
> a stately gothic ship has run aground.
> So what do you think you'll get for your four pounds?
> Sandstone, intricate carvings, dizzy heights,
>
> stories annealed in glass, a thousand years
> of arches, columns, potted history,
> an unexpected sense of mystery?
> One in a thousand pauses, listens, hears
>
> the heart still beating, beating, an unknown
> bird in this enormous cage of stone.

Although "Chester Cathedral" is in formal terms a sonnet, its content affiliates the text with the genre that Deborah Kennedy calls "the ruined abbey poem."[11] The Anglican cathedral of the present gives way in Rudd's verses to the medieval abbey of the past: St. Werburgh's is first a monastic "shrine" and then "a stately gothic ship." But Chester's *navis ecclesiae* "has run aground," acquiring the character of a shipwreck. Its physical fabric ("Sandstone, intricate carvings, dizzy heights") is still intact, but St. Werburgh's is effectively a ruin, "potted history" available for an entry fee of "four pounds."

These details correlate with those that Kennedy identifies as typical of the ruined abbey poem:

> A visit to an abbey would often take place at night, the speaker would be presented as solitary, and the natural surroundings would include ivy, moss, and owls. In addition, the monastic site would often bring to mind the monks or nuns who lived there. They might be written of with respect, or with pity, or with scorn. The speaker might imagine hearing their choir or even seeing their ghosts walk by, though not all poems accentuated these sensational effects.[12]

As line 5's reference to "a crowded bay of lights" indicates, Rudd's speaker does invoke a nighttime setting. There are even more than a few hints of the supernatural in "Chester Cathedral": like Edgar Allen Poe's tell-tale heart, the "heart" of St. Werburgh's is "still beating, beating" somewhere beneath the flagstones of the nave and its "enormous cage of stone." Only a few visitors ("One in a thousand") are capable of responding to the "unexpected sense of mystery" that this heartbeat represents. Isolated in the midst of a crowd, this unique sightseer assumes the identity of the ruined abbey poem's "solitary" speaker.

Anne Janowitz treats post-Restoration English ruin poems as enunciations of national identity: "Castle or abbey, peasant or aristocratic dwelling, the ruin is an image that often appears when 'Britishness' is evoked."[13] The ruin poem "provides an historical provenance for the conception of the British nation as immemorially ancient, and through its naturalization subsumes cultural and class difference into a conflated representation of Britain as nature's inevitable product."[14] According to Janowitz, the eighteenth-century demand for "images of a coherent British polity" required the services of "a ruin poem whose focus was the ideological homogenization of the nation."[15] The preservation of local and regional histories—the *sine qua non* of the chronicle history poem, the ruin poem's predecessor—yields to "a progressive diminishment of time," one in which "the histories which the ruins tell are only of the individual who contemplates them, rather than of the violent events of the past which have taken place in them."[16] In the majority of the ruin poems studied by Janowitz, region collapses into self, transforming the nation into a uniform zone populated by discrete individuals.

Rudd's haunted cathedral represents a supernatural challenge to "the project of naturalizing the nation" that Janowitz detects in eighteenth- and nineteenth-century poetry.[17] The "unknown bird" that replaces the ruined abbey poem's ubiquitous owl is, in a sense, the eagle standard carried by the Roman soldiers who built Chester, "drilling into line / a grid of narrow streets." The bird's still-beating heart implies that the Cestrian community founded by the Romans remains alive today—captured in the cathedral's stone "cage," but not killed.[18] Those who take the time to pause and listen can establish a connection with the local past, reviving it in the present. The poem implies this point in its third quatrain: there the rhyme linking "potted history" with "sense of mystery" suggests that Rudd is not opposed to history— only to superficial histories presented to tourists looking to check off another historical attraction on their lists. A deeper, more meaningful history—one reaching all the way back to Chester's Roman founders— is there for those rare individuals who care to appreciate it.

The organizers of the 2007 St. Werburgh Festival took a more communal approach to their celebration of the city's monastic heritage. To commemorate the eleven hundredth anniversary of the 907 transfer of St. Werburgh's relics, the festival committee staged a reenactment of the saint's *translatio*. Dressed up as monks, a group of local dignitaries (including festival chairman David Pickering and Canon Chris Humphries of the Cathedral) escorted the relics of the saint from Hanbury to Chester.[19] The seventy-three mile journey—explicitly identified in press releases as a "pilgrimage"—began on Sunday, 17 June, and ended on Thursday, 21 June, the day traditionally celebrated in Chester as Werburgh's feast day. Another press release provides an itinerary for would-be pilgrims:

> For those who wish to join the monks on Thursday in recreating this piece of Chester's history, the pilgrims are scheduled to leave

The Old Trooper Inn, Whitchurch Road, Christleton at 2pm and walk along the canal leading into the city. The less fervent can join the procession at 3.30pm when the pilgrims will walk up Bridge Street, Eastgate Street and St. Werburgh Street to Town Hall Square where they will be met by more than 200 pupils from local primary and secondary schools.

At 4pm, the Lord Mayor of Chester Cllr Jim Latham will receive the Relics of St. Werburgh and the Lord Mayor, pilgrims, children and congregation will enter the Cathedral, where there will be a Festival Service to celebrate the return of the Relics to their rightful home. The Service will start at 4.45pm and The Lord Mayor of Chester will present the Relics to the Dean of Chester Prof Gordon McPhate.

The planned spectacle reads like Bradshaw's account of the 907 *translatio* procession in his *Life of Saint Werburge*:

> Thus with great worship, decoure and dignite
> Of all the clergie, lordis and cite3ens
> She was receyued with great humilite
> Into the cite with humble reuerence,
> The clergie syngyng with mycle diligence,
> The comons prayeng with loue feruent,
> Folowynge this relique after their entent.
>
> (2.337–43)

These superficially similar processions are nonetheless motivated by distinctly different ideologies. As I noted in chapter 1, Bradshaw's *Life* reasserts the abbey's rights in the face of increasing civic resistance. His medieval procession is therefore a model of lay submission to clerical authority. The modern procession took the opposite tack, giving lay power pride of place over devotion. Pickering makes it clear in the official festival brochure that the 2007 pageant is the centerpiece of an explicitly civic celebration: "The Works and miracles of St Werburgh are both a fascinating story and a timely reminder for us in this wonderful city. As we undertake a renaissance here in Chester, with the advent of our Culture Park programme and the creation of Chester Festivals, it is worth reminding ourselves of the strengths of the past that created this great city. St Werburgh is that reminder."[20] Pickering's equation of saint and city here reminds us of Lucian, but his mention of specific civic initiatives also makes it clear that the secular authorities are now calling the shots.

The festival's civic sponsorship compensated for the absence at the pageant's center: the relics the modern-day pilgrims brought from Hanbury to Chester are virtual relics, artifacts generated solely through the performance of the pilgrimage and procession. They bear no direct connection to the contents of Werburgh's medieval shrine, torn down in the Reformation and eventually turned into a base for the throne of one of Chester's seventeenth-century bishops.[21] Canon Humphries has to use quotation marks when he describes the casket holding the modern relics in the August 2007 issue of Chester Cathedral's monthly newsletter: "St Werburgh came to the fore when we arrived back in Chester on Thursday 21st June, carrying the 'Feretory' covering the special box representing the saint's relics."[22] Indeed, in the June 2007 issue of the newsletter, Vice Dean Trevor Dennis explicitly acknowledges the new relics' status as mimetic recreations, placeholders for a lost past: "It [the casket] will not contain the real relics of Werburgh, of course. Those have never been recovered. Instead, there will be a small piece of tapestry inside, embroidered with the Chester Cross, and with it messages of goodwill from other cathedrals around the world."[23] The pilgrims' passage through the city streets on 21 June 2007 (figure 7) was thus an ironic reenactment of the earlier monastic processions reported in Lucian and Bradshaw. The festival reincorporated Chester's body politic on the basis of a simulacrum.

The relics' virtual nature is not a particularly difficult challenge to community formation. Medieval Chester faced a similar dilemma: the ca. 907 dissolution of Werburgh's inviolate flesh into its constituent elements (described in 1.3456–3511 of the *Life*) meant that there was no body during the original *translatio* either, only a shrine designated as a "riall relique of reuerence" (2.260). According to Bradshaw, Werburgh's dissolution is an improvement on the spiritual might of her former physicality: "But gretter was the hope of the eterne renouacion / In her body resolued to naturall consumption" (1.3509–10). For Catherine

FIGURE 7   The "pilgrims" escort the "relics" of St. Werburgh's through the streets of Chester (21 June 2007). Photograph by Nicholas Fry. © Marketing Projects, 2009.

Sanok, this "promise of continued, essential identity, to be reclaimed in the resurrection of the body, underwrites Werburge's ultimate role in stabilizing national identity," especially since it anticipates Benedict Anderson's "recognition that nationalism is a secular analog to the 'homogenous,' divine temporality of eschatology."[24] But the saint's relics (and the rituals making use of them) are not only useful for the creation of a "static and self-evident Englishness that persists through historical change."[25] As the St. Werburgh Festival demonstrates, they can also serve as a basis for a local or regional identity capable of constant historical redeployment.

An additional irony emerges in media accounts of the pilgrims' reception at the walls of Chester. The press release describing the relics' return states that "a throng of Roman legions and Vikings met the monks at Newgate, allowing the monks to enter the city."[26] Played by local Cestrians, the Roman soldiers are a routine fixture of modern Chester's tourism scene, guiding sightseers around the city walls and the extant Roman ruins. The Vikings were a special treat prepared just for the festival, part of "a two-day Viking invasion" and "living history encampment" scheduled to begin the celebration on 16 and 17 June.[27] The pilgrims' ability to "convince" the pagans to let the saint enter her city could be construed as a Cestrian victory, but the staging of a Viking greeting party directly reverses the spatial dynamic of similar encounters with pagans presented in Bradshaw's *Life*. As I indicated in chapter 1, Bradshaw places Werburgh's shrine at the city gates, preventing the Danes and the Scots from entering Chester. He also makes it clear that Werburgh's relics only leave Hanbury for Chester in the first place as a means of avoiding their despoliation at the hands of "cruell paynyms and tyrauntes" from Denmark and Norway (2.197). In Bradshaw's account of 907, Chester coalesces around the body of its patron saint, and the Vikings are the other against which the Cestrian polity is defined. In 2007, the Northmen were literally in the city, camping on Dean's Field in the former abbey precincts. This "bit of historical license" (Canon Humphries' phrase) writes the Vikings into Chester history and thus into the Cestrian community.[28] Once again, amalgamation and adaptation serve the ends of local culture.

Rudd's "Chester Cathedral" and the 2007 St. Werburgh Festival are historically engaged projects, creatively revising the regional past to meet the needs of the present. In this they are no different than any of the other texts and performances discussed in this book: local identity is a constantly renegotiated process, whether it takes the form of Lucian shifting Chester streets to fit his monastic allegory or the Stanleys rewriting Bosworth to comment on the family's current relation to the Tudor dynasty. At the same time, all of these works are responding to the demands of regional topography: Cestrian space shapes the expression of Cestrian identity, channeling it in ways no different than those employed by the "big designators" mentioned in the introduction. The regional networks of armorials on display in Scrope-Grosvenor destabilize the national and international claims of the chivalric class, while the Whitsun plays' various meanings are inflected by their sites of performance. As the extra-Cestrian poems in *Lines on the Map* demonstrate, local space has a memory. The Wirral may now administratively belong to Merseyside, may even function in practice as a transriverine suburb of Liverpool.[29] But the peninsula is geographically contiguous with Cheshire, a topographical continuity with residual cultural power—such as the authority to reconstitute the pre-1972 county community in verse.

An online anthology of mostly middling poetry may not seem like an effective standard bearer for Cestrian identity in the twenty-first century. For example, the print edition of *Lines on the Map* cannot be found on the British version of Amazon.com; it can only be purchased from the Cheshire County Council's website.[30] However, the ability of a Midwestern American academic to access this regional anthology via the Internet suggests that local culture is finding ways to make itself known through channels of publication beyond those traditional media concentrated in national centers. *Lines on the Map* certainly participates in the centuries-old tradition of Cestrian response to administrative centralization and national consolidation.

I want to end this book by exploring the center's latest challenge to Cestrian identity: the British Labour government's 26 October 2006 publication of "Strong and Prosperous Communities: The Local Government White Paper."[31] Designed "to give local people and local communities more influence and power to improve their lives," the White Paper invited county governments to provide Westminster with locally generated schemes for reorganization.[32] Factions of the various Cheshire councils submitted two competing proposals. In the first, the district councils of Chester City, Ellesmere Port and Neston, Vale Royal, and Macclesfield suggested two new unitary authorities: Cheshire West and Chester (comprised of the districts of Chester, Ellesmere Port and Neston, and Vale Royal), and Cheshire East (Congleton, Crewe and Nantwich, and Macclesfield). In the second, Cheshire County Council argued for the streamlining of the existing two-tier system of authorities (six district councils and a county council) into a single unitary authority. Put another way, the County Council would take over the responsibilities of the district councils, bringing all of Cheshire into its jurisdiction. On 25 July 2007, John Healey, Minister of State for Local Government, issued a statement identifying the first proposal—the

two-authority plan—as one of the "[p]roposals we are minded to imple-
ment."[33] That decision was reaffirmed on 18 December 2007 by Hazel
Blears, Secretary of State for Communities and Local Government.[34]
Parliamentary attempts to overturn the government's decision were
defeated by votes of 278 to 151 in the House of Commons on 27 February 2008, and 83 to 72 in the House of Lords on 5 March 2008.[35] Elec-
tions for both of the new councils are scheduled for 1 May 2008, and
their authority begins on 1 April 2009.[36] As I write these words, Cheshire
has less than a year left of existence as a nonmetropolitan county.[37]

I have no desire to consider in detail the bureaucratic and financial merits of the competing proposals. Instead, what interests me most
about them is not the controversy they generated, but the language in
which that altercation was couched. For example, the "One Cheshire"
website that the County Council established in defense of its position nominally defines resistance to the districts' two-authority plan in
terms of the economic benefits that a single county-wide administration would provide Cestrians.[38] However, the Council supplements its
rational "value for money" argument with an emotional conflation of
identity and topography:

> "We believe there is no evidence to support the idea of the
> economic split at present but if the Government implements
> this change then it will only be a matter of time before the new
> Councils for East Cheshire and West Cheshire find they cannot
> defend local interests and our historic identity against their big
> city neighbours" explained the County Council's chief executive
> Jeremy Taylor.

> "And at that point there will in effect be a Merseyshire and a
> Manshire—and Cheshire will cease to exist".[39]

Exemplifying this nightmare scenario of "Merseyshire" and "Manshire"
is a graphic at the top of a "Questions and Answers" page that offers
Cestrians a choice between two maps of Cheshire. The first depicts the
diminished but still intact Cheshire of the post-1972 era, while the second tears the county in two.[40] A 25 July 2007 news release responds
to Healey's statement of the government's preference by demonizing

the dual-authority plan in the politically and postcolonially loaded language of "partition."[41]

The Parliamentary debates similarly evoke place and locality. Those
arguing against the government's decision repeatedly resort to somatic
metaphors, playing center against periphery and treating Cheshire as
a holistic body subjected to a surgeon's knife—or a butcher's cleaver.
Identifying himself in the House of Commons as someone "born in
Cheshire," Simon Hughes, Liberal Democrat MP for North Southwark
and Bermondsey, states, "This proposal, yet again, does a further job
of breaking up a historic shire community that has already been sliced
off at one edge around Manchester and sliced off at the other edge."[42]
George Osborne, Conservative MP for Tatton (a Cheshire constituency),
insists that "democratic arrangements and local government structures
should be based on identities that people have in their hearts, not in
the minds of Whitehall Departments."[43] Osborne connects the hearts
of the Cestrian people with the land they inhabit: "Although bits have
been chopped off over the past 30 years . . . the historic heart of the
county remains and there is a county council based on that."[44]

In the House of Lords, the Earl of Selborne, a Conservative peer
from Hampshire, continues this trend of identifying body with landscape: "I am very clear that people see their county being dismembered
for research which may or may not be valid but which certainly does not
take into account the reality, as people see it, on the ground."[45] Baroness
Walmsley, a Liberal Democrat peer from West Derby in Merseyside,
bluntly derides the government's decision in favor of the two-authority
plan as "a carve-up which has been steamrollered through another
place."[46] Finally, Lord Harrison, a Labour peer from Chester, applies the
somatic metaphor to the opposition with somewhat ironic results. He
begins his remarks on "the ancient, proud and historic location of the
county of Cheshire" by noting that Lewis Carroll was born a Cestrian:

> For tonight the Government plan to take us into Alice's
> Wonderland, to wipe the smile off the face of the Cheshire cat
> and to create two artificial entities of west and east Cheshire: two
> entities that have no friends, no heart, no history and no bottom,
> solidity or definition; two entities entirely devoid of that which
> gives communities and individuals character, place, definition

and support. Tonight we forge two entities entirely bereft of location, location, location.[47]

Lord Harrison's attempt to depict Cheshire West and Cheshire East as heartless automatons with no organic connection to the land is not entirely successful. Based on the assumption of a solid, wholly natural Cheshire, his metaphors are nonetheless destabilized by his decision to compare the county to the only intermittently substantial Cheshire Cat. They are also undermined by his subsequent identification of Cheshire as a mechanical "Rolls-Royce of a county, with a big engine, running smoothly, proudly and effectively at its heart, and a real place."[48] But his emphasis on what he later calls "locus, or location" is of a piece with his allies' arguments in both houses.[49] Even Lord Greaves, a Liberal Democrat peer from Lancashire who ultimately abstained from voting on the Cheshire question, agrees that "[t]he questions of what kind of place Cheshire is is crucial."[50] While skeptical of the Cheshire County Council assertion that a region as large as Cheshire can be governed as a single locality ("I would challenge whether such an authority could any longer be called 'local'"), Lord Greaves is also cognizant of the claims of history and topography: "I worry that authorities have to be given names such as East Cheshire or Cheshire East, West Cheshire or Cheshire West and Chester because you cannot think of sensible names to give them that people would know referred to that particular area."[51]

The Parliamentary supporters of the two-authority plan augment their economic data with appeals not to space but to time. In part this tactic is a reaction to the unitary-authority supporters' frequent reference to Cheshire's territorial antiquity: Lord Harrison notes that the county "has been here for a thousand years," a claim anticipated by the County Council's online declaration in 2007 that, "if this option is accepted by the Government it will weaken our 1,000 year old links with the Cheshire name and proud identity over time."[52] One proponent of the two-authority plan, Andrew Miller, Labour MP for Ellesmere Port and Neston, echoes this *longue durée* language when he states that he has "received a number of e-mails telling me that I am destroying 1,000 years of history."[53] To Miller, such complaints ignore history: "The notion that this proposal is splitting Cheshire is fallacious . . . Cheshire started to change geographically a considerable time ago."[54] In support of his position, he points first to the 1998 designation of the Cheshire boroughs of Halton and Warrington as unitary authorities and then to "the 1974 local government reorganisation, when a substantial part of Cheshire was separated off—that was not quite 1,000 years ago."[55] The East Anglian Labour peer Baroness Hollis of Heigham makes a similar point in the House of Lords: "the notion that Cheshire has been an unchanging historic entity over the centuries does not conform to my understanding . . . These things change over time as populations and business pressures change, and as needs alter."[56]

In these remarks from both sides of the controversy, we see the same issues of cultural continuity and rupture that inform this book. Supporters of the County Council's unitary-authority proposal emphasize the topographic features that shape Cheshire's history; these "natural boundaries" (as the Bishop of Chester calls them) provide the county community with a spatial coherence that serves to ground its culture over time.[57] Backers of the two-authority proposal stress the historical malleability of that countryside, its ever-shifting geopolitical designation. As I have argued throughout *Against All England*, the production of regional culture is a dialectic between these two positions: cultural continuity lies not in transhistorical essence but in the deliberate assertion of a connection to a past community (or to a present one on the other side of a boundary). Continuity must be performed, not assumed. Lord Wade of Chorlton, a Conservative Cheshire peer in support of unitary authority, admits that "One interesting thing has happened in those areas on the periphery of Cheshire that have been sloughed off into other areas or into their own unitary authorities is that they still think of themselves as Cheshire; they want to be part of Cheshire."[58] These expatriate Cestrians are akin to the extra-Cestrian contributors to Rudd's *Lines on the Map*, individuals asserting community in the face of jurisdictional *translationes*.

Indeed, these assertions are not extraordinary, a point made by Baroness Andrews, a Labour peer from Southover in East Sussex. As Parliamentary Under Secretary of State for the Department for Communities and Local Government, it was Baroness Andrews's duty to present the government's recommendation to the House of Lords. In doing so, she acknowledges that "Cheshire is a powerful idea" with "a long, complex and changing history."[59] But she resists what she calls the "apocalyptic language" of partition, observing that Cheshire is not alone in possessing such cultural continuity:

> There has been a history of change, as there has been across this country. I come from East Sussex, a powerful and terrific county, but that does not make me any less conscious of the identity and history of Sussex itself. For all the reasons given by noble Lords, I cannot believe that what has been suggested will be Cheshire's fate, either. It is too powerful a county.[60]

Baroness Andrews alludes here to a previous county division, that of Sussex into the separate nonmetropolitan counties of East and West Sussex in 1974. By calling the Lords' attention to the possibility of over-lapping regional identities, her statement recontextualizes Cheshire's impending spatial transformation. What Cheshire is about to undergo, Sussex has already survived. Both counties share a common experience, an intranational union that attempts to undercut the center-periphery discourse evoked elsewhere in the debate.

Of course, Baroness Andrews's own regional affiliation cannot completely trump her position as a national politician. The claim that Cheshire will lose nothing vital on 1 April 2009 is no less absurd than the claim that it will lose everything. Cheshire will change—just as it changed in 1237 when the county reverted to the Crown, in 1543 when it gained Parliamentary representation, and in 1830 when the final palatine institutions were abolished. The 2006–9 council controversy is simply the latest of the county community's ongoing negotiations with national authorities. For the foreseeable future, those negotiations will now be three-way. Again this change is nothing new: Cheshire's voice has never been united as a matter of course. We have seen how its various localities differ in opinion, how county unity is itself a product of intraregional conflict and compromise. Baroness Andrews makes precisely this point in her address to the Lords: "We will have two new authorities but within that there will be new local arrangements for local connections and local identities. Those local identities will build on present identities and enable them to flourish."[61] Unlike her opponents, she is confident that the forthcoming east-west split makes sense: "I believe we have that balance right."[62] The baroness may be mistaken in her assessment—only future historians and politicians will know for sure. But she is certainly correct in placing primary responsibility for cultural continuity in the hands of the Cestrians themselves. If Cheshire is to survive into the twenty-first century as a viable locus of regional identity, it will be the locals who do that work.

NOTES

Introduction

1. There are of course other forms of regional continuity besides the geopolitical variety that concerns me here. For a cross-period approach emphasizing religious continuities, see Theresa Coletti, "The Chester Cycle in Sixteenth-Century Religious Culture."

2. All citations from Lucian's *De laude Cestrie* are taken from M. V. Taylor's RSLC edition of the *Liber Luciani de laude Cestrie*. Taylor only edited portions of the complete text: additional citations will be taken from Oxford's Bodleian Library MS Bodley 672. All translations of Lucian are my own.

3. For a discussion of twelfth-century Cheshire as a "Welsh-English interspace" populated by *biformis* or "two-form" bodies, see Jeffrey Jerome Cohen, *Hybridity, Identity and Monstrosity*, pp. 103–4. For similar readings of fourteenth-century Cheshire, see Rhonda Knight, "All Dressed Up with Someplace to Go," pp. 271–72, and Patricia Clare Ingham, *Sovereign Fantasies*, pp. 119–20. None of these three critics refers to Lucian's text in support of their arguments.

4. *Itinerarium Kambriae*, p. 139. The translation is taken from Lewis Thorpe's Penguin Classics edition of Gerald's *Journey through Wales and the Description of Wales*. All subsequent translations from the *Itinerarium* are also by Thorpe.

5. James W. Alexander, "New Evidence on the Palatinate of Chester," p. 727.

6. *VCH: Ches.*, vol. 2, p. 5.

7. Charles Windsor, the current Prince of Wales, became the latest royal Earl of Chester in 1958.

8. *VCH: Ches.*, vol. 2, pp. 34–35. For a detailed account of the palatinate's Tudor-era travails, see Tim Thornton, *Chester and the Tudor State*.

9. For more on the final abolition of Cheshire's palatine institutions, see *VCH: Ches.*, vol. 2, pp. 59–60.

10. Ibid., vol. 2, p. 19.

11. Geoffrey Barraclough, *The Earldom and County Palatine of Chester*, p. 22.

12. Lucian's Forest of Lyme corresponds to the wooded uplands of the Cheshire Pennines and the Staffordshire uplands. Its status as the traditional

eastern boundary of the county can also be seen in the guarantees of the Magna Carta of Earl Ranulf III (dated 1215 or 1216) that no man from *Cestreshyria* can be compelled to do military service *extra Lymam*, "beyond the Lyme"; for the complete clause of the charter, see James Tait, *The Chartulary or Register of the Abbey of St. Werburgh Chester*, pt. 1, p. 105.

13. David Crouch notes that Lucian's combination of the honorific *princeps* and the symbolic *gladium* identifies the earl as "the ruler of a distinct people" who holds "the royal power to discipline and coerce" ("The Administration of the Norman Earldom," pp. 71 and 72).

14. For the details of Ranulf III's life, see James W. Alexander, *Ranulf of Chester*.

15. *VCH: Ches.*, vol. 2, p. 3.

16. Crouch, "The Administration of the Norman Earldom," pp. 82–83.

17. All citations from the *Annales Cestrienses* are taken from Richard Copley Christie's 1887 RSLC edition of the text.

18. Richard Eales, "Ranulf (III)."

19. Thornton, *Cheshire and the Tudor State*, p. 43.

20. All citations from Bradshaw's *Life of Saint Werburge* are taken from Carl Horstmann's 1887 EETS edition of the text.

21. Thornton, *Cheshire and the Tudor State*, p. 44.

22. Ibid., p. 44.

23. Michelle R. Warren, *History on the Edge*, p. 17.

24. Thornton, *Cheshire and the Tudor State*, fn. 15, p. 44. The sword's subsequent fate is unknown: when George Ormerod went looking for it in the British Museum in the 1830s, he could find only an outline drawing of the weapon by Randle Catherall in British Library MS Harley 1988 ("Observations on Ancient Swords," p. 2). Moreover, Ormerod identifies the heraldic devices engraved on the sword's hilt as the arms of Edward, son of Edward IV and Prince of Wales and Earl of Chester from 1471 to 1483, not the arms of Earl Hugh (ibid., p. 3). The blade's fifteenth-century provenance emphasizes the mythological portion of the palatine myth, but it also demonstrates the legend's continued potency well into the seventeenth century.

25. All citations from *Vale-Royall* are taken from the 1972 Collegium Graphicum facsimile edition of Daniel King's text. Since King paginates each chorography separately from the others, I have made sure to indicate the author of each quotation from the book.

26. This engraving appears to be based on an illumination found in a ca. 1603 pedigree of the Earls of Chester (CCALS MS ZCX/2).

27. For a history of Vale Royal, see *VCH: Ches.*, vol. 3, pp. 156–65.

28. The poem also identifies King's collection as what John Barnard calls "a mainstream and conservative political response to the English Revolution" ("London Publishing, 1640–1660," p. 9). Just after the lines quoted above, it

asks: "What Guerdon shall thy studious Reader give / Thee, KING! by whom these Monuments do live? / For had they not been Thus preserv'd, we must / Have left those Trophies groveling in the dust" (A2v). These lines echo John King's comment on the preceding page that "these Times"—the 1650s—are "an Age of Devastation" (A2r). To these passages we should add a consideration of the Royalist politics of King's dedicatee, Sir Orlando Bridgeman: in August 1642, Bridgeman joined his father Dr. John Bridgeman (then Bishop of Chester) in seizing control of Chester for Charles I, and he may have spent the Interregnum spying for Charles II (see Howard Nenner, "Bridgeman, Sir Orlando (1609–1674)"). King's decision to dedicate *Vale-Royall* to Bridgeman was thus more than a courtesy to a local dignitary, and his compilation of Cheshire chorographies more than mere antiquarianism.

29. See the Cheshire County Council's website at http://www.cheshire .gov.uk/aboutcheshire/Crest.htm (accessed 9 August 2007). The site contains a color image of the device.

30. For the history of the present-day Cheshire arms, see *VCH: Ches.*, vol. 2, pp. 96–97. The black-and-white image accompanying this account includes the county badge: "in front of an oval wreath of oak leaves a sword erect, the blade surmounted of a garb, all or" (ibid., p. 97). Like the county arms, then, the county badge deliberately participates in the palatine myth of the sword.

31. R. V. H. Burne, *The Monks of Chester*, pp. 78 and 91.

32. See Alan Thacker, "The Reuse of the Monastic Buildings at Chester."

33. See *VCH: Ches.*, vol. 5, pt. 2, pp. 270–71.

34. David Wallace, ed., *The Cambridge History of Medieval English Literature*, p. xi.

35. James Simpson, *Reform and Cultural Revolution*, p. 1.

36. Perry Anderson, *Lineages of the Absolutist State*, p. 19.

37. Ralph Hanna, *London Literature*, p. 3. Hanna is suspicious of Wallace's "emphasis on the longue duree," seeing it as little more than a reinscription of traditional master-narratives (ibid., p. xiv). While I share his anxiety about the nationalizing focus of English literary history, old or new, I do feel that the *longue durée* can be reclaimed for local studies by splitting it into a number of regionally specific *longues durées*, microcontinuities that vary from space to space.

38. Kathy Lavezzo's *Angels on the Edge of the World* identifies a similar series of strategies whereby English writers (including the Cheshire monk Ranulf Higden) transform the marginal position granted to them in the geography of classical antiquity into self-empowering discourses of cultural centrality.

39. Thornton, *Cheshire and the Tudor State*, p. 252.

40. Philip Schwyzer and Simon Mealor, eds., *Archipelagic Identities*, p. 4. For the classic statement of the archipelagic approach, see J. G. A. Pocock, "British History."

41. David J. Baker and Willy Maley, "Uncertain Union," p. 20.

42. Two of these essays focus on Devonshire: Kate Chedgzoy, "This Pleasant and Sceptred Isle," and Gillian Wright, "Whose Pastorals?" The third such paper, Melanie Ord's "Provincial Identification," looks at Somerset.

43. David J. Baker and Willy Maley, eds., *British Identities and English Renaissance Literature*, p. 1.

44. Philip Schwyzer, *Literature, Nationalism, and Memory*, p. 3. Here Schwyzer includes a chapter exploring Robert Aske's defense of Northern identity against Thomas Cromwell's 1530s "rationalization of national space" (p. 56). However, Aske's failure as a regional rebel is simultaneously the success of Cromwell's jurisdictional revolution—the same narrative of centralizing triumph seen in Wallace and Simpson. Thornton reads Cromwell's ambitions differently, seeing "not a vision of uniformity but of supreme sovereignty projected into varied jurisdictions" (*Cheshire and the Tudor State*, p. 242).

45. Geraldine Heng, *Empire of Magic*, p. 84.

46. Ibid., fn. 35, p. 345.

47. *Sovereign Fantasies*, p. 188.

48. Ibid., pp. 10, 202.

49. Ibid., p. 117. The present-day Wirral is no longer officially part of Cheshire: in the Local Government Act of 1972, the peninsula was transferred to the metropolitan county of Merseyside (*VCH: Ches.*, vol. 2, p. 96).

50. Jeffrey Jerome Cohen, "The Flow of Blood in Medieval Norwich," p. 50.

51. Thornton, *Cheshire and the Tudor State*, p. 252.

52. Jeffrey Jerome Cohen, ed., *The Postcolonial Middle Ages*, p. 8.

53. Michael J. Bennett makes the case first in *Community, Class, and Careerism*; John M. Bowers follows up in *The Politics of Pearl*.

54. For more on Cheshire as a principality, see R. R. Davies, "Richard II and the Principality of Chester 1397–9."

55. Bennett, *Community, Class, and Careerism*, p. 250.

56. Bowers, *The Politics of Pearl*, p. 191.

57. Ibid., p. 191.

58. Thornton, *Cheshire and the Tudor State*, p. 62.

59. Ibid., p. 62.

60. Thorlac Turville-Petre, *England the Nation*, p. 142.

61. Richard Helgerson, *Forms of Nationhood*, p. 138.

62. All citations from *Bosworth Field* are taken from the edition of the poem found on pp. 233–59 of vol. 3 of J. W. Hales and F. J. Furnivall's *Bishop Percy's Folio Manuscript: Ballads and Romances*.

63. For more on the interdependence of medieval and early modern Cheshire and Lancashire, see Bennett, *Community, Class, and Careerism*, pp. 7–20.

64. For the participation of county figures in civic government during the years 1230–1550, see *VCH: Ches.*, vol. 5, pt. 1, pp. 45, 62–63, and 79–80; for mercantile pursuit of landed status during the same period, see ibid., pp. 53–55.

65. See Clopper's "Lay and Clerical Impact."

66. See Peter Womack, "Imagining Communities."

67. Heng, *Empire of Magic*, p. 7.

68. Turville-Petre, *England the Nation*, p. 4.

69. Ibid., p. 12.

70. Ibid., p. 8.

71. British Library MS Harley 2252, fol. 47.

CHAPTER 1.   *From Cloister to Corporation*

1. For a concise overview of the abbey's history, see *VCH: Ches.*, vol. 3, pp. 32–46. For an account of the medieval abbey's textual output, see Elizabeth Danbury, "Intellectual Life," pp. 107–20.

2. Lavezzo uses these phrases to describe fourteenth-century Chester monk Ranulf Higden's *Polychronicon* in her *Angels on the Edge of the World*, pp. 90, 74. But they also apply to Lucian's project in *De laude Cestrie*: see Catherine A. M. Clarke, *Literary Landscapes*, pp. 98–100.

3. Previous scholarship on Chester's monastic topography has focused almost exclusively on Higden, the most famous of St. Werburgh's Benedictine writers. For particularly effective studies of Higden's regional patriotism, see Jane Beal, "Mapping Identity," and Lavezzo, *Angels on the Edge of the World*, pp. 71–92.

4. For more on the medieval genre of *descriptio*, see Antonia Gransden, "Realistic Observation," and John Scattergood, "Misrepresenting the City."

5. For a definition of medieval *encomium urbis*, see Ernst Robert Curtius, *European Literature*, p. 157.

6. For more on the predominantly local focus of monastic writing throughout medieval Europe, see Jean Leclerq, *Love of Learning*, pp. 187–88.

7. In the RSLC edition, Taylor substitutes brief synopses for most of Lucian's text, stating in her introduction that the work is "interlarded . . . with irrelevant sermons" and "padded" (p. 17). She also laments *De laude Cestrie*'s exegetical method, what she calls its unfortunate tendency to make the topographical features of Chester into "texts for sermons" (p. 20). Lucian's seemingly endless attention to religion at the expense of extensive "historical" detail has meant that his book routinely plays second fiddle to William Fitzstephen's 1173 *Descriptio nobilissimae civitatis Londoniae* ("The Description of the Most Noble City of London") in critical accounts of medieval English

history writing. For example, Danbury finds it "unsurprising" that Taylor's edition presents only excerpts from Lucian's "turgid and repetitive" book ("Intellectual Life," p. 110), while John Scattergood comments that *De laude Cestrie*'s "frequent homilies *interrupt* the general praise" ("Misrepresenting the City," p. 25, my italics). But it should be noted that Fitzstephen's description of London is itself only the prologue to his lengthy *Vita Sancti Thomae*, a hagiographic life of Thomas Becket. Restoring Fitzstephen to his manuscript context reveals a text that, like Lucian's, primarily focuses on the intersection of the urban and the spiritual. For H. E. Butler's translation of the *Descriptio Londoniae*, see Fitzstephen, *Norman London*, pp. 47–67.

8. See the endpapers of R. V. H. Burne's *The Monks of Chester* for a seventeenth-century plan of the abbey (front endpaper) and a map depicting the monks' Cheshire properties (back endpaper).

9. Lucian refers to Job 5:6 a second time on p. 55. With the exception of passages directly quoted by Lucian in the text of *De laude Cestrie*, all quotations from the Latin Vulgate Bible are taken from Alberto Colunga and Laurentio Turrado's edition of the *Bibla Sacra*. My translations of the Vulgate are based on those of the Douay-Rheims Bible.

10. This and all other transcriptions and translations of Bodleian Library MS Bodley 672 are my own. Citations of *De laude Cestrie* from Bodley MS 672 are distinguished from Taylor's edition by the use of folio and page numbers respectively. Note that the marginal gloss accompanying this passage reads *Scriptor ad cives* ("The writer to the citizens").

11. The first phrase refers to Lucian's patron, an anonymous clerk of St. John's, Chester's collegiate church.

12. Lucian establishes this typological point earlier in *De laude Cestrie*, noting that "Idem tunc Deus agnoscebatur; cuius et nunc potencia sapentia bonitas non mutatur. Qui tunc pauit Ierosolimam, ipse nostram nunc pascit et Cestriam" ("The same God was recognized then, and his power, wisdom, and goodness have not changed now—he who fed Jerusalem in the past feeds our Chester in the present," fol. 11r). Lucian's parallel syntax supports his parallel temporalities here.

13. *VCH: Ches.*, vol. 5, pt. 2, p. 94.

14. Ibid., p. 100.

15. St. John's position outside the eastern walls of Chester makes it an ideal spot from which to contemplate the city as a whole.

16. Note how Lucian uses the first-person plural (*miramur Cestrenses*) to identify himself as a Cestrian here, even though he elsewhere refers to himself as a *regionis alumpnus* ("a foster-son of the province," p. 53), and a *monachus extraneus* ("a stranger-monk," p. 67). This passage is essentially self-congratulation disguised as objectivity: Lucian is not so much speaking with his fellow citizens

here as he is ventriloquizing them in ways that augment the abbey's dominance over lay affairs.

17. The Vulgate version of Job 18:18 reads in its entirety: "Expellet eum de luce in tenebras, et de orbe transferet eum" ("He shall drive him out of light into darkness, and shall remove him out of this world").

18. See Curtius, *European Literature*, pp. 495–500.

19. Lucian returns to this point on p. 58.

20. *Tuens urbem* is echoed elsewhere in the text: at one point, he defines Werburgh's function as *civem tuendo, civitatem tenendo contra adversa omnia* ("guarding the citizen and holding the city against all misfortunes," p. 42).

21. J. R. Clark Hall and Herbert D. Meritt, *Concise Anglo-Saxon Dictionary*, p. 60.

22. For more on the equation of civic space and maternal body in Christian tradition, see Sarah Stanbury, "Body and the City in *Pearl*."

23. At first glance, this overcrowded space appears to be purely ecclesiastical, but the phrase *aula veneranda* does echo the earlier description of the earl's court as *aula principis*.

24. Lucian's compliment to his fellow Cestrians here is a backhanded one, preserving as it does the superiority of the (monastic) *literati* to the (lay) *illiterati*.

25. For an extended account of the allegorical connections between St. Peter, St. Peter's church, and Cestrian topography, see Clarke, *Literary Landscapes*, pp. 103–4.

26. The "prophets" whom Lucian paraphrases here include Ezekiel 5:5 ("Ista est Hierusalem, in medio gentium posui eam, et in circuitu eius terras" or "This is Jerusalem, I have set her in the midst of the nations, and the countries round about her") and Psalm 73:12 ("Deus autem rex noster ante saecula, / Operatus est salutes in medio terrae" or "But God is our king before ages: he hath wrought salvation in the midst of the earth").

27. Once again Lucian deforms geographical space for ideological ends: when locating Cheshire between England and Wales on p. 65, he places the two nations on a horizontal axis—one that places Wales to the west of Chester. Here he shifts Wales to a vertical, north-south axis. Place is subordinate to purpose in *De laude Cestrie*.

28. Clarke, *Literary Landscapes*, p. 99.

29. Christleton's inclusion within *De laude Cestrie*'s exegetical scheme gives us a glimpse of the material and social underpinnings of Lucian's allegorical efforts on the monastery's behalf. The chapel of Christleton manor, the spiritual center of Lucian's *Villam Christi*, is also part of the original 1092 endowment of St. Werburgh's, given to the monastery by Robert Fitz-Hugh. See Burne, *The Monks of Chester*, p. 197.

30. For more on the avowry system, see R. Stewart-Brown, "The Avowries of Cheshire."

31. Again, looking at the abbey's charters reveals that St. Werburgh's received "four bovates of land in Hoole" from one Herbert the Jerkin-Maker (Burne, *The Monks of Chester*, p. 199). Lucian's allegorical description, with its insistent binary of *Villam Christi* and *Vallem Demonum*, mystifies the abbey's own involvement in manorial economies and legal jurisdiction. Going by the charters, St. Werburgh's has a stake in both heaven and hell.

32. Lucian's reflections on the cruciform city retroactively explain his *forum* spectator's curious motions on p. 47. As the spectator spins in place, he not only reenacts Christian history, but literally makes the sign of the Cross: the shift from the east (St. John's) to the west (St. Peter's) mimics the upright beam, while the turn from the north (St. Werburgh's) to the south (St. Michael's) imitates the shorter transverse beam. A rotation of 360 degrees in one direction would be simpler, but less symbolically significant.

33. For Stanlaw abbey's medieval designation as *locus benedictus*, see *VCH: Lancs.*, vol. 2, p. 131.

34. Catherine Sanok disagrees with the traditional early sixteenth-century dating of the *Life*: "Bradshaw's plea for the preservation of the abbey's rights, especially concerning the fair (2.1786–93), would be hopelessly belated after 1509, when the 1506 changes [to the abbey's jurisdiction vis à vis the corporation's] were confirmed by the king" (*Her Life Historical*, p. 204). Her preference is for a date of 1485–93, the abbacy of Simon Ripley, "the only abbot whose relationships with the city and local gentry was positive" (ibid.). She bases her decision on the presence of an acrostic signature found in "An other balade to saynt werburge," a poem appended to Bradshaw's text in the 1521 Pynson edition of the *Life*. The final stanza of "An other balade" contains an acrostic signature reading "BVLKELEYC," and Sanok links this to "composition in the fifteenth century, when the Bulkeley family was particularly active in the affairs of the monastery" (ibid.). But Tim Thornton identifies another, later candidate for the identity of BVLKELEYC: Christopher Bulkeley, the abbey's master of works in 1515 ("Opposition Drama," p. 32). In addition, Bradshaw's explicit mention of "preignaunt Barkley nowe beyng religious" (2.2024) in a list of famous English poets makes a late 1480s date untenable: Alexander Barclay's first major work, an English translation of Sebastian Brant's 1494 *Narrenschiff*, was published by Richard Pynson in 1509—sixteen years after the end of Abbot Ripley's tenure. Moreover, Barclay only became "religious" upon entering the Benedictine priory at Ely cathedral sometime between 1509 and 1513. My decision to date the poem ca. 1506–13 (i.e., sometime between the Great Charter's assault on the abbey's rights and Bradshaw's death) acknowledges this evidence.

35. My analysis of Bradshaw's *Life* concentrates on Book 2 and the Cestrian phase of Werburgh's cult. For an excellent reading of Book 1 (the portion

of the text devoted to Werburgh's *vita* proper), see Sanok, *Her Life Historical*, pp. 89–105.

36. Accounts of these attacks can be found at 2.681–729 and 2.758–99. I discuss both of them in more detail below.

37. This is the charter cataloged as CCALS ZCH/5. There is also an earlier, royal charter related to the rights of Chester's burgesses (CCALS ZCH/1): this document, granted by Henry II ca. 1175–76, only reaffirms the trading privileges of Cestrians in the markets of Dublin.

38. The sheer abundance of Bradshaw's economic vocabulary here points to the abbey's political crisis and its need to openly address such matters—especially when compared to Lucian's vague *pro causis et utilitatibus monasterii*. In *De laude Cestrie*, "business and profit" are preliminaries to be disposed of immediately in favor of monastic reflection. In Bradshaw's *Life*, they openly inform the text as a whole.

39. This term of "a hundred yere and one" fits the chronology established earlier in this essay: the 1092 founding of St. Werburgh's takes place a century before Earl Ranulf III's ca. 1190–93 civic charter.

40. Eamon Duffy, *Stripping of the Altars*, p. 79.

41. For more on St. Werburgh's fair, see *VCH: Ches.*, pp. 100–101.

42. For a transcription and translation of the 1506 charter (CCALS ZCH/32), see *CPTR*, pp. 524–40.

43. Ibid., p. 524. The city's establishment as a county is part and parcel of the Tudor reorganization of local space discussed in the introduction.

44. William Dugdale, *Monasticon Anglicanum*, vol. 2, p. 385. The ca. 1120–28 abbey charter of Earl Hugh Lupus's great-nephew, Earl Ranulf I, includes an even stronger clause in support of the abbey's court: "Et ut ego comes darem exemplum posteris veni ipse propter unum placitum in curiam abbatis, audiens et siscipiens ibi meum judicium, non a meis sed a judicibus abbatis, ut in omnibus haberet beata Wereburga jus suae dignitatis imperpetuum" ("And so that I, the earl, might serve as an example to posterity, I myself came to the court of the abbot on account of a certain plea, hearing and receiving my judgment there, not from my own judges but from those of the abbot, so that St. Werburgh's might have perpetual right of dignity in all matters," ibid., p. 387). I believe that Bradshaw has these (or similar) clauses in mind when he states that "the place that tyme was made as fre / As the sayd erle was in his castell" (2.1329–30). These lines also appear to refer to the 1506 charter's exemption of royal space from civic control, arguing in support of a similar privilege for the abbey.

45. The mayor and the city sheriffs were often accused of similar offenses by the abbey. The Pentice Cartulary (CCALS ZCHB/2) includes "the articles of which thabbott and conuente of the howse of Seint Warburge of Chester fynde theim greved or present by the maior and commynaltie of the saide citie"

(fols. 84r–84v). This undated document notes that "the saide maior and the commynaltie haue made their mynysters to make dyuers attachmentes within the saide Abbey to come to their courte of pentice where they oughte not eny thinge to meddle to make or attachmentes within thabey aforseid."

46. *CPTR*, p. 58.

47. For specific details of this incident, see Burne, *The Monks of Chester*, p. 145, and *CPTR*, p. 134.

48. For the complete text of the 1509 award (taken from fol. 454 of British Library Harley MS 1989), see Dugdale, *Monasticon Anglicanum*, vol. 2, p. 375.

49. Ibid., p. 375.

50. The debate between monastery and mayor over access to the city walls via the abbey precincts dates back at least two centuries prior to the 1506–9 controversy. The Pentice Cartulary (CCALS ZCHB/2) contains a memorandum dated 1 August 1322 in which we learn of the "discord which was betweene the Abbott and Covent of theone partie and the saide maior and Commynaltie of Chester of thother partye by reasoun of stoppinge of the posterne of the saide Abbaye in the saide Cittie" (fol. 79r). This is the same postern gate mentioned in the 1509 award.

51. For the history of the Pentice, see *VCH: Chester*, vol. 5, pt. 1, pp. 17–19.

52. Interestingly enough, the living of St. Peter's was apparently under the abbey's control from the twelfth century to the Dissolution (see Burne, *The Monks of Chester*, pp. 9 and 201). Building the Pentice on the side of St. Peter's is thus more than an appropriation of a general ecclesiastical space—it too can be read as part of the history of the abbey and the city's mutual antagonism.

53. Mills, *Recycling the Cycle*, p. 30.

54. For an account of the Dissolution in Chester, see Burne, *The Monks of Chester*, pp. 158–85.

55. For more on the city government's appropriation of monastic space in the years after the Dissolution, see Alan Thacker, "Reuse of the Monastic Buildings at Chester." Note as well that the abbey's 1541 transformation into an Anglican cathedral fails to put a stop to jurisdictional conflicts between civic and ecclesiastical authorities in Chester. These debates continue well into the seventeenth century: see Carl B. Estabrook, "Ritual, Space, and Authority," pp. 603–5, and Catherine F. Patterson, "Corporations, Cathedrals and the Crown," pp. 552–55.

56. Gee's Assembly Book is CCALS ZAB/1. For a discussion of Gee and the Assembly Book's creation, see Mills, *Recycling the Cycle*, p. 50.

57. Quoted on pp. 210–211 of *CPTR*.

58. For an analysis of Bradshaw's role in the monastic reconceptualization of *lytterature* in the fifteenth and sixteenth centuries, see Christopher Cannon, "Monastic Productions."

59. "An other balade" can be found on pp. 200–202 of Horstmann's EETS edition of the *Life*; "An other balade to saynt werburge," on pp. 202–3.

60. For more on the talismanic and reliquary function of hagiographic books, see Jennifer Summit, *Lost Property*, p. 115.

61. Ibid., p. 134. For a more detailed account of Tudor anti-Lutheranism, see Richard Rex, "The English Campaign against Luther."

62. Cecilia A. Hatt, *English Works of John Fisher*, p. 78.

63. For the complete text of Warham's letter, see Henry Ellis, ed., *Original Letters, Illustrative of English History*, pp. 239–42. Rex dates the letter to 1527 ("The English Campaign against Luther," fn. 27, pp. 89–90), but Hatt makes a convincing counterargument for the 1521 date: see her *English Works of John Fisher*, fn. 8, p. 51.

64. Quoted in ibid., p. 50.

65. Quoted in ibid., p. 50.

66. Rex, "The English Campaign against Luther," p. 86.

67. In his 1521 sermon, Fisher explicitly likens Luther to a man who "is neuer lyke to entre in to the port of euerlastynge rest whiche all we desyre and couet to come vnto" (ibid., p. 97). The analogy is explicitly aimed at Luther's heresy and the ultimate fate of his soul, but it has intriguing connections to the insular rhetoric of Bradshaw's *Life* and Warham and Tunstall's letters.

68. Rex, "The English Campaign against Luther," p. 86.

69. Ibid., p. 86. Fisher promised his audience that "the kynges grace our souerayne lorde in his owne persone hath with his pen so substanuncyally foghten agaynst Martyn Luther that I doute not but euery true christen man that shal rede his boke shall se those blessed sacramentes clered and delyuered from the sklaunderous mouthe and cruel tethe that Martyn Luther hath set vpon them, wherin al Englond maye take grete comforte and specially al those that loue lernynge" (Hatt, *English Works of John Fisher*, p. 85). Note how easily Fisher moves here from the universalizing phrase "euery true christen man" to the specifically national mention of "al Englond."

70. Rex, "The English Campaign against Luther," p. 88.

71. For a list of these texts, see H. S. Bennett, *English Books and Readers*, pp. 74–75.

72. Sanok, *Her Life Historical*, p. 112.

73. For Summit's overview of Catholic print culture in Tudor England, see *Lost Property*, pp. 112–13.

74. Ibid., p. 135.

75. Sanok argues similarly that "[t]he legend oscillates throughout between a local focus and a national one . . . in a way that represents Chester as a metonym for England itself" (*Her Life Historical*, p. 84). However, Sanok's 1485–93 dating of the *Life* leads her to imagine not an anti-Lutheran nationalism at work

in the text, but instead "an English Christian identity that bypasses the crisis in dynastic authority and lineage of fifteenth-century England and creates an idea of Englishness independent of the legitimacy of the current monarch" (ibid.). In the context of 1521, this independent Englishness finds itself deployed on behalf of a Tudor Englishness that relies heavily on its subordination to Henry VIII and his status as *defensor fidei*.

76. I am not convinced by Thornton's argument that Christopher Bulkeley, master of works and purported author of "An other balade," had the *Life* printed in London "as part of a propaganda campaign in support of the privileges of the monastery and the abbot's own position" against Wolsey ("Opposition Drama," p. 44). The hypothesis is an interesting one, but Thornton provides no positive evidence of an anti-Wolsey stance within the text of Bradshaw's poem. Indeed, the supposedly Bulkeley-authored "An other balade" makes no reference to Wolsey, concentrating instead on the personal expression of devotion to St. Werburgh. The only political references in the poem are those participating in the discursive contexts of 1520s anti-Lutheranism: the "dedes catholique" and "catholique papall" mentioned above.

CHAPTER 2.   *Grounds of Grace*

1. Smith's text takes pains to emphasize this point: earlier on the same page of *Vale-Royall*, he describes the Pentice in almost identical terms as "a place builded of purpose, where the Maior useth to remain, and one may from thence see into the Four principal Streets or Markets of the City" (p. 39).

2. Evidence for a fourth, albeit minor, moment can be found in the List of Mayors that Smith includes in *Vale-Royall*. The entry for 1489 (John Barrow's mayoralty) includes a curious detail: "This year St. *Peters* Steeple was pointed, and by the Parson and others, a Goose was eaten upon the Top thereof, and part cast into the 4. streets" (p. 76). I have yet to determine the precise fifteenth-century politics of the parson's goose, but the casting of its bones into each of the four streets does suggest the continuing effect of Chester's cruciform topography upon the urban imagination of its citizens.

3. All citations of the Whitsun plays are taken from R. M. Lumiansky and David Mills' EETS edition of *The Chester Mystery Cycle*.

4. We can date this speech (5.272–79) to 1575 because it is found only in what Lumiansky and Mills have called the Group version of Play 5 (*Chester Mystery Cycle*, vol. 1, p. xxviii), the text found in MSS Huntington 2 (Hm), British Library Additional 10305 (A), British Library Harley 2013 (R), and Bodley 175 (B). For the argument linking the Group's Play 5 with the 1575 performance of the cycle and its four day schedule, see David Mills, "Two Versions of Chester Play V," pp. 119–21.

5. The Group version of the play does not explicitly state which direction Balaack and Balaam face when they initially *ascendent in montem* or "climb the mountain" (Group SD 5.271+). However, given that the stage direction following immediately thereafter (*Tunc Balaham versus austram dicat* or "Then let Balaam speak toward the south," SD 5.279+) fails to imply further motion on the part of the performers, it is possible to suggest that Balaack and Balaam both face south as they climb to the top of the pageant wagon's mountain set. Such an orientation accounts for the Group text's mention of "Cittye, castle, and ryvere," features of Chester visible to an actor facing south. The performers are then directed to turn north (Balaack's command "To this north side thow shall gone," 5.302, is supported by the stage direction given at SD 5.303+) and finally east (*Tunc Balaham vertit se ad orientalem in plagam montis* or "Then let Balaam turn toward the east while atop the mountain," SD 5.319+). This final, eastern orientation is a particularly appropriate introduction to the "sterre of Jacobb" prophecy that follows it (5.322). If we agree with Lawrence M. Clopper that the 1575 performance of the cycle was limited to the second or Pentice station only ("History and Development," fn. 48, pp. 234–35), then what we have in the Group version of Play 5 is a pageant carefully calibrated to fit its performance site.

6. Lumiansky and Mills tentatively concur, noting that the passage's translation of Numbers 24:5–6 is a concretization of biblical simile and therefore "perhaps appropriate to the urban surroundings of the performance" (*Chester Mystery Cycle*, vol. 2, p. 71). Their caution is unnecessary: as this chapter shows, the Cestrian localization of sacred history pervades the Whitsun plays.

7. Lumiansky and Mills consider Bedford's *walles* to be "erroneous" (ibid., vol. 2, p. 71). However, their argument in *E&D* that the cycle "is a convenient abstraction . . . a text that perhaps from the outset incorporated a number of different possibilities and that in any case was subject to frequent revision" (p. 41) undercuts their editorial judgment here. If the Chester play text was characterized by "choice and change" (p. 41), then it becomes possible that Bedford's reading is no error, but an accurate transmission of another, alternate text of the pageant. Finally, even if we read Bedford's *walles* as an antiquarian's belated attempt to correct his exemplar, we are still left with the idea of a Cestrian reader following the cues set for him by the pageant and further localizing the play. In this scenario, it would seem perfectly logical to Bedford that *walles* would be an appropriate reading for a pageant so clearly referencing the urban setting of its performance.

8. Clopper, "Lay and Clerical Impact," p. 105.

9. The exploration of the cycle's investment in local culture and politics nevertheless remains a vital task, especially given the formalist emphasis of much Chester cycle criticism during the last several decades. For a brief yet cogent summary of the problem, see Richard Emmerson, "Contextualizing

Performance," pp. 93–94. Emmerson's essay represents the most thoroughly historicized study of the Whitsun plays currently available; my goal in this chapter is to supplement his temporal survey of divergent religious contexts for response with a consideration of the cycle's spatial dimensions.

10. Patricia Badir, "Playing Space," p. 276.

11. Ibid., p. 276.

12. Of course, the stations are not hermetically sealed environments. Each site is marked by the traffic (ceremonial, economic, political, quotidian) that crosses it, accumulating meaning over time. The activities taking place at one station affect those occurring at other stations, and all of the Whitsun stations are subject to intrusions, both ideological and material, from locations outside the socio-spatial network created by and during the performance (some from other networks inside Chester, some from commercial, cultural, and political networks as far away as York, London, Dublin, or even Gascony and Spain).

13. Sarah Beckwith, "Ritual, Theater, and Social Space," p. 76.

14. For a short account of this transitional period, see Clopper, "History and Development," pp. 220–22. The texts of the 1521 agreement and Newhall's proclamation can be found in *E&D*, pp. 210–12 and 213–17 respectively.

15. For Clopper's argument in favor of the Passion play hypothesis, see "History and Development," p. 231. David Mills refuses to fully endorse Clopper on this point, but agrees that the pre-1472 records of the Corpus Christi play "suggest that the Passion of Christ was a central feature" (*Recycling the Cycle*, p. 108).

16. For a detailed discussion of Chester's Corpus Christi procession and play, see Mills, *Recycling the Cycle*, pp. 106–12. Clopper finds an emergent Protestant emphasis on "the salvific words of Christ" in the cycle's 1520s shift to a Whitsuntide schedule ("Lay and Clerical Impact," p. 111), while Alan Nelson suggests that the change took place for a more prosaic reason: to avoid a scheduling conflict in 1519 with Chester's Midsummer Watch and Show (*The Medieval English Stage*, p. 156).

17. All quotations of the Early Banns are taken from the edition found on pp. 278–84 of *E&D*.

18. The Early Banns are quick to credit the civic corporation with the procession's genesis: they tell us that "maister maire of this citie / with all his bretheryn accordingly, / a solempne procession ordent hath he" (lines 156–58).

19. *E&D*, p. 263. Lawrence Clopper dismisses the possibility of a fifth station, concluding that the High Cross station is the most likely candidate for an Eastgate Street stop ("Staging of the Medieval Plays," p. 66). But John Marshall uses the evidence of the Smiths' accounts for 1561 to argue in support of a fifth station further east on Eastgate Street ("'The Manner of These Plays,'" p. 38).

20. Mills, *Recycling the Cycle*, p. 120. The "older centres" were not entirely ignored by the post-1532 cycle: Clopper reminds us that the Banns were performed at both the city's Northgate jail and the palatinate's prisons in Chester

Castle, a recognition of "the two major legal jurisdictions" in the city ("Lay and Clerical Impact," p. 106).

21. Clopper, "Lay and Clerical Impact," p. 105.

22. John D. Cox draws a connection between the northern cycles' processional drama and the parish perambulations of Rogationtide ("Devil and Society," pp. 409–10). He emphasizes both processions' investment in spectacles of "social cohesion" and concludes that the Devil's role "was therefore to define what the community was *not*" (ibid., p. 410). However, Cox overlooks the equally powerful similarities between cycle plays and civic perambulations; the society he discusses is an abstract one, a generic idea of "community" spread out over four mystery cycles as opposed to a specific locality like Chester or York.

23. Beckwith, "Ritual, Theater, and Social Space," p. 66. Anne Higgins makes a similar argument in "Streets and Markets," pp. 77–92. Also relevant here, especially for its recognition of the connection between sixteenth-century economic collapse, social competition, and the cycle plays' emphasis on Christ's shattered body, is Peter W. Travis, "Social Body of the Dramatic Christ." For a general overview of the economic situation confronting the cycles, see John C. Coldewey, "Some Economic Aspects."

24. Beckwith, "Ritual, Theater, and Social Space," p. 75.

25. Sponsler, "The Culture of the Spectator," p. 27.

26. Ibid., p. 28.

27. Ibid., p. 27.

28. Beckwith, "Ritual, Theater, and Social Space," p. 76; "Making the World," p. 268.

29. Beckwith, "Ritual, Theater, and Social Space," p. 76.

30. Ibid., p. 76.

31. See Marvin Carlson, *Places of Performance*, pp. 14–37.

32. Beckwith, "Ritual, Theater, and Social Space," p. 77.

33. *E&D*, p. 271. This particular passage comes from the 1637 version of Rogers's *Brevary*.

34. For examples of this tendency, see Clopper, "History and Development," p. 234; Emmerson, "Contextualizing Performance," pp. 104 and 108; and Mills, *Recycling the Cycle*, p. 148.

35. Mills, *Recycling the Cycle*, p. 27.

36. Ibid., p. 79.

37. Lawrence M. Clopper, *Drama, Play, and Game*, p. 147.

38. Evidence exists for a Tudor wool market in Northgate Street ca. 1548–1549 (Annette M. Kennett, ed., *Tudor Chester*, p. 18, and *CPTR*, p. 398), suggesting that the corn market area was a more or less general site of exchange. The corn market was also home to the city shambles; Morris notes on p. 297 of *CPTR* that this shambles was built in 1578 to replace the older butchers' shops in Watergate Street. He also observes (p. 279) that butchers' shops could

be found in Northgate Street as early as 1557. The point here is that North-gate Street (like any of Chester's four main streets) contained a heterogeneous assemblage of trades and guilds—a diversity capable of inflecting performance of the Whitsun plays in conjunction with the shifting fortunes of the trades-men and burgesses dwelling or working alongside the pageant stations.

39. Kennett, *Tudor Chester*, p. 18. For the complete text of Gee's order, reconfirmed in 1556 by Mayor John Webster, see *CPTR*, p. 397.

40. *CPTR*, p. 397.

41. The prevalence of forestalling in sixteenth-century Chester (buying goods and foodstuffs prior to their being brought to the official marketplace) suggests that Chester's citizens and freemen were not above violating the socio-spatial boundaries of the city in order to make a bargain, whether they illic-itly purchased the goods in secret locations (ibid., p. 400) or in the suburbs beyond the city walls (ibid., p. 403). This resistance to the corporation's orders in favor of private interest provides a possible model for understanding how individual spectators might likewise resist the authoritative interpellations of the Whitsun plays.

42. Burne, *The Monks of Chester*, pp. 142–43.

43. *CPTR*, p. 298. Transcriptions of several of the documents concerning the controversy can be found on pp. 298–300 of the same volume.

44. Ibid., p. 298. This record serves as a useful reminder that spatial dis-putes over the Abbey Gate area did not end with the monastery's 1540 dissolu-tion and its 1541 reconstitution as an Anglican cathedral.

45. Ibid., p. 299.

46. This point assumes that Clopper is correct in suggesting that the 1575 Midsummer performance was limited to the second station at the High Cross ("Staging of the Medieval Plays," p. 66). He elsewhere posits that the decision to forego a fully processional production and stick to the civic zone of the Pen-tice was part of an attempt "to reckon with potential clerical displeasure," but also proposes that the ongoing Midsummer fair would have made the Abbey Gate station unavailable in any event ("History and Development," pp. 234–35). However, there is currently no extant evidence to corroborate Randle Holmes III's note on fol. 40v of British Library MS Harley 2125 that the 1575 cycle was played "at midsomer to the great dislike of many because the playe was in on part of the citty," and the choice of the Pentice as the lone site of performance remains at best a highly plausible conjecture—Mills points out that the Smiths, the Painters, and the Coopers all make reference to pageant wagons in their accounts for the year, leaving open the possibility of some processional ele-ment (*Recycling the Cycle*, p. 150). Even so, it does seem likely that performance outside the Abbey Gate was no longer politically or practically viable in 1575.

47. This includes targets within Chester's own oligarchic class: the 17 January 1575 decision to rescind Dutton's order and return the corn mar-

ket house to its original site came during the mayoralty of his immediate successor, Sir John Savage. The language of Savage's order ("whereby suites & other inconveniences *have alredy growen*," my italics) suggests that the new civic administrators may have been frustrated by Dutton's decision to seek out conflict with the dean—or, alternatively, that they were covering for him in the aftermath of an unsuccessful grab for local power. Dutton's successful 15 April 1575 "motion . . . to have an assuraunce to him & his heires of all the buildings in the Northgate Streete called the Corne market howse lately by him shifted" supports both possibilities: he received guarantees of ownership but also acquired full responsibility for the removal of the house. Coincidentally, both Dutton and Savage proved to be strong supporters of cycle drama. For Dutton's interest in festival and performance, see Mills, *Recycling the Cycle*, p. 36; for Savage's, see Emmerson, "Contextualizing Performance," p. 91.

48. Martin Stevens, *Four Middle English Mystery Cycles*, p. 50. Stevens is speaking here of the York Skinners' *Entry into Jerusalem* pageant (in its self-referential performance of procession, it becomes "the ultimate York play," p. 51), but his remarks apply equally well to Chester's use of the same episode (14.137–224). By immediately following the Entry episode with the Cleansing of the Temple, the Chester pageant achieves an additional effect: the conflation of early modern Chester and biblical Jerusalem assists the audience in establishing connections between the Jewish merchants of the Gospel narrative and their own economic activity in the corn market location.

49. For more on the difference in tone between the York and Chester versions of the Entry episode, see Peter W. Travis, *Dramatic Design*, pp. 165–66. Travis's p. 164 remarks on money's thematic importance in Play 14 are germane here as well.

50. While the Pharisees are most easily read as clerics (assisted no doubt by the practice of using church vestments as costumes), Play 14 leaves open the possibility of simultaneously understanding them as secular authorities. For example, Judas refers to them as "Syr Cayphas and his companye" (14.297), while Caiaphas and the Pharisees self-identify as "Lordinges, lookers of the lawe" (14.305). That latter phrase—"lookers of the lawe"—is particularly interesting, given Chester's own civic office of leavelooker, the position responsible for licensing foreigners to trade within the city. If there is a political allusion to be had here, it enables audience members to view the Pharisees as corrupt officials who let foreigners (i.e., moneylenders) illicitly buy and sell within God's house/city.

51. The Cordwainers' and Shoemakers' accounts for 1549–50 indicate that "ssetteng op of oure stepoll & ffor tember" cost the guild "xvij d" (*REED: Cheshire*, p. 92).

52. Ibid., p. 92.

53. The prop tables may themselves be actual market or shop tables borrowed for the purposes of the pageant. These tables might travel with the wagon

from station to station—or perhaps they could simply be commandeered at the site of performance. In any event, we have no clear reference to tables in the Shoemakers' 1550 accounts, and the symbolic benefits of staging the episode atop the wagon (Christ literally drives the moneylenders from the space identified as temple) are ultimately no greater than those of playing it in the street (and thus implicating the performance site in the moral critique).

54. The Cleansing of the Temple episode still holds some relevance for performance at the High Cross. For example, it is possible to envision Sir John Savage, mayor of Chester, and many of the aldermen watching the pageant in 1575 from the steps of the Pentice and thinking back on the Abbey Gate and the corn market incident of 1574, still unresolved at the time of the cycle's final performance—especially since many of the official spectators at the second station will have been the same individuals who supported Mayor Dutton in his decision to shift the corn market house in the first place. Even more speculative—but within the realms of probability—is the chance that someone in the audience might recognize the parallel function of both the Pentice and the moneylenders' tables as secular thresholds to the sacred spaces of (respectively) St. Peter's and the Temple.

55. Before the 1545 removal of the city's portmote court to the new Common Hall in the chapel of St. Nicholas, the play would also have been performed in Chester's judicial center (excepting of course the rival jurisdictions of the palatine and ecclesiastical courts). The city sheriffs' (or Pentice) court continued to meet in the Pentice until the renovations of 1573 transferred it to the common hall as well. These details remind us that time is as necessary an element in the localization of the Whitsun plays as is space. For more on the relationship between the city courts and the Chester cycle, see below.

56. For details of the Pentice feasts involving the Stanleys, see the city treasurers' accounts listed in *CPTR*, fn. 4, pp. 80–81.

57. *REED: Cheshire*, p. 871.

58. *REED: Chester*, pp. 194 (Essex) and 304–7 (James). The records of the 1617 royal entry specifically trace the king's path through the city: James entered Chester from the east and was subsequently met by "the Major and Aldermen standing on a scaffold in their scarlett gownes in the Eastgate street near the honey stairs, the companyes of this Cittie attending with their Banners" (ibid., p. 306). He then went on horseback to St. Werburgh's and attended a service in the choir. Afterwards, he walked to the Pentice on foot (via Northgate Street and Shoemakers' Row). This royal itinerary calls into question Mills's assertion that "the usual route into the city was from the south" (*Recycling the Cycle*, p. 32).

59. It might also remind spectators of the city's vexed relations with the Crown's palatine administrators; see below for a discussion of the 1570s jurisdiction dispute as it relates to Play 1.

60. John Marshall, "'The Manner of These Playes,'" p. 36.

61. Meg Twycross, "'Places to Hear and Play.'"

62. David Mills, "Chester's Mystery Cycle," p. 13.

63. Ibid., pp. 13–14. For more on the Chester city government's status as a close corporation, see Kennett, *Tudor Chester*, pp. 9–10, and *VCH: Ches.*, vol. 2, pp. 110–11.

64. The text of the memorandum can be found on pp. 219–20 of *E&D*.

65. In "Women, Work, and Plays," Mary Wack reads the dispute as an explicit debate over who actually gets to sit in the windows of the Bridge Street house ("good seats—that is, a privileged perspective on the shows—were valuable and contested," p. 38), and it is indeed possible that Whitmore wanted Webster's seats for the 1568 plays. But I am inclined to agree with Lumiansky and Mills that this is primarily an argument about ownership and access (*E&D*, p. 183). However annoying the lost opportunity to view the cycle may have been, Whitmore appears to have been far more upset at Ireland and Webster's challenge to his status as landlord and feudal tenant. For the identification of Webster's "mansion" as the Blackhall, see Marshall, "'The Manner of These Playes,'" p. 43. For the Blackhall's location at the intersection of Bridge and Pepper Streets, see *VCH: Ches.*, vol. 5, pt. 1, p. 55.

66. For Webster, see Marshall, "'The Manner of These Playes,'" p. 48; for Whitmore, see Nelson, *The Medieval English Stage*, p. 160.

67. *CPTR*, pp. 578–79 and 580–81. The 1542 list can be found on pp. 236–37 of the same volume.

68. Ibid., p. 234. This is the record that causes Marshall to identify Webster's "mansion" as the Blackhall.

69. Marshall, "'The Manner of These Playes,'" pp. 41–43.

70. Ibid., p. 43.

71. Ibid., p. 43.

72. For a discussion of the range of women's participation in the production of the Chester cycle, see Wack, "Women, Work, and Plays," pp. 36–38.

73. *CPTR*, pp. 397, 398. The use of the exclusionary phrases "his or there" and "he and they" in the 1533 ordinance suggests that gender was already at stake there as well.

74. The 1556 order continues with the requirement that the citizen ("every person and persons") designate "one discryte man or woman and no more for one houshoulde" as his buyer and that he register this individual with the mayor "upon payne of forfyture of ther bodyes at his will and pleasure" (ibid., p. 398). As we shall see below in our discussions of disenfranchisement and vagrancy, the vocabularies of licensing and punishment found in this statute are ubiquitous in early modern Chester.

75. Wack, "Women, Work, and Plays," p. 39. Morris provides the text of two Assembly orders (dated, interestingly enough, 1573–74 and 1574–75)

detailing the shot custom on pp. 381–82 of *CPTR*. Both orders indicate the presence of dissension even within the most exclusive levels of Cestrian society: two of the signatories to the first order explicitly refuse to consent to all of the document's clauses, and the second order openly rejects its predecessor, naming it "utterly voide & of none effect" (p. 382).

76. Recent archival research has identified another female spectator (one Margaret Rodon) watching the plays from locations that effectively serve as sixth and seventh stations. Testifying at a 1569–70 legal action involving Rodon, John Boland, "sherman dwellyng in chester," stated that, "that same yeare [1566–67] yat sir william sneade was mayre of chester," he "hath sene the same wyddox Rodon at the grene vnder the walles by the mynster at a reherse of a playe which was to be played; at whytsontyde followyng and . . . haith allso sene her at the new tow[er] on a nother tyme, when there was a nother play. rehersed" (*REED: Cheshire*, pp. 130–31). Imprisoned for debt, Rodon was nonetheless apparently able to get permission from the town sheriffs to see dress rehearsals for two of the plays enacted in the 1567 performance of the cycle. If we take Boland's testimony to indicate that play rehearsals were open to the public, we could therefore feasibly add the Abbey Green (located inside the northeast corner of Chester's walls) and the New Tower (extending out from the walls' northwest corner) to our list of performance sites.

77. For Mrs. Noah, see Wack, "Women, Work, and Plays," see pp. 43–46; for the Alewife, see pp. 38–43.

78. Ibid., p. 43. More detailed accounts of these statutes can be found on pp. 40–41 of the same essay.

79. For example, in his brief discussion of her potential status as Mayor John Webster's widow, Marshall notes in passing that Webster's apprentice, William Pixley, was listed in the freeman rolls of 1568 as a mercer ("'The Manner of These Playes,'" p. 48). Webster was himself most likely a mercer as well, and this allows us to think about Anne Webster's possible reactions to or roles in the production and performance of Play 9, the Mercers' elaborate *Offerings of the Three Kings*.

80. For a brief but trenchant critique of the formalist tendency in Whitsun play scholarship, see Emmerson, "Contextualizing Performance," pp. 92–94. The formalist critics' emphasis on what Emmerson terms "the text as authored by a unifying literary sensibility" (ibid., p. 93) seems particularly compatible with the city government's own desires for a homogenous response to the plays.

81. See Kathleen M. Ashley, "Divine Power," and Stevens, *Four Middle English Mystery Cycles*, pp. 272–76. In *Dramatic Design*, Travis concludes that "Pagina I is a pageant fairly easily interpreted because the foundation of its dramatic hermeneutics is essential non-temporal," that, "once the mimetic action of the cycle has fallen into time, a complex hermeneutics in all likelihood will obtain" (p. 75). My contention here is that Play 1 has already "fallen into time"

long before its performance: the pageant's decision to depict the heavenly city in an embodied fashion encodes human (and thus historical) social activities. Performance on the streets of Chester only adds to the play's politics.

82. Jean Q. Seaton, "Source of Order or Sovereign Lord," p. 205. Seaton goes on to refer to Lucifer as "baron" and "tyrant" (p. 211), arguing that his rebellion is "treason" and a violation of "the oath of fealty" he makes to God (p. 215).

83. Norma Kroll, "Cosmic Characters and Human Form," p. 33.

84. Cox, "Devil and Society," pp. 426 and 413 respectively.

85. Clopper, "History and Development," p. 243.

86. Clopper, "Lay and Clerical Impact," p. 105.

87. Lumiansky and Mills, *Chester Mystery Cycle*, vol. 2, p. 7.

88. For the central role played by civic defenses in late medieval urban self-imagination and representation, see Colin Platt, *The English Mediaeval Town*, pp. 49–50. See also Patricia Badir's discussion of the early sixteenth-century walls of Kingston-upon-Hull in "The Garrison of the Godly."

89. Lumiansky and Mills take issue with the theological impossibility of the passage's second line: "God has no need of defense" (*Chester Mystery Cycle*, vol. 2, p. 7). Their comment reflects the problems caused by a continuing critical emphasis on the cycle play as a vehicle for the presentation of a consistent theology. The real God may prove impervious to harm, but the mimetic God on stage in Chester has as much to do with the presentation of a civic ideology as he does with any specific theological point.

90. As Kroll observes in "Cosmic Characters and Human Form," God's *compasse* "strongly suggests not natural boundaries but official or political limits to the area that He [God] chooses to rule" (p. 35).

91. For the record of the 1574 perambulation, see *CPTR*, pp. 212–15.

92. For more on the generation gap structuring oligarchic government, see Charles Phythian-Adams, "Ceremony and the Citizen."

93. With its emphasis on the careful demarcation of space and the establishment of social prohibitions (punishable by expulsion from the blessed site), Play 1 thus replicates the processes which produce what Badir refers to as "bureaucratized" space ("Playing Space," p. 263). God's ability to effectively locate transgression—he immediately returns to Heaven the moment that Lucifer breaks his command and sits on his throne in 1.213—might thus be made analogous to the mayor's own practice of urban surveillance (as exemplified by Smith in *Vale-Royall*).

94. For a variety of documents concerning admission to the freedom of Chester, see *CPTR*, pp. 443–52. Note the regular use in these records of spatial metaphors to describe the process: "admyttyd into the fraunches of this citie" (p. 445), "shalbe enfrachessed and made fre within the said citie" (p. 446), "admyttyd into ye liberties and fraunches of ye citie of Chester" (p. 446),

"meete men to enter into the fredom of this citie and be freemen" (p. 447), and "receyved into the fraunches of the saide cittie" (p. 448).

95. The phrase "in paine of heaven your forefeyture" participates in urban guild discourse going all the way back to the Norfolk guild returns of 1389: there we learn "þat no brother no sister ne shulle discuss þe counseil of þis fraternite to no straungere, vp þe payne of forfeiture of þe fraternite for euermore" (J. T. Smith, L. T. Smith, and L. Brentano, eds., *English Gilds*, p. 76).

96. For an exhaustive list of the institutions and bodies with some claim to authority in Chester, see W. J. Jones, "Exchequer of Chester," pp. 124–25.

97. For a list of several of these orders, see *CPTR*, fn. 1, p. 198. Kennett dates one such order to 1540, quite possibly during the period of civic assertion and self-definition promoted by Henry Gee's mayoralty (*Tudor Chester*, p. 11).

98. For the mayoral license, see Jones, "Exchequer of Chester," p. 157. For the disenfranchisement penalty, see Kennett, *Tudor Chester*, p. 11.

99. *CPTR*, p. 198; Jones, "Exchequer of Chester," p. 158.

100. For a brief history of the Aldersey family, see D. M. Woodward, *The Trade of Elizabethan Chester*, pp. 106–9. For John Aldersey's disenfranchisement, see *CPTR*, p. 198, and Kennett, *Tudor Chester*, p. 11. Detailed accounts of the 1572–74 charter controversy can be found in Jones, "Exchequer of Chester," pp. 157–59; Kennett, *Tudor Chester*, p. 11; and *VCH: Ches.*, vol. 2, p. 39.

101. Kennett, *Tudor Chester*, pp. 10 and 11. Jones is of the opinion that "the possibly genuine question of jurisdictional rights was really only a weapon being wielded by rival factions in the city" ("Exchequer of Chester," p. 158).

102. It may also have been helped along by William's 1553 acquisition of a charter for the newly formed Chester Merchant Adventurers Company: that document effectively denied the other companies, all nominally members of the city's guild merchant, access to foreign trade, forcing them to go through the merchants for goods from overseas. For details of the resulting rancor, see Woodward, *The Trade of Elizabethan Chester*, pp. 73–75.

103. *CPTR*, p. 185.

104. Ibid., p. 251.

105. The city charter of 1564 was surrendered and replaced with a new charter in which the palatinate exchequer's (and thus the earldom's) authority in and over the city was clarified; see Kennett, *Tudor Chester*, p. 11, and *VCH: Ches.*, vol. 2, p. 39. The palatinate also received a guarantee that Chester's Newgate would be open on a regular basis; this gate had been ordered shut by the Assembly in 1573 due to "divers enconvennences" (*CPTR*, p. 238). Local tradition has it that the Assembly's decision was due to the use of the Newgate in the kidnapping of Ellen Aldersey, daughter of alderman Ralph Aldersey (a relative of William's), but whatever the cause, the dispute over the closing of the gate points once again to the extensive role played by issues of space and access in early modern urban politics and culture. In spite of their symbolic function in

Play 1, Play 5, and elsewhere in the cycle, the city walls were not under the total control of the corporation.

106. R. W. Hanning, "'You Have Begun a Parlous Pleye,'" p. 37.

107. Ibid., p. 38.

108. Ibid., p. 33.

109. Travis, *Dramatic Design*, pp. 156–62.

110. Mills, *Recycling the Cycle*, p. 174.

111. Play 13's audience has already seen just such a vagabond in Play 2, the Drapers' *Adam and Eve; Cain and Abel*: there Cain's initial identity as "tyllman" (2.514) gives way (via his murder of Abel) to a new identity: "to all men thou shalt be unleeffe, / idell and wandringe as a theyfe / and overal set at nought" (2.630–32). Cain's redesignation as vagabond is confirmed at several other points in the play. For example, he responds to God's sentence of exile with the assertion that "I will from place to place / and looke where is the best" (2.667–68) and ends the play by observing that "owt of land I will flee. / A losell aye I muste bee, / for scapit I am of thryfte" (2.698–700). Phrases like these echo the concerns of Tudor anti-vagabond discourse: the uncontrolled movement of the able poor across jurisdictional boundaries, the *thryfte* wasted by vagabond idleness, paupers' inclinations toward crime, and so on. Moreover, Cain's vagabondage has direct implications for the Cestrians watching his play: in 2.674–75, he laments that, "whether I bee in house or hall, / 'cursed Cayne' menn will me call." One of the Chester cycle's five extant manuscripts (British Library MS Harley 2124) contains a variant reading of 2.674: "where ever I stand in street or stall." "Street or stall" eschews the private domesticity of "house or hall," shifting Cain to the public streets of the city—the very streets occupied by his spectators. Like Caecus, Cain acknowledges their presence, albeit with a curse instead of a petition: "And now I flee, all yee may see. / I grant you all the same gifte" (2.703–4). Threatening the audience with the possibility of their own descent into vagabondage and crime (an ever-present possibility in the turbulent sixteenth-century economy), Cain assumes the role of defiant vagabond with a vengeance. Caecus will therefore have to work hard to overcome Cain's bad example.

112. Commenting on a 1452–53 ordinance of the Coventry Weavers' Guild concerning the requirements for apprenticeship, noting that a man could only gain access to the guild if he was both "an Englelysch man borne" and possessed of "all his ryght lymes," Travis concludes that "To be a foreigner and to be physically incomplete were similar conditions of existence" ("Social Body of the Dramatic Christ," p. 23). Given that "foreigner" was also a term applied to those individuals excluded from the freedom of the medieval and early modern city, we might read the statement "he could never bye nor sell" as an indication of Caecus's own lack of franchise and, more generally, the problematic relationship of the urban poor to the city's hierarchies of labor. Lumiansky and Mills note the "added significance" this phrase might acquire

"when uttered by a guildsman in a medieval town who was authorized to trade by virtue of his guild status" (*Chester Mystery Cycle*, vol. 2, p. 189). For more on the somatics of labor in English cycle drama, see Claire Sponsler, *Drama and Resistance*, pp. 138–40.

113. Mills's discussion of the Whitsun plays' engagement with contemporary politics in *Recycling the Cycle* (the chapter section entitled "The City as Actor," pp. 173–78) is an exclusively synchronic affair, setting the cycle in an undifferentiated sixteenth-century Chester. No dates appear in the main text of this section, generating an overall sense of an urban culture free of any significant change. Given the historical specificity and diachronic narrative of the rest of *Recycling the Cycle*, "The City as Actor" stands out as a curious anomaly.

114. For overviews of Tudor poor law, see A. L. Beier, *Problem of the Poor* and *Masterless Men*; John Pound, *Poverty and Vagrancy*; and Paul Slack, *Poverty and Policy*.

115. For details of the 1531 Act, see Beier, *Problem of the Poor*, p. 39; Pound, *Poverty and Vagrancy*, p. 37; and Slack, *Poverty and Policy*, p. 118.

116. Slack, *Poverty and Policy*, p. 31.

117. Tudor poor law did gradually move toward the recognition of a third class of paupers, those unemployed through lack of work and not through any deficiency of their own (physical or moral): for a discussion of the "labouring poor," see ibid., pp. 27–31.

118. For the complete text of the order, see *CPTR*, pp. 355–56.

119. Slack notes that his discussion of poverty legislation is "directed towards the centre . . . In the end, embellished and adapted as it was to fit local circumstances, the poor law was a poor law. The centre called the tune. The centre also composed it" (*Poverty and Policy*, p. 114). However, local authorities could (and did) resist national directives: Pound describes the refusal of many provincial magistrates to enforce the harsher provisions of the 1547 Act (*Poverty and Vagrancy*, p. 40). The enactment of early modern poor law is therefore perhaps better seen as a multidirectional effort to achieve accommodation between center and periphery: "Policy was most likely to be effective when rule-makers and enforcers were in agreement" (Beier, *Masterless Men*, p. 147).

120. For the text of Gee's "tabull," see *CPTR*, pp. 257–58.

121. The "tabull" listing the wards combines these two functions: the description of each ward's boundaries includes the number of paupers licensed to beg therein, and several of the entries end by noting that these "pore ffolk" are "admytted by the Maire for the yere being with consent of thalderman of the same Warde" (ibid., p. 257).

122. It also resembles the punishment meted out to disenfranchised citizens as described above in William Aldersey's 1574 petition to Leicester.

123. For more on the 1536 Act, see Slack, *Poverty and Policy*, pp. 118–19.

124. For the complete text of Smith's order, see *CPTR*, pp. 356–57.

125. The "great number and multitude of valient idlle persones and vacabunges which be stronge and able to serve and labur for ther Lyvnge" (ibid., p. 356) were already forbidden from begging "in any plase within Cittie . . . upon payne of imprisonment by Stockes and other ponishment as by any statute of this Reallme is for that case provyded" (ibid., p. 357).

126. In *Poverty and Policy,* Slack provides examples of individual critiques of Elizabeth I's 1572 Act by an Essex husbandman (p. 106) and the Worcestershire MP Miles Sandys (p. 124).

127. For the history of the High Cross, see *VCH: Ches.,* vol. 5, pt. 2, p. 20.

128. I suspect that citizens and sturdy beggars share punishments in the 1539 order due to their bodily similitude: both are assumed to be healthy and capable of labor, whereas the impotent pauper's physical impairments place him or her into a different category altogether (and thus subject him or her to different punishments for violating town statute).

129. See *CPTR,* pp. 192–93.

130. Quoted in Kennett, *Tudor Chester,* p. 26.

131. See Beier, *Problem of the Poor,* pp. 30–31.

132. For more on the play's interest in dynamics of revelation, see Travis, *Dramatic Design,* pp. 145 and 157.

133. Given the earlier establishment of Caecus's lack of free status ("hee could never bye nor sell," 13.187), "hart free" could be read here as indicative of admission to the freedom of Christ's New Jerusalem, an economic system superior to that of Chester.

134. On p. 97 of *Poverty and Policy,* Slack discusses aliases and forged passports, vagabond dodges which necessitated further levels of scrutiny and identification by the authorities. For examples of Cestrian surveys of the poor, see *CPTR,* pp. 357 (Mayor Hugh Aldersey's survey of either 1528–29, 1541–42, or 1546–47), 360–61 (1567), and 362–63 (Mayor John Hanky's 1572 order to survey the poor—the same year as the cycle's penultimate performance).

135. Quoted in Slack, *Poverty and Policy,* p. 125.

CHAPTER 3.   Chester's Triumph

1. All citations of the text of *Chester's Triumph* are taken from Thomas Corser's 1844 Chetham Society edition of the show. Corser's edition is a facsimile of the original 1610 pamphlet, so it provides only signatures, not page numbers. For greater ease of reference, I have followed his lead here.

2. The St. George's Day race belongs to a long-standing tradition of Chester horse racing: see *VCH: Ches.,* vol. 5, pt. 2, pp. 255–60.

3. The route outlined above is conjectural. The only locations explicitly named in both the pamphlet version of the show and the British Library MS

Harley 2150 list of its contents are the High Cross and the Roodee. For the text of this list, see *REED: Cheshire*, pp. 351–52.

4. There is no direct evidence that the mock-battle was staged on the Roodee instead of at the High Cross. However, since the pamphlet text describes the dragon chasing the savages into "their Denne" (A3v), I have located their encounter on the spacious Roodee instead of in the crowded streets of the city proper. Mills concurs with this placement on p. 137 of *Recycling the Cycle.*

5. The winners of both race and tilt also received monetary prizes: for the specific "Articles" of the 1610 race, see *REED: Cheshire*, pp. 349–50.

6. Ibid., p. 579.

7. John Nichols, ed., *Progresses . . . of King James the First*, vol. 2, pp. 307–8. For more on Henry's involvement with the construction and launching of the *Prince Royal*, see Gregory Vaughan McNamara, "'A Perfect Diamond Set in Lead,'" pp. 265–77.

8. David M. Bergeron, *English Civic Pageantry*, p. 92; Mills, *Recycling the Cycle*, p. 138.

9. Mills, *Recycling the Cycle*, pp. 138 and 139.

10. Amery appears to have had no local publishing options: the first book known to be printed in Chester is Randle Holme III's 1688 *Academy of Armory* (ibid., p. 194).

11. Bergeron, *English Civic Pageantry*, p. 64; Kipling, "Triumphal Drama," p. 42. Kipling includes retinues within his expanded mimetic field: "Even the henchmen marching with the *triumphator* in procession often donned costumes and performed crucial mimetic actions" (p. 44).

12. Bergeron, *English Civic Pageantry*, p. 6.

13. Ibid., p. 64.

14. Ibid., p. 6.

15. In 1610 Chester, the city magistrates seated at the Pentice would have had a holistic experience of Amery's show—they were the objects of its various orations and actions. The more partial experience described by Bergeron would have been reserved for those Cestrians outside the civic elite.

16. Stephen Orgel, "Poetics of Spectacle," p. 378. For an important qualification of the sociopolitical effectiveness of Jones's perspectival method, see Russell West, "Perplexive Perspectives."

17. Kipling qualifies this sense of hierarchy, arguing that the *triumphator* "can be made to perform a mimetic action predetermined by the dramatic craft of the civic dramatist" ("Triumphal Drama," p. 45). In this way, local space and civic interests can direct the *triumphator*'s spectacle of authority to their own ends, even as they rely upon the authoritative presence to underwrite and activate such goals. Of course, monarchs could resist the interpellations of urban pageant poets and control their own performances: James's refusal to stay and hear many of the various orations and shows intended for

performance at his 1604 royal entry into London is a prime example of the conflict inherent in pageantry's politics of presence. For a general discussion of the reciprocity inherent in the pageants' dramatic manipulation of royal presence, see Gail Kern Paster, "Idea of London," p. 52; for specific comments on Thomas Dekker's response to James's reluctance to play the part of *triumphator*, see David M. Bergeron, "Stuart Civic Pageants," p. 167.

18. See Bergeron, *English Civic Pageantry*, pp. 74–75 and 104, and Kipling, "Triumphal Drama," pp. 54–55.

19. Roy Strong, *Cult of Elizabeth*, pp. 174–75. Celebrating St. George's Day after the death of Henry in 1547 became difficult: see Muriel C. McClendon, "Moveable Feast," pp. 15–25. As McClendon points out, even Garter knights required "special permission" from Parliament in 1552 to continue celebrating the feast (p. 17).

20. Strong, *Cult of Elizabeth*, p. 175.

21. For descriptions of the St. George's Day celebrations held in these locations, see ibid., p. 175. For more on pageantry's investment in fantasies of political union, see Gordon Kipling, *Enter the King*, p. 47.

22. Indeed, it appears that both Amery and Davies originally expected Henry to be created Prince of Wales and Earl of Chester on St. George's Day. Camber states this explicitly within the show: "Whose *Grace* is thought vpon this present day, / Which day Saint *George* hath blisfully created, / To take his Birth-right" (C1r). The civic documents related to the pageant's production concur: the race "articles" mention "St George his day beinge the three and twentieth day of Aprill" (*REED: Cheshire*, p. 349), and Amery's British Library MS Harley 2150 "maner of the showe" refers to "St Georges day next being the 23th of Aprill 1610" (ibid., p. 351). The historical evidence supports these assumptions: for a discussion of the repeated deferral of the Crown's initial plans for a February 1610 creation, see Pauline Croft, "Parliamentary Installation," pp. 185–86. Davies's post-show preface for *Chester's Triumph* apologizes for "jumping the gun" by observing that this "glorious Triumph, with much more, was meerely intended (as it was then thought) for the ioyfull celebration of *Cambers* boundlesse glory" (A2v).

23. See Glynne Wickham, *Early English Stages*, vol. 2, pt. 1, p. 224. Wickham places Henry in Chester on St. George's Day, stating that "A dragon spouting fire was killed for Prince Henry's amusement in Chester in April 1610."

24. The limitations of presence become clear in the British Library MS Harley 2150 transcription of a speech welcoming the Earl of Leicester to Chester in 1584. Written by Clerk of the Pentice William Knight and delivered by local schoolboy Thomas Throp, the speech addresses "your honour, the Cheefe mentayn<..> defendour and patrone" of Chester, identifying him as "Righte honorable Erle" (*REED: Cheshire*, p. 873). However, a note appended to the speech testifies to the slipperiness of these designations: "it was not well liked

of because he did direct it to Earle darby [Henry Stanley, fourth Earl of Derby, present at Leicester's side]: & hauinge ended sayd God blesse the Earle of darby" (p. 874). The *REED: Cheshire* editors comment that "Thomas seems to have become confused" (p. 868) and accordingly classify the speech's misdirection as an error. Barry Coward has a different suggestion, one more in line with my argument in this chapter: he notes that "Stanley influence in Chester was weakened by the loss of the office of chamberlain of the county palatine from 1564 to 1589 to the earl of Leicester . . . The earls of Derby may have had to share the role of patron in the city, but they had their body of support there" (*The Stanleys*, p. 133). Thomas's mistake may therefore have been a deliberate one, honoring Derby and dismissing Leicester as an outsider and usurper. If physical presence fails to guarantee authority, how can virtual presence do any better?

25. In maintaining James's pride of place, *Chester's Triumph* reveals itself to be as cautious as the various masques and court entertainments celebrating the prince and his creation during the first half of 1610. Ben Jonson and Inigo Jones's *Barriers* and Samuel Daniel's *Tethys' Festival* are both careful not to slight the king, undermining their functions as tributes to Prince Henry: for more on the court politics surrounding Henry's creation, see Norman Council, "Ben Jonson"; Orgel, "The Poetics of Spectacle"; Graham Parry, "The Politics of the Jacobean Masque"; and John Peacock, "Jonson and Jones Collaborate."

26. The passage's secondary division of the elite spectators into groups of old and young recalls the father-son dynamic of its royal references. As I will suggest below in my discussion of Envy, generational difference, whether at court or in the mercantile institutions of the city, is a locus of competition and discord. Chester's description of the magistrates and gentlemen also calls to mind class divisions and antagonisms as it separates the "blisfull crew" of the elite from "the vulgar view" of those Cestrian spectators situated outside the city franchise or the ranks of the gentry (B3v).

27. For more on Jacobean pageantry's increased use of dialogue, see Bergeron, *English Civic Pageantry*, p. 66.

28. For the historical and dramatic continuity linking civic pageants and morality plays, see ibid., pp. 7–8; for a discussion of Envy's role within Elizabethan and Jacobean civic ceremonies, see pp. 281–82. Countering Bergeron's moralistic approach to the vice is M. C. Bradbrook's exploration of the ways in which Envy is "secularized" by seventeenth-century pageant poets ("The Politics of Pageantry," p. 68). My analysis of Envy in this chapter takes a similarly political tack.

29. For a description of the Lord Mayor's Show route, see Theodore B. Leinwand, "London Triumphing," pp. 137–38.

30. See James Knowles, "The Spectacle of the Realm," p. 173.

31. Once again, see Platt, *The English Medieval Town*, pp. 49–50. Chester's long history as an English garrison in the Welsh Marches gives even greater

resonance to Peace's mention of "vnshaken walls," while "litigious braules" brings to mind the jurisdictional battles I discussed in chapter 2.

32. Arguing that Envy is "routed," Bergeron thus fully agrees with the ostensible outcome of the show's pre-race portion (*English Civic Pageantry*, p. 282).

33. For a description of Chester's particular sequence of offices, see *VCH: Ches.*, vol. 5, pt. 1, pp. 97–99.

34. All citations from *Triumphs of Re-United Britannia* are taken from Arthur F. Kinney's *Renaissance Drama* edition of the show.

35. For more on James and Henry's vexed relationship, see David M. Bergeron, *Royal Family, Royal Lovers*, pp. 104–5.

36. McClendon makes a similar point: "In the sixteenth century, when Saint George's Day was marked by the riding of the Banns, humble citizens of Chester, such as the members of the guild of cordwainers and shoemakers, took part in the celebration. Amery's horse race permanently sidelined the lower orders from participation in the commemoration of the day. Their role was now confined to that of spectator, as the gentry riders became the focal point of the celebration" ("Moveable Feast," p. 25). My only caveat here is her designation of the guildsmen as "humble citizens." In a city ruled by a guild merchant oligarchy, the citizens were anything but humble. Indeed, shoemakers held the office of mayor from time to time during the early modern period (*VCH: Ches.*, vol. 5, pt. 1, p. 99). We therefore need to read Amery's show with a more nuanced understanding of social divisions within McClendon's so-called "lower orders": gentry-aligned freemen on the one hand, disenfranchised foreigners on the other.

37. Appealing to Henry, soon to be Earl of Chester and thus chief officer of the Cheshire palatinate, might thus be seen as analogous to the common Chester practice (discussed in chapter 2) of suing one's fellow freemen not in the mayor's portmote court but in the earldom's exchequer court—a practice for which Amery was called to task on at least one occasion (see below).

38. Davies goes along with this assessment, insisting in the pamphlet preface that "Loue deuis'd" the show (A2v).

39. Envy's list includes the anti-civic, self-consuming desire "To see a City burnt" (C3v). Can we read this as the logic of civic emulation taken to its metaphorical extreme?

40. Davies announces in his preface to the pamphlet text that "The chiefest part of this people-pleasing spectacle, consisted in three Bees, *viz. Boyes, Beasts,* and *Bels . . . Boyes* of rare Spirit, and exquisite performance" (A2v).

41. Christina M. Fitzgerald's work on the masculinity of guild culture in Chester's sixteenth-century Whitsun plays applies equally well to this seventeenth-century civic triumph. For more information, see her "Of Magi and Men." Civic status depends in part on a publicly secure gender identity: by linking criticism of the show to the Medusa-like Envy, Amery pre-defines his opponents as effeminate (and thus lesser in nature).

42. J. H. E. Bennett, ed., *Rolls of the Freemen*, p. 78. Amery's father was sheriff in 1586–87 (*CPTR*, p. 583); his grandfather, sheriff in 1554–55 (ibid., p. 582), figures in John Foxe's *Book of Martyrs* as one of the men escorting Protestant martyr George Marsh to his execution (ibid., pp. 71–72).

43. CCALS ZAB/1, fol. 282d; CCALS ZMB/28, fol. 243; and CCALS ZAB/1, fol. 305.

44. CCALS ZMB/29, fols. 169 and 242. Amery's will (CCALS WS Amery 1613) survives, revealing to us that he lived on Bridge Street in St. Bridget's parish.

45. CCALS ZQSF/56, item 41. The charge was dismissed.

46. CCALS ZAB/1, fol. 287d. It is not clear what penalty, if any, was levied against Amery and his fellows in this case.

47. Ibid., fol. 316d.

48. Ibid., fol. 316. Button's wealth was extensive: at his death in 1618, he was worth £713 (*VCH: Ches.*, vol. 5, pt. 1, p. 102).

49. Button's election as alderman allowed him to outdo Amery once more: in 1616, four years after Amery's death, he was elected mayor of Chester (*VCH: Ches.*, vol. 5, pt. 2, p. 314).

50. Due to the *REED: Cheshire* editors' redating of many of the records related to the 1610 show (as well as their discovery of a previously unknown pageant document), the following account of civic response to *Chester's Triumph* differs from that given in my "Absent *Triumphator*" essay.

51. For the complete text of this record, see *REED: Cheshire*, pp. 351–53.

52. The "maner of the showe" order is not the same as that given in the published pamphlet: see the appendix (pp. 208–10) of my "Absent *Triumphator*" essay for a precise accounting of the two lists' differences.

53. Corser claims in his notes to *Chester's Triumph* that Harley 2150 is "drawn up in the hand-writing of Mr. Amery himself" (no page number given). A look at the manuscript confirms that "the maner of the show" is written in a hand other than Holme's, a point with which Clopper agrees (*REED: Chester*, p. 260). But it does not follow that this unknown hand is Amery's own: Margaret Groombridge notes in the introduction to her *Calendar of Chester City Council Minutes* that professional scribes were routinely hired to write clean copies of petitions to the Assembly (p. vii).

54. *REED: Cheshire*, p. 352.

55. Ibid., p. 352.

56. *OED*, sense 1.

57. Ibid., sense 4.

58. *REED: Cheshire*, pp. 352–53. The phrase "now all is done" suggests that at least the poem, if not the entire "maner of showe," was written down after 23 April 1610.

59. Ibid., p. 353.

60. Ibid., p. 353.

61. *OED*, sense 2.

62. For a still relevant introduction to petitionary verse, see J. A. Burrow, "The Poet as Petitioner."

63. *REED: Cheshire*, pp. 350–51. The document in question (CCALS ZAF 8/38, fol. 2) is undated: as Groombridge notes, petitions to the Assembly "were never dated by the petitioner, who sometimes had to apply several times before he obtained an answer to his request" (*Calendar of Chester City Council Minutes*, p. viii). The *REED: Cheshire* editors date the petition to 1609–10. We can be more precise than that: as the petition's use of the phrase "did lately" with reference to Amery's staging of the triumph indicates, the show is over and done with. I would therefore date the document to sometime after 23 April and before mid-October 1610: the petition names William Leicester as mayor of Chester, and his 1609–10 term would have ended with Thomas Harvey's election to the office on the Friday after the feast of St. Denis (9 October).

64. *REED: Cheshire*, p. 350.

65. Ibid., p. 350.

66. Ibid., p. 350.

67. Ibid., p. 350.

68. Ibid., p. 350.

69. Ibid., p. 351.

70. Groombridge's description of the petitionary process suggests that it had its performative elements: "it was often advisable to provide entertainment if support was wanted for a measure" (*Calendar of Chester City Council Minutes*, p. vii). For example, in 1603–4, representatives of the Painters' company spent eight pence to buy "wyne at Thomas Alertons tavern" for the clerk of the Pentice, the civic official responsible for presenting petitions to the Assembly (ibid., p. viii). This sort of bribe may not initially seem performative until we remember the Chester "shot" (as discussed in chapter 2).

71. For the complete text of this petition, see *REED: Cheshire*, pp. 358–59.

72. Ibid., p. 358.

73. Ibid., p. 358.

74. Ibid., p. 355.

75. Ibid., p. 357.

76. Ibid., p. 360.

77. Ibid., p. 371.

78. I base my figures here on a St. George's Day race proclamation dated ca. 1609 (*REED: Cheshire*, pp. 347–48). This document summons twenty-six companies to the Roodee "vpon St Geor<..>s day Anno 1609" (ibid., p. 348). The year "1609" is actually an interlinear insertion after "Anno," so it's possible that the document, originally prepared for a later running of the race, has been backdated to the mayoral year 1609–10. But a 1610 date seems equally

likely. The proclamation includes the Beerbrewers and the Drawers of the Dee as a single company for the purposes of the race (ibid., p. 347), and I have counted them accordingly.

79. CCALS ZAB/1, fol. 327.

80. *REED: Cheshire*, pp. 375–76.

81. Ibid., p. 374.

82. For information on the wider cultural background of Stuart-era opposition to games and "recreation," see Leah S. Marcus, *The Politics of Mirth.*

83. *REED: Cheshire*, p. 374.

84. Edward Arber, ed., *Transcript of the Registers of the Company of Stationers*, vol. 3, p. 436.

85. A fourth such text is Daniel Price's sermon *The Creation of the Prince*, printed by George Eld for Roger Jackson and entered by Jackson into the Stationers' Register on 14 June 1610, two days after *Chester's Triumph* (ibid., vol. 3, p. 436).

86. *REED: Cheshire*, p. 579.

87. Ibid., p. 579.

88. The paratext of *Chester's Triumph* generates a similar presence effect: on signature A1v, just across from a dedicatory poem written by Davies, the pamphlet includes an image of the Prince's heraldic device (the ostrich-feathers-and-coronet badge accompanied by the motto "Ich dien"). Like the shields included in Amery's show, this image offers readers a heightened level of virtual presence to compensate for the lack of the Prince's physical presence.

89. Womack, "Imagining Communities," p. 105.

90. See Bergeron, "Stuart Civic Pageants," p. 168, and Paula Johnson, "Jacobean Ephemera," pp. 161–62. For a counterargument concerning the commercial potential of masque and pageant publication, see Lauren Shohet, "The Masque as Book."

91. These and all other citations of Munday's *London's Love* and Dekker's *Troia-Nova Triumphans* are taken from the EEBO versions of the two pageants.

92. Johnson, "Jacobean Ephemera," p. 162.

93. Westminster masques and London pamphlets did occasionally acquire a nonlocal audience: for specific instances, see Shohet, "The Masque as Book," pp. 162–63.

94. For more on the court-focused aspects of London pageants, see Lawrence Manley, *Literature and Culture in Early Modern London*, pp. 212–93, and Nancy E. Wright, "'Rival Traditions.'" In addition, although Knowles makes a compelling counterargument for London pageantry's pursuit of a national audience in "The Spectacle of the Realm," he nonetheless acknowledges that the shows' nationalizing rhetoric is largely a defensive response to the provinces' "anti-metropolitan polemic" (p. 167). *Chester's Triumph* should thus be read in relation to regional antagonism toward London.

95. *VCH: Ches.*, vol. 2, p. 36.

96. *MED*, sense 3a of *dever*.

97. For more on the triumph as Advent, see Kipling, *Enter the King.*

98. Womack, "Imagining Communities," p. 104.

99. See McNamara, "'A Perfect Diamond Set in Lead,'" pp. 278–87.

100. The decision to pit English ships against Turkish pirates is a deliberate nod to Prince Henry's desire to lead a new Crusade against the Turks. For more on Henry's Protestant militarism (particularly in relation to his masquing identity as Meliadus, the *miles a Deo*), see Parry, "The Politics of the Jacobean Masque," and Peacock, "Jonson and Jones Collaborate."

101. Paster, "Idea of London," p. 49.

102. Ibid., p. 49.

103. For example, we have an account of Bristol's 1613 entertainment for Anne of Denmark (published that same year in London), which clearly makes use of strategies similar to those deployed in *Chester's Triumph.* For a copy of the text, see Nichols, *Progresses . . . of King James the First*, vol. 2, pp. 648–66. A single passage suffices to convey the fact of Bristol's urban self-consciousness: impressed by the spectacle of the city's soldiery, the Queen tells her entourage that "Brave Bristoll men from all the Land have borne the prize away" (ibid., p. 654).

104. *VCH: Ches.*, vol. 2, p. 36.

105. Womack, "Imagining Communities," p. 107.

106. Neither of the two main modern anthologies of medieval English drama—David Bevington's *Medieval Drama* and Greg Walker's *Medieval Drama*—include civic ceremonies. The situation is only slightly better in Renaissance studies: while Bevington's *English Renaissance Drama* features only "plays," Kinney's *Renaissance Drama* does contain two royal entries and a Lord Mayor's Show (Munday's *Triumphs*).

107. *REED: Cheshire*, p. 442.

108. McClendon would locate that end earlier: "The Marian observance of the 23 April feast simply disappeared after 1558. The craft guilds that had made gifts of money to local prisoners on that day no longer did so, and the churchwardens of Holy Trinity parish ceased to make payments to have a banner carried in procession on that day. For the following half century, Saint George's Day passed without any attention from the corporation of Chester, the local church, or the city's craft guilds" ("Moveable Feast," p. 24). But the guild accounts referencing the riding of the Banns make no explicit mention of St. George's Day either before 1558 or after that year. The Banns are simply ridden before every performance of the plays up to (and including) 1575, and payments are made to cover the costs of the riding. Without any positive evidence of a post-1558 shift in the riding's date, I am inclined to accept Rogers's account at face value and cut McClendon's era of neglect in half.

109. See Mills, *Recycling the Cycle*, pp. 88–89.
110. Ibid., pp. 90–95.

CHAPTER 4.   *Heraldic Devices/Chivalric Divisions*

1. Arguing that the scribe's dialect must be distinguished from that of the poet, H. N. Duggan places *SGGK* in Staffordshire proper, "well south of . . . the Cotton Nero A.x scribe" and his proximity to the Cheshire-Staffordshire border ("Meter, Stanza, Vocabulary, Dialect," p. 241). Ad Putter and Myra Stokes disagree: in their recent reexamination of the dialectal profile used by Duggan and others to locate *SGGK* in Staffordshire (the so-called "southern drift"), they conclude that the poem's language is more accurately attributed to "a home dialect somewhat north of Staffordshire" ("*The Linguistic Atlas* and the Dialect of the *Gawain* Poems," pp. 488 and 489). In other words, Putter and Stokes tentatively return the poem to Cheshire. Such debates about *SGGK*'s provenance have little immediate bearing on my argument in this chapter: in what follows, I rely more on the poem's explicit location of Gawain's adventures in regional Cheshire than on any necessary belief in the poet's Cestrian credentials. The poem's discourse of regionalism matters more to me than its precise point of origin.

2. For a concise summary of the authorship debate up to 1997, see Malcolm Andrew, "Theories of Authorship." The search for the poet's true identity continues: for one of the most recent hypotheses, see Leo Carruthers, "The Duke of Clarence and the Earls of March." John Bowers analyzes this scholarly quest, detecting in much of it an academic anxiety about the place of anonymous poetry within the author-driven canon of British literature (*The Politics of Pearl*, pp. 5–10).

3. R. W. V. Elliott, "Landscape and Geography," p. 113. This essay is based on the much larger body of work Elliott assembles in *The Gawain Country*. In both studies, Elliott identifies the Cheshire-Staffordshire border landmark of Ludchurch as his choice for the Green Chapel's historical referent; he also posits nearby Swythamley Park as the model for Hautdesert's topography. My own study of *SGGK*'s regionalism steers away from Elliott's reflectionist approach, reading the poet's citation of local features not as a response to topographical inspiration but as an element in a politically targeted discourse of provinciality.

4. For the fullest statement of Bennett's historical thesis, see his *Community, Class, and Careerism*.

5. See Bowers, *The Politics of Pearl*, pp. 69–76 and 187–95.

6. See James R. Hulbert, "A Hypothesis Concerning the Alliterative Revival"; Thorlac Turville-Petre, "The 'Pearl'-Poet in His 'Fayre Regioun'"; and Ingham, *Sovereign Fantasies*, pp. 107–36.

7. It is perhaps appropriate to note at this point that the *MED* entries for the terms *province* and *provincial* are value-neutral. Indeed, *province* is an effective synonym for "nation" throughout the late Middle Ages; see *MED* sense b of *province* for examples as recent as the second half of the fifteenth century. In addition, according to the *OED*, the *provinces* (that portion of the nation separate from the capital) are first cited as late as 1638 (*province*, sense I.6), and the dismissive connotations of *provincial* as "backwards" or "countrified" date to the early 1700s (*provincial*, senses A.6 and B.8). To be sure, Middle English terms like *uplondish* perform similar, derogatory functions within the culture, but there is a sense in which regional difference has not yet been demonized or subsumed under the category of rural idiocy. Therefore, throughout this chapter, I will be somewhat perversely using "provinciality" as nothing more than a synonym for "regionality" or "locality."

8. All citations from *SGGK* are taken from the fourth edition of Malcolm Andrew and Ronald Waldron's *The Poems of the Pearl Manuscript*.

9. See Andrew and Waldron's note for lines 698ff. (ibid., p. 234).

10. Elliott, *The Gawain Country*, pp. 65–66.

11. Michael J. Bennett, "The Historical Background," p. 89. In *Community, Class, and Careerism*, Bennett links the experience of traversing the route to a final stage of poetic composition: "In all likelihood the *Gawain*-poet was one of their number, and on his return home sat down to re-work a poem first conceived, commissioned and composed at court" (p. 235). This idea of nostalgic revision ("he wrote for a world which had been shattered," p. 235) seems more a critical fantasy than a "likelihood," especially given both our inability to precisely date the poem and the route's historical association with Anglo-Welsh conflict.

12. Ingham, *Sovereign Fantasies*, p. 116. Curiously, Ingham's list leaves out Edward I's advances along this line in the Anglo-Welsh wars of 1277, 1282–83, and 1294–95, a sequence of battles and castle-raisings that ended in the subjugation of *Wallia pura* and the 1301 establishment of the Principality of Wales.

13. Ibid., pp. 116 and 131.

14. For Knight's comment that Gawain's "journey begins in England, continues into Wales and then . . . crosses the border back into England," see "All Dressed Up with Someplace to Go," p. 272. For my own prior discussion of the route, see "Writing from the Marches," p. 206.

15. By locating Hautdesert in the middle of the sequence "Troy (Camelot [Wirral { Hautdesert } Green Chapel] Camelot) Troy," *SGGK* offers readers an intriguing inversion of the center-periphery binary that informs the poem's politics. That which the narrative proper presents as marginal actually occupies the majority of the audience's attention—a customary strategy in chivalric romance.

16. Both Elliott (*The Gawain Country*, p. 41) and Turville-Petre ("The 'Pearl'-Poet in His 'Fayre Regioun,'" p. 288) agree that the inclusion of known

sites within this passage of *SGGK* functions as a signal to readers, that the naming of mundane places in the midst of traditional romance topography is meant to stop the audience short. I concur: the sort of geographical orientation I am discussing here is encouraged by the poem and not an imposition upon it. The *Gawain*-poet mentions familiar toponyms so that we are well aware of Gawain's precise location leading up to his testing at Hautdesert.

17. Traditionally, the River Severn marks the western border of Logres (England): as Geoffrey of Monmouth says in his *Historia Regum Britanniae*, "Has duas prouincias [Loegria and Cornubia] seiungit sabrina kambria id est gualia" ("the Severn separates the provinces of Logres and Cornwall from Cambria or Wales," p. 330). However, in the *Itinerarium Kambriae*, Gerald of Wales grants the Dee a similar border status: "Trasvadato tandem Deiae fluvio sub Cestria, quem Kambri Deverdoeu dicunt, feria tertia ante Pascha, die videlicet absolutionis, Cestriam venimus. Sicut enim Waia ab austro sub castro Strigulensi, sic Deia a borea sub Cestrensi castro Galliam ab Anglia seperat et secernit" ("Below Chester we crossed a ford over the River Dee, which the Welsh call Dwfr Dwy, and so came to Chester itself on the Day of Absolution, the third day before Easter. Just as the River Wye separates Wales from England in the south, near Striguil Castle, so the River Dee divides the two countries in the north at Chester Castle," p. 139). As we saw in the introduction, Gerald's Dee is an ambiguous boundary, shifting its topography in relation to the ongoing status of the English colonial project. But it nonetheless remains a border: once Gawain crosses the river, he is back in England.

18. See Ingham, *Sovereign Fantasies*, pp. 119–20.

19. Ibid., pp. 117 and 118. Christine Chism makes a similar argument: "Gawain falls off the map and into a landscape untouched by human nomenclature or history. Only nature has left its traces there" (*Alliterative Revivals*, p. 75). She goes on to note that "In this passage the poet portrays the desolation of the uncleared oak forests of the North West Midlands, virtually untouched by the late fourteenth century" (ibid.). However, the late fourteenth-century Wirral was anything but "untouched": "The forest of Wirral was created in a region where there was little recorded woodland in 1086 and a relatively high density of population" (*VCH: Ches.*, vol. 2, p. 167).

20. Like Ingham, Chism overlooks these human *frekez*, restricting the region's "natural inhabitants" to the pitiful (and animalistic) birds of lines 746–47 (*Alliterative Revivals*, p. 75).

21. Given the intervening phrases "gates straunge / In mony a bonk vnbene" (lines 709–10) and "contrayez straunge" (line 713), it could be argued that the desolate wasteland Gawain crosses in lines 713–39 belongs outside the space designated by "þe wyldrenesse of Wyrale." However, even if the Wirral does extend its reach to take in "dragons, trolls, and giants," it is nevertheless a problematically wild space, one which is both inhabited and empty of civilization.

22. See Andrew and Waldron's note for lines 701ff. (*The Poems of the Pearl Manuscript*, p. 234). A brief sampling from my personal library alone (note the repetition of "notorious"): Charles Moorman calls the Wirral "a notorious resort of criminals" (*The Works of the Gawain-Poet*, p. 331); Ralph Elliott, "part of a notoriously lawless corner of fourteenth-century England" (*The Gawain Country*, p. 34); Helen Cooper, "a notorious refuge for outlaws" (in Keith Harrison's Oxford World's Classics translation of *SGGK*, p. 99); Christopher Baswell and Anne Howland Schotter, "a wild area and resort of outlaws" (*The Longman Anthology of British Literature*, vol. 1A, p. 202). For Henry L. Savage's claim and his designation of the Wirral as "a lawless locality," see "A Note of *Sir Gawain and the Green Knight* 700–2," p. 456. Savage attributes the 20 July 1376 disafforestation of the Wirral to a royal policy aimed at exposing criminals and outlaws (p. 455). However, as R. Stewart-Brown had pointed out previously, the charter in question contains no mention of human malefactors, but instead seeks relief from the damage to property caused by the *savagyns* or "wild beasts" protected by forest law ("The Disafforestation of Wirral," p. 166). In spite of the Stewart-Brown's charter evidence, Savage argues that "it is reasonable to believe that the civil authority might not wish to admit that it found law enforcement difficult" and, in an instance of circular reasoning, posits lines 700–702 of *SGGK* as support for his argument about the intended allusion of lines 700–702 ("A Note of *Sir Gawain and the Green Knight* 700–2," pp. 455–56)! It is perhaps time for the Wirral (advertised in 1999 on a bumper sticker I saw in the window of the Wirral Country Park Visitor Centre at Thurstaston as "The Leisure Peninsula") to receive a second look.

23. Bennett, *Community, Class, and Careerism*, p. 225. There was a local disturbance in 1381, traditionally linked to the Rising in the southeast; for a record of the Wirral rebellion, see R. B. Dobson, ed., *The Peasants' Revolt of 1381*, pp. 297–99. However, Bennett's analysis of the Wirral *nativi* and their "revolt" uncovers "no specific allegations of violence," just "responsible men of solid means, who were finding their dues and disabilities irksome and were aiming at their reduction or abolition through legal action rather than armed rebellion" (Bennett, *Community, Class, and Careerism*, pp. 94–95). While it is possible to imagine lines 701–2 as a winking reference to and dismissal of men such as these, it is also equally likely that the poem's "wyldrenesse of Wyrale" is less a reflectionist allusion than it is a transformation of familiar ground into romance terrain.

24. Turville-Petre, "The 'Pearl'-Poet in His 'Fayre Regioun,'" p. 288.

25. For the texts of the depositions and many of the other documents produced by the dispute, see Nicholas Harris Nicolas, *De controversia in curia militari inter Richardum le Scrope et Robertum Grosvenor milites*. All subsequent citations from the case records are taken from vol. 1 of Nicolas's edition. Translations of the records are my own, albeit with some help from the various summaries included in J. G. Nichols, "The Scrope and Grosvenor Controversy."

26. Bennett, "The Historical Background," p. 72.

27. For the poem's partial erasure of France from its opening series of imperial conquests, see Ingham, *Sovereign Fantasies*, pp. 115–16.

28. Grosvenor's Norman origin story has little basis in fact: as R. Stewart-Brown indicates, no evidence exists linking Grosvenor's line to that of any of William the Conqueror's companions ("The Scrope and Grosvenor Controversy, 1385–1391," pp. 11–12). However, for my purposes, the only fact that matters is Grosvenor's belief in that origin and the extent to which it was shared by the deponents testifying on his behalf. The prestige of a Norman and (perhaps more important) imperial origin is what counts here.

29. Joel Rosenthal notes that "For virtually every deponent, testimony that rested on visual memory was key" (*Telling Tales*, p. 66).

30. For the list of Grosvenor's armorials, see ibid., pp. 17–19. The Rector of Medeburn's list appears on pp. 222–26 of Nicolas's edition.

31. Although the "home de comuns" or "man of the commons" (p. 40) is expressly excluded from testifying in the case (the Constable cannot imagine a commoner capable of exercising "conissaunz darmes," "knowledge of arms," p. 40), it is nevertheless quite possible that the commissioning and production of armorials was ultimately intended for more than just a self-reflective aristocratic audience. Here I depart slightly from Lee Patterson's account of Scrope-Grosvenor in *Chaucer and the Subject of History*. On p. 175, he argues that chivalry was "a form of life that was autonomous and self-sustaining, complete in itself and requiring no authentication from outside." He later makes reference to aristocratic anxieties over "the extension of the [heraldic] system beyond the nobility" (p. 182). I agree that the primary audience for heraldic displays was fellow armigers, that "the chivalric community of honor" (p. 183) was most invested in exhibiting itself to itself. But the inscription of arms on tombs and in church windows (and over tavern doors in London, as Chaucer's testimony reveals) suggests that the nobility saw some benefit in presenting their self-images for wider, less class-specific consumption. Moreover, once the image is public, total control over the conditions of its reception is lost—anyone viewing the arms is free to read it in conjunction with their own horizon of expectations. As Patterson says (and here I concur), "Because of its visibility, its location in the contingency of the material sign, rather than in an intangible, inner realm, it [chivalric identity] is always vulnerable to depredation and decay" (p. 186).

32. Ibid., p. 185.

33. Quoted in Stewart-Brown, "The Scrope and Grosvenor Controversy, 1385–1391," pp. 8–9. Bennett sees Gaunt's decision to use English instead of the Court of Chivalry's customary French as evidence that "Grosvenor may not have been entirely at home in the language" ("The Historical Background," p. 71). That supposition is crucial, for it permits Bennett to assert that "Grosvenor almost certainly sought Scrope's pardon in the dialect of the *Gawain*-poet"

(ibid., p. 71). However, as Duggan details on pp. 240–42 of "Meter, Stanza, Vocabulary, Dialect," there may have been substantial differences between the dialects of the poet (Duggan suggests north-central Staffordshire) and of the scribe (the Cheshire-Staffordshire border area near Grosvenor's seat of Hulme). Moreover, Gaunt's use of English might have been directed at members of Parliament as much as at Grosvenor.

34. Depositions like these contradict Bennett's statement that "there is no mention at all of written records, books of hours, heraldic texts or literary works" in the testimony on Grosvenor's behalf ("The Historical Background," p. 74). We might also consider a document transmitted to the Constable on 21 January 1390 by the commissioners in charge of Grosvenor's appeal: in it, they request delivery of a number of charters and "diverses cronicles" submitted as evidence on Sir Robert's behalf and still in the custody of the Court of Chivalry (p. 334).

35. Patterson, *Chaucer and the Subject of History*, p. 185.

36. The socio-spatial effectiveness of such armorials is due to their immobility, their fixed positions within the physical and cultural landscape. They offer the armiger a stable chivalric identity. The smaller, portable armorials—such as Grosvenor's escutcheon or the sign he hangs out on Friday Street in London for Chaucer to notice (see below)—might be best understood as tactically useful extensions of that identity, temporary expansions of the knight's honor.

37. Many of the knights and esquires who testified for Grosvenor were his relatives, reminding us that a regional community was frequently coterminous with a familial one. This was especially true in the Cheshire-Lancashire region: Bennett notes, "Certainly the Cheshire and Lancashire population was more than usually inbred. Between 1374 and 1427 a quarter of all the papal dispensations granted to English couples for consanguineous marriages were issued to residents of the archdeaconry of Chester" (*Community, Class, and Careerism*, pp. 11–12).

38. Writing about the presence of Grosvenor's arms on Friday Street in London (part of Geoffrey Chaucer's testimony on Scrope's behalf), Paul Strohm argues in similar terms to my own: "A newcomer has staked his claim; first territorial and then seigneurial and genealogical. Surprising, in other words, is not the mere fact of Grosvenor's accomodation, or even its ostentatious announcement, but its encroachment, both upon this street and upon the symbolic terrain of the Scropes" (*Theory and the Premodern Text*, p. 7).

39. While Grosvenor's commissioners display their familiarity with the topography of the Chester venue for depositions ("lesglise de Seint Johan de Cestre en le suburbe de Cestre joust le rivere de Dee," "the church of Saint John of Chester in the suburb of Chester next to the River Dee," p. 246), Scrope's representatives refer to it twice as "lesglise de Seint Johan dehors lez mures de

West Chestre" (pp. 78, 79, my italics). The addition of *West* to *Chestre* suggests an outsider's point of view and perhaps speaks to the Scrope commissioners' sense that they were making an incursion into unfriendly and, in at least one case, hostile territory: Sir William Brereton, a cousin of Grosvenor's, refused three summons to testify on 4 September 1386 and ended up being fined £20 for his "grande contumace" (p. 83). Brereton happily testified on his cousin's behalf shortly thereafter (pp. 262–63). Brereton's resistance to the Constable's orders may represent the sort of "contestation" Ingham detects in the Green Knight's own refusal to acknowledge Arthur's authority at Camelot (*Sovereign Fantasies*, p. 125).

40. See Bennett, *Community, Class, and Careerism*, pp. 5–20. There Bennett comments on the "regional solidarity of the knightly class" demonstrated by Grosvenor's deponents (p. 16).

41. For a list of the Coventry deponents, see p. 360 of Nicolas's edition; the text of their depositions is no longer extant.

42. Bennett mentions Owain Glyndwr and Bagot on p. 16 of *Community, Class, and Careerism*, making much the same point as I do above, but fails to include Tudor Glyndwr in this list of outsiders.

43. Bennett, "The Historical Background," p. 77.

44. Ibid., p. 77.

45. It should be noted that the London area's effective status as national capital was called into question during the early 1390s, particularly during the king's financial dispute with the city. For more information on Richard's threats and plans to relocate the capital elsewhere, see Caroline M. Barron, "The Quarrel of Richard II with London, 1392–97," and John H. Harvey, "Richard II and York." For a brief discussion of late 1390s "rumours that Richard intended to rule from Wales and Ireland and that he would never return to England," see R. R. Davies, "Richard II and the Principality of Chester 1397–9," pp. 273–74.

46. For a summary of Grosvenor's military exploits, see Bennett, *Community, Class, and Careerism*, p. 166.

47. Patterson, *Chaucer and the Subject of History*, p. 186.

48. Like Patterson, Rosenthal considers the knightly communities at odds in the controversy as members of a national chivalric class: "Though they were now scattered across the kingdom, necessitating hearings in many venues, this community—the veterans of foreign wars—was reconstituted through speech acts" (*Telling Tales*, p. xxiii). His acknowledgment that "North-country identity, of course, was a strong feature of the sense of community" informing the Scrope depositions literally ends up as a footnote to his larger argument about transregional culture (ibid., fn. 38, p. 183).

49. Quoted in Stewart-Brown, "The Scrope and Grosvenor Controversy, 1385–1391," p. 9.

50. Ibid., p. 9.

51. Ibid., p. 8.

52. Ibid., p. 8.

53. Ibid., p. 9.

54. Ibid., p. 9.

55. Differences like Gloucester's plain silver bordure were often used in late medieval English heraldry to designate cadency, a son's status within a given family. In rejecting the symbolic imputation of a familial connection to Scrope, Grosvenor is not only denying any participation in Scrope's particular affinity, but refusing the suggestion of junior status that a mark of cadency usually communicates. For discussions of bordures as marks of difference that make explicit reference to the Scrope-Grosvenor dispute, see Arthur Charles Fox-Davies, *A Complete Guide to Heraldry*, pp. 138–41 and 481–83.

56. Stewart-Brown, "The Scrope and Grosvenor Controversy, 1385–1391," p. 6.

57. Gerald Grosvenor, the sixth and current Duke of Westminster (as well as Sir Robert's distant descendant), still bears this device, and it can be seen throughout modern Chester and Cheshire—most prominently on the facade of the Grosvenor Hotel, Chester's swankiest hostelry, and in the windows above the south aisle of Chester Cathedral. For more on the romance history of "Randolf Erl of Chestre," see J. W. Ashton, "Rymes . . . of Randolf, Erle of Chestre," and Sharon Kinoshita, "Male-Order Brides," pp. 66–69.

58. For an account of the Scottish campaign of 1385 and King Richard's summons of the levy, see Nigel Saul, *Richard II*, pp. 144–45.

59. Scrope had served as Richard's chancellor in 1377–79 and 1381–82, being dismissed by the king in 1382 over a monetary dispute: see ibid., p. 111. Scrope's various royal offices (and the affiliation with national concerns that they might represent) do not necessarily erase or overwhelm his regional identities: in July 1379, he received permission to crenellate his seat at Bolton Castle, an indicator of a continued interest in his local, Yorkshire honor. As I will argue repeatedly throughout this chapter (and indeed throughout the entire book), the point is not that the national and the regional are exclusive categories, but that they are simultaneous, that the individual subjects existing within their discursive sway are capable of practicing multiple spatio-cultural identities, selves whose hierarchy of dominance is situational and contextual.

60. The deponents' use (on both sides) of the language of "publik vois et fame" has implications for the study of public poetry in late medieval England. What if the public poet of the fourteenth and fifteenth centuries is reconceived as not only a national but a regional figure? Can public poetry emerge in the provinces along with its more customary location in the London-centered circles of writers like Chaucer, Gower, and Langland?

61. Even such pro-Cestrian scholars as John Bowers share in this sentiment. When Bowers writes that early fifteenth-century patronage of Southeastern

writers "eventually succeeded at establishing an official canon of English poets known by full name [as well as] excluding from the official pantheon those shadowy provincials such as William Langland and, far more effectively, the nameless Cheshire author of *Pearl*" (*The Politics of Pearl*, p. 195), he is essentially postdating Turville-Petre's Ricardian transition to a Lancastrian moment that is more congenial to his own narrative of suppression and loss. Again, while I do not wish to dispute the increasing importance over time of London and the Southeast in literary production and consumption, I do want to reiterate that reading and writing soldier on in the provinces—that (as we have seen throughout this book) a shift in political and economic power does not necessitate the cessation of regional voices. The texts produced in the Northwest during the fifteenth and sixteenth centuries may not meet the exacting standards of the official, London-centered canon, but those texts were still produced and still consumed.

62. Ralph Hanna III, "Sir Thomas Berkeley and His Patronage," p. 913.

63. We can complicate the situation further, replacing the multiregional triangulation of Cheshire, Yorkshire, and Westminster with a four-coordinate system that adds Cornwall to the mix: deponents for both Scrope and Grosvenor described prior encounters that each man had with members of the Carminowe family, a Cornish clan who also bore the arms *azure a bend or*. For a summary of the testimony on the Carminowe claim to the device, see Stewart-Brown, "The Scrope and Grosvenor Controversy, 1385–1391," pp. 15–16.

64. Turville-Petre, "The 'Pearl'-Poet in His 'Fayre Regioun,'" p. 289. There is a certain cognitive dissonance to be found here in Turville-Petre's use of an international discourse to shore up national identity: he never makes it clear how sharing a class-centered affinity with "frenkysch fare" (line 1116) heightens one's sense of feeling English as opposed to feeling Cestrian. Indeed, Turville-Petre has recently abandoned his arguments for a nationalizing *SGGK*, linking the romance's investment in "a court culture that is international" to a cosmopolitan Ricardian "attachment to European culture" ("Afterword: The Brutus Prologue to *Sir Gawain and the Green Knight*," pp. 345, 340).

65. Patterson, *Chaucer and the Subject of History*, p. 188.

66. Turville-Petre, "The 'Pearl'-Poet in His 'Fayre Regioun,'" p. 289. The modern equation between "provincial" and "apish" informs Turville-Petre's comment here: provincial Hautdesert and central Camelot share the same court culture, but Hautdesert is definitely the junior partner of the two courts (the inconclusive "strove to imitate" versus the wholly realized sense of "eminently exemplified").

67. Ibid., p. 289. Here Turville-Petre once again reads *SGGK*'s provinciality through an anachronistic lens: as we have seen above, *prouinces* is not limited to "region" in Middle English, but can also be used as a term for "nation." This is certainly the case in *Cleanness*, one of *SGGK*'s fellow British Library MS Cotton Nero A.x poems. There we see the elite Israelite captives, victims of

Babylonian imperial aggression, referred to as "Þe pruddest of þe prouince" (line 1300). One of those prisoners is Daniel, "A prophete of þat prouince and pryce of the worlde" (line 1614) and "Profete of þat prouince þat prayed my fader" (line 1624). *Cleanness* certainly depicts Israel as an area in the process of being provincialized (as we understand the term today), but it also seems implicitly clear to me that Israel is more than just a dependent region—it is instead a foreign nation conquered by an alien foe. The *prouinces* of *SGGK* may carry the same national connotation.

68. Here we should remember Ingham's point about the elision of the Normans from the history traced in *SGGK*'s first stanza (*Sovereign Fantasies*, pp. 115–16). Only by removing the French conquerors outside the boundaries of the British body politic can the fiction of a continuous Trojan-British gene-alogy be maintained. The Normans become a "French flod" located just out-side the Britains' field of honor.

69. See Clare R. Kinney, "The (Dis)Embodied Hero."

70. I say "British" here because "England" is as marginal in the poem as "France," if not more so. "England" shows up but once, in the description of the pentangle: there we are told that "Englych hit [the pentangle] callen / Oueral, as I here, 'þe endeles knot'" (lines 629–30). The *Gawain*-poet's use of *Englych* here is reminiscent of the first line of *Saint Erkenwald*: "At London in Englond" (line 1). John Burrow has argued that this line indicates an authorial location outside England proper, a position near the Welsh border in Cheshire ("*Saint Erkenwald* Line 1," p. 22). I would suggest that a similar strategy may be at work in *SGGK*: the poet can say that the English call the pentangle "the endless knot" because he in some sense identifies as other than English. The modify-ing phrase "as I here" increases the perceived gap between the poet and the English, attributing his knowledge of the vernacular translation to hearsay.

71. As we shall shortly see, the *Gawain*-poet routinely puns on the mul-tiple meanings of terms like *armes*. He is concerned to blur the boundaries between knight's equipment and knight's body, between the material bases of chivalry and the subjectivity they protect from dissolution.

72. The Green Knight does tell us where his armor is: "I haue a hauberghe at home and a helme boþe, / A schelde and a scharp spere, schinande bry3t, / Ande oþer weppenes to welde, I wene wel, als: / Bot for I wolde no were, my wedez ar softer" (lines 268–71). We never see any of these arms, however—the poem withholds the Green Knight's heraldic information all the way to the end (a point I will discuss further below).

73. *The Gawain-Poet*, pp. 178–79.

74. His question ("Wher is . . . Þe gouernour of þis gyng?") is perhaps the clearest example of his apparent insolence. Helen Cooper grants him some lee-way in her note on the passage: "Arthur is out of his place at the High Table, so cannot be immediately located" (p. 93 of her introduction to Keith Harrison's

translation of *Sir Gawain and the Green Knight*). But she immediately admits that, since the king is most likely wearing a crown, "the Green Knight clearly does not take the trouble to look far" (ibid., pp. 93–94). What interests me most about this implied insult is the way in which it plays upon the knight's own unintelligibility: he makes a deliberate point of staging Camelot's insecure position within the heraldic sign system. The poet also uses the same verb to describe the two parties' attempts at recognition: in lines 230–31, we learn that the Green Knight "stemmed and con *studie* / Quo walt þer most renoun" (my italics), while in line 237 the court does likewise ("Al *studied* þat þer stod and stalked hym nerre," my italics).

75. By setting this condition, the Green Knight is reversing his own, earlier practice. When Gawain agrees to take part in the beheading game, the Knight insists on first learning his challenger's name: "Fyrst I eþe þe, haþel, how þat þou hattes / Þat þou me telle truly, as I tryst may" (lines 379–80). Gawain readily complies: "'In god fayth,' quoþ þe goode kny3t, 'Gawain I hatte'" (line 381). Needless to say, the Knight does not subsequently follow his own advice. This discrepancy may be one more indication of the extent to which the Green Knight inverts or resists standard chivalric practice (initially signaled by his refusal of Arthur's hospitality in lines 252–57, a point to which I will return below).

76. The end of the pentangle passage revisits these lines, signaling the completion of a traditional ring structure: "Þerfore on his schene schelde schapen watz þe knot, / Ryally wyth red golde vpon rede gowlez, / Þat is þe pure 'pentaungel' wyth þe peple called / With lore" (lines 662–65). This symbolic unit is thus meant to hold our attention, to cause us to linger on the presentation of Gawain's arms and their equation with both his social body (his honor) and his physical form—something the *Gawain*-poet admits at the start of the passage: "And quy þe pentangel apendez to þat prynce noble / I am in tent yow to telle, þof *tary* hyt me schulde" (lines 623–24, my italics).

77. Ross G. Arthur notes that "it is clear that a man's heraldic device was seen in the medieval period as a simple sign for the man himself" (*Medieval Sign Theory*, p. 48).

78. *Accordez* will become important at the poem's end, when it appears three times in relatively rapid succession, all in connection with issues of inter- and intraregional hospitality. I have already commented on the semantically rich range of *armez*; I would just like to note here that its modification by *cler* points toward the questions of reputation and intercultural renown which brought the Green Knight to Camelot in the first place (or so he says at the beginning of *SGGK* in lines 258–64). The *MED* entry for *cler* (adj.) includes sense 3b, "praiseworthy, illustrious, glorious," and gives citations for this usage going back to 1300. In addition, sense 6c, "unrestricted; of possession or title: unconditional, absolute; of land: clear as to title; of descent: undisputed,"

emerges in the first half of the fifteenth century; this sense may have some potential applicability to *SGGK*, given its use in the phrase "cler of ames," "fully entitled to bear arms." Finally, senses 5b ("of objects: clearly visible"), 5d ("of knowledge, understanding: clear, certain"), and 5e ("of words, speech, etc.: readily understood, plain, lucid") all point directly to the questions of intelligibility and chivalric reputation I have been discussing above: Gawain's "cler armez" are thus meant to be recognized by all who see them.

79. Heraldic devices nevertheless function arbitrarily, just like other humanly produced signs: "In practice a man may have more than one sign, just as one thing may be signified by more than one word; similarly, a sign may be attached to more than one man, just as a word may refer to a variety of things" (Arthur, *Medieval Sign Theory*, p. 55). The applicability of this point to the Scrope-Grosvenor case is obvious, but it also holds true for the pentangle and *SGGK*. The poet goes to great lengths here to present us with a complete and stable set of significations for the pentangle, but the necessarily arbitrary (and sociohistorical) connection between signifier and signified undermines the poet's attempts to control meaning.

80. Gawain's failure to live up to the pentangle's promise has become a mainstay of *SGGK* criticism, but that is not my focus here—and thus the specific use of the phrase "heraldic task." I am not concerned in this chapter with the question of Gawain's flaws and faults; instead I am interested in exploring how the heraldic economy and its accompanying rituals of recognition break down over the course of the poem.

81. See Felicity Heal, "Reciprocity and Exchange," p. 186.

82. Gawain's anonymity is less threatening to Hautdesert, but this is primarily due to his courteous decision to play by the rules of hospitality, his willingness to submit to being moved through what Heal identifies as "a series of ceremonial moments" (ibid., p. 186). My reading here runs counter to Spearing's claim for "the poet's notable failure to make the Green Knight consistently 'intelligible,' either by giving him any openly interpreted symbolic device like Gawain's pentangle, or by letting us see the poem for more than a moment through his eyes" (*The Gawain-Poet*, pp. 235–36). As "openly interpreted" as the pentangle might be, it does not serve to make Gawain any more intelligible in Bertilak's castle, and thus Spearing's sense of a clear opposition between Gawain and the Green Knight is not as strong as it first appears.

83. These lines do suggest that class identity does successfully cross regional boundaries, but knowing that Gawain is an aristocrat is not the same as knowing which aristocrat he is.

84. The Green Knight's "absolution" of Gawain in lines 2390–99 discusses the green girdle via a lexicon similar to that used to describe the pentangle (key words like *poynt, pured, golde,* and *token* recur), but the effect of such a speech is to locate the girdle within heraldic discourse, setting the stage for

Gawain's own riffs on it as a device, not to demonstrate the Green Knight's knowledge of the pentangle.

85. Andrew and Waldron report that this is J. A. W. Bennett's reading; see their note for line 636, "Forþy þe pentangel nwe." However, Norman Davis's revised edition of J. R. R. Tolkien and E. V. Gordon's edition of the poem instead argues that "it is probably no more than 'newly painted'" (p. 94). Andrew and Waldron agree.

86. Helmut Nickel describes Gawain's usual arms as either *argent, a canton gules* or *purpure, a double-headed eagle Or, armed axure* ("Arthurian Armings," p. 14). But he also notes the fourteenth-century custom of carrying both a shield for war and a shield for peace: "The triangular 'War' shield bore the family arms, to be carried in battle; the 'shield for Peace' was a squarish *targe* designed for tournament use, and it displayed the badge. Since he does not go to war, Sir Gawain quite correctly takes his 'shield for Peace' on his quest" (ibid.).

87. Christine Chism points out the danger inherent in this disarming scene: "In romance traditions, moments of knightly relaxation or disarming before the climactic encounter usually signal a dangerous temptation" (*Alliterative Revivals*, p. 94).

88. The lady's ambiguous pun on *tale* in this passage is of a piece with her subsequent assurance that Gawain is "welcum to [her] cors" (line 1236). She may have only courteous conversation in mind—or she may be offering Gawain a more physical delight.

89. It is true that both Bertilak and his lady (as well as Morgan le Fay) are well aware that their guest is Sir Gawain of Camelot, that the seduction attempts are part of the chivalric test that is the exchange game. A second reading therefore offers some sense of security: Gawain may be threatened by their doubts, but we know that they know his identity is not in doubt. Nevertheless, whether we read the scene as seduction or test, the questioning of Gawain's selfhood is still an issue: will Gawain succumb to the romance-self the lady offers? will he give in and disgrace the high reputation of the Round Table? are variants of the same question.

90. See p. 344 of Andrew and Waldron's edition. The *MED* entry for *sheld* indicates that "shield" was a technical term used in boar hunting: see senses 4a ("The tough hide at the shoulders and neck of a wild boar, the shield of a boar") and 4b ("a slab of boar meat") for citations from the fourteenth and fifteenth centuries (including *SGGK*'s use of the term).

91. This self-inflicted division of pentangular individuality will be reprised at poem's end when the knights of the Round Table adopt the green girdle as their new device, literally filling the halls of Camelot with the "hundreth of seche" Gawain mentions here.

92. Gawain's "cler armez" may be referenced here—or at least come to the audience's mind.

93. The fox's coat functions in a similar fashion. At the end of the third day's hunt, Bertilak and his men "tyruen of his cote" (line 1921), subsequently giving it to Gawain, who just happens to be dressed in a brilliant *surkot* of his host's (line 1929). The juxtaposition of the two coats—the "foule fox felle" (line 1944) and the "softe . . . furred" garment (line 1929)—reminds us that Gawain is not wearing his own surcoat, embroidered as it is with the pentangle. Again our knight is caught without his heraldry, and again the threat to his self is made clear.

94. Note that Gawain's arrival at the Green Chapel, like the other two entries we have already discussed, is announced with the use of *wyȝe*: "'Gawayn,' quoþ þat grene gome, 'God þe mot loke! / Iwysse þou art welcom, wyȝe, to my place'" (lines 2239–40). Interestingly enough, it is on this occasion that we finally achieve recognition of the guest-knight's identity—precisely at the moment when Gawain will realize the full implications of his earlier self-alienation at Hautdesert.

95. Although the Green Chapel may ultimately be considered part of Bertilak's domain, it is nonetheless important to remember that neither Gawain nor the poem's audience know that fact at the start of Fitt 4. What we have there is a spatial triangulation similar to the one at work in the Scrope-Grosvenor controversy: Camelot, Hautdesert, and the Green Chapel form an interregional network equivalent to the one made up by Westminster, Cheshire, and Yorkshire.

96. To be fair, the idea of the girdle as a heraldic device is initially Bertilak's: he offers it to Gawain as a keepsake of his adventure, "a pure token / Of þe chaunce of þe Grene Chapel" (lines 2398–99). But Bertilak's *token* is one to bear "Among prynces of prys" and "at chevalrous knyȝtez" (lines 2398, 2399), not a "token of vntrawþe." For more on the difficulty of fixing the girdle's meaning, see Arthur, *Medieval Sign Theory*, pp. 106–12.

97. John Burrow, "The Two Confession Scenes," p. 79.

98. David Aers, *Community, Gender, and Individual Identity*, p. 172.

99. The court's subsequent adoption of the green girdle thus represents a second attempt (the first was Bertilak's) to establish an assimilative accord with Gawain, a process that deemphasizes individual difference in favor of class solidarity. As we will see, Gawain accepts accord with his fellow Camelot knights even as he rejects it with regional Bertilak.

100. Turville-Petre, "The 'Pearl'-Poet in His 'Fayre Regioun,'" p. 288.

101. Ibid., p. 290. My critique of Turville-Petre holds up against his more recent cosmopolitan reading of the poem in "Afterword: The Brutus Prologue": while Hautdesert and Camelot can share internationally intelligible chivalric values, the mere fact of that sharing does not automatically invalidate other, conflicting identities.

102. Spearing, *The Gawain-Poet*, p. 229.

103. See p. 311 of Andrew and Waldron's edition.

104. Spearing, *The Gawain-Poet*, p. 236.

105. Gawain's rejection of Bertilak's chivalric hospitality is also a rejection of somatic identity with the provinces. When Bertilak reveals to Gawain that the old woman dwelling at Hautdesert is Morgan le Fay, he uncovers a familial connection between Gawain and his regional court: "Þe auncian lady . . . is euen þyn aunt, Arþurez half-suster" (lines 2463–64). Gawain's refusal to return to the castle and greet his aunt is therefore a dismissal of a blood relationship, one akin to Grosvenor's decision to reject the *bordure argent* and its implication of junior status within Scrope's family.

106. We should remember here that, for the Middle Ages and for the *Gawain*-poet in particular, translation was never far from imperial desire.

107. Chism, *Alliterative Revivals*, p. 88.

108. For the extent to which the household served as the model for English nation-building in the late Middle Ages, see Heal, "Reciprocity and Exchange," p. 179.

109. Ibid., p. 186.

110. Ibid., p. 187.

111. Ibid., p. 190.

112. Chism, *Alliterative Revivals*, p. 97.

CHAPTER 5.   *Two Shires against All England*

1. Barry Coward, *The Stanleys*, p. 10. Thomas's younger brother Sir William Stanley of Holt was far more aggressive: his intervention at a crucial moment in the battle helped to give the Stanleys credit for the victory—even as it also permitted his brother to maintain his quiescence.

2. For Clopper's take on periodization and early English drama, see *Drama, Play, and Game*, pp. 268–93; for Summit's account of Catholic printing, see *Lost Property*, pp. 109–61.

3. Coward, *The Stanleys*, p. 4.

4. Ibid., pp. 101 and 102.

5. Ibid., p. x.

6. *The Stanley Poem* is the one exception here, appearing nowhere in the Percy Folio manuscript.

7. David Lawton, "*Scottish Field*," p. 51.

8. There is no mention of Sir William Stanley's 1495 execution for treason in *Rose of England*, placing the poem's composition sometime during the decade prior to that event.

9. All citations of the Percy Folio Stanley poems (*The Rose of England*, *Bosworth Field*, *Lady Bessy*, *Scottish Field*, and *Flodden Field*) are taken from the

first three volumes of John W. Hales and Frederick J. Furnivall's *Bishop Percy's Folio Manuscript.*

10. For more on Henry's dragon device, see Ian F. Baird, *Scotish Feilde,* p. 39.

11. The allegory demands that the rosebush represent Edward IV and his children—yet in depicting Edward as another "rose soe redd" (line 7), it deliberately violates heraldry, replacing the white rose of York with the red rose of Lancaster. The poet seems forced into this heraldic error as a result of his desire to depict Henry as the legitimate heir of both lines and thus the true claimant to the throne: if Henry is a red rose, then Edward IV must have been one as well.

12. Sir William's intervention was a crucial part of Henry's victory over Richard, but Thomas Stanley appears to have stayed on the sidelines until the battle's conclusion; for more on the Stanley role in the battle, see Coward, *The Stanleys,* pp. 12–13.

13. Like *Rose of England, Bosworth Field* makes no mention of Sir William's 1495 execution.

14. The anachronistic reference to James I at the end of this late fifteenth-century poem demonstrates the ongoing interest in the Stanley romances during the early modern period. Indeed, since the version of *Bosworth Field* mentioning James is subsequently recopied by the Percy Folio scribe during the 1640s, we are looking at approximately 150 years of reception history here.

15. This exchange is another pro-Stanley fiction: as mentioned above, Thomas Lord Stanley took no part in the planning or execution of the Tudor battle strategy at Bosworth.

16. Helen Cooper, "Romance after 1400," p. 711.

17. Cooper, "Romance after Bosworth," p. 156.

18. According to Lawton, *Lady Bessy* "may safely be dated only to the first part of the sixteenth century" ("*Scottish Field,*" p. 47).

19. Even then the poem simply borrows wholesale a number of combat passages from *Bosworth Field,* one of its source texts. For example, lines 1035–50 of *Lady Bessy* contain a slightly variant version of the *Bosworth Field* horse episode (lines 585–96).

20. Cooper, "Romance after Bosworth," p. 154.

21. Ibid., p. 156.

22. The poem stresses this point: when Humphrey Brereton arrives at Holt, Sir William Stanley asks for news of his brother "That lately was made the Erle of darby" (line 314). The Stanleys' status as magnates is in no way dependent on the Tudors—at least within the imaginative confines of the dynastic romance tradition.

23. Cooper, "Romance after Bosworth," p. 155. For more on the fifteenth- and sixteenth-century Breretons, see ibid., pp. 155–56, and Lawton, "*Scottish Field,*" p. 47.

24. The one reward that Humphrey does reject—Henry's line 765 offer of 100 marks—comes after the porter's display of generosity. Couched in language similar to that of the porter ("I will none of thy gold . . . nor yett none of thy ffee," lines 789–90), Humphrey's refusal to take Henry's money might therefore be understood as a lesson learned at the hands of a lower-ranking man—and thus another example of cross-class affinity within the poem.

25. The *Lady Bessy* in British Library MS Harley 367 substitutes "queene" for "Kinge" at this point. Coupled with Lawton's dating of the Harley 367 scribe's hand to the years ca. 1560–80 (*"Scottish Field,"* p. 46), this reading suggests an Elizabethan audience for at least one version of the text.

26. All citations from *The Stanley Poem* in this chapter are taken from the transcription of the Bodleian Library MS Rawlinson Poet. 143.II version of the poem provided in James Orchard Halliwell's *Palatine Anthology*.

27. The statement in *The Stanley Poem* that "Thomas Lord Mountegle, sonne to Edward . . . Hath lefte behinde him on memoriall sure" (p. 258) places the text's *terminus a quo* in 1560, the year of Lord Thomas's death. A subsequent reference to "Edward that right noble Earle of Darby" (p. 259) as still living gives the poem a *terminus ad quem* of 1572, the year of Earl Edward's death.

28. Isabel of Lathom's historical father was Sir Thomas Lathom. Replacing Sir Thomas with Oskell in the second fitt is a way for *The Stanley Poem* to incorporate Lathom dynastic romance into the Stanley legendary: Oskell is the mysterious orphan "miraculouslye" (p. 217) found in an eagle's nest by the childless Lord Lathom—and thus the source of the Stanleys' eagle device.

29. The poet may be referring here to the tax levied by the Crown in 1489, one that—in explicit violation of palatine privilege—included Cheshire in its purview: for more on the reaction to this subsidy, see Thornton, *Cheshire and the Tudor State*, p. 75.

30. Andrew Taylor, "*The Stanley Poem*," p. 103.

31. For details about non-Stanleyite accounts of Flodden Field, see Ian F. Baird, "The Poems Called *Flodden Field*," and John Scattergood, "A Defining Moment." For details of the battle itself (and its immediate historical context), see Baird, *Scotish Feilde*, pp. xv–xx.

32. Flodden's position in an ongoing history of Anglo-Scots antagonism qualifies John Scattergood's observation that "[i]n this poem a national event is made to serve local interests and family rivalries" ("A Defining Moment," p. 77). The battle (and all subsequent accounts of it) require a triangulation of identities, imperial/archipelagic as well as national and regional.

33. Lawton, "*Scottish Field*," p. 45.

34. For the 1515 date of *Scottish Field*, see Baird, *Scotish Feilde*, pp. ii–iii.

35. For more on the Leghs of Baguley, see Lawton, "*Scottish Field*," p. 44, and Baird, *Scotish Feilde*, pp. vii–viii.

36. Baird, *Scotish Feilde*, p. vii.

37. Ibid., p. vii.

38. For the argument in favor of a 1521 *terminus ad quem* for *Flodden Field*, see Baird, *Scotish Feilde*, p. iv.

39. This reference to a Stanley-Howard feud provides the poem with an alternate *terminus ad quem*: the 1528 marriage of Edward Stanley, the third Earl of Derby, to Dorothy Howard. As Baird notes, the marriage "would probably have made such strong feelings unacceptable to the poem's likely audience" (*Scotish Feilde*, p. iv).

40. There is no evidence for this incident, but Jamie Garsed did exist: for details, see Baird, *Scotish Feilde*, p. 74.

41. The Percy Folio version of *Flodden Field* augments these awards with an interpolated narrative absent from the other extant copies of the poem. In this passage (lines 439–507), the Cheshire knight Sir Rowland Egerton convinces the king to reward him with "a litle grange house, / in the Lordshippe of Rydeley" (lines 482–83). Lawton identifies the Egerton account as "a fabulous 'ancestral romance' ending in the second half of the sixteenth century to associate the poem with the pedigree of the Egertons of Ridley" ("*Scottish Field*," p. 49). The overall effect of its inclusion in *Flodden Field* is to further elevate the needs of the region over those of the nation or empire: Tudor war in France, a cross-Channel clash, is ultimately waged so that the Egertons can aquire property amounting to little more than "a cote with one eye" (line 485).

42. Joseph Donatelli, "The Percy Folio Manuscript," p. 116.

43. Ibid., p. 129.

44. Ibid., p. 129.

45. Gillian Rogers, "The Percy Folio Manuscript Revisited," p. 44.

46. Donatelli, "The Percy Folio Manuscript," p. 129.

47. J. S. A. Adamson, "Chivalry and Political Culture," p. 182.

48. Ibid., pp. 191–92.

49. Alex Davis, *Chivalry and Romance*, pp. 191–92.

50. For details of the Earl's wartime performance, see Coward, *The Stanleys*, pp. 172–76.

51. Adamson, "Chivalry and Political Culture," p. 183.

52. Lois Potter, *Secret Rites*, p. 73.

53. For a summary of the different stages of the siege, see Katherine A. Walker, "Military Activities," pp. 48–51.

54. All citations from *A Briefe Journall* are taken from George Ormerod's edition of the text in *Tracts Relating to Military Proceedings in Lancashire*. Citations from *A True and Genuine Account* are taken from the online ECCO version of Seacome's *Memoirs*.

55. For more on the romance Amazons and *femmes fortes* of seventeenth-century France, Countess Charlotte's homeland, see Ian Maclean, *Woman Triumphant*.

56. Thomason Tracts E45(10), 20 April 1644.

57. All citations from *The Turke and Sir Gawain* are taken from Thomas Hahn's edition in *Sir Gawain: Eleven Romances and Tales.*

58. Walker notes that Charlotte's French heritage would have worked against her in this regard: "During the seventeenth century the expressions 'whore' and 'Babylon' seem to be used in relation to Roman Catholic and foreign, particularly French, influence" ("Military Activities," p. 48).

59. Potter, *Secret Rites*, p. 73.

60. Thomason Tracts E49(4), 13–20 May 1644.

61. Thomason Tracts E50(7), 27 May–3 June 1644. In the same issue, Hall implies that Birkenhead is another one of the Countess's lovers: "you will not let the *Countesse* be quiet in her Castle, but father such *prodigious*, and masculine *Sallies* upon the *Countesse*, (that the Earle vowes) if all be true I hear, never to appear for them again."

62. Thomason Tracts E52(8), 17–24 June 1644.

63. Thomason Tracts E44(18), 26 April–1 May 1644.

64. Thomason Tracts E45(11), 29 April–6 May 1644.

65. Ibid.; Thomason Tracts E50(7).

66. Thomason Tracts E45(11).

67. Potter, *Secret Rites*, p. 80.

68. Adamson, "Chivalry and Political Culture," p. 194.

69. Walker, "Military Activites," p. 52.

70. Thomason Tracts E311(19), 3–10 December 1645.

71. Ormerod, *Tracts Relating to Military Proceedings in Lancashire*, p. 316.

72. Ibid., p. 321.

73. For Earl Charles's struggle to reclaim his patrimony, see Coward, *The Stanleys*, pp. 70–79.

Epilogue

1. See http://entertainment.timesonline.co.uk/tol/arts_and_entertainment/books/article838217.ece (accessed 11 April 2008).

2. Ibid.

3. Simon Armitage, *Sir Gawain and the Green Knight*, p. vi.

4. *VCH Ches.*, vol. 5, pt. 2, p. 257.

5. For more on the plays' twentieth-century revival, see Mills, *Recycling the Cycle*, pp. 211–19.

6. See http://www.chestermysteryplays.com/ (accessed 11 April 2008).

7. For Garner's own reflections on his Cestrian identity, see the essays and lectures collected in *The Voice that Thunders* (especially "Achilles in Altjira," pp. 39–59).

8. Created in 2002, the position of the Cheshire Poet Laureate has two official purposes: "to provide an opportunity for local poets to have their individual profiles raised" and "to use the appointed poet to assist in raising the profile of poetry across the county of Cheshire" (http://www.cheshire.gov.uk/ ReadersAndWriters/Writers/poetlaureate/writerspoetbackground.htm, accessed 11 April 2008). While these are nominally local goals, the decision to couch them in the nationally oriented language of laureateship has broader implications. The United Kingdom may have a Poet Laureate, but so does Cheshire county.

9. See http://cheshirepoetlaureate.blogspot.com/2006/03/lines-on-map_ 06.html (accessed 11 April 2008).

10. See http://www.cheshire.gov.uk/ReadersAndWriters/Writers/lines onthemap/ (accessed 11 April 2008).

11. Deborah Kennedy, "The Ruined Abbey in the Eighteenth Century," p. 509.

12. Ibid.

13. Anne Janowitz, *England's Ruins*, p. 1.

14. Ibid., p. 4.

15. Ibid., p. 59.

16. Ibid., p. 7.

17. Ibid.

18. While the overall thrust of the poem is to treat Chester Cathedral as a numinous space, its characterization as an "enormous cage" qualifies such praise. Rudd's mention of the £4 admission fee a few lines earlier may be a similar qualification. There has been some local resistance to the imposition of the fee: on his *Virtual Stroll Around the Walls of Chester* website, Chester photographer (and amateur historian) Steve Howe critically compares the admission charge to the money exchanged in Jerusalem's Temple. Referring to the "money-takers at the door sitting in judgement," Howe notes that "One is reminded how their boss dealt with their like" and quotes Matthew 21:12–13 (http://www .bwpics.co.uk/cathedral3.html, accessed 11 April 2008). Whether or not Rudd shares Howe's opinion here is less important than the reminder that local communities are not utopias free from internal strife. Twenty-first-century Chester is no less riven than medieval or early modern Chester.

19. Pickering grew a beard for this performance, adopting the character of Cedric the Conversus, "a bearded trainee monk" (http://www.marketing projects.co.uk/clientpo/90/news/701, accessed 11 April 2008). In doing so, he consciously connected the 2007 festival to an earlier instance of Chester historical pageantry: as the same press release tells us, "Cedric was the name of a character in Episode 11 of the Chester Historical Pageant 1937" (ibid.). For the subsequently quoted press release, see http://www.marketing projects.co.uk/clinetpo/90/news/708 (accessed 11 April 2009). For more on

twentieth-century English historical pageant-plays, see Joshua D. Esty, "Amnesia in the Fields."

20. I downloaded the 2007 festival brochure on 18 September 2007. At the time of writing, the brochure is no longer available online, having been replaced by an entry for the 2008 St. Werburgh's Festival (http://www.chesterfestivals .co.uk, accessed 11 April 2008). Pickering's use of "renaissance" in the brochure resonates with "The Chester Renaissance," the title of the Chester City Council's ongoing "programme of major development and investment which will transform the Chester area over the next 10 years, respecting our culture & heritage" (http://www.chesterrenaissance.co.uk/faqs.htm, accessed 11 April 2008).

21. *VCH: Ches.*, vol. 5, pt. 2, p. 191. The shrine's remains were reassembled and installed in the cathedral's Lady Chapel in 1888.

22. "To Be a Pilgrim" (http://web.archive.org/web/20070823065931/ http://www.chestercathedral.com/Website_Pages/monthlynewsletter.asp, accessed 11 April 2008).

23. "The Festival of St Werburgh" (http://web.archive.org/web/200706 21054328/http://www.chestercathedral.com/Website_Pages/monthlynewsletter .asp, accessed 11 April 2008).

24. Sanok, *Her Life Historical*, p. 102.

25. Ibid.

26. See http://www.marketingprojects.co.uk/clientpo/90/news/710 (accessed 11 April 2008).

27. See http://www.chesterstandard.co.uk/chesternews/City39s-Viking-invasion.2969868.jp (accessed 11 April 2008).

28. "To Be a Pilgrim." Of course, Norsemen were always already a part of medieval Cestrian culture: see *VCH: Ches.*, vol. 1, pp. 248–59. The value of the Vikings' inclusion in 2007 is its overwriting of the pagan-Christian dichotomy structuring the work of Lucian, Bradshaw, and other early Cheshire historians.

29. Strangely enough, the citation accompanying the *OED* definition of "transriverine" is a 1900 reference to the Wirral community of Birkenhead.

30. See http://www.cheshire.gov.uk/PoetryEShop/writerspoetpublications .aspx (accessed 11 April 2008). Priced at £3.99, the print version of the anthology contains only a selection of the poems published online.

31. See http://www.communities.gov.uk/publications/localgovernment/ strongprosperous (accessed 11 April 2008).

32. Ibid.

33. See http://www.communities.gov.uk/statements/corporate/local-government (accessed 11 April 2008).

34. See http://www.chesterstandard.co.uk/chesternews/New-council-to-rule-Chester.3605469.jp (accessed 11 April 2008).

35. For the House of Commons debate, see http://news.bbc.co.uk/1/hi/ england/staffordshire/7267605.stm (accessed 11 April 2008). For the House of

Lords debate, see http://news.bbc.co.uk/1/hi/england/7279147.stm (accessed 11 April 2008).

36. For the Cheshire West and Chester Joint Committee website, see http://www.cheshirewestandchester.gov.uk/ (accessed 11 April 2008). For the Cheshire East Joint Committee site, see http://www.cheshireeast.gov.uk/ (accessed 11 April 2008).

37. Its continued existence as a ceremonial county appears to be unthreatened by the administrative split.

38. At the time of writing, this website (http://www.cheshire.gov.uk/onecheshire/) has been replaced by a new "Local Government Reorganisation" page (http://www.cheshire.gov.uk/LocalGovReorg/, accessed 11 April 2008). The full version of the "One Cheshire" page is on its way to oblivion, having slipped temporarily into Google's cache (http://64.233.167.104/search ?q=cache:SRkiTrZNdRwJ:www.cheshire.gov.uk/onecheshire/onecheshire council.htm&hl=en&ct=clnk&cd=2&gl=us&client=safari, accessed 11 April 2008). Whether or not the page will be archived for future reference is unclear. The same is true for many of the online documents under discussion in this epilogue. For example, once the new unitary authorities are in place in April 2009, the existing County Council website will no longer serve any official purpose. If its servers are taken offline or put to other use, its contents—sites like *Lines on the Map* and the poems contained therein—will vanish from public view.

39. See http://web.archive.org/web/20070825090147/http://www.cheshire .gov.uk/onecheshire/ (accessed 11 April 2008). "Merseyshire" and "Manshire" are satirical responses to the economic rationale informing the two-authority scheme: the argument that twenty-first-century Cheshire's economy naturally divides into two zones, one dependent on Merseyside (the proposed Cheshire West and Chester) and the other on Greater Manchester (Cheshire East).

40. I first accessed this page (http://www.cheshire.gov.uk/onecheshire/ Questions+and+Answers.htm) on 18 September 2007. When I revisited it on 29 November 2007, I discovered that the static image had been replaced by an animated one in which a map of Cheshire is torn in two before the viewer's eyes and then replaced with the ominous all-caps question "THE FUTURE?" A third visit on 11 April 2008 revealed that the page has subsequently disappeared.

41. See http://www.cheshire.gov.uk/PR/2007/july07/293-07.htm (accessed 11 April 2008).

42. Commons *Hansard*, 26 February 2008, col. 1043. This and all other quotations from Commons *Hansard* are taken from the online edition at http://www.publications.parliament.uk/pa/pahansard.htm (accessed 11 April 2008).

43. Commons *Hansard*, 26 February 2008, col. 1059.

44. Ibid.

45. Lords *Hansard*, 4 March 2008, col. 1053. This and all other quotations from Lords *Hansard* are taken from the online edition at http://www.publications .parliament.uk/pa/pahansard.htm (accessed 11 April 2008).

46. Lords *Hansard*, 4 March 2008, col. 1050.

47. Lords *Hansard*, 4 March 2008, col. 1039.

48. Ibid.

49. Lords *Hansard*, 4 March 2008, col. 1062.

50. Lords *Hansard*, 4 March 2008, col. 1054.

51. Lords *Hansard*, 4 March 2008, cols. 1054 and 1055 respectively.

52. Lords *Hansard*, 4 March 2008, col. 1043. The County Council's statement (now offline) was originally available at http://www.cheshire.gov.uk/ onecheshire/Questions+and+Answers.htm (accessed 29 November 2007).

53. Commons *Hansard*, 26 February 2008, col. 1053.

54. Ibid.

55. Ibid.

56. Lords *Hansard*, 4 March 2008, col. 1051.

57. Lords *Hansard*, 4 March 2008, col. 1044. The Bishop opposes such landscape divisions to the "purely arbitrary line that is drawn to separate east and west in the way that is proposed" (col. 1046). But his catalog of topographical features is not entirely natural: the Bishop lists "the Welsh border" alongside "the River Tame, the River Mersey, [and] the Derbyshire hills" (col. 1044). Cheshire's borderline with Wales is the product of centuries of imperial aggression; like the divide between Cheshire West and Cheshire East, the Welsh boundary has always been an arbitrary political decision imposed upon a contiguous, nonethnic landscape and the intermixed Anglo-Welsh population inhabiting that terrain.

58. Lords *Hansard*, 4 March 2008, col. 1037.

59. Lords *Hansard*, 4 March 2008, col. 1060.

60. Ibid.

61. Ibid.

62. Ibid.

BIBLIOGRAPHY

Chester
Cheshire and Chester Archives and Local Studies MS WS Amery 1613
Cheshire and Chester Archives and Local Studies MS ZAB/1
Cheshire and Chester Archives and Local Studies MS ZAF 8/38
Cheshire and Chester Archives and Local Studies MS ZCH/1
Cheshire and Chester Archives and Local Studies MS ZCH/5
Cheshire and Chester Archives and Local Studies MS ZCH/32
Cheshire and Chester Archives and Local Studies MS ZCHB/2
Cheshire and Chester Archives and Local Studies MS ZCX/2
Cheshire and Chester Archives and Local Studies MS ZMB/28
Cheshire and Chester Archives and Local Studies MS ZMB/29
Cheshire and Chester Archives and Local Studies MS ZQSF/56

London
British Library MS Additional 27879
British Library MS Harley 1989
British Library MS Harley 2125
British Library MS Harley 2150
British Library MS Harley 2252

Oxford
Bodleian Library MS Bodley 672

Andrew, Malcolm, and Ronald Waldron, eds. *The Poems of the Pearl Manuscript.*
    4th ed. Exeter: University of Exeter Press, 2002.
Arber, Edward, ed. *Transcript of the Registers of the Company of Stationers,*
    1554–1640 AD. Vol. 3. New York: P. Smith, 1950.

Armitage, Simon, trans. *Sir Gawain and the Green Knight.* London: Faber and Faber, 2007.

Baird, Ian F., ed. *Scotish Feilde and Flodden Feilde: Two Flodden Poems.* New York: Garland Publishing, 1982.

Baswell, Christopher, and Anne Howland Schotter, eds. *The Middle Ages.* Vol. 1A, *The Longman Anthology of British Literature.* 3rd ed. New York: Pearson Longman, 2006.

Bergeron, David M., ed. *Pageants and Entertainments of Anthony Munday: A Critical Edition.* New York: Garland Publishing, 1985.

Bevington, David, gen. ed. *English Renaissance Drama: A Norton Anthology.* New York: W. W. Norton, 2002.

———, ed. *Medieval Drama.* Boston: Houghton Mifflin, 1975.

Christie, Richard Copley, ed. *Annales Cestrienses: or, Chronicle of the Abbey of S. Werburg at Chester.* The Record Society of Lancashire and Cheshire, vol. 14. London, 1887.

Colunga, Alberto, and Laurentio Turrado, eds. *Bibla Sacra.* 7th ed. Madrid: Biblioteca de Autores Christianos, 1985.

Corser, Thomas, ed. *Chester's Triumph in Honor of Her Prince As It Was Performed Upon St. George's Day 1610 in the Foresaid Citie.* Chetham Society, vol. 3. Manchester, 1844.

Davis, Norman, ed. *Sir Gawain and the Green Knight.* 2nd ed. Oxford: Clarendon Press, 1968.

Ellis, Henry, ed. *Original Letters, Illustrative of English History.* Vol. 1. London, 1846.

Fitzstephen, William. *Norman London.* Trans. H. E. Butler. New York: Italica Press, 1990.

Geoffrey of Monmouth. *The "Historia regum Britanniae" of Geoffrey of Monmouth.* Ed. Acton Griscom. London: Longmans, Green, and Co., 1929.

———. *The History of the Kings of Britain.* Trans. Lewis Thorpe. Harmondsworth: Penguin Books, 1966.

Gerald of Wales. *Itinerarium Kambriae et Descriptio Kambriae.* Ed. James F. Dimock. *Giradli Cambrensis opera,* vol. 6. London, 1868.

———. *The Journey through Wales and the Description of Wales.* Trans. Lewis Thorpe. Harmondsworth: Penguin Books, 1978.

Hales, John W., and Frederick J. Furnivall, eds. *Bishop Percy's Folio Manuscript: Ballads and Romances.* 3 vols. London, 1867–68.

Halliwell, James Orchard, ed. *Palatine Anthology: A Collection of Ancient Poems and Ballads, Relating to Lancashire and Cheshire.* London, 1850.

Hahn, Thomas, ed. *Sir Gawain: Eleven Romances and Tales.* Kalamazoo, MI: Medieval Institute Publications, 1995.

Harrison, Keith, trans. *Sir Gawain and the Green Knight.* Oxford: Oxford University Press, 1998.

Hatt, Cecilia A., ed. *English Works of John Fisher, Bishop of Rochester.* Oxford: Oxford University Press, 2002.

Horstmann, Carl, ed. *The Life of Saint Werburge of Chester, by Henry Bradshaw.* Early English Text Society, original series, 88. London, 1887.

King, Daniel. *The Vale-royall.* The Printed Sources of Western Art, vol. 20. Portland, OR: Collegium Graphicum, 1972.

Kinney, Arthur F., ed. *Renaissance Drama: An Anthology of Plays and Entertainments.* Oxford: Blackwell Publishers, 1999.

Lumiansky, R. M., and David Mills, eds. *The Chester Mystery Cycle.* 2 vols. Early English Text Society, supplementary series, 3 and 9. London: Oxford University Press, 1974 and 1986.

Moorman, Charles, ed. *The Works of the Gawain-Poet.* Jackson: University of Mississippi Press, 1977.

Nichols, John, ed. *The Progresses, Processions and Magnificent Festivities of King James the First.* Vol. 2. London, 1828.

Nicolas, Nicholas Harris, ed. *De controversia in curia militari inter Richardum le Scrope et Robertum Grosvenor milites.* 2 vols. London, 1832.

Ormerod, George, ed. *Tracts Relating to Military Proceedings in Lancashire during the Great Civil War.* London, 1844.

Smith, Joshua Toulmin, Lucy Toulmin Smith, and Lujo Brentano, eds. *English Gilds.* Early English Text Society, original series, 40. London, 1870.

Tait, James, ed. *The Chartulary or Register of the Abbey of St. Werburgh Chester.* The Chetham Society, vol. 82. Manchester, 1920.

Taylor, M. V., ed. *Extracts from the MS. Liber Luciani de Laude Cestrie.* The Record Society of Lancashire and Cheshire, vol. 64. Edinburgh, 1912.

Walker, Greg, ed. *Medieval Drama: An Anthology.* Oxford: Blackwell, 2000.

PRIMARY SOURCES (ONLINE)

Dekker, Thomas. *Troia-Nova Triumphans.* London, 1612. Early English Books Online. http://eebo.chadwyck.com.

Munday, Anthony. *London's Love to the Royal Prince Henry.* London, 1610. Early English Books Online. http://eebo.chadwyck.com.

Rudd, Andrew. "Chester Cathedral." Cheshire County Council. http://www .cheshire.gov.uk/ReadersAndWriters/Writers/linesonthemap/chester .htm (accessed 11 April 2008).

———, ed. *Lines on the Map.* Cheshire County Council. http://www.cheshire .gov.uk/ReadersAndWriters/Writers/linesonthemap/ (accessed 11 April 2008).

Seacome, John. *Memoirs; Containing a Genealogical and Historical Account of the Ancient and Honourable House of Stanley.* Liverpool, 1741. Eighteenth

Century Collections Online. Gale Group. http://gale.com/Eighteenth Century.

The Thomason Tracts. Early English Books Online. http://eebo.chadwyck.com/thomason_browse.

Secondary Sources (Print)

Adamson, J. S. A. "Chivalry and Political Culture in Caroline England." In *Culture and Politics in Early Stuart England,* ed. Kevin Sharpe and Peter Lake, 161–97. Stanford: Stanford University Press, 1993.

Aers, David. *Community, Gender, and Individual Identity: English Writing, 1360–1430.* London: Routledge, 1988.

Alexander, James W. "New Evidence on the Palatinate of Chester." *English Historical Review* 85 (1970): 715–29.

———. *Ranulf of Chester: A Relic of the Conquest.* Athens: University of Georgia Press, 1983.

Anderson, Perry. *Lineages of the Absolutist State.* London: New Left Books, 1974.

Andrew, Malcolm. "Theories of Authorship." In Brewer and Gibson, *A Companion to the Gawain-Poet,* 23–33.

Arthur, Ross G. *Medieval Sign Theory and "Sir Gawain and the Green Knight."* Toronto: University of Toronto Press, 1987.

Ashley, Kathleen M. "Divine Power in the Chester Cycle and Late Medieval Thought." *Journal of the History of Ideas* 39 (1978): 387–404.

Ashton, J. W. "Rymes . . . of Randolf, Erl of Chestre." *English Literary History* 5 (1938): 195–206.

Badir, Patricia. "The Garrison of the Godly: Antitheatricalism and the Performance of Distinction in Early Modern Hull." *Journal of Medieval and Early Modern Studies* 27 (1997): 285–316.

———. "Playing Space: History, the Body, and Records of Early English Drama." *Exemplaria* 9 (1997): 255–79.

Baird, Ian F. "The Poems Called *Flodden Field.*" *Notes and Queries,* n.s., 28 (1981): 15–19.

Baker, David J., and Willy Maley, eds. *British Identities and English Renaissance Literature.* Cambridge: Cambridge University Press, 2002.

———. "An Uncertain Union (A Dialogue)." In Schwyzer and Mealor, *Archipelagic Identities,* 8–24.

Baldwin, Elizabeth, Lawrence M. Clopper, and David Mills, eds. *Cheshire including Chester.* 2 vols. Records of Early English Drama. Toronto: University of Toronto Press, 2007.

Barnard, John. "London Publishing, 1640–1660: Crisis, Continuity, and Innovation." *Book History* 4 (2001): 1–19.

Barraclough, Geoffrey. *The Earldom and County Palatine of Chester.* Oxford: Blackwell, 1953.

Barrett, Robert W., Jr. "The Absent *Triumphator* in the 1610 *Chester's Triumph in Honour of Her Prince.*" In *Spectacle and Public Performance in the Late Middle Ages and the Renaissance,* ed. Robert E. Stillman, 183–210. Leiden: Brill, 2006.

———. "Writing from the Marches: Cheshire Poetry and Drama, 1195–1645." Ph.D. diss., University of Pennsylvania, 2001.

Barron, Caroline M. "The Quarrel of Richard II with London, 1392–97." In Du Boulay and Barron, *The Reign of Richard II,* 173–201.

Beal, Jane. "Mapping Identity in John Trevisa's English *Polychronicon*: Chester, Cornwall, and the Translation of English National History." In *Fourteenth-Century England III,* ed. William Mark Ormrod, 67–82. Cambridge: Boydell, 2004.

Beckwith, Sarah. "Making the World in York and the York Cycle." In *Framing Medieval Bodies,* ed. Sarah Kay and Miri Rubin, 254–76. Manchester: Manchester University Press, 1994.

———. "Ritual, Theater, and Social Space in the York Corpus Christi Cycle." In Hanawalt and Wallace, *Bodies and Disciplines,* 63–86.

Beier, A. L. *Masterless Men: The Vagrancy Problem in England, 1560–1640.* London: Methuen, 1985.

———. *The Problem of the Poor in Tudor and Early Stuart England.* London: Methuen, 1983.

Bennett, H. S. *English Books and Readers, 1475–1557.* 2nd ed. Cambridge: Cambridge University Press, 1969.

Bennett, J. H. E., ed. *The Rolls of the Freemen of the City of Chester, Part I: 1392–1700.* The Record Society of Lancashire and Cheshire, vol. 51. Edinburgh, 1906.

Bennett, Michael J. *Community, Class, and Careerism: Cheshire and Lancashire Society in the Age of "Sir Gawain and the Green Knight."* Cambridge: Cambridge University Press, 1983.

———. "The Historical Background." In Brewer and Gibson, *A Companion to the Gawain-Poet,* 71–90.

———. "*Sir Gawain and the Green Knight* and the Literary Achievement of the North-West Midlands: The Historical Background." *Journal of Medieval History* 5 (1979): 63–88.

Bergeron, David M. *English Civic Pageantry, 1558–1642.* London: Edward Arnold, 1971.

———, ed. *Pageantry in the Shakespearean Theater.* Athens: University of Georgia Press, 1985.

———. "Stuart Civic Pageants and Textual Performance." *Renaissance Quarterly* 51 (1998): 163–83.

————. *Royal Family, Royal Lovers: King James of England and Scotland.* Columbia: University of Missouri Press, 1991.

Bowers, John M. *The Politics of Pearl: Court Poetry in the Age of Richard II.* Cambridge: D. S. Brewer, 2001.

Bradbrook, M. C. "The Politics of Pageantry: Social Implications in Jacobean London." In *Poetry and Drama, 1570–1700: Essays in Honour of Harold F. Brooks*, ed. Antony Coleman and Antony Hammond, 60–75. London: Methuen, 1981.

Brewer, Derek, and Jonathan Gibson, eds. *A Companion to the Gawain-Poet.* Cambridge: D. S. Brewer, 1997.

Briscoe, Marianne, and John C. Coldewey, eds. *Contexts for Early English Drama.* Bloomington: Indiana University Press, 1989.

Burne, R. V. H. *The Monks of Chester: The History of St. Werburgh's Abbey.* London: Society for Promoting Christian Knowledge, 1962.

Burrow, J. A. "The Poet as Petitioner." *Studies in the Age of Chaucer* 3 (1981): 61–75.

————. "*Saint Erkenwald* Line 1: 'At London in Englond.'" *Notes and Queries* 238 (n.s., 40) (1993): 22–23.

————. "The Two Confession Scenes in *Sir Gawain and the Green Knight.*" *Modern Philology* 57 (1959): 73–79.

Cannon, Christopher. "Monastic Productions." In Wallace, *The Cambridge History of Medieval English Literature*, 316–48.

Carlson, Marvin. *Places of Performance: The Semiotics of Theatre Architecture.* Ithaca, NY: Cornell University Press, 1989.

Carruthers, Leo. "The Duke of Clarence and the Earls of March: Garter Knights and *Sir Gawain and the Green Knight.*" *Medium Aevum* 70 (2001): 66–79.

Chedgzoy, Kate. "This Pleasant and Sceptred Isle: Insular Fantasies of National Identity in Anne Dowriche's *The French Historie* and William Shakespeare's *Richard II.*" In Schwyzer and Mealor, *Archipelagic Identities*, 25–42.

Chism, Christine. *Alliterative Revivals.* Philadelphia: University of Pennsylvania Press, 2002.

Clarke, Catherine A. M. *Literary Landscapes and the Idea of England, 700–1400.* Oxford: D. S. Brewer, 2006.

Clopper, Lawrence M., ed. *Chester.* Records of Early English Drama. Toronto: University of Toronto Press, 1979.

————. *Drama, Play, and Game: English Festive Culture in the Medieval and Early Modern Period.* Chicago: University of Chicago Press, 2001.

————. "The History and Development of the Chester Cycle." *Modern Philology* 75 (1978): 219–46.

————. "Lay and Clerical Impact on Civic Religious Drama and Ceremony." In Briscoe and Coldewey, *Contexts for Early English Drama*, 102–36.

———. "The Staging of the Medieval Plays of Chester: A Response." *Theatre Notebook* 28 (1974): 65–70.

Cohen, Jeffrey Jerome. "The Flow of Blood in Medieval Norwich." *Speculum* 79 (2004): 26–65.

———. *Hybridity, Identity and Monstrosity in Medieval Britain: On Difficult Middles.* London: Palgrave Macmillan, 2006.

———, ed. *The Postcolonial Middle Ages.* New York: St. Martin's Press, 2000.

Coldewey, John C. "Some Economic Aspects of the Late Medieval Drama." In Briscoe and Coldewey, *Contexts for Early English Drama*, 77–101.

Coletti, Theresa. "The Chester Cycle in Sixteenth-Century Religious Culture." *Journal of Medieval and Early Modern Studies* 37 (2007): 531–47.

Cooper, Helen. "Romance after 1400." In Wallace, *The Cambridge History of Medieval English Literature*, 690–719.

———. "Romance after Bosworth." In *The Court and Cultural Diversity: Selected Papers from the Eighth Triennial Congress of the International Courtly Literature Society, the Queen's University of Belfast, 26 July–1 August 1995*, ed. Evelyn Mullally and John Thompson, 149–57. Cambridge: D. S. Brewer, 1997.

Council, Norman. "Ben Jonson, Inigo Jones, and the Transformation of Tudor Chivalry." *English Literary History* 47 (1980): 259–75.

Coward, Barry. *The Stanleys, Lords Stanley, and Earls of Derby, 1385–1672: The Origins, Wealth, and Power of a Landowning Family.* Chetham Society, 3rd series, vol. 30. Manchester: Manchester University Press, 1983.

Cox, John D. "The Devil and Society in the English Mystery Plays." *Comparative Drama* 28 (1994–95): 407–38.

Croft, Pauline. "The Parliamentary Installation of Henry, Prince of Wales." *Historical Research* 65 (1992): 177–93.

Crouch, David. "The Administration of the Norman Earldom." In *The Earldom of Chester and Its Charters: A Tribute to Geoffrey Barraclough*, ed. A. T. Thacker, 69–95. Journal of the Chester Archaeological Society, vol. 71. Chester: Chester Archaeological Society, 1991.

Curtius, Ernst Robert. *European Literature and the Latin Middle Ages.* Trans. Willard R. Trask. London: Routledge, 1953.

Danbury, Elizabeth. "The Intellectual Life of the Abbey of St Werburgh, Chester, in the Middle Ages." In *Medieval Archaeology, Art and Architecture at Chester*, ed. Alan Thacker, 107–20. Leeds: British Archaeological Association, 2000.

Davies, R. R. "Richard II and the Principality of Chester 1397–9." In Du Boulay and Barron, *The Reign of Richard II*, 256–79.

Davis, Alex. *Chivalry and Romance in the English Renaissance.* Studies in Renaissance Literature, vol. 11. Cambridge: D. S. Brewer, 2003.

Dobson, R. B., ed. *The Peasants' Revolt of 1381.* 2nd ed. London: Macmillan Press, 1983.

Donatelli, Joseph. "The Percy Folio Manuscript: A Seventeenth-Century Context for Medieval Poetry." *English Manuscript Studies 1100–1700* 4 (1993): 114–33.

Du Boulay, F. R. H., and Caroline M. Barron, eds. *The Reign of Richard II: Essays in Honour of May McKisack.* London: University of London–Athone Press, 1971.

Duffy, Eamon. *The Stripping of the Altars: Traditional Religion in England, c. 1400–c. 1580.* New Haven, CT: Yale University Press, 1992.

Dugdale, William. *Monasticon Anglicanum.* Vol. 2. London, 1846.

Duggan, H. N. "Meter, Stanza, Vocabulary, Dialect." In Brewer and Gibson, *A Companion to the Gawain-Poet,* 221–42.

Elliott, R. W. V. *The Gawain Country.* Leeds: University of Leeds School of English, 1984.

———. "Landscape and Geography." In Brewer and Gibson, *A Companion to the Gawain-Poet,* 105–17.

Emmerson, Richard K. "Contextualizing Performance: The Reception of the Chester Antichrist." *Journal of Medieval and Early Modern Studies* 29 (1999): 89–119.

Estabrook, Carl B. "Ritual, Space, and Authority in Seventeenth-Century English Cathedral Cities." *Journal of Interdisciplinary History* 32 (2002): 593–620.

Esty, Joshua D. "Amnesia in the Fields: Late Modernism, Late Imperialism, and the English Pageant-Play." *English Literary History* 69 (2002): 245–76.

Farrer, William, and J. Brownbill, eds. *The Victoria History of the County of Lancashire.* Vol. 2. The Victoria History of the Counties of England. London: Constable, 1906.

Fitzgerald, Christina M. "Of Magi and Men: Christ's Nativity and Masculine Community in the Chester Mystery Cycle." In *Varieties of Devotion in the Middle Ages and Renaissance,* ed. Susan C. Karant-Nunn, 145–62. Turnhout: Brepols, 2003.

Fox-Davies, Arthur Charles. *A Complete Guide to Heraldry.* Rev. ed. London: T. C. & E. C. Jack, 1925.

Garner, Alan. *The Voice that Thunders: Essays and Lectures.* London: Harvill Press, 1997.

Gibson, Gail McMurray. *The Theatre of Devotion: East Anglian Drama and Society in the Late Middle Ages.* Chicago: University of Chicago Press, 1989.

Gransden, Antonia. "Realistic Observation in Twelfth-Century England." *Speculum* 47 (1972): 29–51.

Groombridge, Margaret, ed. *Calendar of Chester City Council Minutes, 1603–1642.* The Record Society of Lancashire and Cheshire, vol. 106. Blackpool, 1956.

Hall, J. R. Clark, and Herbert D. Meritt, eds. *A Concise Anglo-Saxon Dictionary.* 4th ed. Toronto: University of Toronto Press, 1960.

Hanawalt, Barbara, and David Wallace, eds. *Bodies and Disciplines: Intersections of Literature and History in Fifteenth-Century England.* Minneapolis: University of Minnesota Press, 1996.

Hanna, Ralph, III. *London Literature, 1300–1380.* Cambridge: Cambridge University Press, 2005.

———. "Sir Thomas Berkeley and His Patronage." *Speculum* 64 (1989): 878–916.

Hanning, R. W. "'You Have Begun a Parlous Pleye': The Nature and Limits of Dramatic Mimesis as a Theme in Four Middle English 'Fall of Lucifer' Cycle Plays." *Comparative Drama* 7 (1973): 22–50.

Harris, B. E., C. P. Lewis, and A. T. Thacker, eds. *A History of the County of Chester.* 5 vols. The Victoria History of the Counties of England. Oxford: Oxford University Press, 1979–2005.

Harvey, John H. "Richard II and York." In Du Boulay and Barron, *The Reign of Richard II*, 202–17.

Heal, Felicity. "Reciprocity and Exchange in the Late Medieval Household." In Hanawalt and Wallace, *Bodies and Disciplines*, 179–98.

Helgerson, Richard. *Forms of Nationhood: The Elizabethan Writing of England.* Chicago: University of Chicago Press, 1992.

Heng, Geraldine. *Empire of Magic: Medieval Romance and the Politics of Cultural Fantasy.* New York: Columbia University Press, 2003.

Higgins, Anne. "Streets and Markets." In *A New History of Early English Drama*, ed. John D. Cox and David Scott Kastan, 77–92. New York: Columbia University Press, 1997.

Hulbert, James R. "A Hypothesis Concerning the Alliterative Revival." *Modern Philology* 28 (1931): 405–22.

Ingham, Patricia Clare. *Sovereign Fantasies: Arthurian Romance and the Making of Britain.* Philadelphia: University of Pennsylvania Press, 2001.

Janowitz, Anne. *England's Ruins: Poetic Purpose and the National Landscape.* Oxford: Basil Blackwell, 1990.

Johnson, Paula. "Jacobean Ephemera and the Immortal Word." *Renaissance Drama*, n.s., 8 (1977): 151–71.

Jones, Douglas. *The Church in Chester, 1300–1540.* Chetham Society, 3rd series, vol. 7. Manchester, 1957.

Jones, W. J. "The Exchequer of Chester in the Last Years of Elizabeth I." In *Tudor Men and Institutions: Studies in English Law and Government*, ed. Arthur J. Slavin, 123–70. Baton Rouge: Louisiana State University Press, 1972.

Kennedy, Deborah. "The Ruined Abbey in the Eighteenth Century." *Philological Quarterly* 80 (2001): 503–23.

Kennett, Annette M., ed. *Tudor Chester: A Study of Chester in the Reigns of the Tudor Monarchs, 1485–1603.* Chester: Chester City Record Office, 1986.

Kinney, Clare R. "The (Dis)Embodied Hero and the Signs of Manhood in *Sir Gawain and the Green Knight*." In *Medieval Masculinities: Regarding Men in the Middle Ages*, ed. Clare A. Lees, 47–57. Minneapolis: University of Minnesota Press, 1994.

Kinoshita, Sharon. "Male-Order Brides: Marriage, Patriarchy, and Monarchy in the *Roman de Silence*." *Arthuriana* 12 (2002): 64–75.

Kipling, Gordon. *Enter the King: Theatre, Liturgy, and Ritual in the Medieval Civic Triumph*. Oxford: Clarendon Press, 1998.

———. "Triumphal Drama: Form in English Civic Pageantry." *Renaissance Drama*, n.s., 8 (1977): 37–56.

Knight, Rhonda. "All Dressed Up with Someplace to Go: Regional Identity in *Sir Gawain and the Green Knight*." *Studies in the Age of Chaucer* 25 (2003): 259–84.

Knowles, James. "The Spectacle of the Realm: Civic Consciousness, Rhetoric and Ritual in Early Modern London." In Mulryne and Shewring, *Theatre and Government under the Early Stuarts*, 157–89.

Kroll, Norma. "Cosmic Characters and Human Form: Dramatic Interaction and Conflict in the Chester Cycle 'Fall of Lucifer.'" *Medieval and Renaissance Drama in England* 2 (1985): 33–50.

Lancaster, Charles. "'Learned, Judicious, and Laborious' Gentlemen: Collectors of Genealogies and Gentry Histories in Later Seventeenth-Century England." *Limina* 5 (1999): 76–92.

Lawton, David. "*Scottish Field*: Alliterative Verse and Stanley Encomium in the Percy Folio." *Leeds Studies in English* 10 (1987): 42–57.

Lavezzo, Kathy. *Angels on the Edge of the World: Geography, Literature, and English Community, 1000–1534*. Ithaca, NY: Cornell University Press, 2006.

Leclercq, Jean. *The Love of Learning and the Desire for God: A Study of Monastic Culture*. Trans. Catharine Misrahi. 2nd rev. ed. New York: Fordham University Press, 1974.

Leinwand, Theodore B. "London Triumphing: The Jacobean Lord Mayor's Show." *Clio* 11 (1982): 137–53.

Lindenbaum, Sheila. "London Texts and Literate Practice." In Wallace, *The Cambridge History of Medieval English Literature*, 284–309.

Lumiansky, R. M., and David Mills. *The Chester Mystery Cycle: Essays and Documents*. Chapel Hill: University of North Carolina Press, 1983.

MacLean, Ian. *Woman Triumphant: Feminism in French Literature, 1610–1652*. Oxford: Clarendon Press, 1977.

Madan, Falconer, and H. H. E. Craster. *A Summary Catalogue of Western Manuscripts in the Bodleian Library at Oxford*. Vol. 2, Part 1. Oxford: Clarendon Press, 1922.

Manley, Lawrence. *Literature and Culture in Early Modern London*. Cambridge: Cambridge University Press, 1995.

Marcus, Leah S. "City Metal and Country Mettle: The Occasion of Ben Jonson's *Golden Age Restored*." In Bergeron, *Pageantry in the Shakespearean Theater*, 26–47.

———. *The Politics of Mirth: Jonson, Herrick, Milton, Marvell, and the Defense of Old Holiday Pastimes*. Chicago: University of Chicago Press, 1986.

Marshall, John. "'The Manner of These Playes': The Chester Pageant Carriages and the Places Where They Played." In *Staging the Chester Cycle*, ed. David Mills, 17–48. Leeds: University of Leeds School of English, 1985.

McClendon, Muriel C. "A Moveable Feast: Saint George's Day Celebrations and Religious Change in Early Modern England." *The Journal of British Studies* 38 (1999): 1–27.

McNamara, Gregory Vaughn. "'A Perfect Diamond Set in Lead': Henry, Prince of Wales and the Performance of Emergent Majesty." Ph.D. diss., West Virginia University, 2000.

Mills, David. "Chester's Mystery Cycle and the 'Mystery' of the Past." *Transactions of the Historic Society of Lancashire and Cheshire* 137 (1987): 1–23.

———. *Recycling the Cycle: The City of Chester and Its Whitsun Plays*. Toronto: University of Toronto Press, 1998.

———. "The Two Versions of Chester Play V: Balaam and Balak." In *The Chester Mystery Cycle: A Casebook*, ed. Kevin J. Harty, 119–25. New York: Garland Publishing, 1993.

Morris, Rupert H. *Chester in the Plantagenet and Tudor Reigns*. Chester, 1893.

Mulryne, J. R., and Margaret Shewring, eds. *Theatre and Government under the Early Stuarts*. Cambridge: Cambridge University Press, 1993.

Nelson, Alan H. *The Medieval English Stage: Corpus Christi Pageants and Plays*. Chicago: University of Chicago Press, 1974.

Nickel, Helmut. "Arthurian Armings for War and for Love." *Arthuriana* 5 (1995): 3–21.

Nicols, J. G. "The Scrope and Grosvenor Controversy." *The Herald and Genealogist* 1 (1863): 385–400.

Ord, Melanie. "Provincial Identification and the Struggle over Representation in Thomas Coryat's *Crudities* (1611)." In Schwyzer and Mealor, *Archipelagic Identities*, 131–40.

Orgel, Stephen. "The Poetics of Spectacle." *New Literary History* 2 (1971): 367–89.

Ormerod, George. "Observations on Ancient Swords of State Belonging to the Earldom of Chester." *Vetusta Monumenta*, vol. 5, plate L, 1–4. London, 1835.

Parry, Graham. "The Politics of the Jacobean Masque." In Mulryne and Shewring, *Theatre and Government under the Early Stuarts*, 87–117.

Paster, Gail Kern. "The Idea of London in Masque and Pageant." In Bergeron, *Pageantry in the Shakespearean Theater*, 48–64.

Patterson, Catherine F. "Corporations, Cathedrals and the Crown: Local Dispute and Royal Interest in Early Stuart England." *History* 85 (2000): 546–71.

Patterson, Lee. *Chaucer and the Subject of History.* Madison: University of Wisconsin Press, 1991.

Peacock, John. "Jonson and Jones Collaborate on Prince Henry's *Barriers.*" *Word and Image* 3 (1987): 172–94.

Phillips, A. D. M., and C. B. Phillips, eds. *A New Historical Atlas of Cheshire.* Chester: Cheshire County Council, 2002.

Phythian-Adams, Charles. "Ceremony and the Citizen: The Communal Year at Coventry, 1450–1550." In *The English Medieval Town: A Reader in English Urban History, 1200–1540,* ed. Richard Holt and Gervase Rosser, 238–64. London: Longman, 1990.

Platt, Colin. *The English Mediaeval Town.* London: Paladin-Granada Publishing, 1979.

Pocock, J. G. A. "British History: A Plea for a New Subject." *The Journal of Modern History* 47 (1975): 601–21.

Potter, Lois. *Secret Rites and Secret Writing: Royalist Literature, 1641–1660.* Cambridge: Cambridge University Press, 1989.

Pound, John. *Poverty and Vagrancy in Tudor England.* 2nd ed. London: Longman, 1986.

Putter, Ad, and Myra Stokes. "*The Linguistic Atlas* and the Dialect of the *Gawain* Poems." *Journal of English and Germanic Philology* 106 (2007): 468–91.

Rex, Richard. "The English Campaign against Luther in the 1520s." *Transactions of the Royal Historical Society* 39 (1989): 85–106.

Rogers, Gillian. "The Percy Folio Manuscript Revisited." In *Romance in Medieval England,* ed. Maldwyn Mills, Jennifer Fellows, and Carol M. Meale, 39–64. Cambridge: D. S. Brewer, 1991.

Rosenthal, Joel T. *Telling Tales: Sources and Narration in Late Medieval England.* University Park: Pennsylvania State University Press, 2003.

Sanok, Catherine. *Her Life Historical: Exemplarity and Female Saints' Lives in Late Medieval England.* Philadelphia: University of Pennsylvania Press, 2007.

Saul, Nigel. *Richard II.* New Haven, CT: Yale University Press, 1997.

Savage, Henry L. "A Note on *Sir Gawain and the Green Knight* 700–2." *Modern Language Notes* 46 (1931): 455–57.

Scattergood, John. "A Defining Moment: The Battle of Flodden and English Poetry." In *Vernacular Literature and Current Affairs in the Early Sixteenth Century: France, England and Scotland,* ed. Jennifer Britnell and Richard Britnell, 62–79. Studies in European Cultural Transition, vol. 6. Aldershot: Ashgate, 2000.

———. "Misrepresenting the City: Genre, Intertextuality and Fitzstephen's *Description of London (c.* 1173)." In *Reading the Past: Essays on Medieval and*

Renaissance Literature, ed. John Scattergood, 15–36. Dublin: Four Courts Press, 1996.

Schwyzer, Philip. *Literature, Nationalism, and Memory in Early Modern England and Wales*. Cambridge: Cambridge University Press, 2004.

———, and Simon Mealor, eds. *Archipelagic Identities: Literature and Identity in the Atlantic Archipelago, 1550–1800*. Aldershot: Ashgate, 2004.

Seaton, Jean Q. "Source of Order or Sovereign Lord: God and the Pattern of Relationships in Two Middle English 'Fall of Lucifer' Plays." *Comparative Drama* 18 (1984): 203–21.

Shohet, Lauren. "The Masque as Book." In *Reading and Literacy in the Middle Ages and Renaissance*, ed. Ian Frederick Moulton, 143–68. Turnhout: Brepols, 2004.

Simpson, James. *Reform and Cultural Revolution*. The Oxford English Literary History, vol. 2. Oxford: Oxford University Press, 2002.

Slack, Paul. *Poverty and Policy in Tudor and Stuart England*. London: Longman, 1988.

Spearing, A. C. *The Gawain-Poet: A Critical Study*. Cambridge: Cambridge University Press, 1970.

Sponsler, Claire. "The Culture of the Spectator: Conformity and Resistance to Medieval Performances." *Theatre Journal* 44 (1992): 15–29.

———. *Drama and Resistance: Bodies, Goods, and Theatricality in Late Medieval England*. Minneapolis: University of Minnesota Press, 1997.

Stanbury, Sarah. "The Body and the City in *Pearl*." *Representations* 48 (1994): 30–47.

Stevens, Martin. *Four Middle English Mystery Cycles: Textual, Contextual, and Critical Interpretations*. Princeton, NJ: Princeton University Press, 1987.

Stewart-Brown, R. "The Avowries of Cheshire." *English Historical Review* 29 (1914): 41–55.

———. "The Disafforestation of Wirral." *Transactions of the Historic Society of Lancashire and Cheshire* 59 (1907): 165–80.

———. "The Scrope and Grosvenor Controversy, 1385–1391." *Transactions of the Historic Society of Lancashire and Cheshire* 89 (1937): 1–22.

Strohm, Paul. *Theory and the Premodern Text*. Minneapolis: University of Minnesota Press, 2000.

Strong, Roy. *The Cult of Elizabeth: Elizabethan Portraiture and Pageantry*. London: Thames and Hudson, 1977.

———. *Henry, Prince of Wales and England's Lost Renaissance*. London: Thames and Hudson, 1986.

Summit, Jennifer. *Lost Property: The Woman Writer and English Literary History, 1380–1589*. Chicago: University of Chicago Press, 2000.

Taylor, Andrew. "*The Stanley Poem* and the Harper Richard Sheale." *Leeds Studies in English*, n.s., 28 (1997): 99–121.

Thacker, Alan. "The Reuse of the Monastic Buildings at Chester, 1540–1640." *Transactions of the Historic Society of Lancashire and Cheshire* 145 (1995): 21–43.

Thornton, Tim. *Chester and the Tudor State, 1480–1560.* Woodbridge: Boydell Press, 2000.

———. "The Integration of Cheshire into the Tudor Nation State in the Early Sixteenth Century." *Northern History* 29 (1993): 40–63.

———. "Opposition Drama and the Resolution of Disputes in Early Tudor England: Cardinal Wolsey and the Abbot of Chester." *Bulletin of the John Rylands University Library of Manchester* 81 (1999): 25–47.

Travis, Peter W. *Dramatic Design in the Chester Cycle.* Chicago: University of Chicago Press, 1982.

———. "The Social Body of the Dramatic Christ in Medieval England." *Acta* 13 (1985): 17–36.

Turville-Petre, Thorlac. "Afterword: The Brutus Prologue to *Sir Gawain and the Green Knight.*" In *Imagining a Medieval English Nation,* ed. Kathy Lavezzo, 340–46. Minneapolis: University of Minnesota Press, 2004.

———. *England the Nation: Language, Literature, and National Identity, 1290–1340.* Oxford: Clarendon Press, 1996.

———. "The 'Pearl'-Poet in His 'Fayre Regioun.'" In *Essays on Ricardian Literature: In Honour of J. A. Burrow,* ed. A. J. Minnis, Charlotte C. Morse, and Thorlac Turville-Petre, 276–94. Oxford: Clarendon Press, 1997.

Twycross, Meg. "'Places to Hear and Play': Pageant Stations at York, 1398–1572." *Records of Early English Drama Newsletter* 2 (1978): 10–33.

Wack, Mary. "Women, Work, and Plays in an English Medieval Town." In *Maids and Mistresses, Cousins and Queens: Women's Alliances in Early Modern England,* ed. Susan Frye and Karen Robertson, 33–51. New York: Oxford University Press, 1999.

Walker, Katherine A. "The Military Activities of Charlotte de la Tremouille, Countess of Derby, during the Civil War and Interregnum." *Northern History* 38 (2001): 47–64.

Wallace, David, ed. *The Cambridge History of Medieval English Literature.* Cambridge: Cambridge University Press, 1999.

———. *Chaucerian Polity: Absolutist Lineages and Associational Forms in England and Italy.* Stanford, CA: Stanford University Press, 1997.

Warren, Michelle R. *History on the Edge: Excalibur and the Borders of Britain, 1100–1300.* Minneapolis: University of Minnesota Press, 2000.

West, Russell. "Perplexive Perspectives: The Court and Contestation in the Jacobean Masque." *The Seventeenth Century* 18 (2003): 25–43.

White, Paul Whitfield. "Reforming Mysteries' End: A New Look at Protestant Intervention in English Provincial Drama." *Journal of Medieval and Early Modern Studies* 29 (1999): 121–47.

Wickham, Glynne. *Early English Stages.* Vol. 2, pt. 1. London: Routledge, 1959.

Womack, Peter. "Imagining Communities: Theatres and the English Nation in the Sixteenth Century." In *Culture and History, 1350–1600: Essays on English Communities, Identities and Writing,* ed. David Aers, 91–145. Detroit, MI: Wayne State University Press, 1992.

Woodward, D. M. *The Trade of Elizabethan Chester.* Hull: University of Hull, 1970.

Wright, Nancy E. "'Rival Traditions': Civic and Courtly Ceremonies in Jacobean London." In *The Politics of the Stuart Court Masque,* ed. David Bevington and Peter Holbrook, 197–217. Cambridge: Cambridge University Press, 1998.

Secondary Sources (Online)

BBC News. "Bid to Halt Council Change Fails." 5 March 2008. http://news.bbc.co.uk/1/hi/england/7279147.stm (accessed 11 April 2008).

———. "MPs Back Cheshire Council Split." 27 February 2008. http://news.bbc.co.uk/1/hi/england/staffordshire/7267605.stm (accessed 11 April 2008).

Cheshire County Council. "Background to the Scheme." http://www.cheshire.gov.uk/ReadersAndWriters/Writers/poetlaureate/writerspoetbackground.htm (accessed 11 April 2008).

———. "Crest." http://www.cheshire.gov.uk/aboutcheshire/Crest.htm (accessed 11 April 2007).

———. "Government's Conditional Recommendation to Partition County Worst Choice for People of Cheshire Say County Leaders." http://www.cheshire.gov.uk/PR/2007/july07/293-07.htm (accessed 11 April 2008).

———. "Local Government Reorganisation." http://www.cheshire.gov.uk/LocalGovReorg (accessed 11 April 2008).

———. "One Cheshire Council." http://64.233.167.104/search?q=cache:SRkiTrZNdRwJ:www.cheshire.gov.uk/onecheshire/onecheshirecouncil.htm&hl=en&ct=clnk&cd=2&gl=us&client=safari (accessed 11 April 2008).

———. "One Council for Cheshire." http://web.archive.org/web/20070825090147/http://www.cheshire.gov.uk/onecheshire/ (accessed 11 April 2008).

———. "Questions and Answers." http://www.cheshire.gov.uk/onecheshire/Questions+and+Answers.htm (accessed 29 November 2007).

Cheshire East Joint Committee. http://www.cheshireeast.gov.uk/ (accessed 11 April 2008).

Cheshire West and Chester Joint Committee. http://www.cheshirewestandchester.gov.uk/ (accessed 11 April 2008).

Chester City Council. "The Chester Renaissance—Frequently Asked Questions." http://www.chesterrenaissance.co.uk/faqs.htm (accessed 11 April 2008).

Chester Festivals. "Chester Festivals . . . the Beating Pulse of Our Vibrant City."
http://www.chesterfestivals.co.uk (accessed 11 April 2008).

Chester Mystery Plays Ltd. "Chester Mystery Plays." http://www.chestermystery
plays.com/ (accessed 11 April 2008).

The Chester Standard. "New Council to Rule Chester." 19 December 2007. http://
www.chesterstandard.co.uk/chesternews/New-council-to-rule-Chester
.3605469.jp (accessed 11 April 2008).

Communities and Local Government. "Strong and Prosperous Communities: The Local Government White Paper." http://www.communities.gov
.uk/publications/localgovernment/strongprosperous (accessed 11 April
2008).

Dennis, Trevor. "The Festival of St Werburgh." "Chester Cathedral—Monthly
Newsletter," June 2007. http://web.archive.org/web/20070621054328/
http://www.chestercathedral.com/Website_Pages/monthlynewsletter.asp
(accessed 11 April 2008).

Eales, Richard. "Ranulf (III), Sixth Earl of Chester and First Earl of Lincoln
(1170–1232)." In *Oxford Dictionary of National Biography*, ed. H. C. G. Matthew and Brian Harrison. Oxford: Oxford University Press, 2004. http://
www.oxforddnb.com/view/article/2716 (accessed 11 April 2008).

Garner, Alan. "Benighted Verse." *Times Online*, 27 December 2003. http://
entertainment.timesonline.co.uk/tol/arts_and_entertainment/books/
article838217.ece (accessed 11 April 2008).

Hansard. http://www.publications.parliament.uk/pa/pahansard.htm.

Healey, John. "Local Government: Statement by John Healey MP on
25 July 2007." http://www.communties.gov.uk/statements/corporate/
local-government (accessed 11 April 2008).

Howe, Steve. "Chester Cathedral 3." http://www.bwpics.co.uk/cathedral3.html
(accessed 11 April 2008).

Humphries, Chris. "To Be a Pilgrim." "Chester Cathedral—Monthly Newsletter," August 2007. http://web.archive.org/web/20070823065931/http://
www.chestercathedral.com/Website_Pages/monthlynewsletter.asp
(accessed 11 April 2008).

Marketing Projects. "Pilgrim's Progress—May 25, 2007." http://www
.marketingprojects.co.uk/clientpo/90/news/701 (accessed 11 April 2008).

———. "Return of the Pilgrims." http://www.marketingprojects.co.uk/client
po/90/news/708 (accessed 11 April 2008).

———. "St. Werburgh's Relics Return." http://www.marketingprojects.co.uk/
clientpo/90/news/710 (accessed 11 April 2008).

The Middle English Dictionary. http://quod.lib.umich.edu/m/med.

Murdoch, Alain. "City's Viking Invasion." *The Chester Standard*, 21 June 2007.
http://www.chesterstandard.co.uk/chesternews/City39s-Viking-invasion
.2969868.jp (accessed 11 April 2008).

Nenner, Howard. "Bridgeman, Sir Orlando (1609–1674)." In *Oxford Dictionary of National Biography*, ed. H. C. G. Matthew and Brian Harrison. Oxford: Oxford University Press, 2004. http://www.oxforddnb.com/view/article/3392 (accessed 11 April 2008).

The Oxford English Dictionary. http://www.oed.com.

Rudd, Andrew. "Cheshire Poet Laureate 2006: Lines on the Map." http://cheshirepoetlaureate.blogspot.com/2006/03/lines-on-map_06.html (accessed 11 April 2008).

INDEX

Clopper, Lawrence (*continued*)
236nn15–16, 236nn19–20,
238n46, 252n53
Cohen, Jeffrey Jerome, 14
Combermere Abbey (Cheshire), 42
Compton, Sir William, 191, 195
Constable of England, Lord High,
141, 143, 147, 151, 260n31,
261n33, 261n39, 263n53
Cooper, Helen, 178, 180–82, 259n22,
265n74
Coopers Company (Chester), 238n46
corn market (Chester), 11, 68–72,
76–77, 93, 237n38, 238n47,
239n48, 240n54
Cornwall, 258n17, 264n63
Corser, Thomas, 252n53
court, Cheshire, 4
Court of Chivalry, 138, 140–41,
143–44, 147, 151, 165, 260n33,
261n34
Cox, John, 80, 237n22
Cromwell, Thomas, 226n44
Crouch, David, 224n13

Dacre, Thomas (second Lord Dacre),
187, 190, 192
Danbury, Elizabeth, 227n7
Davies, Richard (poet), 97, 111,
120–24, 126, 249n22, 251n38,
251n40, 254n88. *See also Chester's
Triumph in Honor of Her Prince*
(Amery and Davies)
Davies, R. R., 137
Davis, Alex, 196–97
Davis, Norman, 268n85
Dee, River, 2–3, 5, 28, 60–61, 67,
97, 118, 136, 254n78, 258n17,
261n39
Dekker, Thomas, 107, 121–23, 127.
See also Troia-Nova Triumphans
(Dekker)

Dennis, Trevor (Vice Dean of Chester
Cathedral), 213
Derby, Earls of. *See* Stanley, family of
Descriptio nobilissimae civitatis Londoniae
(Fitzstephen), 227n7
Dieulacres Abbey (Staffordshire),
135–36
disenfranchisement, 19, 62, 82–86,
107, 113, 241n74, 246n122
Dissolution, 9, 11, 19, 29, 50–51,
232n52, 232n55, 238n44
Donatelli, Joseph, 196
Drawers of the Dee (Chester), 118,
254n78
Dudley, Robert (Earl of Leicester),
74, 83, 246n122, 249n24
Duffy, Eamon, 47
Duggan, H. N., 256n1, 260n33
Dutton, Richard (Mayor of Chester),
69–70, 75–76, 79, 81, 84, 238n47,
240n54

Eastgate (Chester), 10, 39, 64
Eastgate Street (Chester), 39, 41, 49,
77, 94, 96, 212, 236n19, 240n58
Edward I, 4, 9, 148, 257n12
Edward II, 4, 148
Edward IV, 185, 224n24, 271n11
Edward VI, 93
Egerton, Sir Ralph, 191, 195
Egerton, Sir Rowland, 273n41
Elizabeth I, 93, 99, 101, 247n126,
272n25
Elizabeth of York, 180–82, 197–98
Elliott, Ralph, 133, 135–36, 256n3,
257n16, 259n22
Emmerson, Richard, 235n9, 242n80
encomium, familial, 173–75, 180–82,
186–88, 195
encomium urbis, 2, 19, 29, 61
Envy (allegorical personification),
20, 98, 105–13, 116, 118–19,

ROBERT W. BARRETT, JR., is associate professor of English and medieval studies at the University of Illinois at Urbana-Champaign.